BASIC CRIMINAL LAW

The U.S. Constitution, Procedure, and Crimes

Anniken Davenport, Esq.

Harrisburg Area Community College

Pearson
Prentice Hall
Legal Series

PEARSON
Prentice
Hall

Upper Saddle River, New Jersey 07458

Library of Congress Cataloging-in-Publication Data

Davenport, Anniken.
  Basic criminal law / by Anniken Davenport.
    p. cm.
  Includes bibliographical references and index.
  ISBN 0-13-079771-5
1. Criminal law—United States. I. Title.
  KF9219.3.D38 2006
  345.73—dc22   2004021227

Director of Production and Manufacturing: Bruce Johnson
Executive Editor: Elizabeth Sugg
Consulting Editors: Enika Schulze and Nancy Blanchette/Athena Group, Inc.
Editorial Assistant: Cyrenne Bolt de Freitas
Marketing Manager: Leigh Ann Sims
Managing Editor—Production: Mary Carnis
Manufacturing Buyer: Ilene Sanford
Production Liaison: Denise Brown
Production Editor: Melissa Scott/Carlisle Publishers Services
Composition: Carlisle Communications, Ltd.
Design Director: Cheryl Asherman
Senior Design Coordinator: Christopher Weigand
Cover Design: Kevin Kall
Cover Printer: Phoenix Color
Printer/Binder: Courier Westford

The information provided in this text is not intended as legal advice for specific situations, but is meant solely for educational and informational purposes. Readers should retain and seek the advice of their own legal counsel in handling specific legal matters.

Pearson Education LTD.
Pearson Education Singapore, Pte. Ltd
Pearson Education, Canada, Ltd
Pearson Education—Japan

Pearson Education Australia PTY, Limited
Pearson Education North Asia Ltd
Pearson Educación de Mexico, S.A. de C.V.
Pearson Education Malaysia, Pte. Ltd

10 9 8 7 6 5 4 3 2 1
ISBN 0-13-079771-5

DEDICATION

No book is ever written alone. This one is no exception. I am blessed to be surrounded by many talented and hardworking students and a wonderful family who helped make this book possible. First, thanks to my muse Albert Davenport. Without his keen eye for historical details, this book would be just another dry textbook. My talented daughter, Morgan Horton, contributed many hours of research into the current events that are featured in the book.

Thanks also to my student intern from Wilson College, Stephanie Lingle, who read hundreds of Supreme Court opinions and meticulously updated cases and citations over a long summer. You and the other Wilson women I had the pleasure of teaching over the last five years have enriched my life more than you know.

Anniken Davenport

CONTENTS

CHAPTER 4:   *Constitutional Rights Before Arrest*   59

CHAPTER 5:   *Constitutional Rights After Arrest*   81

CHAPTER 9:   *Crimes Against the Person: Violence*   159

CHAPTER 10:   *Crimes Against Property*   185

CHAPTER 11:   *Treason, Terrorism, and Wartime Criminal Justice*   208

**APPENDIX A: *The Constitution of the
United States of America***   **285**

PREFACE

Today, criminal law and procedure is at the forefront of public discourse. Not a day goes by that a criminal case doesn't make the news. The public debate includes the imposition of the death penalty on juveniles and the mentally handicapped, the use of the insanity defense by mothers accused of killing their children, the release of prisoners on death row who are cleared of criminal responsibility by new scientific evidence, and the question of how to treat those suspected of engaging in terrorist activities against U.S. citizens.

These subjects under discussion in the nation's homes and schools are complicated. Without a basic understanding of the legal system, the Constitution, and the origins of our criminal laws, the public, and sometimes the journalists reporting the stories, can't make much sense of the news. In the classroom, I regularly have to explain how there can be a civil and a criminal trial for the same act (O. J. Simpson always comes up). Students think double jeopardy means that can't happen. They don't understand why "the American Taliban" can't be charged with treason or why we can't hold an American citizen suspected of plotting a terror attack or fighting with Muslim extremists indefinitely without a hearing. Despite numerous television cop and lawyer shows, students don't understand the right to remain silent or the right to be free from unreasonable searches. Nor do they understand the structure and function of the criminal justice system.

I am convinced that to really understand criminal law students need a grounding in three things. The first is the history of the American criminal law system. That history gives perspective to the public debate and helps us understand not just what the law is today, but why it is what it is. Therefore, the first unit in this book focuses on the history of the criminal justice system and its organization.

The second unit covers what is commonly referred to as criminal procedure. It focuses on the right all citizens have under the Constitution when we are suspected of, charged with, or being punished for a crime. This unit covers rights before arrest, rights at trial, and rights after conviction. Finally, the third unit covers specific crimes and common defenses to those crimes. Each chapter in this unit also includes a section "Practice Pointers" with advice and resources for those working in the criminal justice system.

No introductory criminal law textbook can cover it all. We are, after all, a nation of over 50 governments, each with its own set of criminal laws. Fortunately, we are all bound by the United States Constitution and our common history. It is only with a grounding in that history that students can develop a fundamental appreciation for and understanding of criminal law. With that as a foundation, they can begin to explore the law in their jurisdiction and build upon the fundamental knowledge this book delivers.

ACKNOWLEDGMENTS

The author and editors wish to thank the reviewers who contributed greatly to the quality of the final product:

Initial Reviewers (May 1999)

Lisa Rieger, JD, Justice Center, Unviersity of Alaska, Anchorage, AK Thomas E. Wright, JD, School of Justice Studies, Roger Williams University, Warren, RI Lisa Duncan, JD, Business Dept., Central Carolina Community College, Holly Springs, NC Laura Barnard, JD, Program Director, Lakeland Community College, Kirtland, OH John LeLeo, Criminal Law Professor, Central Penn College, Summerdale, PA

Final Reviewers (November 2003)

Taylor L. Morton, JD, educational consultant, Altadena, CA Robert N. Diotalevi, PhD, Esq., Florida Gulf Coast University, Fort Myers, FL Kent D. Kauffman, JD, Ivy Tech State College, Ft. Wayne, IN Cheryl K. Bullard, Jd, Auburn University, Montgomery, AL

ABOUT THE AUTHOR

Ms. Davenport is an attorney with many years of experience in administrative law as well as general practice. She holds a Bachelor's Degree in Public Policy from the Pennsylvania State University and earned her law degree from The Dickinson School of Law of the Pennsylvania State University.

As a labor consultant, she negotiated collective bargaining agreements. She has represented government agencies in workers' compensation, unemployment compensation, civil service, medical licensure, and discrimination cases and has represented clients in private practice.

Ms. Davenport formerly headed the legal studies program at Wilson College, Chambersburg, PA. She also is a member of the adjunct faculty at Harrisburg Area Community College and Penn State. She teaches Business Law, Real Estate Law and Human Resource Management. She is also a senior contributing editor to several human resource newsletters.

CHAPTER 1
What Is Criminal Law?

CHAPTER OBJECTIVES

After studying this chapter, you should be able to:

- Explain the concept of English common law
- Explain *stare decisis*
- Explain *mala in se* and *mala prohibita*
- Explain the term *jurisprudence*
- List and explain the major theories of law and schools of jurisprudence
- List and explain the difference between criminal and civil law
- List the three categories of crimes
- Explain the federal system and federalism
- Explain how a criminal case is processed through the criminal justice system
- Explain checks and balances
- Explain the Supremacy Clause
- Explain the Commerce Clause
- Explain police power
- List and explain the sources of American law

CHAPTER CONTENTS

> *We hold these truths to be self-evident, that all men are created equal, that they are endowed by their Creator with certain unalienable rights, that among these are life, liberty and the pursuit of happiness.*
>
> *Declaration of Independence* 1776

INTRODUCTION AND HISTORICAL BACKGROUND

Every society, from the most remote tribe to the most technologically advanced culture, has rules by which it operates. Most societies have written rules governing behavior and a set of punishments for those who break the rules. These can be called the society's laws. The **law** is defined as the body of rules of conduct created by government and enforced by the authority of government. Without any rules of behavior, life in a group would be difficult, if not impossible. **Jurisprudence** is the study of law. Criminal law is a specialized part of the study of jurisprudence.

In order to master criminal law, you must understand the context in which criminal law exists. In this chapter, we will take a look at the American legal system as a whole. Once you have a good grasp of the structure and form of that system, you will find it easier to visualize the criminal law system as a subpart of the whole.

The United States has a system of law derived from the English system of **Common Law.** As the original English settlers arrived in the New World, they took with them a well-developed system of justice. The law they brought with them was common to all men and all areas in the English Empire, so it came to be referred to as the Common Law. Common Law is founded on the idea that if one set of facts yields a decision in one case, the same set of facts should yield the same decision in the next case. So, if a judge in Essex ruled that stealing a cow was a crime, a judge in Londonderry should rule the same way. Under Common law, judges look at similar cases decided before and decide new cases the same way. This makes the legal system predictable and stable. Using previous decisions in similar cases to decide a current case is called following the rule of ***stare decisis.*** *Stare decisis* means "to stand by the decision." The earlier case that the court relies on as *stare decisis* is called a **precedent.**

THEORIES OF LAW AND SCHOOLS OF JURISPRUDENCE

The role of law in society depends on the society. It varies from era to era, culture to culture, country to country, region to region, and sometimes even town to town. Different cultures have different ideas of what is right and wrong and what should be legal or illegal. Recall that jurisprudence is the study of law. Over the years, philosophers, lawyers, and social scientists have developed theories about how laws develop and are accepted by cultures. These theories of law are referred to as "schools of jurisprudence." Some of the major theories and schools are described in the following text. As you study these, ask yourself how each theory is reflected in the laws that affect you daily. For example, which theory do you think best reflects the almost universal prohibition against sexual relationships between blood relatives? Which theory explains laws against jaywalking or spitting on public streets?

DURKHEIM'S CONSENSUS THEORY

Emile Durkheim (1858–1917) was a Frenchman who is often referred to as the father of sociology. Durkheim developed what he called the **consensus theory.** He thought that laws develop out of a society's consensus of what is right and wrong.

According to Durkheim, crimes are crimes because the society decides they are, not because some things are wrong and other things are right. In his classic work, *The Division of Labor in Society*, Durkheim wrote:

> Even when a criminal act is certainly harmful to society, it is not true that the amount of harm that it does is regularly related to the intensity of the repression which it calls forth. In the penal law of most civilized people, murder is universally regarded as the greatest of crimes. However, an economic crisis, a stock-market crash . . . can disorganize the social body more severely than an isolated homicide. (T)he only common characteristic of all crimes is that they consist . . . in acts universally disapproved of by members of each society. . . . [1]

In Durkheim's view, the collective membership of society decides what is a crime and what isn't. Likewise, society can change its mind. This happens when the values of the society change to the point that behavior that was seen as a crime no longer is seen as such. The behavior is then decriminalized. For example, a state that passes a referendum (a change in the law that occurs when the majority of voters vote to make the change) that makes it legal to grow marijuana for personal consumption is making a collective judgment that growing marijuana isn't worthy of being considered a crime, and a state that legalizes prostitution is doing the same.

MARX'S RULING CLASS THEORY

While Durkheim saw criminal laws as agreed upon societal norms, the sociologist Karl Marx (1818–1883) saw things very differently. He taught that laws are a reflection of the interests or ideology of the ruling class. Under Marxist theory, laws are a manifestation of ongoing class conflict. They exist merely to protect property interests of the **bourgeoisie,** or the group that controls industrial production. Private property rights are viewed as a tool of oppression of the **proletariat,** or the working classes.[2] This theory is referred to as the **elite or ruling class theory.** Related to this theory is the **Command School** theory.[3] The Command School believes that law is a set of rules developed by the ruling class or elite and imposed on the society. Under this theory, laws will change when those in power change.

BLACKSTONE'S THEORY

The great English legal analyst Sir William Blackstone (1723–1780) theorized that there are two different types of crime. Some acts are crimes because the behavior is inherently bad or evil. A crime that is bad in and of itself is defined by the Latin term ***mala in se.*** Other acts are crimes because society has chosen to make some behaviors crimes. A crime that is a crime because society decides it is is called a ***mala prohibita.***[4] For example, murder is *mala in se*, or inherently evil. Driving a car with an expired inspection sticker, however, isn't inherently evil. Most traffic and auto code violations are *mala prohibita.* Think of *mala prohibita* crimes as violations of those rules your mother enforced over your objections with "because I said so, that's why."

THE NATURAL LAW SCHOOL OF JURISPRUDENCE

The **Natural Law School** believes that people have natural rights and that laws are based on what is right. They adhere to the **moral theory of law,** the belief that law is based on morality. Much of English law reflects this school.[5] The English political philosopher John Locke (1632–1704) spoke of the natural rights of man and profoundly influenced Thomas Jefferson (1743–1826) in the writing of the Declaration of Independence. Both the Declaration of Independence and the U.S. Constitution reflects the Natural Law School of jurisprudence. For example, the introductory quote in this chapter is from the *Declaration of Independence.* Note the references to self-evident truths and unalienable rights. These are hallmarks of the Natural Law School of jurisprudence.

THE HISTORICAL SCHOOL

The **Historical School** of jurisprudence states that law is merely the accumulation of a society's social traditions. Historical School legal theorists believe that laws evolve to accommodate changes in society.[6] Historical legal scholars will look to previous decisions, and then determine if the norms reflected by those decisions are still the norms of the society. In other words, precedent is only relied on if the society's current social norms support the rationale underlying the decision in the case.

The Historical School would likely support overturning precedent if times have changed. For example, assume that the courts have regularly ruled that children born out of wedlock can't inherit from their fathers. The Historical School would look to society's current views on illegitimate births. If such births have become commonplace and accepted by a large segment of society, the Historical School would support overturning precedent. Like Durkheim's consensus theory, the Historical School recognizes that society influences what is or should be legal and illegal.

THE ANALYTICAL SCHOOL

The **Analytical School** of jurisprudence holds that logic determines what is law. Analytical philosophers will apply theories of logic to the facts of a case to make a decision.[7]

Emotional appeals hold little sway. Analytical adherents will tend to focus on the logic of a legal decision rather than on popular opinion or changing values.

THE SOCIOLOGICAL SCHOOL

The **Sociological School** of jurisprudence holds that law is a way of achieving sociological goals within a society. Also known as **realists,** sociological theorists believe that the purpose of law is to shape societal behavior.[8] Because of their activist approach, they are unlikely to place much emphasis on prior decisions. Realists propose new laws designed to shape behaviors they consider desirable for society. For example, realists seeking to encourage religious tolerance might urge the passage of laws banning religious hate crimes such as church burnings and the desecrations of houses of worship. In effect, realists decide on a public policy and then mold laws to achieve that policy.

THE CRIT AND THE FEM-CRIT SCHOOL OF JURISPRUDENCE

Another theory of jurisprudence that emerged in the twentieth century is the Critical Legal Studies School, or the **Crits.** Crits believe that the legal system is arbitrary and artificial, that legal neutrality and objectivity are myths to maintain the current status quo, and that the legal system perpetuates social inequality and oppression of those not in power. The **Fem-Crits** are an offshoot of the Crits. Fem-Crits apply the crit theory of oppression and control to women, arguing that the legal system perpetuates the oppression of women in society.[9]

WHICH THEORY FITS THE AMERICAN SYSTEM?

No one theory of jurisprudence explains or describes the American legal system perfectly. There are elements of each theory in our legal system. For example, the introduction of a new bill to encourage more fathers to pay child support can be seen as the work of realists who want to encourage more fathers to support their children by penalizing those who don't. The law could also be the work of Analytical School proponents who see increased child support as logically reducing dependence on government aid. Or the law could be the work of proponents of the Historical School who see increased child support collection as a necessary measure in a society that accepts a high divorce and illegitimacy rate. Or the law could be the work of proponents of the Natural Law School, who see a child's right to support as the natural and moral obligation of his or her father. Finally, the law could be seen by the realists and the Fem-Crits as a way of addressing a societal problem of children living in poverty and a correction of the unequal earning power of single mothers.

CRIMINAL LAW VS. CIVIL LAW

Legal proceedings are classified as either criminal or civil. Criminal and civil law each have a unique set of functions, procedures, and consequences. Generally speaking, criminal law is designed to protect and vindicate public rights, while civil law is used to resolve private disputes. Criminal law seeks to protect society as a whole from the aberrant (as defined by the law) behavior of some members of that society. A **crime** is a wrong against society.

CRIMINAL LAW PROTECTS PUBLIC RIGHTS

When a murder, assault, rape, or other crime directed at a person is committed, a victim is harmed and the public order is disturbed. People assume that a civilized society has an interest in protecting the physical safety of its citizens. Thus, actions that threaten physical safety are crimes.

This same public interest is often also attached to property rights. In societies that believe that property can be owned (and that's not a universally held belief), it's assumed that stable property rights produce a stable society. That stability is threatened when members of the society appropriate property for their own use without permission or payment. Theft of property is therefore also a wrong against society.

Because criminal laws protect public interests, criminal prosecutions are brought on behalf of all of us. Charges in criminal proceedings are brought by a representative of the state. The prosecutor is always a public figure, not a representative of the victim of the crime. Thus, a Pennsylvania rape case is prosecuted by a district attorney and the case is captioned *"Commonwealth of Pennsylvania v. John Doe."* A federal case is brought by a U.S. attorney and is captioned as *"United States v. Jane Doe."* Both the district attorney and the U.S. attorney represent all of us as a whole.

CIVIL LAW PROTECTS PRIVATE RIGHTS

While criminal law deals with crimes, civil law deals with **torts,** contracts, estates, and family matters. A tort is a private or civil wrong, or injury resulting from a breach of a legal duty. It can be an intentional tort, such as an assault, or an unintentional one, such as an automobile accident. A person who commits a tort is called a **tort feasor.** Civil suits are filed by individuals seeking redress of private grievances, be they personal injuries, breach of contract, divorce and custody actions, or the administration of estates.

Sometimes one act can be both a crime and a tort. For example, a physical assault is both a crime and a tort. The criminal law seeks to punish the assailant on behalf of all of us, and the civil law seeks to reimburse the assault victim for any loss he or she had because of the assault. Because different rights are at stake, the assailant can be sued in both criminal court and in civil court for the same assault.

Perhaps no event in American history better explains the rights vindicated by the criminal and civil system than the terrorist bombings of the Pentagon and World Trade Center on September 11, 2001. The aftermath left the entire nation in grief and feeling at least a little less secure than before. Clearly, the terrorists' acts harmed us all. Those same acts also killed almost 3,000 innocent men and women, whose survivors each have a potential civil tort action against the terrorists, those that financed their operations, and perhaps other parties responsible for security.

CRIMINAL LAW PENALTIES AND THE BURDEN OF PROOF

The punishment for a crime is imprisonment or death. Sometimes a fine is added to the punishment. Criminal punishments are meant to vindicate the public interest by either removing the convicted criminal from society for a period of time, or permanently in the case of death or a life sentence. In the American criminal law system, it is always the government that has the **burden of proof,** or has to prove that the allegations against the defendant are true. The criminal defendant is presumed innocent until proven guilty.

Because the consequences of conviction are so great, the prosecution has a heavy burden of proof. In criminal cases, that burden is proof **beyond a reasonable doubt** that the defendant did commit the criminal act he or she was charged with. (See Chapter 4 for a full discussion of the meaning of "beyond a reasonable doubt.")

TORT PENALTIES AND THE BURDEN OF PROOF

The remedy in tort actions is a payment of money to the victim, an order to stop doing something (such as polluting a stream), or an order to do something (such as clean up an industrial waste site). A tort feasor stands to lose money if he or she must pay a damage award or stop production. The loser in a civil trial is in no danger of imprisonment. Because only money is at stake, a different burden of proof is used in civil trials. A **plaintiff** (the person bringing the suit) in a civil case need only prove his or her case by a **preponderance of the evidence.** This concept can best be explained by picturing a blindfolded statue of justice holding her scales. If the scales tip under the weight of evidence ever so slightly to one side or the other, the side to which it tips wins the case.

Unlike criminal cases, which are prosecuted by a representative of the state or federal government, civil cases are brought by private attorneys retained to represent the plaintiff. As in criminal cases, the person bringing the suit has the burden of proving the case.

TYPES OF CRIMES

Crimes are classified as **summary offenses, misdemeanors,** and **felonies.** Summary offenses are minor violations such as speeding tickets, parking violations, and littering. They carry only the possibility of a short prison term, generally under 90 days, and are usually punishable by the payment of a fine. Summary offenses are often tried at the lowest level of the judicial system, often in a streamlined procedure. In many states, summary cases are tried before a district magistrate or justice of the peace. A person charged with a summary offense may not receive all the procedural safeguards a defendant charged with a more serious crime receives. For example, he or she will not have the case tried by a jury.

HISTORICAL HIGHLIGHT
Different Burdens of Proof = Different Verdicts

On June 12, 1994, Nicole Brown Simpson and Ron Goldman were brutally murdered outside of Nicole Simpson's condominium in the Brentwood section of Los Angeles. Nicole was the former wife of football star and sportscaster O. J. Simpson. Bloody footsteps led from the scene. When police arrived at O. J.'s house, they found his white Ford Bronco parked on the street with blood stains trailing from it toward the house. Scaling the fence, Detective Mark Fuhrman claimed he found a bloody glove matching one recovered at the scene of the crime. Simpson was not home, having left earlier in the evening for a business trip to Chicago.

Upon his return from Chicago, Simpson was questioned. Suspicion quickly fell on him because the police were familiar with the violence of the Simpsons' marriage. The police made arrangements for Simpson to turn himself in, but he didn't show up. That evening a low-speed chase took place on the freeways of Los Angeles. The chase was televised live across the United States. Simpson's friend A. C. Cowlings drove the white Ford Bronco as a despondent Simpson threatened suicide in the back seat. The nation watched as the chase ended peacefully at Simpson's house when he surrendered.[10]

Simpson retained a legal "dream team" of high-profile attorneys to defend him against the charges. The prosecution expressed confidence in its ability to convict Simpson. The evidence presented by the prosecution was at first compelling. Bloody footprints at the crime scene matched exclusive, high-fashion shoes belonging to Simpson. Blood stains in the haphazardly parked Bronco and a blood-stained sock found in Simpson's bedroom all pointed to Simpson's guilt.

The "dream team," however, found holes in the prosecution's case. The Bronco was left unsecured in police custody. In a dramatic in-court demonstration, the prosecution had Simpson try on the bloody glove, and it was too small. That led Simpson attorney Johnny Cochran to say in his summation, "If the glove doesn't fit, you must acquit." A DNA expert testified that DNA belonging neither to Simpson nor the victims was found in the blood removed from under Nicole's fingernails. And when Detective Fuhrman was called to testify about the circumstances under which he found the glove, he refused to answer on the ground that the answer might incriminate *him*. In a stunningly short deliberation, the jury returned a "not guilty" verdict. The district attorney had been unable to prove beyond a reasonable doubt that O. J. Simpson had murdered his ex-wife.

Months later, Simpson was sued civilly by Nicole's parents and the family of Ron Goldman. Much the same evidence was presented. But this time Simpson lost. A judgment for $33.5 million was entered against Simpson. Why the different verdicts? The answer is that different burdens of proof are required in a criminal and a civil trial.

The prosecutors in the criminal trial had to prove that Simpson committed the murders beyond a reasonable doubt. In the civil trial, the plaintiffs merely had to prove that most of the evidence showed that Simpson was responsible for the deaths of Nicole Simpson and Ron Goldman. The "dream team" could create enough doubt to get an acquittal. The private attorneys representing Nicole Brown Simpson and Ron Goldman were able to persuade the second jury by a preponderance of the evidence that O. J. Simpson was responsible for their deaths.

Misdemeanors are more serious crimes, but crimes that are not as serious as felonies. A defendant convicted of a misdemeanor offense may serve a prison term, generally less than one year. The length of possible imprisonment varies from crime to crime and state to state. Most theft offenses are misdemeanor offenses unless they involve several thousand dollars. In some cases, repeat offenders are charged with felonies rather than misdemeanors.

Felonies are the most serious crimes. Murder, rape, and robbery are considered felonies in most states. Felonies are punishable by long prison sentences or death. Felony trials occur in state or federal courts. Procedural safeguards are more closely monitored in felony trials because of the serious nature of the potential punishment. A convicted felon faces lifelong consequences. Felons generally cannot serve in public office or on a jury, and often cannot hold professional licenses. They also can't vote while imprisoned, and sometimes for long periods after release. They may also lose other important benefits such as access to student grants and loans for college.

THE AMERICAN JUDICIAL SYSTEM

THE FEDERAL SYSTEM

The American government is a **federal system.** A federal system is one in which the task of governing is divided between different levels of government. The United States has a national government, 50 state governments, and numerous local governments as well as the District of Columbia. In addition, Puerto Rico and the U.S. Virgin Islands are governed by American law.

The Constitution of the United States lays out the structure of the federal government, including its court system. In addition, the Constitution guarantees that American citizens and legal aliens shall enjoy liberties such as freedom of speech and religion and freedom from discrimination on the basis of race, religion, and national origin. In many instances, these rights are even extended to those in the United States illegally. The Constitution provides important procedural safeguards for individuals charged with crimes, including the right to counsel, right to a jury trial, and freedom from cruel and unusual punishments. You will learn more about these guarantees in later chapters.

The Constitution establishes three branches of government. These three are the **legislative,** the **executive,** and the **judicial.** The legislative branch makes laws, the executive branch enforces the laws, and the judicial branch interprets the laws. The judicial branch is headed by the U.S. Supreme Court. The Supreme Court has the last say on the constitutionality of laws. Its decisions establish the law of the land.

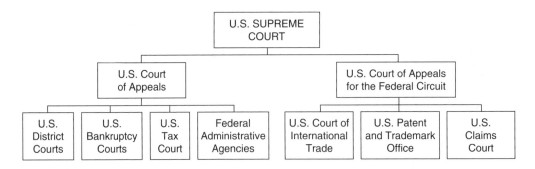

The Federal Court System

The U.S. Supreme Court hears appeals from the federal court system and appeals from state court systems if the issue concerns the interpretation of federal law or the U.S. Constitution or a conflict between states or citizens of different states. Very few cases are actually heard by the Supreme Court. That's because the court can choose those cases that it wants to hear. A litigant who wants to take his or her case to the U.S. Supreme Court must file a **petition for** *certiorari,* requesting that the court hear the case. If the court decides it wants to hear the case, it issues a ***writ of certiorari.*** Generally, the Supreme Court only hears cases it considers important to the national interest.

The ability of the court to declare laws unconstitutional is part of the **checks and balances** system between the branches of government. The legislative branch consists of the Senate and the House of Representatives. Together, these two bodies are referred to as Congress. Congress makes law. The Senate must also approve all judges appointed to the federal bench, including to the Supreme Court, in a process called **confirmation.**

Supreme Court justices and all other federal judges are appointed for life. A federal judge or a justice of the Supreme Court can only be removed from office through **impeachment.** The Constitution specifies that a judge or justice can be impeached if he or she is convicted of "high crimes or misdemeanors." Charges are brought in the House of Representatives. If enough evidence of wrongdoing is found, the House can pass a bill of impeachment. A trial is then held in the Senate. If the judge is convicted by a two-thirds vote of the Senate, he or she is removed from office.

The executive branch of the government is responsible for enforcing the laws enacted by Congress and the protections granted us by the Constitution. The president of the United States heads the executive branch. Under his jurisdiction are numerous agencies, each responsible for enforcing laws under its jurisdiction. For example, the Department of Justice is responsible for enforcing federal criminal laws, the Department of Labor wage and hour laws, and the Food and Drug Administration laws governing foods and pharmaceuticals.

THE FEDERAL JUDICIARY

In addition to the Supreme Court, there are U.S. District Courts and U.S. Courts of Appeals. Federal crimes are tried in the U.S. District Courts and appealed to the U.S. Courts of Appeals, and ultimately to the U.S. Supreme Court. Federal courts try cases when federal laws have been broken, and in other areas where the federal government has been given **exclusive jurisdiction.** For example, the federal court system has exclusive jurisdiction over patent cases, federal crimes, most admiralty cases, and federal bankruptcy cases. Federal courts also have **concurrent jurisdiction** with state courts over some matters. For example, a federal court can decide a civil lawsuit filed by a citizen of one state against a citizen of another state.

The federal system is organized into **Federal Circuits.** There are 13 circuits in all. Within each circuit, there are U.S. District Courts and a U.S. Court of Appeals. The number of U.S. District Courts in a circuit depends on the size of the geographic area covered by the circuit. Each circuit has only one U.S. Court of Appeals. Within each circuit, the District Court must follow the law as interpreted by the Court of Appeals for that circuit, and the rulings of the U.S. Supreme Court. That is, it must abide by *stare decisis* and rely on precedents if any are available.

The Circuit Courts of Appeals must follow the rulings of the U.S. Supreme Court, but don't have to follow the decisions of the other 12 U.S. Court of Appeals. That means that there can be up to 13 different interpretations of a law. These differences are referred to as "splits in the circuits." The U.S. Supreme Court often accepts cases for review to resolve these splits.

There are also special federal courts that handle specific subject matter. For example, the U.S. Tax Court handles federal tax questions and the U.S. Bankruptcy Court handles bankruptcy cases.

The Constitution gives specific powers to the federal government. All other powers are reserved to the states and their citizens. The powers given by the states to the federal government are called the **enumerated powers.** These powers are primarily in areas of national and international interest. Some of the enumerated powers are described in the following sections.

THE SUPREMACY CLAUSE

The **Supremacy Clause** of the Constitution establishes it as the supreme law of the land. The concept that federal law must take precedence over state and local law is called the **preemption doctrine.** When the U.S. Constitution or a federal law addresses an area within the federal government's exclusive jurisdiction, federal law is said to preempt the state or local law.

All states have their own constitutions, but state constitutions can't give the state's citizens fewer rights than given under the U.S. Constitution. In other words, states can give their citizens greater rights than the U.S. Constitution gives, but never fewer rights. The U.S. Constitution serves as the minimum standard below which the states may not go.

THE COMMERCE CLAUSE

Initially, the jurisdiction of the federal courts was very limited. However, as transportation and communications linked the states more closely, some standardization of laws was necessary. The Constitution gives the federal government jurisdiction over matters of **interstate commerce.** In the early days of the republic the **Commerce Clause** of the Constitution was interpreted narrowly. However, as commerce grew more complex, the federal government assumed jurisdiction over anything affecting interstate commerce. For example, the

HISTORICAL HIGHLIGHT

Acquitted in State Court but Convicted in Federal Court

Early in the morning of March 2, 1991, Rodney King and two friends were drinking and apparently decided to go for a ride. Driving erratically and at high speed, King soon drew the attention of the California Highway Patrol and some Los Angeles Police Department officers. After a high-speed chase down the freeway, King headed down city streets. While driving at a moderate rate of speed, he ran several red lights in an attempt to elude the police. Eventually he pulled over.

The police ordered the men out of the car. King's two friends quickly complied, but King did not. Slowly, he got out of the car while yelling at police and refusing to comply with their orders to lie down on the ground. Sergeant Stacey Koon tried to get King to lay down by administering an electrical charge from a Taser. The shock had no effect. Finally, King lay down. At that point, a resident of the area, Mr. George Holliday, began to videotape the scene. King attempted to run away. As he ran, Officer Laurence Powell struck him on the side of the head and he fell. King was still trying to escape as other officers struck him with their batons.

King eventually rolled over and Officer Koon reached for his handcuffs. Then Officer Theodore Briseno stomped on King's chest, and other officers struck and kicked King as he lay on the ground. A full minute passed from the time Koon reached for his handcuffs and when King was restrained. Throughout that period the officers were beating and kicking King.[11]

Initially, criminal charges were filed against the police officers. Their trial took place in rural Simi Valley, California, before an all-white jury. The case focused attention on racial tensions in Los Angeles. Many African Americans felt that King was treated brutally simply because he was black. When the Simi Valley jury returned a "not guilty" verdict, South Central Los Angeles erupted in violence.

Soon after federal criminal charges were filed against the officers. The indictment accused the police officers of violating King's civil rights, a criminal offense under federal law. Koon and Powell were convicted; Wind and Briseno were acquitted. Koon and Powell were sentenced to 30 months in jail.

This was not the first time that defendants have been prosecuted on federal charges for the same behavior they had previously been acquitted of at the state level. Although the practice dates back to the 1920s, prosecuting at the federal level was a popular tactic during the civil rights movement of the 1950s and 1960s when it became obvious that local juries were intimidated into acquitting white supremacists who carried out violent attacks on civil rights activists. The most famous case from that period was the murder of three civil rights workers in Philadelphia, Mississippi, with the complicity of local law enforcement officers. When a local jury acquitted them, federal civil rights charges were filed and the culprits were convicted in the federal trial.[12]

The legal doctrine that allows this prosecution is called **"dual sovereignty."**[13] Under dual sovereignty, persons may be prosecuted by the different "sovereigns" without violating the double jeopardy provisions of the Constitution's Fifth Amendment.

HISTORICAL HIGHLIGHT
Heart of Atlanta Motel v. United States, *379 U.S. 241 (1964)*

Facts: The Civil Rights Act of 1964 was passed pursuant to Congress's power to regulate interstate commerce. The Act provides that "All persons shall be entitled to the full and equal enjoyment of the goods, services, facilities, privileges, advantages, and accommodations of any place of public accommodation . . . without discrimination or segregation on the ground of race, color, religion, or national origin." The Heart of Atlanta Motel was a 216-room motel located in downtown Atlanta. It was easily accessible from several interstate highways. The motel advertised nationally in magazines and on billboards along interstate highways in the South. About 75 percent of its guests were from out of state. The Heart of Atlanta Motel had a policy of refusing to rent rooms to African Americans. After the Civil Rights Act passed, the motel sued the United States. The owner said he was denied the right to choose with whom he wanted to associate. He sought to have the law declared invalid.

Issue: Did Congress have the power under the Commerce Clause to dictate to whom a Georgia motel rented rooms?

Decision: Yes. The motel's refusal to rent to African Americans affected interstate commerce.

Reasoning: Because lack of lodging along interstate highways made it difficult for African Americans to travel, refusal to rent to African Americans effectively prevented many from traveling across state lines. That affected interstate commerce since those who stayed home did not spend money that they would otherwise have spent on lodging, meals, and other attractions throughout the South. Therefore, the enactment of the Civil Rights Act was a valid exercise of the Commerce Clause.

Civil Rights Act of 1964, which guarantees equal civil rights to all regardless of race, sex, religion, or national origin, was passed by Congress under the authority of the Commerce Clause.

As the federal government's role expanded, so did the number of federal laws. Crimes that involved interstate flight posed problems for state and local law enforcement. The advent of the automobile made flight easier, and created a whole new category of crime, auto theft. Interstate flight problems became so large that a federal law enforcement body was needed. This organization eventually became the Federal Bureau of Investigations.

POLICE POWER

What does it mean when we say a government has the right to regulate an activity? We mean that a government has the power to enforce existing laws, and punish those who break them. This is commonly referred to as the government's exercise of its **police**

HISTORICAL HIGHLIGHT
Birth of a National Police Force

Until 1908, there was no national law enforcement agency. States and cities all had their own police forces. But as travel became easier, crime became more mobile. The advent of the automobile changed old-fashioned notions about law enforcement. Criminals could now easily cross state lines and elude prosecution. Local police departments often lacked training and were unable to coordinate investigations that crossed county and state lines. In some cases, police corruption also interfered with the ability to effectively control crime.

President Roosevelt and his Attorney General, Charles Bonaparte (a descendant of Napoleon I), realized the need for a law enforcement body that could cross state lines to apprehend criminals, coordinate the investigations of local police forces, and do it in a professional way with no trace of corruption. Bonaparte created a corp of special agents who were chosen strictly on the basis of their qualifications.

The force was small and tightly controlled by Congress. The idea of a national police force was very controversial. States were wary of this federal intrusion into an area that was traditionally the purview of states, counties, and municipalities. Many feared a national police force as a first step toward widespread federal control of state affairs.

Gradually, events led to a widening of the special agents' jurisdiction. In 1910 the Mann Act was passed into federal law. It is also known as the "White Slave" Act. White Slavery refers to the practice of abducting or luring away rural Southern girls and forcing them into prostitution in Northern cities. Since White Slavery abductions took place across state lines, local police forces were ill-equipped to stop these lucrative operations. Special agents became adept at investigating the trade in young girls.[14]

During World War I, the force was again expanded and charged with investigating violations of the Espionage, Selective Service, and Sabotage Acts. After the war, a series of bombings highlighted the need for the Bureau of Investigations, as the agency was now called. On the evening of June 2, 1919, U.S. Attorney General A. Mitchell Palmer heard a thud at his front door as he was going upstairs to bed. A second later an explosion ripped through the front of his house. No one in the Palmer household was injured, but the bomber was killed. The explosion scattered the anarchist political leaflets the bomber was carrying throughout the neighborhood. America's first "red scare" was on.

The explosion was the first in a series of bombings to take place across the country. The Bureau of Investigation began large-scale arrests of immigrants believed to be communists. These mass arrests became known as "Palmer Raids." The Palmer Raids were organized and carried out by an ambitious law school graduate, J. Edgar Hoover.

Hoover would rise very quickly to assume control of the Bureau in 1926. Until his death in 1972, Hoover would run the FBI with the shrewd ability to manipulate, cajole, and influence Congress and the White House to gain increased funding and greater power. Although some of his methods have been criticized, he managed to build a law enforcement agency that has garnered national and international respect and praise. Today the FBI remains a vital part of the nation's policing forces and an integral part of the nation's homeland security.

power. A state's police power allows it to regulate the health, safety, morals, and the general welfare of its citizens.

Most states have an extensive system of laws and regulations that govern how business is done within the state. The police powers are also exercised through the enactment of criminal laws to protect the public. Whereas federal crimes cover crimes affecting interstate commerce or interfering with the civil rights given all citizens in the Constitution, state criminal laws cover **intrastate** crime, or crime that occurs within the state's borders.

States are also free to delegate some of their police powers to local governments like counties and municipalities. These can then pass laws, usually called ordinances, to protect health, safety, morals, and the general welfare of people in the county or municipality. Ordinances are sometimes classified as criminal laws. For example, it is fairly common for cities to have in place extensive building codes. Violating these may be a summary offense.

THE CRIMINAL TRIAL PROCESS

The criminal trial process is a carefully orchestrated journey from suspicion to conviction to final appeal. For many, the process doesn't end there. Defendants may serve their sentence in full or be granted early release or *parole* after serving just part of the sentence. Defendants may go through a lengthy period of post-release supervision. In addition, they may need to pay fines and penalties and make restitution to victims. This is where theory meets practice, where concepts of punishment, rehabilitation, and restorative justice come together.

Whether you are a paralegal working in the district attorney's office, a parole officer working for the county, or an investigator working with defense attorneys, you will be dealing with people who are facing some of the darkest hours of their lives. Those who haven't "been in trouble with the law" before may (rightfully so) be very frightened. For the first time in their lives, they are staring at the power of the state. Even the rich and famous are awed by the process. Before her trial on charges she lied about her sale of Imclone stock, Martha Stewart told Larry King on his show *Larry King Live* that " . . . no one is ever strong enough for such a thing . . . you have no idea how much worry and sadness and grief it causes."

Others who are more "experienced" may seem nonchalant or even unconcerned about the criminal process. Either way, as a legal professional, you may be one of the few sources of reliable information for defendants facing criminal charges. How you handle questions about the process may help reduce anxiety and let the defendant better help in his or her defense.

The criminal process falls into four distinct phases. They are:

- Investigation, arrest, and pretrial
- Trial
- Appeal
- Serving the sentence

INVESTIGATION, ARREST, AND PRETRIAL

The criminal process begins when authorities are alerted to the possibility that a crime has taken place. This may be something as simple as a police officer observing an illegal act or as complicated as an auditor questioning a company's financial transactions and alerting appropriate authorities. Either way, the criminal process begins.

Once the government authority responsible for enforcing the law for the type of offense has enough information to institute criminal proceedings, an arrest may be made. In the case of an officer observing an illegal act, the arrest may take place immediately. Because probable cause must be present for all arrests, the officer will have to justify his decision with a sworn statement or complaint after the fact. The officer need not, however, wait for a magistrate to authorize the arrest. This, of course, is based on the practical reality that the offender might be long gone before a magistrate's permission could be obtained.

A police officer may also issue a citation if the offense is minor. If you've ever been caught speeding or running a stop sign, you were probably issued a citation. Citations usually allow the defendant to plead guilty and send in a fine or elect to have a hearing before a district justice or magistrate. If the officer finds illegal narcotics or the driver fails a sobriety check, it's more likely that the driver will be arrested on the spot rather than cited, given the more serious nature of the offense.

Naturally, police officers don't catch every defendant "red-handed" so that an immediate arrest or citation is possible. Sometimes an arrest is made only after a long investigation, weeks or months after the offense was allegedly committed. In that case, the arrest is usually carried out by the use of an **arrest warrant.** To get an arrest warrant, a police officer must apply for one with the local judiciary—usually a district magistrate or other judge assigned to oversee arrest warrants. The application includes a police officer or investigator's sworn statement or affidavit about what he or she believes happened and who committed the offense. Before an arrest warrant is issued, the magistrate or judge must be convinced that there is probable cause to believe the offense took place and the defendant committed it based on what the officer alleges in the affidavit or statement.

Armed with a signed arrest warrant, police officers can arrest the defendant and bring him or her to a central processing center, usually located at the police station, municipal building, or local jail. There, the defendant is held temporarily while being processed. Processing may include fingerprinting and a thorough search. If the police officers haven't already done so, they will now read the defendant the *Miranda warning.* They may then also question the defendant—who, of course, is free to refuse to answer or to demand an attorney be present during questioning.

In most jurisdictions the defendant will be brought before a magistrate soon after arrest. This is generally referred to as the **preliminary arraignment.** At that point, the magistrate may rule on whether bail should be granted. Whether and how much bail is set depends on the seriousness of the charges and the likelihood that the defendant will appear for trial if he is released. The more serious the offense, the less likely bail will be granted and the higher bail is likely to be. In some cases, bail may be nothing more than the defendant's promise to appear for trial. This is usually referred to as being released on one's own recognizance. Defendants with close ties to the community and no prior criminal convictions are most likely to be released on bail. Sometimes conditions are attached to bail, such as surrendering a passport to prevent flight to another country.

The next legal proceeding the defendant will face is the **preliminary hearing.** The preliminary hearing is the first stage in the criminal process in which the government is required to present actual evidence. In most cases, the state is represented by the arresting police officer. He or she will act as the government's representative and call any witnesses needed to prove that there is probable cause to hold the defendant over for trial. Sometimes, especially in cases where the defendant is mounting an aggressive defense, the district attorney or prosecutor will handle the preliminary hearing for the government.

In high-profile cases, preliminary hearings may become something akin to a minitrial. For the defense, the preliminary hearing may be a good opportunity to look at the evidence the state has against a client. This is especially important if the defense wants to gauge how well a witness handles being on the witness stand. It also gives the defense an opportunity to get a transcript of the witnesses' statements and be able to use those transcripts later if their version of the story changes later. The defense usually does not present any evidence at the preliminary hearing. If the government's case is weak, the case may even be dismissed after the preliminary hearing.

The evidentiary standard the government needs to meet at the preliminary hearing is simply that there is **probable cause.** Put succinctly, the government needs to prove that it is more likely than not that an offense took place and that it was the defendant who committed it. If the magistrate or district justice hearing the case believes the government has proven that it is more likely than not that the defendant committed the crime, the defendant will be ordered bound over for trial.

Even after the preliminary hearing, the defendant has not been officially charged with a crime. The government must jump yet another hurdle—it must either convince a **grand jury** that the defendant committed a crime or it must persuade the prosecutor of the same. A grand jury is a body of citizens whose job it is to determine if a crime has been committed and if a person should be charged with that crime based on probable cause. In many jurisdictions, the decision to formally charge a defendant with a crime is left to the district attorney or state attorney. He or she has the authority to file an **information,** which formally charges the defendant with a crime and begins the next phase of the process—the actual trial phase. The information is very specific and names the penal sections of the law that the defendant is accused of violating. Very often it will include the most serious crimes the defendant is charged with as well as any other lesser included offenses. For example, a defendant may be charged with rape, indecent assault, aggravated assault, and simple assault. If the prosecution is unable to prove the more serious crime, he or she may still get a conviction for one of the lesser offenses. In addition, the inclusion of the lesser offenses allow some room for maneuvering if the prosecution and the defense decide to engage in **plea bargaining.** Plea bargaining is the practice of negotiating with a defendant and his attorney concerning the terms of a guilty plea. For example, a defendant might be persuaded to plead guilty to indecent assault but not rape because he knows if convicted of rape he faces a much longer sentence than if he is sentenced on the indecent assault charge.

If the jurisdiction uses a grand jury to commence criminal trials, the charging document is referred to as an **indictment.** There is great flexibility in whether a defendant is charged with a crime. A district attorney has the discretion to decline to prosecute cases in most jurisdictions. The district attorney also typically can drop a case at any stage if he or she believes that would be in the interest of justice. This is done with a *nol pros* motion, which stands for the Latin *nolle prosequi,* translated loosely as no prosecution. Requiring an indictment or an information before people can be tried for a crime is another way to assure that innocent persons are not subjected to the power of the state without good reason. It is another check and balance on the power of the state over its citizens.

After the defendant is formally charged by indictment or information, he or she is then formally **arraigned.** At arraignment, the formal charges are read to the defendant and he or she must enter a formal response to the charges, or a **plea.** The plea may be not guilty, guilty, *nolo contendere,* or not guilty by reason of insanity.

A caution is in order. All jurisdictions have strict time limits that require the government to move the criminal process forward in a timely fashion. Those limits are designed to prevent the government from holding defendants for extended periods of time without having the opportunity for a trial on the charges. For example, in many states, defendants must be brought to trial within 180 days of being charged if imprisoned or 360 days if free on bail. Any continuance requested by the defendant is excluded from the count. If the case isn't brought in a timely fashion, the penalty is dismissal of the charges.

There are some exceptions, most notably for those who have been arrested on the battlefield in Afghanistan in the "war on terror" or are suspected terrorists picked up elsewhere in the world and held at Guantanamo Bay in Cuba. In addition, Americans suspected of terrorist activities and picked up on the battlefield or in the United States have been designated as "enemy combatants" by the president of the United States. At the time of this writing, the Supreme Court ruled 6–3 that foreign nationals held at Guantanamo Bay, Cuba, have the right to have federal courts determine whether they are being held illegally. The Court, in *Rasul et al. v. Bush,* 124 S.Ct. 2686 (2004), remanded their cases to the lower court for an opportunity to challenge their detention. The Court also decided, in *Hamdi v. Rumsfeld,* 124 S.Ct. 2633 (2004), that an American citizen caught on the battlefield in Afghanistan is entitled to a limited judicial inquiry into the legality of his detention. The Court did not specify how or when the detainees or Hamdi can exercise those rights. Hamdi's attorneys negotiated for his release; the government did not charge him. Mr. Hamdi returned to Saudi Arabia and renounced his U.S. citizenship.

TRIAL

As a practical matter, most criminal cases never make it to trial. Most cases are disposed of by guilty pleas through plea bargaining. Plea bargaining in one form or another takes place in every jurisdiction. If the defendant doesn't plead guilty or no plea bargain is entered into, the case will proceed to trial.

Most jurisdictions hold special sessions of criminal court. Defendants who want a trial may select either trial by judge or trial by jury. Which a defendant chooses depends on many factors such as the reputation of the judge who would hear the case and the type of crime the defendant has been charged with. A separate jury pool is called from the community for each criminal session. Jurors for individual cases are selected from the pool. If you are called to jury duty, you may hear several cases.

If the defendant chooses a jury trial, he or she may assist in the selection of jurors from the jury pool. Sometimes the defense will even hire jury consultants, who are specially trained psychologists or sociologists well versed in human psychology who predict which jurors may favor one side over the other and who understand group dynamics.

The process of selecting jurors starts with voir dire, which involves asking potential jurors questions to determine whether they can judge the case fairly and impartially. Voir dire also helps to eliminate jurors who know too much about the case or who are related to the defendant, the victim, or any of the witnesses or attorneys or police officers involved in the case.

Both the prosecution and the defense help choose the jurors. Either side may challenge the selection of a juror. The attorneys can reject an unlimited number of jurors *for cause*. For example, a juror who admits he has followed the case closely in the press and has already concluded that the defendant is guilty will be dismissed for cause. Attorneys can also reject potential jurors using a *peremptory challenge*. Peremptory challenges are essentially wild cards available to either side. When used, the attorney need not state a specific reason. Usually, there is a set number of peremptory challenges allowed. For more information on the jury process, see Chapter 6, The Constitutional Right to Trial by Jury.

After a jury has been selected, it's time for the prosecution and the defense to address that jury through *opening statements*. Because the government has the burden of proof to show the defendant is guilty beyond a reasonable doubt, the government makes its opening statement first. The government's opening statement usually outlines what the prosecutor expects to prove and who the jurors can expect to hear testify for the prosecution. Essentially, the government tries to give the jury a road map of the case, orienting them.

The defense may make its opening statement next, or it may choose to wait until after the prosecution has rested its entire case. Many defense attorneys think it's better to wait until later, when they have already heard the government's witnesses and evidence. They can then tailor their opening to the weaknesses in the government's case.

After opening, the government presents its witnesses for *direct examination* and the defense *cross-examines* them. Either party may then ask questions again by *redirect exam* and *recross exam*. Redirect and recross questions are limited to subject matter raised in the last cross or redirect exam.

Because the government has the burden of proof and the defendant is considered innocent until proven guilty, the government must prove each element of the crime charged. That is, they must prove beyond a reasonable doubt that the defendant intentionally committed the act charged. Many prosecutors use a checklist of the elements of the crime charged and cross off each element as the evidence is presented. For example, in a theft case, the prosecutor would have to present evidence of who owned the stolen goods and that the item was taken without the owner's permission. Finally, the prosecution would have to show that it was the defendant who physically took the owner's property, intending to permanently deprive the owner of it.

At the end of the prosecution's case, the government rests. If the defense thinks that the prosecution failed to prove an element of its case, it may ask for the charges to be dismissed. If the motion is denied, the defense may present its case. It is not required to do so, since the burden is on the prosecution to prove the case beyond a reasonable doubt. If the defense does present evidence or witnesses, the prosecution has a chance to cross-examine them. Recall that the defendant is not required to testify against himself, and therefore may not testify. The jury will be instructed that it cannot consider the defendant's decision not to testify as evidence of guilt. The decision to testify or remain silent depends on the case and on the defendant. If his or her testimony is likely to be sympathetic, it may be best to testify. If not, the best option may be to stay silent.

If the defense does have witnesses testify, the prosecution may present rebuttal evidence to disprove the evidence.

Finally, the attorneys present closing arguments. The prosecution goes first, usually outlining what it believes its evidence has proven. The defense then closes. The prosecution then has one last chance to address the jury.

The jury then retires to the jury room and elects a foreperson to help direct its deliberations. In high-profile cases, the jury may be sequestered both during trial and deliberations to avoid tainting their process with outside news or opinions. If the jury is unable to reach a decision, the jury is said to be *hung*. The jury can judge the defendant guilty or not guilty. Its decision is the **verdict.** In a case in which the defendant has raised insanity as a defense, the jury can also find the defendant not guilty by reason of insanity. In some states, they can also find the defendant guilty but mentally ill. For more on the insanity defense, see Chapter 14, Common Law Defenses.

After the jury has rendered a verdict, the court will enter the judgment in the record. In those cases where the judge is deciding the case, he or she will announce the verdict and enter judgment.

The defendant may be sentenced immediately or after pre-sentence investigation and recommendations. There may be sentence guidelines or mandatory sentences. In the case of a capital crime tried by a jury, there will be a sentencing phase of the trial.

APPEAL

Every defendant is entitled to an appeal of some sort. In state criminal cases, those appeals go though the state system and may include a trip to the state's highest court or even the U.S. Supreme Court. Only the defendant may appeal. If the jury concludes that the defendant is not guilty, that is the end of the matter. Appeals generally must be filed within 30 days of sentencing.

The defendant's appeal may attack any defect in the trial or evidence. Generally, however, the issue appealed must have been preserved during the trial by an objection on the record. For example, if the defense believes a piece of evidence should not have been admitted, it must have challenged the admission at the time to preserve the issue on appeal.

Once all direct appeals are exhausted, the defendant may still have an opportunity to be heard. He or she can do so through a process called *habeas corpus*. A *writ of habeas corpus* is an order by federal court to "bring the body" of the prisoner to the court. It is an old right designed to protect citizens from abusive government practices. A *writ of habeas corpus* may be filed years into a defendant's sentence and raise issues that weren't raised earlier such as ineffective counsel. It may also be raised if there is new evidence of innocence such as a DNA test that clears the defendant or proof of some form of corruption during the trial.

SERVING THE SENTENCE

The defendant may begin serving the sentence immediately after trial or may be free pending appeal. Once direct appeals are over, the defendant will have to start his sentence. He or she will get credit for any time already served while awaiting trial.

Most defendants will serve a minimum sentence (generally half of the bottom range of the sentence). In some cases, the sentence range cannot be deviated from. Parole boards generally consider when the defendant may be released. Defendants may also ask the parole board or the governor (or president) for a pardon under limited circumstances.

Once parole is granted or the defendant has served his sentence, the defendant is released. In the case of parole, he or she will be supervised for as long as the maximum sentence would have been. If he or she has served the maximum sentence, there is no additional supervision unless he or she is a sexual predator as defined under that state's laws.

SOURCES OF LAW

As you have already learned, the Constitution and the laws Congress passes pursuant to its powers are the supreme law of the land. But they aren't the only source of law in the United States. Law is also created by treaties signed with foreign governments, laws enacted by state and local legislatures, regulations of administrative agencies, executive orders, and judicial decisions.

TREATIES

Treaties with foreign governments have the force of law. Any treaty negotiated by the president or his representatives must be ratified by the U.S. Senate to become law. This is part of the Senate's **advise and consent** duty under the Constitution. The most common way treaties affect criminal law is through the power of **extradition.** Countries with an extradition treaty with the United States have agreed to send an accused criminal to the United States where he or she can be charged with a crime and tried. Likewise, the United States is the signatory to many treaties that obligate it to return persons accused of a crime in another country to that country for trial. Not all countries have extradition treaties with the United States.

CODIFIED LAWS

Codified laws are laws passed by either a federal or state legislature. These laws are collected and classified by topic. Laws passed by the U.S. Congress become part of the U.S. Code. State laws are published in the various state codes. Local governments are said to be "creatures of the state" in that they draw their power from state governments. They may pass local laws or ordinances within the bounds of their charters.

HISTORICAL HIGHLIGHT
Treaty Obligations and Criminal Law

Under the U.S. Constitution, treaties negotiated by the president and his representatives and ratified by the Senate have the same force of law as the Constitution itself. In theory, treaty provisions should have priority over state laws. But states have seldom been willing to abide by treaties they were not specifically a party to.

A case in point is the execution of a Paraguayan national by the name of Angel Francisco Breard (pronounced BRAY-ard). Breard was arrested for the stabbing death and sexual assault of Ruth Dickie, his neighbor. Under the Vienna Convention, an international treaty signed by 130 nations including the United States and Paraguay, police are required to notify the consular office of a nation if they arrest a foreign national. Virginia police never did so.

Mr. Breard confessed to the crime, but claimed that the reason he committed the stabbing was that his father-in-law had put a satanic curse on him. Breard had the benefit of court-appointed attorneys who advised him not to testify at his trial, and probably didn't endorse the satanic curse defense. Breard testified anyway, and was sentenced to death. The government of Paraguay sued Virginia officials in federal court complaining that Breard had been denied his rights under the Vienna Convention.

The case worked its way through to the Supreme Court. The Court ruled in a 6–3 decision that because Breard had not raised the Vienna Convention violation in his initial defense, he could not raise it now. Paraguay presented the case to the International Court of Justice. The International Court of Justice hears cases involving international treaties. It is also known as the World Court and is a part of the United Nations. The International Court of Justice agreed to hear the case and scheduled argument for the fall of 1998, well after Breard's scheduled April 14, 1998, execution date.

Secretary of State Madeline Albright personally requested that Virginia authorities delay Breard's execution until the International Court could hear the case. She cited possible repercussions for Americans charged with crimes overseas. After all, if the United States refused to comply with the treaty, why should other signatory nations? Virginia refused and executed Breard on April 14, hours after the Supreme Court denied his final appeal for a stay of execution.[15] Since then, other foreign nationals have been executed for crimes committed on American soil without having been given the opportunity to consult with their embassies when arrested.

Foreign diplomats traveling or working in the United States enjoy **diplomatic immunity.** Foreign diplomats cannot be charged with a crime or imprisoned unless they or their government agree. Some treaties also have specific guidelines for the arrest of foreign nationals accused of crimes. All of the states of the union have extradition agreements with each other.

HISTORICAL HIGHLIGHT
Waiving Diplomatic Immunity

Foreign diplomats working or traveling in the United States are protected from arrest and imprisonment by diplomatic immunity. Some large American cities have a continuous problem with foreign diplomats who exercise their right to diplomatic immunity. The problem is particularly big in New York City, home to the headquarters of the United Nations, and Washington, D.C., home to over a hundred foreign embassies. For example, in New York City, diplomats from Belarus managed to amass over $41,000 in overdue traffic fines during the first half of 1996. Overdue parking tickets may be frustrating to city officials in major cities where parking is hard to come by, but diplomatic immunity creates greater problems when diplomats commit crimes. In some cases, a foreign government will waive immunity and allow its consular employees to be prosecuted and imprisoned.

On January 3, 1997, 16-year-old Joviane Waltrick was killed in a five-car crash along Diplomat Row in Washington, D.C. The accident was caused by a Gueorgui Makharadze, a high-ranking diplomat of the Republic of Georgia. He was driving under the influence of alcohol and weaving through cars while traveling at a speed of nearly 85 miles per hour through crowded city streets. The Republic of Georgia waived diplomatic immunity for the criminal charges, but not the civil charges. Makharadze pleaded guilty to involuntary manslaughter and four counts of aggravated assault, but relatives of the victims could not recover civil damages in court.[16] Makharadze is now serving his sentence in a U.S. jail.[17]

Another instance in which diplomatic immunity was waived occurred in 1989 when a Belgian army sergeant was charged with murdering two homosexual men in Fort Lauderdale, Florida. Belgium agreed to waive immunity after the prosecutors pledged not to seek the death penalty. He is now serving two 25-year sentences.

The United States has not been quick to waive diplomatic immunity for *its* diplomats, though. In 1993, an American envoy stationed in Moscow killed a pedestrian while driving down a dark street. He was accused of driving drunk, but U.S. officials insisted the accusation was false. The United States did not waive diplomatic immunity, and instead sent the diplomat home.

REGULATIONS

Regulations are written by administrative agencies. At the national level these become part of the Code of Federal Regulations (CFR). When Congress passes a law, it often instructs an appropriate administrative agency to develop regulations to give guidance on how the law should be enforced. For instance, regulations dealing with counterfeiting are developed by the Department of the Treasury, the agency that is responsible for the legitimate printing of bills and coinage. Regulations that are consistent with the law under which they are promulgated are also law.

Executive Orders

The president and the governors of the states have the power to issue executive orders. The power to issue executive orders comes from the power delegated by legislatures to the executive branch to enforce the laws.

Judicial Decisions

As you learned earlier in this chapter, the doctrine of *stare decisis* is employed by judges to create common law. Much of American common law can be traced back to English common law.

Stare decisis lends uniformity and consistency to legal decisions, at least within a state. A court is bound to follow a precedent of a higher court in its system. For example, a state trial court is bound to follow the decision of that state's supreme court. But a state does not have to follow the precedence of another state's highest court. Thus, *stare decisis* promotes uniformity within a jurisdiction, but not necessarily across different jurisdictions.

Priority of Law

The U.S. Constitution is the supreme law of the land. Any treaty ratified by the Senate carries the same weight as the Constitution. Federal statutes take precedence over federal regulations. Federal law will take precedence over state law.

Most state legal systems are a mirror image of the federal structure. The state constitution is the highest state law. State statutes supersede state regulations, and state laws take precedence over local laws and ordinances. Most state court systems also mirror the federal judicial system. Each state has a set of courts that are responsible for trials and another set that handles intermediate appeals. All 50 states also have a state supreme court, although it may go by another name.

CHAPTER SUMMARY

Every society has a body of laws. Laws govern the behavior of members of society. Laws are created and enforced by government. The United States has a system of law derived from the English common law.

Common law relies on *stare decisis* and precedent to decide cases. Courts must follow earlier decisions when faced with a new case. This makes the legal system predictable and stable.

Jurisprudence is the study of law. There are many theories of law, or schools of jurisprudence. The consensus theory holds that society decides what is a crime and what isn't. The ruling class theory and the Command School theory posit that the ruling classes decide what is legal and what is illegal. Blackstone classified crime into two types: those that are *mala in se*, or inherently evil, and those that are *mala prohibita*, or illegal because society decides they are. The Natural Law School believes that people have natural, inherent rights and that laws are based on what is right. The Historical School sees laws as changing to accommodate changes in the society. The Analytical School relies on logic. The

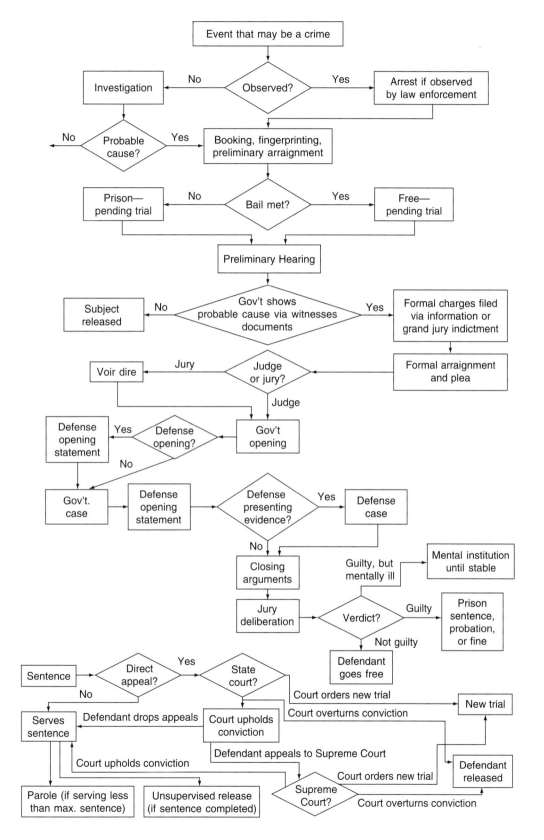

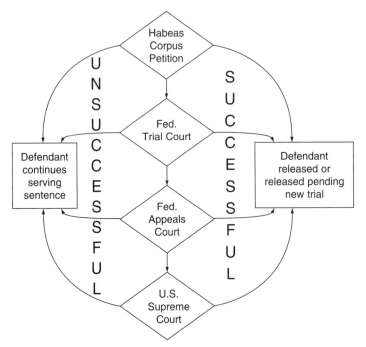

Procedure When Defendant Is Serving Sentence

Sociological School, or the realists, believe that law should be created to shape societal behavior. Finally, the Critical Legal Studies School and the Fem-Crits believe that laws are arbitrary rules to enforce the status quo and oppress and control those not in power.

A crime is a wrong against society. Criminal law differs from civil law in several important ways. First, criminal law seeks to protect all of society from lawbreakers while civil law deals with vindication of individual, private rights. Second, criminal cases are always brought in the name of the people by a representative of the government, while civil cases are brought by the private representatives of the litigants. Third, in order to win a criminal case, the prosecutor must prove the case beyond a reasonable doubt, a very high standard. Private plaintiffs need only prove their case by a preponderance of the evidence, a much lighter burden of proof.

Crimes are classified in order of their relative seriousness. Summary offenses are minor violations, usually punishable by either a short period of imprisonment or a fine. Misdemeanors are more serious offenses and carry a penalty of up to a year in prison. Felony offenses are the most serious, and are punishable by a long prison sentence or death.

The American judicial system is part of a federal system of government. The United States has a national government, 50 state governments, and numerous local governments. The framework for our federal system is found in the United States Constitution. It established three branches of government: the legislative to make law, the executive to enforce laws, and the judicial to interpret laws. Each of the three branches serves as a check and balance on each other.

The Supreme Court, federal laws, and treaties are the supreme law of the land. The federal judiciary is headed by the U.S. Supreme Court. The system is divided into 13 circuits. Each circuit has trial courts called U.S. District Courts and an intermediate appellate court called the U.S. Court of Appeals. Justices of the Supreme Court and other federal judges serve for life. They can only be removed by impeachment. Federal courts have exclusive jurisdiction over some subject matter and concurrent jurisdiction with the states over other matters. Some areas of exclusive jurisdiction include patents and federal tax cases.

State court systems parallel the federal judicial system in many ways. Each has a trial court, at least one intermediate appellate court, and a supreme court. State courts follow the same hierarchy as federal courts. That is, the lower courts must follow the decisions previously handed down by the Supreme Court and the intermediate appellate court. The intermediate appellate court must follow the state supreme court's decisions. And all state courts must abide by decisions made by the U.S. Supreme Court.

The Supremacy Clause of the Constitution establishes that federal law takes precedence over state and local law. The Commerce Clause allows the federal government to pass laws that regulate interstate commerce. Both the federal government and state and local governments have police powers. Through its exercise of police powers, government can regulate the health, safety, morals, and welfare of its citizens.

The legal system provides many safeguards for persons thought to have committed a crime. These safeguards exist at every level of the criminal process. For example, persons can only be arrested for a crime if a law enforcement officer has either observed the accused committing the crime or has probable cause to convince a magistrate or judge that the accused committed the crime and a warrant is issued. The defendant must then be formally charged with the crime and be given an opportunity early on to defend against the charges.

A defendant is entitled to a trial at which the prosecution must prove beyond a reasonable doubt that he or she has committed the crime. The convicted defendant may then appeal the verdict. He or she can also challenge the verdict later under some circumstances such as newly discovered evidence.

There are many sources of law. The Constitution is one source. Others include treaties, codified laws, regulations, ordinances, executive orders, and judicial decisions.

KEY TERMS

Advise and consent: The Constitutional relationship of the Senate to the president regarding the selection of federal judges and other duties.

Analytical School: The school of jurisprudential thought that believes laws are based on logic.

Arraignment: The stage of a criminal case at which the defendant is first formally charged with a specific crime.

Arrest warrant: Document approved by a magistrate or judge attesting that there is probable cause to believe that someone has committed a specific crime and authorizing that person's arrest.

Beyond a reasonable doubt: The burden of proof the prosecution must meet in a criminal case in order to convict the accused.

Bourgeoisie: In Marxist theory, the class in society that controls the means of production.

Burden of proof: The duty to go forward to prove an allegation with facts.

Checks and balances: The system of restraints built into the U.S. Constitution that prevent one branch of government from dominating the others.

Command School: The school of jurisprudential thought that posits that laws are dictated to the society by the ruling class of that society.

Commerce Clause: The clause of the U.S. Constitution that gives the federal government the right to regulate interstate commerce. Article I, Section 8, Clause 3.

Common Law: The system of jurisprudence, originated in England and later applied in the United States, that is based on judicial precedent rather than legislative enactments.

Concurrent jurisdiction: Jurisdiction shared by two or more courts.

Confirmation: The process of approval of presidential nominees by the Senate.

Consensus theory : A theory developed by Emile Durkheim that postulates that laws develop out of a society's consensus of what is right and wrong.

Crime: A wrong against society.

Defendant: In a civil case the person against whom a suit is filed. In a criminal trial, the person accused of a crime.

Diplomatic immunity: The courtesy afforded all diplomats while in foreign countries that allow them to be immune from prosecution for crimes they commit.

Dual sovereignty: The legal doctrine that allows a person to be prosecuted by different "sovereigns" or governmental entities for the same action or set of actions. Most commonly prosecution by both the federal and state government for the same action

Elite theory: Also known as the "ruling class" theory, it is the theory put forth by Karl Marx that postulates laws exist only as a means of class oppression.

Enumerated powers: The powers explicitly given to the federal government in the U.S. Constitution.

Exclusive jurisdiction: A court with exclusive jurisdiction is the only court that can hear the case.

Executive: One of the three branches of government; the branch charged with enforcing the law.

Extradition: The process of returning an accused criminal to the jurisdiction in which he or she is charged.

Federal Circuit: One of 13 federal judicial districts, each with a U.S. District Court and a U.S. Court of Appeals.

Federal system: A system of governing where government is divided into different levels.

Felonies: The most serious classification of crimes punishable by long prison sentences or death.

Fem-Crits: A school of jurisprudence that holds the legal system perpetuates the oppression of women in society.

Grand jury: A body of citizens whose job it is to determine if a crime has been committed and if a person should be charged with that crime based on probable cause.

Historical School: The school of jurisprudential thought that believes that law is an accumulation of societal traditions.

Impeachment: The process by which Congress may charge a sitting judge, president, or vice president with "high crimes and misdemeanors" and convict that person in a trial before the Senate. A conviction results in removal from office.

Indictment: A formal charge by which the defendant has been charged with a crime, usually as the result of a grand jury inquiry.

Information: A formal document signed and filed by a district attorney or prosecutor that charges an individual with a specific crime.

Interstate commerce: Commerce that occurs between states as opposed to strictly within a state's borders.

Intrastate: Occurring within a state's border.

Judicial: One of the three branches of government; the branch charged with interpreting the law.

Jurisdiction: The power to hear and decide a case. Jurisdiction can be divided as to subject matter, parties, or territory.

Jurisprudence: The study of law.

Law: The body of rules of conduct created by government and enforced by the authority of government.

Legislative: One of the three branches of government; the one charged with making the law.

Mala in se: According to Blackstone, a category of crimes that are bad in and of themselves.

Mala prohibita: According to Blackstone, a category of crimes that are crimes because society has decided they are crimes.

Misdemeanors: Crimes punishable by relatively short prison sentences, or fines. Misdemeanors are less serious than felonies.

Moral theory of law: A theory subscribed to by Natural Law adherents stating that laws are based on the moral code of the society.

Natural Law School: The school of jurisprudential thought that teaches that laws are based on morality and ethics, and that people have natural rights.

Petition for *certiorari*: Request by a litigant that the U.S. Supreme Court hear his or her appeal.

Plaintiff: The party who files a lawsuit.

Plea: A formal response to criminal charges. A plea may be not guilty, guilty, nolo contendere, or not guilty by reason of insanity.

Plea bargaining: The practice of negotiating with a defendant and his attorney about the terms of a guilty plea.

Police power: The power of a government to enforce laws and regulate the health, safety, morals, and welfare of the population.

Precedent: Prior decision that a court must follow when deciding a new, similar case.

Preemption doctrine: This concept that federal law must take precedence over state and local law.

Preliminary arraignment: An accused's first official notification of the charges against him or her. The preliminary arraignment generally occurs shortly after arrest.

Preliminary hearing: A formal hearing that is the first occasion at which the government must produce evidence against the defendant. The prosecutor must convince the judge or magistrate hearing the case that it is more likely than not that the defendant committed the crime he or she is charged with.

Preponderance of the evidence: Evidence that is more convincing than the opposing evidence; enough evidence to tip the scales of justice.

Probable cause: A low standard of proof in a criminal case used to justify an arrest or hold a defendant over for trial after a preliminary hearing. The standard requires that there be sufficient proof to convince a reasonable person that it is more likely than not that he or she committed the crime charged.

Proletariat: In Marxist theory, the working class who must sell their labor in order to survive.

Realists: Belonging to the Sociological School of jurisprudence. Realists believe that the purpose of law is to shape societal behavior.

Sociological School: Adherents of the Sociological School of jurisprudence believe that the purpose of law is to shape societal behavior. Believers are called realists.

Stare decisis: To stand by that which was decided; rule by which courts decide new cases based on how they decided similar cases before.

Summary offenses: Minor offenses such as parking tickets, or minor traffic violations.

Supremacy Clause: The clause in the U.S. Constitution that states that the Constitution, federal law, and treaties are the supreme law of the land. Article VI, Section 2.

Tort: A private or civil wrong or injury independent of contract, resulting from a breach of a legal duty.

Tort feasor: A person who commits a tort.

U.S. Courts of Appeal: The federal court system's intermediate appellate courts.

U.S. District Courts: The federal court system's trial courts.

U.S. Supreme Court: The highest court in the United States.

Verdict: A judge or jury's decision at the end of a trial. The verdict in a civil case must be by at least a preponderance of the evidence, while the verdict in a criminal case must be beyond a reasonable doubt.

Writ of certiorari: Notice from the Supreme Court that the court will hear a case.

DISCUSSION QUESTIONS

1. What do you see as the advantages and disadvantages of a Common Law system?
2. Durkheim felt that laws were agreed upon standards of a society, but Marx felt that laws were put in place by a society's elite to serve the elite's interest. Which do you think is closer to the truth and why?
3. What are the major differences between criminal law and civil law?
4. In what ways is the judiciary restrained by the legislative and executive branches? What power does the judiciary have to restrain the other branches?
5. What is police power? Can you think of ways that states have abused the police power? What is it that makes a police power legitimate?
6. Does the American policy of giving ratified treaties the force of law put the United States at a disadvantage internationally?
7. What do you think has been the impact of the Supreme Court's decision on African Americans who choose to travel through several states?

FOR FURTHER READING

1. Hamilton, J., Madison, J., & Jay, J. *The Federalist Papers*. For the student who wants to develop an understanding of the Constitution as the founding fathers saw it, this classic work is essential reading. Written by Alexander Hamilton, James Madison, and John Jay, the work was originally circulated to argue for the ratification of the Constitution.
2. Young, A. (ed.) (1976). *The American Revolution: Explorations in the History of American Radicalism*. Dekalb, IL: Northern Illinois University Press. This collection of essays by historians explores the ideologies of the men who created the American Revolution.
3. DeTocqueville, A. (1969). *Democracy in America* (rev. ed.). New York: Harper Collins. This classic study of what makes American democracy unique was first published in the 1800s by a Frenchman who traveled extensively through the new United States. His observations on American democracy are regarded as some of the most insightful ever made.
4. Maier, P. (1997). *American Scripture*. New York: Alfred A. Knopf. This work analyzes the Declaration of Independence and the attitudes that shaped its framers' thoughts.

5. Burger, W. (1995). *It Is So Ordered: A Constitution Unfolds.* New York: William Morrow. Written by former chief justice of the U.S. Supreme Court Warren E. Burger, this book analyses some of the most important cases to have been decided by the Supreme Court in layperson's terms.

QUOTATIONS FOR CHAPTER ONE

1. *Let us consider the reason of the case. For nothing is law that is not reason.*
   John Powell, English judge (1645–1713)

2. *The basis of a democratic state is liberty.*
   Aristotle, *The Politics* (343 B.C.)

3. *Men being . . . by Nature, all free, equal and independent, no one can be put out of this Estate, and subjected to the Political Power of another, without his own consent.*
   John Locke, *The Second Treatise on Government* (1690)

4. *Governments . . . deriv(e) their just powers from the consent of the governed.*
   Thomas Jefferson, *Declaration of Independence* (July 4, 1776)

5. *We may define a republic . . . as a government which derives all its powers directly or indirectly from the great body of the people, and is administered by persons holding their offices during pleasure, for a limited period, or during good behavior.*
   James Madison, *The Federalist* (January 16, 1788)

6. *The people made the Constitution, and the people can unmake it. It is the creature of their own will, and lives only by their will.*
   John Marshall, *Cohens v. Virginia* (1821)

7. *Democracy is not so much a form of government as a set of principles.*
   Woodrow Wilson, *Atlantic Monthly* (March 1901)

8. *"We the People" tell the government what to do, it doesn't tell us. "We the people" are the driver, the government is the car. And we decide where it should go, and by what route, and how fast.*
   Ronald Reagan, farewell address (January 11, 1989)

ENDNOTES

1. E. Durkheim, *The Division of Labor in Society* (New York: Free Press, 1933; original work published 1893).

2. K. Marx and F. Engels, *The Communist Manifesto: A Modern Edition* (New York: Verso, 1998; original work published 1848; original English version 1888).

3. D. R. Coquillette, *Ideology and Incorporation III: Reason Regulated—The Post-Restoration English Civilians, 1653–1735+*, 67 B. U. L Rev. 289 (1987).

4. Blackstone, *Commentaries on the Laws of England,* ed. Cooley (1899).

5. Coquillette, *Ideology and Incorporation III.*

6. Ibid.

7. Ibid.

8. Ibid.

9. D. L. Rhode, *Feminist Critical Theories.* 42 Stan. L. Rev. 617 (1990).

10. Cable News Network, *The Murder* (1995)
    http://www.cnn.com/US/OJ/murder/index.html.

11. *United States v. Koon, Powell, Wind, and Briseno,* 833 F. Supp. 769 (C. D. Cal, 1993).

12. *United States v. Price, et al.,* 383 U.S. 787 (1966).

13. *United States v. Lanza,* 260 U.S. 377 (1922).

14. Federal Bureau of Investigation, *A Short History of the Federal Bureau of Investigation* (Washington, DC 1998) *http://www.fbi.gov/history/hist.htm.*

15. J. R. Schmertz Jr., and M. Meier, Despite requests for stay of execution from International Court of Justice, U.S. Supreme Court denies habeas corpus relief to convicted Paraguayan citizen for citizen's failure to raise violation of Consular Convention before Virginia Courts. *International Law Update,* Vol. 4, no. 4 (1998, April).

16. "Georgian Diplomat Wins Immunity Claim," *Legal Times* (June 8, 1998) Update Section, page 12. American Lawyer Newspapers Group Inc.

17. "Georgian Diplomat Gets Up to 21 Years in Fatal Crash," *The Daily Record* (Baltimore, MD) (December 22, 1997), page 17.

CHAPTER 2
The Origins of American Criminal Law

CHAPTER OBJECTIVES

After studying this chapter, you should be able to:

- Explain the tribal origins of criminal law
- Explain the impact of the Norman Invasion on the development of criminal laws
- Explain the nature of ecclesiastical courts and list the types of cases they heard
- Explain the significance of the Norman Invasion on the development of the Common Law
- Explain the significance of the Charter of Liberties in establishing the concept that no man is above the law
- Explain the significance of the Constitutions of Clarendon in establishing the right to trial by jury
- Explain the significance of the Assize of Northampton in establishing the idea of *stare decisis*
- Explain the significance of the Magna Carta in establishing the right to due process of law
- Explain the significance of the English Bill of Rights on the development of the Bill of Rights in the U.S. Constitution.

CHAPTER CONTENTS

> *Or think of a young citizen in a toga . . . coming out here in the train of some prefect. . . . Land in a swamp, march through the woods, and in some inland post feel the savagery, the utter savagery has closed around him.*
>
> **Marlow speculating on Roman soldier's reaction to first-century England in Joseph Conrad's**
>
> *Heart of Darkness*

INTRODUCTION

By modern-day standards, or by Roman standards for that matter, England of the first century A.D. was a savage place. It was inhabited by fierce warring tribes, in the process of slowly settling into an uneasy peace with one another. It was the land of Stonehenge and nature-worshipping Druid priests.[1] For the next millennium, England was the site of a series of invasions. Each onslaught would bring refinements to its legal system as the conquerors assimilated into the conquered. Ultimately these refinements would make it a less savage place.

The American legal system is patterned after the English system. This chapter and the next are designed to provide a thumbnail sketch of the history of the English system of criminal law and its offspring, the American criminal system. This history is designed to provide more than just interesting historical anecdotes. It is here to explain why.

As you learned in Chapter 1, the English and American systems of criminal law use the concept of *stare decisis*. Judicial decisions are based on precedents, or previous rulings in similar cases. These decisions constitute the **Common Law.** The rulings made in courtrooms today in America may have their origins in decisions made in England centuries ago. Thus, understanding how these precedents were established helps us understand our current system of laws.

ANGLO-SAXON TRIBAL LAW TO 1066

The Romans left England largely as they found it. Despite their intentions to incorporate it into the greater Roman Empire, military defeats in other parts of the empire made the island too costly for the Romans to maintain. At the same time, the Roman Empire was in decline. Although they brought a certain amount of stability to the island, they were unable to maintain a presence. As more pressing crises threatened the empire, the Roman legions withdrew to fight Germanic tribes on the continent. At the same time, tribes invaded from what are now Ireland, Scotland, and Germany. By the 400s A.D., the most powerful of the invading tribes, the Anglos and the Saxons, controlled the island.

These Anglo-Saxon newcomers viewed crimes not as acts against the state, but as acts against the family. They did not look beyond the immediate harm a crime caused an individual to the harm crime caused society.

This does not mean the Anglo-Saxons worked out criminal proceedings between themselves. They had a sophisticated structure for vindicating crimes. The kingdom was divided into **shires** (now counties) and further subdivided into **hundreds.** The hundreds were groups of one hundred freemen who were further divided into groups of ten called **tithings.** They were headed by a hundredman and a tithingman, respectively. Above the hundredman and tithingman was the shire-reeve (later shortened to sheriff), who was the king's representative. It was an efficient system of local control.[2]

Although the hundredmen and tithingmen reported happenings in the shire to the shire-reeve, they were not responsible for apprehending criminals like modern-day law enforcement officers. If such action was necessary, they would organize the effort. Usually men of the hundred actually chased down criminals.

The typical way in which an accused criminal was brought to court was by a complaint made by the victim or his family. In fact, in most cases it was the victim's responsibility to bring the accused to court. While this may seem unusual to us in modern times, it is important to bear in mind that the hundreds represented very close-knit tribal communities. If a person attempted to flee a hundred, there simply was nowhere to go. He couldn't lose himself in the anonymity of a large urban area. Each person's ability to make a living and perhaps his entire life was tied up in the hundred.

The hundred court would meet every four weeks and hear cases. The appropriate king's reeve would usually preside. Unlike modern-day courts, no distinction was made between civil and criminal cases. All cases were brought before the hundred court on the same day. First, the plaintiff presented his version of the facts to the court. The court then decided whether the case should be heard. If the court decided it would hear the case, a future date was set.

Occasionally the court would decide it wasn't appropriate for the hundred court to hear the case, because it dealt with issues outside of the interest of the hundred. The case was then sent to the shire court that met twice a year. The shire court would be presided over by the ealdorman (later earl), the bishop, the king's senior reeve in the area, and the shire-reeve.[3]

A criminal who was convicted of a crime was never imprisoned in Anglo-Saxon England because prisons didn't exist yet. He could be executed for particularly heinous crimes, he could be tortured, or more likely he would simply have to compensate the victims. This compensation fell into three categories, *wergild, bot,* and *wite.* **Wergild** was compensation paid to a family group if a member of that family was killed or suffered severe injury. In murder cases, the amount was determined by the social standing of the person murdered. The cause or circumstances of the crime were irrelevant. **Bot** was compensation paid for minor injuries. **Wite** was a public fine payable to a lord or tribal chieftain. This was then used for the benefit of the entire tribe. If the offender was too poor to pay, the fine would be assessed in livestock.[4]

During this period, one king in particular left a mark on law. King Alfred, who died in 899 A.D., helped unify the many tribes and issued a book of laws, or **dooms.** These would serve as a basis for common law.[5] In the next 170 years, England was ruled by a succession of Saxon and Danish kings until the Norman Invasion of 1066.

HISTORICAL HIGHLIGHT
The Anglo-Saxon Way to the Truth: Oath-Helpers and Trial by Ordeal

In the tribal society of Anglo-Saxon England, two very important things were a man's reputation and the perceived "will of God." A person's reputation was measured by the number of "oath-helpers" he could find to speak on his behalf when accused of a crime.

If a person was accused of a crime and maintained his innocence, he could bring in oath-helpers. They would take an oath swearing that the accused was telling the truth. The oath read: "*In the name of Almighty God, so I stand here by N in true witness, unbidden and unbought, as I saw with my eyes and heard with my ears that which I pronounce with him.*" The oath-helper was not required to testify or present evidence; he merely stated that he believed the accused. In most cases, this was enough for charges to be dropped.

However, if the court still had reason to doubt the accused's innocence, it could employ trial by ordeal. Trial by ordeal was administered by the Church. It was seen as a way of determining the will of God. The trial began with three days of fasting and a mass. The accused had the opportunity to confess if he chose. If he insisted he was innocent, he was offered the choice between the water or iron ordeal.

The water ordeal came in two varieties, hot and cold. The cold water ordeal involved the accused drinking holy water, and then being thrown into a river. If he floated, he was guilty. If he was innocent, he sank. With any luck, the innocent were fished out before they drowned.

The hot water ordeal involved the accused reaching into boiling water to retrieve a stone. In the iron ordeal, the accused had to carry a red hot iron bar nine feet. In both cases the accused's hands were bandaged, and if the wounds did not fester in three days, he was pronounced innocent. Contrary to popular belief, the trial by ordeal was not used to force confessions, but rather as a good faith attempt to ascertain divine truth. All in all, it was probably a good idea to avoid being accused of a crime in the first place.[6]

Trial by ordeal has fortunately disappeared from criminal courts, but the use of "oath helpers" survives in the form of character witnesses.

THE NORMAN INVASION AND ITS AFTERMATH 1066–1215

THE NORMAN INVASION

Upon the death of King Edward in 1066, three different princes claimed the throne of England. One of them, William of Normandy, invaded England and defeated another, Harold Godwin, at the battle of Hastings. The Norman conquest was the first step in the transformation of the English government into a modern state. Eventually it would be said that "the sun never sets on the British Empire."

ECCLESIASTICAL COURTS

William conquered England with the support of the Catholic Church. Consequently, the Church played a large role in the legal life of the country. A parallel system of state and **ecclesiastical courts** developed, each with its own sets of laws and sanctions.[7]

The ecclesiastical courts adjudicated both civil and criminal cases. The civil matters within the ecclesiastical court's jurisdiction were the collection of **tithes,** disputes dealing with the holding of church offices, marriage and divorce, and **probating of wills.** Tithes were in effect church taxes levied on the people.

Criminal matters within the ecclesiastical court's power were heresy, fornication, adultery, and other moral offenses. The Church had the right to excommunicate a person. Excommunication was not merely expelling a person from the Church as we would use the term today. The Church could issue a *writ de excommunicato capiendo.* The subject of the writ was imprisoned until "obedience yielded to the sentence." (That is, until he or she repented.)

The ecclesiastical courts used *stare decisis* to decide cases, but their basis for deciding cases was at first **canon law.** Canon law is the body of law derived from papal edicts and rulings by other church officials. As time went on, where canon law conflicted with English statutory or common law, the English law took precedence. However, canon law remained an influence in ecclesiastical court decisions.

THE EVOLVING COMMON LAW

William attempted to centralize the government in order to consolidate its power. In 1086 he decreed the **Domesday Book.** The Domesday Book is essentially the first universal census in English history. Its purpose was to gather information about the populace in order to assess taxes.

The twelfth and thirteenth centuries saw rapid changes in the legal system during which the king was subject to the law, trials by jury were begun, the rights of the accused were guaranteed, and clearly defined rules were developed to determine where cases were heard (county or king's court).

For the first time, the king bound himself to the law. From this point on, no man would be above the law. That did not mean that the relationship between the king and his subjects would always be smooth. In fact, these changes laid the groundwork for continual struggles between Parliament and the king, and contain the seeds of the American Revolution. The rights of the accused developed in this era would become the basis for both the English and American Bill of Rights. Finally, the multiple levels of courts would be the pattern for American federalism. These changes are chronicled in a series of documents that defined the rights of the king, his noblemen, and other citizens.

THE CHARTER OF LIBERTIES

In 1100 A.D., upon ascending the throne, Henry I issued the **Charter of Liberties.**[8] The charter represents the first document that bound the king to the law. In it:

- The king renounced his right to seize property of the Church and noblemen.
- The noblemen gained the right to will their property to their heirs.
- The noblemen were ordered to obey the same laws that applied to those below them in social stature.

This document served as the basis for the Magna Carta signed by King John in 1215.

THE CONSTITUTIONS OF CLARENDON (1164)

The Constitutions of Clarendon, issued in 1164 by Henry II, gutted the authority of the ecclesiastical courts in England. After 1164, most disputes fell within the jurisdiction of the king. The Constitutions of Clarendon also made reference to a recently adopted practice. Both royal and ecclesiastic judges were to use a panel of 12 lawful men to determine the truth in disputes. This was the beginning of trial by jury.[9]

The Constitutions of Clarendon were designed to resolve the conflict between the Church and the state. However, Thomas à Becket, the archbishop of Canterbury, and highest ranking church official in England, continued to agitate for more papal authority. As Becket's popularity grew, Henry made the comment he "wished to be rid of this meddlesome priest." Four of his knights obliged him by killing Becket in the Canterbury Cathedral in 1170. Despite the fact that Henry II was forced to do penance at Becket's tomb, the supremacy of the state was firmly established by the priest's murder. This was the beginning of the separation of church and state.[10]

THE ASSIZE OF NORTHAMPTON (1176)

The **Assize of Northampton** firmly established *stare decisis* on a widespread basis. It broadened the jurisdiction of the king's court, but established certain laws that had to be followed. At this time, most court cases dealt with land ownership; specifically, the disposition of land upon the death of its owner. Although today we take it for granted that land can be inherited, under the feudal system this wasn't the case. Land was granted to vassals by noblemen in return for pledges of military service. Vassals in turn could pledge to several different lords for different plots of land. The Assize was an attempt to provide uniform guidelines to protect the rights not only of lords, but widows and underage children as well. These guidelines were to be the basis of future decisions.[11]

The Assize changed the legal system in another way. Prior to 1176, the king's court heard only a small percentage of the cases, usually those between two noblemen. Other cases were heard at the county, or hundred level. After the Assize of Northampton, the accused in a criminal trial, or either the plaintiff or defendant in a civil action, could appeal to the king to have the case heard in the king's court. If the king agreed, a **writ** would be

HISTORICAL HIGHLIGHT
The Clash between Church and State: Henry II and Thomas Becket

Thomas Becket was the Paris-educated son of a former sheriff of London. Becket was admired for his administrative abilities. He was politically astute, well connected, universally admired and respected. When introduced to King Henry II, the attraction was immediate. Henry recognized Becket's political skill and strong intellect. Henry would eventually appoint Becket to the position of chancellor.

Henry relied on Becket's advice and considered him an ally in his ongoing power struggle with the Church. When archbishop of Canterbury Theobald died in 1161, Henry appointed Becket to the post. Henry was sure that with Becket in the archbishop's chair, the Church would be subservient to him.

Becket, however, underwent something of a religious conversion after assuming office. He saw his loyalty to the Church in religious terms. He could not, in good conscience, put his allegiance to Henry before his allegiance to God.

The Church in those days would try any clerics accused of wrongdoing in the ecclesiastical courts. Henry was determined that they should be tried in the king's court. The disagreement came to a head when a canon was accused of murder in 1163. The ecclesiastical court acquitted the cleric and the public demanded justice. The king insisted on trying the cleric, but Becket protested. Henry relented in this particular case, but proposed the Constitutions of Clarendon that would extend the king's jurisdiction over the clerics. Becket reluctantly agreed.

Henry began to see Becket as unreliable and disloyal. Henry summoned Becket to his castle at Northampton and demanded to know what he had done with the large sums of money he had handled when he was chancellor. Becket saw the trap set for him and fled to France. His exile lasted six years.

Even in exile, Becket agitated against the king. All the clerics who supported the king were excommunicated by Becket. In 1170, Henry met with Becket in France, and it appeared the rift was healed. Becket returned to his post in Canterbury. Henry requested that Becket reinstate the excommunicated clerics, but Becket refused. Henry, while still in France, is said to have flown into a rage, shouting: "What sluggards, what cowards have I brought up in my court, who care nothing for their allegiance to their lord. Who will rid me of this meddlesome priest?"

Four of the king's knights sailed to England, and confronted Becket in Canterbury Cathedral. When Becket still refused to reinstate the excommunicated clerics, they drew their swords and struck his head repeatedly until the altar was splattered with his brains and blood. Allegedly the stains are still visible today. Henry was despondent when he heard the news. His momentary rage had led to the martyrdom of his nemesis.

> Becket's reputation grew in death far beyond what it was in life. Miracles were said to have occurred at his tomb. Henry was forced to do penance four years later. He wore sack cloth in a procession to Becket's tomb while being flogged by 80 monks. He then spent the night at the tomb. Becket remained a cult figure for centuries. The pilgrimages made by the faithful to his tomb were immortalized in Chaucer's *Canterbury Tales*.

issued ordering the case to be heard in the king's court. To this day, courts in the United States issue writs commanding action.

The Assize of Northampton produced two other changes in the practice of law. The first was that common law required knowledge about earlier cases and the use of writs was complicated. Law required experts. More judges were needed for the expanded docket of the king's court. Second, the larger role for the king's court increased the king's power, but the king and his staff were too small to handle the load. The eventual answer was to create a body to implement the king's power, called the **Parliament.**

THE MAGNA CARTA OF 1215

Henry II's second son, John, assumed the throne in 1199 at the death of his brother, Richard the Lionhearted. John had the misfortune to lose land in northwestern France that had belonged to England for some time. Because this loss represented losses for his noblemen as well, John's popularity suffered. With the provinces in France gone, John devoted his time to the royal courts. He developed a reputation as a tyrant. John also quarreled with the Pope and was unpopular with the Church. When his nobles had enough, they moved to limit his power. He was forced to sign the **Magna Carta,** or Great Charter, in 1215.[12]

The Magna Carta is important because some of its provisions can be found in later documents including the U.S. Constitution. Like the previous documents, most of the Magna Carta dealt with property rights. However, among important emerging criminal law concepts were the following clauses:

- No freeman shall be captured or imprisoned or disseised (disseise means to take away title and possession of property) or outlawed or exiled or in any way destroyed, nor will we (the king and nobles) go against him or send against him, except by the lawful judgment of his peers or by the law of the land.
- We (the king and nobles) will hold the lands of those convicted of a felony only a year and a day, and the lands shall then be given to the lords of the fees (those leasing the land in return for military service or payment).
- To no one will we sell, to no one will we deny or delay right or justice.

Compare the first clause above with this wording from the fifth amendment to the U.S. Constitution: "No person shall be . . . deprived of life, liberty, or property, without due process of law; nor shall private property be taken for public use, without just compensation." See the similarity?

PUTTING THE PERIOD 1066–1215 IN PERSPECTIVE

In a mere 115 years, the English moved from a tribal, erratic legal system to one that provided uniform enforcement of laws. Prior to 1100, there were few rules guiding judges' decisions. This left open the possibility of inconsistent interpretation of laws. An accused in 1215 was entitled to a trial by a jury of his peers; his counterpart a century earlier was not. Although the legal system of 1066 bears little resemblance to ours, by 1215 obvious similarities had emerged.

THE SEVENTEENTH AND EIGHTEENTH CENTURIES

The next period of rapid change in the English legal system was the seventeenth and eighteenth centuries. This period is characterized by dramatic changes in the religious and political makeup of England. As these changes occurred, the legal system had to adapt to a more diverse body of political and religious opinion. In order to accommodate all of its citizens, England had to allow more civil liberties. The belief that these civil liberties were necessary to a functioning society was carried to America with the English settlers of the period.

These changes neither occurred overnight, nor were they accomplished without turmoil and bloodshed. In fact, the England of the seventeenth century appalled its European neighbors with its barbarity.

THE ENGLISH CIVIL WAR AND THE ENGLISH BILL OF RIGHTS

By the seventeenth century, England had been using the concept of common law for over four hundred years. But the first king to ascend the throne in the seventeenth century was James I. James was a Scottish king who believed in the **divine right of kings.** In James's view, kings ruled through a god-given mandate and could rule absolutely without regard to the rule of law.

Obviously, the English tradition of common law ran contrary to this notion. As we have seen, under common law court decisions are based on precedents already established. And previous kings had signed the Charter of Liberties, the Constitutions of Clarendon, and the Magna Carta. These, taken together, bound the king to the rule of law. The divine right of kings and the rule of law were on a collision course.[13]

James's son Charles also believed in the divine right of kings. He continued the feud his father had started with Parliament. Parliament had originally been a body designed to enforce the king's edicts. Through the centuries, Parliament's role had changed. Parliament controlled the kingdom's purse strings much as Congress today approves the federal budget. This severely limited the powers of the king. James, and Charles after him, resented having to share power with Parliament.

By the late 1620s organized opposition to Charles formed from three groups. These groups were composed of lawyers, who understood the workings of common law; **Puritans,** a splinter religious group; and members of the **House of Commons,** the lower house of Parliament.

In 1628 Charles was forced to sign the **Petition of Right.** The Petition of Right was designed to force the king to obey the laws laid out in the Charter of Liberties and Magna Carta. Parliament forced Charles to do this because he had instituted the practice of demanding loans from wealthy landowners. When the landowners refused, they were arrested or sometimes killed without being charged or tried. Parliament saw this as a denial of the due process guarantees of the Magna Carta, and demanded the right of *habeas corpus.* Parliament also sought to reassert its power of the purse by declaring "*that no man hereafter be compelled to make or yield any gift, loan benevolence, tax, or such like charge, without common consent by act of parliament.*"[14]

Charles signed the document, but never had any intention of fulfilling its terms. He refused to allow Parliament to meet from 1629 to 1640. When Parliament did reconvene, it denied the king any tax monies until he agreed to restrictions of his powers. Civil war broke out in 1642 when he refused to give up any of his authority.

Charles was eventually captured by Parliament's army and executed in 1649. England was ruled as a commonwealth under Parliament's control until 1653, when Oliver Cromwell dissolved Parliament and decreed England to be a Protectorate. Cromwell took the title "Lord Protector." Following Cromwell's death in 1658, his son assumed power but lacked the ability to govern. In 1660, new Parliamentary elections were held. Parliament restored the monarchy by placing Charles's son, Charles II, on the throne with limited powers.[15]

Charles II died in 1685 and his brother James II, a Roman Catholic, became king. James II also believed in the divine right of kings, and England once again seemed poised for internal strife. The English did not want another civil war, and tolerated James. The Protestant majority in England placed their hope for peaceful transition in James's daughter, Mary, who was a Protestant. But then James had a son and Mary was no longer next in line for the throne under the laws of **primogeniture.**

Parliament invited Mary and her husband, William of Orange, the ruler of the Netherlands, to invade England with an army and assume the throne. When William and Mary invaded, James left the country without a drop of blood being spilled. Because the change in monarchs happened without violence, it is referred to as the "Glorious Revolution."[16]

Parliament, however, did not intend to import an absolute ruler. Part of the deal was that William and Mary had to agree to a "Bill of Rights." The **English Bill of Rights** of 1689 would prove to be a very influential document in the evolution of the American legal system.

The English Bill of Rights reiterated the king's subservience to the law and the limited role of Parliament. Because monarchs had frequently abused the judicial system to silence political foes, Parliament inserted the following provisions to protect those accused of a crime:

- That excessive bail ought not be required, nor excessive fines imposed; nor cruel and unusual punishments inflicted.
- That jurors ought to be duly empaneled and returned, and jurors which pass upon men in trials of high treason ought to be freeholders.
- That all grants and promises of fines and forfeitures of particular persons before conviction are illegal and void.[17]

The provision about excessive bail became the Eighth Amendment to the U.S. Constitution. The provision about jurors carried over into American law as well. The fines and forfeitures provision refers to the accused being innocent until proven guilty. No fine is due until the person has been convicted of a crime. You will learn more about these and other important Constitutional protections provided to persons accused of a crime in later chapters.

CHAPTER SUMMARY

In this chapter you have gained an overview of the events in England's history that form the basis for many of the Constitutional rights enjoyed by Americans accused of crimes today. These events of long ago have shaped the development of criminal law into what it is today. From the early tribal days to the eighteenth century, England served as the incubator of what would become the U.S. Constitution. By understanding the historical context, you will develop a deeper appreciation for the Constitutional protections provided to every person accused of a crime.

KEY TERMS

Assize of Northampton: The document that firmly established *stare decisis* as the basis for court rulings, and therefore is generally considered the beginning of Common Law.

Bot: In Anglo-Saxon tribes, the compensation paid for minor injuries.

Canon law: The body of law derived from papal edicts and rulings by other Church officials.

Charter of Liberties: An edict issued by Henry I that bound the king to the law. The source of the concept of "no man is above the law."

Common Law: The system of jurisprudence that originated in England and was later applied in the United States; law that is based on judicial precedent.

Constitutions of Clarendon: Documents issued by Henry II establishing the supremacy of the state over the Church. Also the first major document to mention a jury of twelve.

Divine right of kings: The belief that God ordained kings to rule over the people and that the king's rule was therefore absolute.

Domesday Book: A record made in the time of William the Conqueror (1081–1086) consisting of accurate and detailed description of the lands in England and the means by which the alleged owners obtained title.

Doom: Anglo-Saxon word for a law.

Ecclesiastical courts: In medieval times, the court system run by the Church.

English Bill of Rights: The Bill of Rights that Parliament had William and Mary sign as a condition of ascending the throne. This guaranteed various basic concepts of English and later American law, such as "innocent until proven guilty," "trial by jury," and prohibition against excessive bail.

Habeas corpus: Known as the "great writ" and means literally "you have the body." It is a procedure for obtaining a judicial determination of the legality of an individual's custody.

House of Commons: The lower house of Parliament.

Hundreds: Group of one hundred freemen in Anglo-Saxon England responsible for criminal justice administration.

Magna Carta: The Great Charter signed by King John in 1215. This is the first royal guarantee of certain basic rights including that of due process.

Parliament: The legislature of England; Parliament is divided into an upper house, the House of Lords, in which membership is dependent on being a member of the peerage and is passed on through heredity, and a lower house, the House of Commons, where membership is determined by election of the people.

Petition of Right: A document signed by Charles I guaranteeing the right of *habeas corpus* and reaffirming the rights granted by the Magna Carta and the Charter of Liberties.

Primogeniture: The ancient common law of descent in which the eldest son takes all property of the decedent father.

Probating of wills: The act of proving that an instrument purporting to be a will was signed and otherwise executed in accordance with legal requirements.

Puritans: A religious sect that broke away from the Church of England when they sought to "purify" it. They were a political force in the English Civil War, and the dominant group among the English settlers in the New England states.

Shires: In Anglo-Saxon England, a unit of government corresponding today most closely to counties. Shires were divided into hundreds and tithings.

Tithes: Originally meaning one-tenth; the taxes collected by the Church, one-tenth of annual income.

Tithings: In Anglo-Saxon England, the smallest unit of government, consisting of ten freemen. Ten tithings made up a hundred, which in turn made up a shire.

Wergild: In Anglo-Saxon tribes, the compensation paid to a family group if a member of that family was killed or suffered severe injury.

Wite: In Anglo-Saxon tribes, a public fine payable to a lord or tribal chieftain.

Writ: A mandatory order issued by the authority or in the name of the sovereign or the state for the purpose of compelling a person to do something.

Writ de excommunicato capiendo: The ultimate sanction for ecclesiastical courts, this allowed the Church to excommunicate those convicted of heresy or other crimes against the Church. Excommunication consisted of imprisonment until the person had a change of heart.

DISCUSSION QUESTIONS

1. What vestiges of English tribal law are still present in the American judicial system?
2. What impact did the Norman Invasion have on the development of criminal law?
3. What types of cases did the ecclesiastical courts hear? What type of court fulfills those functions today?
4. How did the Charter of Liberties ensure that no man is above the law?
5. How did the Constitutions of Clarendon establish the right to trial by jury?
6. How did the Assize of Northhampton establish *stare decisis*?
7. Explain the significance of the Magna Carta in establishing the right to due process of law.
8. What are the similarities between the English and American Bills of Rights?

FOR FURTHER READING

1. Shakespeare, W. *King John*. A play about the king who signed the Magna Carta.
2. Chaucer, G. *The Canterbury Tales*. Chaucer's classic of the tales told by pilgrims on the way to Becket's Tomb.
3. Malory, Sir Thomas. *Le Morte D' Arthur*. The source of many of the legends of King Arthur and the knights of the round table.

FOR FURTHER VIEWING

1. *The Lion in Winter.* (1968). Peter O'Toole, Katherine Hepburn, Sir Anthony Hopkins. King Henry II and Eleanor of Aquitaine argue over the succession to the English throne.
2. *Becket.* (1964). Richard Burton, Peter O'Toole. The story of Henry II and Becket and their destiny with fate.
3. *Cromwell.* (1970). Sir Alec Guiness, Timothy Dalton, Richard Harris. The story of Oliver Cromwell and the fall of Charles I.

QUOTATIONS FOR CHAPTER TWO

1. *Necessity hath no law.*
   Oliver Cromwell (1599–1658)

2. *The state of monarchy is the supremest thing upon earth: for kings are not only God's Lieutenants upon earth, and sit upon God's throne, but even by God himself they are called Gods.*
   King James I of England, explaining the divine right of kings

3. *You have sat too long for any good you have been doing. Depart, I say, and let us have done with you. In the name of God, go!*
   Oliver Cromwell, dismissing Parliament (1599–1658)

4. *That the king can do no wrong, is a necessary and fundamental principle of the English constitution.*
   Sir William Blackstone, *Commentaries on the Laws of England* (1765)

ENDNOTES

1. T. D. Kendrick, *The Druids* (rev. ed.) (London, England: Random House, 1927).
2. W. Churchill, *History of the English-Speaking Peoples* (rev. ed.) (New York: Random House, 1965).
3. H. R. Loyn, *The Governance of Anglo-Saxon England, 500–1087* (Stanford, CA: Stanford University Press, 1984).
4. J. A. Sigler, *An Introduction to the Legal System* (Homewood, IL: Dorsey Press, 1968).
5. Churchill, *History.*
6. M. Farmer, *The Long Arm of the Law* (1994) http://www.ftech.net/~regia/law.htm. Regia Anglorum Publications.
7. A. B. Smith and H. Pollack, *Criminal Justice: An Overview* (3rd ed.)(West/Wadsworth, 1991).
8. J. Moser, *The Secularization of Equity: Ancient Religious Origins, Feudal Christian Influences, and Medieval Authoritarian Impacts on the Evolution of Legal Equitable Remedies* 26 Cap. U. L. Rev. 483 (1997).
9. J. Biancalana, *For Want of Justice: Legal Reforms of Henry II* 88 Colum. L. Rev. 433 (1988).

10. Churchill, *History.*
11. Biancalana, *For Want of Justice.*
12. Churchill, *History.*
13. Ibid.
14. Ibid.
15. Ibid.
16. Ibid.
17. R. C. Van Caenegem, *An Historical Introduction to Western Constitutional Law* (Cambridge, England: Cambridge University Press, 1995).

CHAPTER 3
The Colonial Period's Influence on American Criminal Law

CHAPTER OBJECTIVES

After studying this chapter, you should be able to:

- List the four distinct areas that were colonized by settlers from the British Isles
- Explain the Puritan approach to criminal law and justice
- Discuss Puritan influences on modern criminal law
- Explain the Quaker approach to criminal law and justice
- Discuss Quaker influences on modern criminal law
- Explain the Chesapeake Bay settlers' approach to criminal law and justice
- Discuss the Chesapeake Bay settlers' influence on modern criminal law
- Explain the Carolinas and Georgian settlers' approach to criminal law and justice
- Discuss the Carolinas and Georgian settlers' influence on modern criminal law
- Explain Thomas Jefferson's concept of "unalienable rights"
- Explain why the Articles of Confederation failed
- Explain the influence of the Napoleonic Code on American criminal law

CHAPTER CONTENTS

INTRODUCTION

England's colonies in the New World were populated by a wide variety of immigrants who came from every part of the British Isles. Four separate regions were settled during this period. These were Massachusetts and the New England Colonies, the Middle Atlantic Colonies of William Penn, the Chesapeake Bay Colonies, and the Southern colonies of the Carolinas and Georgia. Each developed its own criminal law system. As you read this chapter, ask yourself how the character of each region influenced the development of American criminal law.

NEW ENGLAND

> *We, whose names are underwritten, . . . doe, by these presents, solemnly and mutually in the presence of God and one another, covenant and combine ourselves together into a civil body politick, for our better ordering and preservation, and furtherance of the ends aforesaid; and by virtue hereof do enact, constitute, and frame, such just and equal laws, ordinances, acts, constitutions, and offices, from time to time, as shall be thought most meete and convenient for the general good of the Colonie unto which we promise all due submission and obedience.*
>
> **Mayflower Compact (1620)**

The period from 1629 to 1640, when Charles I attempted to rule England without Parliament, is known as "the eleven years tyranny." There was political and religious repression, and poor economic conditions. As a result, over 80,000 people left England. Some went to Ireland, others to the Caribbean, still more to Holland and Germany. Over 21,000 went to Massachusetts.[1]

The Massachusetts colony was founded by Puritans, who sought to establish a society in line with their religious beliefs. Although by modern standards some of the laws of colonial Massachusetts may seem restrictive, they reflected a firm belief in the due process of law. For example, the 1641 Massachusetts *Body of Liberties* guaranteed each accused the right to representation by counsel.

This is not to say that there were no excesses. The famous Salem witch trials of 1692 demonstrate that under certain circumstances the rule of law breaks down. Some of the Puritans' punishments for crimes may seem inhumane to the modern observer. The Puritans had 13 **capital crimes** on the books. Each was based on an Old Testament passage. The following transgressions were punishable by death:

1. Witchcraft
2. Idolatry
3. Blasphemy

4. Homicide
5. Rape
6. Adultery
7. Bestiality
8. Sodomy
9. Rebellion by children
10. Stubbornness by children
11. Hitting or cursing a parent if over age 16
12. Treason
13. Bearing false witness in court in order to convict someone else of a capital crime

Capital punishment was carried out either by burning at the stake or by hanging. New England had few jails. Often criminals were sent to farmers in outlying regions where they were made to work or were imprisoned underground. Public shame was also used. Convicted criminals were forced to wear a letter indicative of their crime; for example, A for Adultery, B for burglary or blasphemy, C for counterfeiting, and so on. Massachusetts law provided for speedy trial and required a four-day interval between sentencing and execution. Compared to today's long death row delays, Puritan justice was certainly swift.

The Massachusetts colony developed its own way of enforcing the laws. Since the New England colonists tended to settle in small towns, each town elected a town constable. The constable could summon the men of the town in times of crisis, and they were required by law to assist him.

THE MIDDLE ATLANTIC COLONIES

> *Liberty without obedience is confusion, and obedience without liberty is slavery.*
>
> **William Penn**

The Quakers were another sect who came to America to establish a colony based on their religious beliefs. They had been persecuted in England because they did not belong to the Anglican Church, and refused to pay the required **tithes.** As you may recall from Chapter 2, tithes were the tax the church collected to fund their activities. In England, the Quakers were often imprisoned and tortured for their refusal to submit to the Anglican Church. Their property was also seized. This experience gave the Quakers a deep belief in the **separation of church and state,** the right to freedom of religion, and an appreciation for the rights of the accused.

Although they were a religious sect, residency in the Quaker colonies (New Jersey, Pennsylvania, and Delaware) was not restricted to only Quakers. The Quakers had experienced firsthand the tyranny of a state religion, and refused to establish one in their colony. Thus, the established government, although at first dominated by Quakers, sanctioned no state religion.

The Quakers allowed and even encouraged members of other religions and sects to live with them in their colonies. As a result, these colonies were the first to receive religious refugees from continental Europe. The Quakers realized very early that freedom of conscience was tied very closely to property rights. Their experience in England of having their property confiscated when they refused to tithe reinforced this belief.

HISTORICAL HIGHLIGHT
When Superstition Overcame Reason: Salem, 1692

It began with a few adolescent girls behaving strangely. They screamed obscenities, had seizures, and went into trancelike states. Doctors in the town of Salem,
Massachusetts, were at a loss for an explanation, and told the town elders the children must be under the influence of Satan. The girls were pressured by their elders to tell what "witch" had put this spell on them. They named three Salem
women: Tituba (a Carib Indian slave), Sarah Good, and Sarah Osborne.

The slave, Tituba, eventually confessed to practicing witchcraft and seeing
apparitions. The other two steadfastly denied any wrongdoing. After Tituba's
confession, more townspeople made accusations. They claimed to have seen
ghosts of their neighbors appear to them at night, and believed this was a sign
that their neighbors had cast spells on them.

The accused were quickly imprisoned, and within six months many were
hung. At trial, the testimony against the "witches" included girls screaming
when the accused tried to speak. This was taken as a sign of the devil's torment,
and was used as evidence of guilt. If a jury found the accused not guilty, they
were required to vote again. In effect, no acquittal was possible once a trial
started. All of the accused were convicted without any physical evidence whatsoever against them.

Within nine months of the girls'"bewitching," 20 people had been executed,
19 by hanging. The only male suspect was pressed to death by heavy rocks.

It was soon obvious that the hysteria had to come to an end. When the governor's own wife was accused of practicing witchcraft, he intervened and dissolved the court. He ruled that intangible evidence such as apparitions and the
screams of adolescent girls were not admissible.

The trials occurred while Increase Mather, the colony's most influential clergyman, was away visiting England. Mather strongly disapproved of the witch trials, and his return in the fall of 1692 helped curb the hysteria. Almost
immediately he began making restitution to the families of the victims. His son,
Cotton Mather, had overseen the trials. His involvement scarred his career as a
clergyman and educator. He had been the likely candidate to succeed his father
as the president of Harvard, but he was passed over in part because of his association with the trials.[2]

Was this an isolated instance? Many have compared the persecution of left-
leaning political activists after World War II, during the so-called "Red Scare,"
to the Salem witch trials. The comparison was made very forcibly in the Arthur
Miller play, *The Crucible.* Miller produced the play about the Salem witch trials during the height of the McCarthy anticommunist era. Could the same type
of occurrence happen in the aftermath of the terror attacks of September 11, 2001?

Quakers had a very enlightened attitude toward criminals by the standards of the day. Their goal was one of **rehabilitation** as opposed to punishment. This was reflected not only in their laws, but in practice as well. The Quakers only had two capital offenses, treason and premeditated murder. All those accused of a crime were guaranteed the right to a speedy trial. Prison sentences were generally short, and very humane even by today's standards. The Quakers even allowed prisoners to leave their cells on hot days.[3]

HISTORICAL HIGHLIGHT
The Origins of "Lynching"

Southern trees bear strange fruit
Blood on the leaves
Blood on the root
Black bodies swinging in the southern breeze
Strange fruit hanging from the poplar trees.
Lyrics from the song "Strange Fruit," sung by Billie Holiday, written by
   Lewis Allen

Most Americans are familiar with the term *lynching*. It generally refers to the hanging of a person without the benefit of a trial. The origins of "lynching" are murky. One theory is that members of the Lynch family of western Virginia were known for dispensing frontier justice without much regard for legal niceties.

One of the stories centers around a Charles Lynch, a Virginia planter during the American Revolution who became fed up with local **Tories**. The Tories, British sympathizers, felt justified in stealing from the farms of "rebels." Lynch is reported to have headed a vigilante group that would either whip or tar and feather the Tories. Often little evidence existed of their guilt.[4]

Another possible source of the term centers around a Captain William Lynch of Virginia, and later South Carolina. William Lynch practiced what came to be known as "Lynch's Law." In the 1760s roving gangs were terrorizing the mountainous regions of western Virginia. Lynch made a formal agreement with his neighbors that they would catch the criminals and punish them on the spot. Many were beaten; some were hanged. Again, this was done without much attention to the rule of law.[5]

Whatever its origins, lynching became synonymous with the oppression of African Americans in the post–Civil War era. Lynching became the tool of the Ku Klux Klan and other White Supremacists well into the twentieth century. Southern blacks learned to fear the knock on the door in the middle of the night. It often meant a loved one was going to be taken and found dangling from a tree in the morning. Only after continued protests forced federal law enforcement officials to act did the number of lynchings decline.

THE CHESAPEAKE BAY COLONIES

The Chesapeake Bay Colonies of Maryland and Virginia were settled by Englishmen who were supporters of the king. They were, for the most part, the second and subsequent sons of noble families who received no inheritance in England (recall from Chapter 2 that England had a system of inheritance based on primogeniture) and came to America to make their fortune. They brought with them a strong sense of hierarchical order and in some cases enforced it ruthlessly.

Tobacco was the mainstay of the Chesapeake Bay Colonies' economy. The plantation owners of Virginia and Maryland made large fortunes from its growth and export. A small elite of landed gentry led the colonies and wrote the criminal laws. Any perceived rebellion against the established order was met with swift and often violent reaction.

In the Chesapeake Colonies, class distinctions were much more obvious than in other American Colonies. For instance, a gentleman accused of a capital offense was often allowed to read a verse from the Bible, which came to be known as the "neck verse" because of the many gentlemen's necks it saved.[6]

By contrast, common criminals convicted of capital offenses were carried to the gallows in a cart. Once at the scene, the noose was placed around the convict's neck as he stood on the cart. After he said his final words, the cart was removed. Often the gallows were erected at the scene of the crime, and the public watched the execution.[7]

Sheriffs were appointed by the landed gentry to enforce the laws in each county. Their duties included organizing the courts, impaneling juries, issuing writs, calling elections, reading royal proclamations, maintaining the peace, protecting the church, administering judicial punishments, running the jail, and keeping county records. The sheriff, of course, was a gentleman too, and could not be expected to perform all these duties himself. He maintained a staff of deputies, jailers, under-sheriffs, county whippers, and clerks.[8]

In addition to imprisonment and capital punishment, colonists in the Chesapeake area employed the **pillory.** In some cases, other criminals were forced to cut the ears off prisoners in the pillory, or even pull the cart out from under fellow criminals at the gallows.

Capital punishment was clearly used as a deterrent to crime in the Chesapeake Colonies. The bodies of executed pirates would often be hung at the river's edge for several days to discourage other would-be pirates. The bodies of less-notorious criminals were given to physicians for dissection, and any property owned by the convict was forfeited to the crown in what is known as the **corruption of the blood**.[9]

THE CAROLINAS AND GEORGIA

The Southern colonies, consisting of North and South Carolina and Georgia, have a unique legal history. Because of its relatively sparse population and widely scattered plantations, there were few formal legal institutions during the colonial period. Despite this, a few environmental factors strongly influenced the early life of the South.

The Carolinas were settled largely as tobacco plantations. When indigo (used to make dye) and cotton became profitable, they were also raised. However, the plantations could only be profitable with slave labor. The legal system soon reflected the need of the white planters to control their black slaves. Because slaves were subject to their own set of laws, an entire separate court system was established to administer crimes by slaves. Slaves never had the same protection under the law that their white owners had, but there were rules that slave owners were required to follow.

The lack of centralized population centers led to localized law enforcement. Local sheriffs and court officials held more influence in the South than they did in the North. A tradition of self-reliance grew and it was common for individuals to resolve disputes between themselves. Often, the law would look the other way.[10]

Georgia was the last English colony to be founded in North America. It was founded by philanthropist James Oglethorpe. Oglethorpe was appalled at the English practice of imprisoning debtors. Throughout England, people unable to pay their debts were incarcerated in what were called **debtor's prisons** while their families were forced to live in the "poor house." Oglethorpe felt that if these debtors were given a fresh start in the new world, they could work off their debts.

Oglethorpe petitioned King George I to take a group of prisoners to the New World to provide them with a fresh start. The king needed colonists to populate the area between the Carolinas and Spanish-held Florida. The area was in dispute, and a permanent English settlement would solidify England's claim. George granted Oglethorpe the land between the Savannah and Altama Rivers. Oglethorpe dutifully named the colony Georgia after the king.

Oglethorpe's altruistic vision didn't last long. Once Oglethorpe's entourage had secured the area from the Spanish and hostile Indians, settlers came streaming in from the Carolinas in search of cheap land. Oglethorpe had prohibited slavery in Georgia, but as the Carolina planters came in with their slaves, it was only a matter of time until that law was changed.

AMERICAN INDEPENDENCE

> *We hold these truths to be self-evident that all men are created equal, that they are endowed by their Creator with certain unalienable rights, that among these are life, liberty, and the pursuit of happiness.*
>
> *The Declaration of Independence*

Each region of the colonies began with very idealistic notions of the relationship between the government and the people. This is the basis of criminal law. Each one had to adapt to new influences as immigrants who were different from the original settlers came in. Despite these adaptations, the founding ideals of each survived in some way and found their way into the American legal system. When the time came for the colonies to band together as a nation, the challenge was to build an overarching framework that could accommodate these different sets of values.

The American Revolution forced the 13 American colonies to become far more interdependent than they had ever intended or possibly wanted to be. Although the colonies had their separate cultures, they all could unite around the idea of what Thomas Jefferson called "unalienable rights." These were the same rights that Englishmen had sought for centuries and considered their birthright. Brought together by a common need for self-determination, the 13 colonies declared themselves free and independent states in 1776 with the signing of the *Declaration of Independence.*

When Jefferson described the right to *life*, he was referring to the right of self-defense against invasion, civil disturbance, or unjust government. *Liberty* is a reference to freedom of religion, speech, assembly, and the vote. Remember that the colonists were subject to the laws of Parliament, but could not vote in Parliamentary elections. The *pursuit of happiness* is probably a reference to the right to own property.[11] This phrase actually is taken from the writings of the English political philosopher John Locke, who used the terms *life*, *liberty*, and *property* to summarize man's unalienable rights.

The members of the Continental Congress were all relatively prosperous landowners who felt they were entitled to the same rights that the English nobility had wrested from the crown. These rights to life, liberty, and property would become the basis for the American legal system. They would be viewed as rights not granted by a government, but as Jefferson said, God-given rights, rights that no government should be able to take away.

At the time, these rights were believed to belong only to the landed male gentry. Other groups would be included later; first, all white men whether they owned property or not, then African American and other nonwhite men, and finally, women.

After the colonies won their independence from England, they had to establish a central government. Their first effort, the **Articles of Confederation,** proved an abysmal failure. The Articles of Confederation created a very weak central government, incapable of raising enough revenue to ensure its ability to govern. It quickly became obvious a more powerful central government was necessary. But the former colonists still feared anything resembling the tyranny they had experienced under the English Monarchy.

In 1787, a Constitutional Convention was convened in Philadelphia. Each state sent representatives in an attempt to establish a strong central government that also safeguarded states' rights. The result was a delicately balanced and intricate federal system of government. You may want to review Chapter 1 now to refresh your understanding of the system.

THE NAPOLEONIC CODE

Most of our discussion has centered on the tradition of English common law. However, there is another major influence on current American criminal law; the French system of civil law based on the **Napoleonic Code**.

The Napoleonic Code was written under Napoleon I. The goals of the Napoleonic Code were to make criminal penalties more consistent and to bring the French government under the rule of law in much the same way the Charter of Liberties, Magna Carta, and the other notable English documents made the English government accountable to the people.

Napoleon had seized power in the aftermath of the French Revolution. The French Revolution had taken place in large part in response to the excesses of the French monarchy. Under the French monarchy, an influential person could issue a *lettre d'cachet;*—a document that directed that a person be imprisoned indefinitely without trial, or even without ever being charged with a crime. Following the revolution, there was the Reign of Terror during which many French nobles and members of the middle class were beheaded. After reeling between the extremes of Royal tyranny on one hand and mob terror on the other, the need for an open and fair legal code was obvious.[12]

In the United States, only Louisiana relies heavily on the Napoleonic Code tradition. Louisiana was purchased by the U.S. government in 1803. Its customs and laws were much more influenced by the French and Spanish than the English.

DIFFERENCES BETWEEN THE NAPOLEONIC CODE AND ENGLISH COMMON LAW

The way courtrooms are organized and run are very different under the two systems. Under the Napoleonic Code or civil law, criminal trials resemble boards of inquiry rather than the adversarial arrangement we are familiar with. Judges in civil law cases may cross-examine witnesses to gather facts. In contrast to the English system, plea bargaining is unknown. The judge does not ratify "deals" made between the prosecuting and defense attorneys. Rather the judge's duty is to conduct an investigation into the circumstances surrounding a crime and render a just verdict.[13]

Many of the legal maneuvers in American criminal trials are designed to protect the rights of the accused and the state. Our system attempts to balance the rights of the individual and the state in an adversarial setting. The civil law system seeks to discover the truth about a crime with all parties participating in the search. Critics of the civil law system charge that it does not offer the same safeguards of individual rights that the English system provides. This may be why so many Louisiana criminal cases reach the highest court of the land, the Supreme Court. (See, for example, Chapter 4 on the right to trial by jury.) The Napoleonic Code tradition is at odds with the English tradition of trial by jury and the right against self-incrimination.

CHAPTER SUMMARY

The development of criminal laws in the United States was heavily influenced by the migration patterns to the New World. The colonists brought with them a viewpoint on morality, and thus on law. For the most part, since the colonists hailed from the British Isles, their views were heavily influenced by the common law tradition. But because each group of colonists left the Continent for the colonies for reasons peculiar to each group, each area differed in their approach to law. The New England colonists' laws were heavily influenced by religious faith. The Mid-Atlantic colonists' laws emphasized religious tolerance and respect for due process. The Chesapeake Bay colonists' laws protected the interests of landed gentry. The Southern colonists' laws reflected the economic reality of slavery. Together, these divergent groups united as they sought independence. The Constitution they eventually ratified contains the compromises necessary to unite the 13 colonies into one nation.

KEY TERMS

Articles of Confederation: The first framework of government in the United States. It created a weak central government. It was replaced by the Constitution.
Capital crimes: Crimes for which the possible punishment is death.
Capital punishment: The death penalty as a punishment for a crime.

Corruption of the blood: The cutting-off of the right to pass property on through inheritance as punishment for criminal activity. All property belonging to the convict was forfeited to the crown and the heirs received nothing.

Debtor's prison: Prison in which debtors were incarcerated until they were able to pay their debts and the cost of their imprisonment.

Napoleonic Code: Also known as the *Code Civil* or the Civil Code, it is a codification of French law made during the reign of Napoleon I. It is the basis for laws in the State of Louisiana.

Pillory: A frame of wood erected on a post, with holes through which a person's head and hands were put. Used to humiliate criminals as punishment.

Rehabilitation: The act of reforming a criminal to prevent recidivism.

Separation of church and state: The belief that the church should be separate from the government, and that government will not unduly restrict the right of citizens to worship in accordance with their beliefs.

Tithes: One-tenth; the amount of income collected by the Church of England to finance its operations.

Tories: Colonists who sided with the British during the American Revolution.

DISCUSSION QUESTIONS

1. Name one or two philosophies from each of the four colonial regions that became incorporated into American criminal law.
2. What were some of the major contributions of the Quakers to our system of criminal law?
3. Now that you have a basic understanding of the ideas and beliefs that the various settler groups brought with them to the colonies, do you think it was difficult for the new states to agree on a Constitution? Why or why not?
4. Do you think the use of the pillory or the practice of wearing a letter representing one's crime was effective as punishment? As a deterrent?
5. Does the civil law system embodied in the Napoleonic Code represent a more just system or simply a more efficient one than the English system?
6. In this chapter we have seen how economics have often determined how laws are written (i.e., slavery). Should laws reflect economic realities or should they be morally based?

FOR FURTHER READING

1. Hawthorne, N. (1850). *The Scarlet Letter*. The classic tale of a Puritan woman, Hester Prynne, who gives birth out of wedlock and must wear a scarlet letter "A" on her dress as punishment for adultery.
2. Miller, A. (1952). *The Crucible*. New York: Penguin Group. The classic play about the hysteria that allowed the Salem witch trials to destroy 20 families.

3. Hawthorne, N. (1851). *The House of Seven Gables.* The story of the Pyncheon House. Colonel Pyncheon obtained the house by accusing its rightful owner of witchcraft. The house became cursed.
4. Wheatley, P. (1784). *Liberty and Peace.* Poem by African-born American poet Phyllis Wheatley, who was bought as a slave by a merchant but later educated.
5. Maier, P. (1997). *American Scripture: Making the Declaration of Independence.* An in-depth look at the writing of the Declaration of Independence and what it represents to American history.
6. Barth, J. (1987). *The Sot-Weed Factor.* A humorous novel about a ne'er-do-well Englishman who is sent to colonial Maryland to manage his father's tobacco plantation. The novel is known for its meticulously accurate portrayal of seventeenth-century American life.
7. Fischer, D. H. (1989). *Albion's Seed: Four British Folkways in America.* A comprehensive study of the cultural and migratory patterns of English settlement in America.
8. Margolick, D. (2000). *Strange Fruit: Billie Holiday, Café Society, and an Early Cry for Civil Rights.* Fascinating look at the career of Billie Holiday and her influence on the early civil rights movement through performance of songs like "Strange Fruit." The song would later be named *Time* magazine's Song of the Century. The composer Lewis Allen (A. K. A. Abel Meeropol) continued in the civil rights movement and would later adopt Julius and Ethel Rosenberg's sons. (See discussion in Chapter 7.)

FOR FURTHER VIEWING

1. *Three Sovereigns for Sarah.* (1985). Vanessa Redgrave, Patrick McGoohan. The story of the Salem witch trials and the aftermath. Based on a true story.

QUOTATIONS FOR CHAPTER THREE

1. *She had returned, therefore, and resumed—of her own free will . . . resumed the symbol of which we have related so dark a tale. Never afterwards did it quit her bosom . . . . the scarlet letter ceased to be a stigma which attracted the world's scorn and bitterness, and became a type of something to be sorrowed over, and looked upon with awe, yet with reverence too.*
   Nathaniel Hawthorne, *The Scarlet Letter*
2. *These are the times that try men's souls. The summer soldier and the sunshine patriot will, in this crisis, shrink from the service of their country; but he that stands it now, deserves the love and thanks of man and woman. Tyranny, like hell, is not easily conquered; yet we have this consolation with us, that the harder the conflict, the more glorious the triumph.*
   Thomas Paine, *The American Crisis* (1780)
3. *Society in every state is a blessing, but government even in its best state is but a necessary evil, in its worst state an intolerable one.*
   Thomas Paine, *Common Sense* (1776)

4. *Great stones they lay upon his chest until he plead aye or nay. They say he give them but two words. "More weight," he says. And died.*
Elizabeth, recounting death by pressing in Arthur Miller's play, *The Crucible*

5. *. . . governments are instituted among men, deriving their just powers from the consent of the governed; that whenever any form of government becomes destructive to these ends, it is the right of the people to alter or abolish it. . . .*
Thomas Jefferson, *Declaration of Independence* (1776)

ENDNOTES

1. D. H. Fischer, *Albion's Seed: Four British Folkways in America* (New York: Oxford University Press, 1989).

2. P. Johnson, *A History of the American People* (New York: Harper Collins Publishers, 1997).

3. Fischer, *Albion's Seed*.

4. F. E. Zimring, Lynching. In *World Book Encyclopedia*, Vol. 12 (Chicago: World Book Inc., 1990).

5. Fischer, *Albion's Seed*.

6. Ibid.

7. Ibid.

8. P. Maier, *American Scripture: Making the Declaration of Independence* (New York: Alfred A. Knopf, 1997).

9. Fischer, *Albion's Seed*.

10. P. Johnson, *A History of the American People* (New York: Harper Collins Publishers, 1997).

11. Fischer, *Albion's Seed*.

12. E. A. Tomlinson, *Symposium: Comparative Criminal Justice Issues in the United States, West Germany, England, and France: Nonadversarial Justice: The French Experience*, 42 Md. L. Rev. 131 (1983).

13. Ibid.

CHAPTER 4
Constitutional Rights Before Arrest

CHAPTER OBJECTIVES

After studying this chapter, you should be able to:

- Explain the constitutional protection against unreasonable searches and seizures
- Give examples of searches that violate the Fourth Amendment
- Explain what proof law enforcement must have before a search warrant will be issued
- Explain the steps that law enforcement officers must take in order to get a search warrant issued
- List areas that can be searched without a warrant
- Explain probable cause
- Explain the exclusionary rule
- Explain the right to remain silent
- Explain double jeopardy
- Define and explain *ex post facto* laws and bills of attainder
- Explain the right to bail

CHAPTER CONTENTS

CHAPTER SUMMARY

KEY TERMS

DISCUSSION QUESTIONS

FOR FURTHER READING

The poorest man may in his cottage bid defiance to all the forces of the Crown. It may be frail, its roof may shake, the wind may blow through it, the storm may enter, the rain may enter, but the King of England cannot enter! All his forces dare not cross the threshold of the ruined tenement.

William Pitt the Elder, Lord Chatham, English statesman in a speech (1763)

The right of the people to be secure in their persons, houses, papers, and effects, against unreasonable searches and seizures, shall not be violated, and no Warrants shall issue, but upon probable cause, supported by Oath or Affirmation, and particularly describing the place to be searched, and the persons or things to be seized.

U.S. Constitution, Fourth Amendment (1791)

The protection guaranteed by the [Fourth and Fifth] Amendments is much broader in scope. The makers of our Constitution undertook to secure conditions favorable to the pursuit of happiness. They recognized the significance of man's spiritual nature, of his feelings and of his intellect. They knew that only a part of the pain, pleasure and satisfactions of life are to be found in material things. They sought to protect Americans in their beliefs, their thoughts, their emotions and their sensations. They conferred, as against the Government, the right to be let alone—the most comprehensive of rights and the right most valued by civilized men.

Justice Louis Brandeis from his dissent in *Olmstead v. United States* (1927)

INTRODUCTION AND HISTORICAL BACKGROUND

As you learned in the last two chapters, the American colonists rebelled against British control over their lives. Although each region in the colonies had its own distinct character, one common characteristic unified them: the desire to control their own destiny without Britain's interference. In the 1760s, it was common practice for British agents to enter American buildings and homes searching for goods on which customs taxes hadn't been paid. These searches took place without the British having to state a reason for suspecting that they would find contraband in the house.

The American colonists resented the expanding British control over phases of American life ranging from religious practices to where and how the colonists were tried if charged with a crime. Put in its simplest terms, the colonists wanted to be left alone. Once they freed themselves from Britain's yoke, they were reluctant to replace the harness with a new one. One reflection of the American spirit of independence is the Constitution's guarantee that the government can't conduct "**unreasonable searches and seizures,**" or arrest citizens except "**upon probable cause.**"

So strong is the populace's resistance to governmental intrusions that evidence obtained in violation of the prohibition against unreasonable searches and seizures generally can't be admitted into evidence, no matter how incriminating the evidence turns out to be. If the police don't follow the law, the consequence may well be that a guilty man or woman goes free.

The Constitution also protects citizens from being tried repeatedly for the same crime after being acquitted, or **double jeopardy.** In the United States, citizens also can't be tried for acts committed before the behavior was made a criminal offense; the government is prohibited from making *ex post facto* laws. Nor can governments pass **bills of attainder.** Bills of attainder are criminal laws that apply only to named individuals or specific, identified groups. These three Constitutional protections help assure that citizens aren't harassed or oppressed by their government through the use of the criminal process and assure that the laws are applied uniformly and fairly.

The Constitution also protects persons charged with crimes from having to incriminate themselves through oral testimony or a confession. The right against **self-incrimination** is an important safeguard that prevents, for example, the use of torture to extract confessions. Persons charged with crimes are also entitled to effective assistance of counsel and a reasonable opportunity to post **bail** so that he or she can assist in the preparation for trial.

As you study this chapter, think about the liberties accorded to all citizens and ask yourself whether the great legal scholar William Blackstone was right when he said, "It is better that ten guilty persons escape than that one innocent suffer." Is that the price we all must pay in order to live in a free society? Does the price become too high in time of war?

WHAT IS AN UNREASONABLE SEARCH?

The Fourth Amendment to the Constitution provides that "*The right of the people to be secure in their persons, houses, papers, and effects, against unreasonable searches and seizures, shall not be violated.*" This right has evolved over the years to protect citizens from overzealous law enforcement officers and judges eager to secure criminal convictions. One of the key words in the Fourth Amendment is "unreasonable." *Reasonable* searches and seizures are allowed; it's only unreasonable ones that are unconstitutional.

EXPECTATION OF PRIVACY

Searches are unreasonable if they unduly interfere with the people's expectations of privacy. Thus, it can be said that people, not places, are protected from unreasonable searches. That is, if a person has a reasonable expectation of privacy in a place, the place may not be searched without a warrant. However, if he or she does not have a reasonable expectation of privacy in a place, the area can be searched without a warrant.

Courts have long held that people have an expectation of privacy in their homes. Police must either get permission to search a home, be in hot pursuit of someone, or obtain a warrant. The Supreme Court has held that ". . . except in certain carefully defined classes of cases, a search of private property without proper consent is 'unreasonable' unless it has

HISTORICAL HIGHLIGHT
The Right to Privacy

The word *privacy* does not appear in the Constitution. So where does the "right to privacy" come from? It is a legal construct based on various amendments to the Constitution. The "right to be let alone" was first noted by Justice Louis Brandeis in a 1927 case challenging the government's right to tap phones.[1]

Brandeis's "right to be let alone" wasn't applied to sexual or reproductive matters. Brandeis specifically refused to invoke it in a case deciding whether the state could forcibly sterilize a "promiscuous" girl. Brandeis concurred in the majority opinion allowing sterilization, apparently with no qualms about its effect on the "right to be let alone."[2]

However, the seed was planted. When the state of Oklahoma wanted to sterilize a career criminal (whose last conviction was for chicken theft) Justice William O. Douglas ruled that the right to have children was a "basic liberty."[3]

In 1961, the Court was faced with a challenge to a Connecticut law that forbade doctors to distribute contraceptives. Noted conservative jurist John Harlan cited the Oklahoma case when he wrote that the due process clause in the Fourteenth Amendment protected the "privacy of the home." When the same doctor challenged the Connecticut law four years later, Justice Douglas wrote that the state could not violate the "zone of privacy" surrounding the marital bedroom.[4]

This right to privacy was further enlarged in the case of *Roe v. Wade*, when the right to privacy was expanded to include a woman's right to have an abortion under certain circumstances.[5]

There have been limits placed on this right to privacy. Subsequent decisions have failed to expand the right. Other types of sexual activity have been ruled to not be covered by the "right to privacy" until recently.

In 1986, a homosexual male sought unsuccessfully to have Georgia's sodomy law overturned. The plaintiff had been arrested for engaging in oral sex with another man in his own apartment. If convicted under Georgia's 1816 anti-sodomy law, he would have faced up to 20 years in prison. The charges were dropped by the district attorney, but the plaintiff sought to have the law declared unconstitutional. The Supreme Court ruled against him on a 5–4 vote, arguing that moral concerns outweighed the "right to privacy" in this case. In effect, the Supreme Court ruled that it was a matter left to the states to regulate.[6]

Recently, the Supreme Court revisited the matter and overturned its earlier ruling in a 6–3 decision. The Court concluded that the right to privacy includes what consenting adults do in the privacy of their own home and due process protects them from criminal prosecution for that conduct, however offensive it may be to other members of the community.[7] The case is seen by some as a major step forward for the gay rights movement.

been authorized by a valid search warrant."[8] (For an explanation of the requirements for obtaining a warrant, see the discussion on probable cause later in this chapter.) Simply put, unless an officer gets permission to enter, is acting in an exigent situation, or gets a search warrant, it's illegal for him or her to enter someone's home or apartment.

The law gets more complicated, however, when the area to be searched isn't the suspect's own home or apartment. For example, when can police search a car? Can they search your desk at work? What about listening in on the calls you make from a public phone booth? Can they read your e-mail? What if you're a guest at someone's home? What about your backyard? Your luggage? The Supreme Court has considered these and other cases on a case-by-case basis. Essentially, the higher the reasonable expectation of privacy, the greater the likelihood that the police can't invade that privacy. For example, a conversation overheard by an off-duty police officer at a restaurant in which the dining companions discuss a murder-for-hire scheme wouldn't be protected, but the same conversation in the privacy of the conspirators' home would be. In the first, the diners have no reasonable expectation that their conversation is private since they are in public. In the last, the speakers can reasonably expect that their conversations aren't being monitored. It is the cases that fall between these extremes that have called for judicial interpretation.

For example, in *Mancusi v. De Forte*[9] the Supreme Court held that a union official had an expectation of privacy in an office he shared with other workers. The warrantless search of his office space was a violation of the Fourth Amendment. For the search to have been valid, the police officers needed to get a warrant *or* the consent of the employer. They had done neither. However, the Supreme Court recently refused to review an Alaska case in which a worker complained that a secret video camera was aimed at her desk. The college she worked at suspected she was stealing money from the college theatre, and local police crawled through the vents in the ceiling and installed a video camera aimed at her desk, all without a warrant. She was caught on tape taking money from an office money bag and putting it in her purse. She asked the Court to suppress the evidence, but the Alaska Supreme Court concluded she had no expectation of privacy in her desk, since it was in an area accessible to other workers.[10]

In another case, *Minnesota v. Olson*,[11] a suspected driver of the getaway car used in a murder took refuge in an apartment rented by two female friends. The police surrounded the apartment and called the occupants. When one of the women answered, police heard a male voice say "tell them I left." Although they had the apartment surrounded, the officers stormed the apartment and arrested Olson. He challenged his arrest, arguing that the officers should have obtained a warrant or permission from the women before entering. The Supreme Court agreed. Olson, as an overnight guest, had a reasonable expectation of privacy. The Court wrote:

> To hold that an overnight guest has a legitimate expectation of privacy in his host's home merely recognizes the everyday expectations of privacy that we all share. Staying overnight in another's home is a longstanding social custom that serves functions recognized as valuable by society. We stay in others' homes when we travel to a strange city for business or pleasure, when we visit our parents, children, or more distant relatives out of town, when we are in between jobs or homes, or when we house-sit for a friend. We will all be hosts and we will all be guests many times in our lives. From either perspective, we think that society recognizes that a houseguest has a legitimate expectation of privacy in his host's home.

> *Minnesota v. Olson,* 495 U.S. 91, 99 (1990)

Persons who use a pay phone and close the door behind them to make a call have a reasonable expectation of privacy. Their conversation can't be intercepted by police officers without a warrant.[12] But no one has a reasonable expectation of privacy in things that are in plain view. For example, if an officer walking down the street sees a marijuana plant growing next to the petunias in your flower bed, he can use the plants as evidence without a warrant. But he can't knock your door down and seize the plants you were also growing in the basement.

Nor can police use a heat-sensing device to sniff out energy use as a way to get probable cause to search for marijuana plants. That's what the Supreme Court ruled in a 5–4 decision in *Kyllo v. United States*.[13] In that case, the Court concluded that the warrantless use of a thermal-imaging device aimed at a private home from a public street to detect relative amounts of heat within a home was an unlawful search within meaning of the Constitution's Fourth Amendment. Justice Scalia, who wrote the Court's opinion, concluded that a device that could tell "at what hour each night the lady of the house takes her daily sauna and bath" surely violated the right to privacy in one's home.

As you can see, each case is evaluated on its own merits. Because the standard of "reasonable expectation" is subjective, search-and-seizure questions are frequently raised in criminal cases. Many of these have reached the Supreme Court. Consider that from 1969 through 1986 the Supreme Court under Chief Justice Warren Burger decided 130 search-and-seizure cases!

EXCEPTIONS TO THE RULE

There are several exceptions to the rule that a search requires a warrant. The most obvious exception is consent. If the person whose home or possessions were searched gave his permission for the search, then the search does not violate the Fourth Amendment. Unsophisticated defendants who are politely asked if the officers can "look around" have waived any right to later object. The police are not required to educate you that you have the right to refuse a search or a stop and frisk if they come without a warrant. It is expected that any reasonable person would know that they have the right to refuse the search.[14]

The same holds true if the owner of the premises you are visiting, or someone else in charge such as an employer, gives permission. But landlords generally can't give consent to the search of a renter's apartment.[15] Three other exceptions we will consider are the automobile exception, the **exigent circumstances** exception, and the **stop and frisk** exception.

Automobiles are by their nature mobile. And with a few exceptions such as large travel trailers, automobiles are generally not homes. There is therefore a reduced expectation of privacy associated with cars and other motorized vehicles. As a result, courts considering whether automobiles could be searched early on concluded that a lower standard was appropriate. Although a man's home may be his castle, his car is only transportation.

The first Supreme Court case to consider a search of an automobile was decided in 1925.[16] The case, *Carroll v. Illinois*, held that if the officer conducting the search had "probable cause" to have a warrant issued, but didn't ask for one, the search was still valid. The chief reason was the mobility of automobiles. By the time the officer could have gotten a warrant, the car, unlike a house, would be long gone.

Over the years, the Supreme Court has continued to allow warrantless searches of automobiles, trunks, and glove compartments on the premise that the car is mobile *and* that there is a reduced expectation of privacy. This is true even if the car has been impounded and the owner jailed. As the Court wrote in *United States v. Ross*:[17]

> In many cases, however, the police will, prior to searching the car, have cause to arrest the occupants and bring them to the station for booking. In this situation, the police can ordinarily seize the automobile and bring it to the station. Because the vehicle is now in the exclusive control of the authorities, any subsequent search cannot be justified by the mobility of the car. Rather, an immediate warrantless search of the vehicle is permitted because of the second major justification for the automobile exception: the diminished expectation of privacy in an automobile.

Another issue that arises with some frequency is the question of whether a roadblock set up by police to stop motorists is a legitimate practice or violates the Fourth Amendment. In 2000, the Supreme Court ruled 6–3 in *Indianapolis v. Edmond*[18] that many such police checkpoints violate the Fourth Amendment. In that case, the Indianapolis police created a roadblock program that was designed to interdict illegal drug activity. The police set up six roadblocks between August and November 1998 on city roads. All told, they stopped 1,161 vehicles and made 104 arrests, 55 for drug-related offenses and the remainder for other crimes. Edmond challenged the roadblocks as warrantless and without probable cause. The Supreme Court agreed, writing

> The Fourth Amendment requires that searches and seizures be reasonable. A search or seizure is ordinarily unreasonable in the absence of individualized suspicion of wrongdoing. . . . We have never approved a checkpoint program whose primary purpose was to detect evidence of ordinary criminal wrongdoing. Rather, our checkpoint cases have recognized only limited exceptions to the general rule that a seizure must be accompanied by some measure of individualized suspicion.

Another case involving roadblocks was decided by the Supreme Court in early 2004. The question posed was whether the police can set up a roadblock at the site of an earlier accident in order to attempt to find a motorist who might have witnessed an earlier fatal accident. The case, *Illinois v. Lidster*, involves a motorist who was arrested for drunk driving after he stopped at the roadblock. This time, a unanimous Court sided with the police. It distinguished earlier cases by pointing out that the police weren't searching for a *suspect* in the earlier crime, but were simply asking if anyone had information about the crime. It was more akin to police officers asking people in a crowd what they may have observed.[19]

Because nearly one hundred cases involving the Fourth Amendment and the search of automobiles have been decided by the Supreme Court since 1925, any questions about the legality of automobile searches and seizures should be carefully researched before concluding that the search was or wasn't legal.

Exigent circumstances sometimes justify a search and seizure without a warrant. Generally speaking, exigent circumstances are those situations in which the law enforcement officer believes that getting a warrant will create the risk of injury or death or result in the destruction of evidence. One example is blood alcohol testing following an accident or arrest, since the level of alcohol in the blood may fall by the time a warrant can be obtained. You will learn more about blood testing and breath analysis in Chapter 5.

The most obvious situation that qualifies as exigent is when a police officer is in hot pursuit of a defendant, either on foot or in an automobile. Obviously, the suspect will get away if the officer had to first get a warrant from a magistrate! However, the circumstance must truly be an emergency or involve the destruction of evidence. Like other search-and-seizure cases, exigent circumstances cases are fact driven; that is, each case is decided on its unique facts. For example, the Supreme Court recently concluded that there is no bright line between conducting a warrantless search of a car with the driver still in the car or outside it. In *Thornton v. United States*,[20] the defendant parked his car before a police officer had a chance to stop him. The defendant got out of the car and was stopped by the officer. Because the defendant had drugs in his pocket, the officer arrested him and then searched the parked car. The officer found a handgun and added a firearms charge.

Thornton asked the Court to suppress the gun evidence on the premise that a warrantless search of a parked car was illegal. The Court disagreed and ruled 7–2 that officers can search a parked car when the occupant recently left the car. Would the result be the same if the driver had parked in his own driveway and had entered his house before the officer pulled up? It's hard to say. The Supreme Court seems to decide a case on the limits of exigent automobile cases every year.

What happens if the car you are riding in is pulled over by police for speeding and during the course of the stop, an officer finds illegal drugs? Can the officer arrest all passengers and wait for one to confess? That's the question the Supreme Court tackled in *Maryland v. Pringle*.[21] In that case, police became suspicious when the driver reached into the glove compartment for his registration information, revealing a wad of cash. He asked the driver if he could look around, and was given permission. The officer found cocaine under the back seat armrest. Pringle, who was seated in the front passenger seat, was arrested along with the driver and another passenger. Pringle finally confessed that the drugs were his and was eventually convicted and sentenced to ten years in prison. He now alleges that the officer had no probable cause to arrest all three and did so only to coerce a confession. The Supreme Court decided the case in late December 2003, again unanimously. It was reasonable, wrote the Court, to arrest all three in the car on the premise that they were engaged in a common criminal enterprise. That the others were released after Pringle confessed was immaterial.[22]

Police officers can also stop and frisk suspicious individuals.[23] In *Terry v. Ohio*, a police officer noticed two African American men in downtown Cleveland in the late afternoon in 1963. The officer later said that they ". . . didn't look right to me." After observing the men looking in windows and pacing back and forth many times, he stopped them and frisked one man. In the man's coat he found a gun. The defendant argued that he had been searched in violation of the Fourth Amendment. The Supreme Court disagreed, and upheld the stop and frisk as Constitutional.

Since then, the right to stop and frisk has been limited. Officers must have more than a suspicion about an individual; they must describe specific suspicious actions. And police can't stop individuals because of their race or appearance unless they match the description of individuals wanted by the police or seen leaving the scene of a crime.[24] In other words, law enforcement officials must have more than a hunch that someone is engaged in criminal activity.

However, the Supreme Court recently explained that citizens are not free to refuse to give police their identity. If an officer conducts a *Terry* stop, the citizen stopped must provide his or her name and faces criminal penalties if uncooperative. The case, *Hiibel v. Nevada*,[25] involved a police officer responding to a report that a woman was being assaulted in a car. The officer responded to the reported location and stopped Hiibel outside a car with a woman inside. The officer asked Hiibel his name and arrested Hiibel when he refused to identify himelf. Hiibel's attorney argued that his client's Fourth Amendment rights included the right to refuse to give his name when he believed he wasn't engaging in criminal conduct. The Supreme Court disagreed and ruled that states can charge un-cooperative persons criminally if they refuse to disclose their name. As long as the stop meets *Terry* standards for reasonableness, the suspect is required to identify himself.

One area of stop and frisk that has recently expanded is that of airport searches. This is partly in response to increased terrorist attacks, and partly as a result of increased drug smuggling. Generally, persons entering the country can be frisked, and even strip-searched, based upon nothing more than their appearance and point of origin.[26]

SEARCH WARRANTS AND PROBABLE CAUSE

How exactly does a police officer go about getting a search warrant? The details of the procedure varies from state to state and jurisdiction to jurisdiction, but the general rule is that he or she must present enough evidence to a magistrate or judge to show that there is **probable cause** to make an arrest or search the premises for evidence of criminal wrongdoing. *Probable cause* is a term that is subject to interpretation. Generally, it means enough evidence to conclude that it is more likely than not that a crime was committed or that the place to be searched is connected with a crime. It is more than a suspicion, but

HISTORICAL HIGHLIGHT
Custom Searches Alleged to Be Discriminatory

In 1998, customs officials at Chicago's O'Hare International Airport were slapped with a class action suit brought by 52 African American women who claimed to have been unreasonably targeted for searches. The women complained of being singled out for invasive body cavity and strip searches. In each case, nothing illegal was found.[27]

However, in the aftermath of the four September 11, 2001 hijackings, searches have become more intrusive, and have met with little public resistance. In what may have been a related incident in December 2001, a man carrying a British passport boarded a plane in Paris en route to Miami. While in mid-air he attempted to light a fuse connected to his shoes. A flight attendant and several passengers restrained the man, and the flight was safely diverted to Boston. Since then, spot-checks of passengers' shoes have become part of airport security.[28]

Although the longer lines and thorough searches are being tolerated for the sake of security, it may not always be that way. Clearly, the American public's tolerance for searches is something that changes over time. And as the war on terror continues, it seems likely that authorities will be given more leeway in determining what is a reasonable precaution in public places like airports and what constitutes an invasion of privacy for travelers.

less than that needed for a conviction.[29] Probable cause is always needed before law enforcement officers can obtain a warrant, conduct a search, or arrest even when one of the exceptions to obtaining a warrant is present.

Once officers have a warrant in hand, they are supposed to "knock and announce" their presence. That is, the right to privacy includes the right to not be surprised by officers who knock down your door and storm in. A case recently decided by the Supreme Court tested the limits of the "knock and announce" requirement. During an afternoon, north Las Vegas police officers in SWAT uniforms raided the apartment of Lashawn Banks, whom they suspected was a drug dealer. Warrant in hand, they knocked and waited about 15 seconds before using a battering ram to gain entrance. Banks, who was showering, heard the loud noise and ran into the living room. There he was ordered to the floor by police officers wearing hoods. He claimed that their actions violated his right to privacy and that the evidence the officers found should be suppressed.

The Ninth Circuit sided with Banks, and the police appealed. A unanimous Supreme Court ruled in late 2003 that under the circumstances, the police were justified in breaking the door down. Given that the officers were executing on a warrant for possession of cocaine, they could reasonably have suspected that the defendant's brief delay in answering the door was due to his efforts to dispose of the evidence.[30]

Police frequently work with informants and others whose reputations for honesty and integrity are suspect. A question that often arises in criminal cases is whether the informant is credible enough to support the issuance of a warrant. The court uses a totality of the circumstances test.

The case that set the standard involved an anonymous letter received by police. The letter claimed that a husband-and-wife team would transport a large amount of drugs in an automobile. The husband was to fly down to Florida while the wife drove the automobile. In Florida, the car was to be loaded with drugs, and the husband was to drive the car back. Acting on the information in the letter, the police found that the husband had reservations to fly to Florida. Acting with Florida police, they discovered that he and a female did drive a car back from Florida. When the couple arrived home, the police were waiting.

The couple challenged the warrant on the basis that the informant was unknown. But the Supreme Court, adopting the totality of the circumstance test, upheld the warrant since independent police work confirmed the information provided in the letter.[31] To meet Constitutional standards, a search warrant must describe specifically "the place to be searched and the persons or things to be seized."[32]

THE EXCLUSIONARY RULE

To discourage the abuse of the rules against unreasonable searches and seizures, the Supreme Court adopted the **exclusionary rule.** The rule makes inadmissible any evidence seized as a result of a violation of the Fourth Amendment, so that the evidence can't be used at trial against the defendant. The Court, in *Mapp v. Ohio*, 367 U.S. 643 (1961), ruled that such evidence is like the "fruit of a poisonous tree," and can't be used against the defendant. The rule has since been modified so that evidence obtained through search warrants obtained in good faith, but which are invalidated for technical reasons, can be used at trial.[33]

HISTORICAL HIGHLIGHT
Police Can Search Indian Reservation with Warrant

The Paiute Palace Casino in Bishop, California, is run by Native American members of the Paiute-Shoshone tribe on tribal lands. The casino has 300 slots and seven game tables and provides much-needed jobs to tribe members. Police in Inyo County became suspicious that some tribe members were collecting welfare benefits while working at the casino, and obtained a warrant to search the premises for evidence of welfare fraud. The casino had previously refused to turn over records, citing confidentiality.

The police officers raided the casino offices and seized employment records. No evidence of fraud was discovered, but the police threatened to enter tribal lands again. That's when tribal leaders sued in federal court, alleging that the police were violating the tribe's sovereign immunity. The tribe won in the Ninth Circuit, but lost in the Supreme Court, 9–0. Police can, using a warrant, enter and search tribal lands. The case is *Inyo County v. Paiute-Shoshone Indians*, 538 U.S. 701 (2003).

DOUBLE JEOPARDY

The Fifth Amendment to the U.S. Constitution provides that no person shall "*be subject for the same offense to be twice put in jeopardy of life or limb. . . .*" Its roots can be traced to Roman times, when the Emperor Justinian declared, "The governor should not permit the same person to be again accused of crime of which he has been acquitted."[34] This Constitutional provision assures that no one can be put on trial a second time for the same offense after a court or jury has decided that the government was unable to prove its case beyond a reasonable doubt. In other words, it doesn't matter if the defendant, after being acquitted, takes out a full-page ad in the local paper declaring that he "did it." He can't be tried again after the jury has spoken.

Prosecutors only have one opportunity to present the case to a jury; if the case is botched or if evidence is uncovered later, the opportunity has been lost. As a practical matter, this means that the government must bring all possible charges arising out of one incident against an individual at one time. The government can't, for example, first try a defendant for murder and later try him for possession of a firearm during the robbery in which the murder took place. If it fails to convict on the murder charge, it can't retry on the weapons charge. "*All the charges against a defendant that grow out of a single criminal act, occurrence, episode, or transaction*" must be tried together.[35]

The guarantee, however, has several well-established exceptions. These include the government's:

- Right to retry a suspect if the jury is deadlocked, or "hung"
- Right to retry a suspect when an appellate court has ordered a retrial because of some error in an earlier trial

- Right to try a suspect in federal court on federal criminal charges if a state court acquitted on state charges and vice versa or to try and convict an individual in both state and federal court if the same act violated both state and federal law
- Right on retrial to ask for and get the death penalty if the defendant was originally sentenced to life in prison but appealed the conviction and won a new trial. Each of these exceptions is discussed below.

RETRIAL AFTER HUNG JURY

When a jury is unable to reach a verdict of guilty or not guilty, the defendant may be, and often is, retried. There is no violation of the double jeopardy clause because both the defendant and the government are entitled to a jury's decision on the case. The Supreme Court explained the issue this way:

> The double-jeopardy provision of the Fifth Amendment, however, does not mean that every time a defendant is put to trial before a competent tribunal he is entitled to go free if the trial fails to end in a final judgment. Such a rule would create an insuperable obstacle to the administration of justice in many cases in which there is no semblance of the type of oppressive practices at which the double-jeopardy prohibition is aimed. There may be unforeseeable circumstances that arise during a trial making its completion impossible, such as the failure of a jury to agree on a verdict. In such event the purpose of law to protect society from those guilty of crimes frequently would be frustrated by denying courts power to put the defendant to trial again.

Wade v. Hunter, 336 U.S. 684 (1949)

RETRIAL AFTER REVERSAL ON APPEAL

When a judge or jury finds a criminal defendant guilty of a crime, the defendant may appeal the decision to an appellate court if he or she believes an error occurred during the trial. Errors include incorrect rulings on the admissibility of testimony, ineffective assistance of counsel, violation of a Constitutional right, and the like. Only the criminal defendant can appeal a conviction; the government can't appeal an acquittal.[36]

The remedy ordered by the appellate court is typically a new trial. That new trial allows the defendant to exclude the erroneously admitted evidence the second time around, to have the assistance of effective counsel, to have evidence admitted, or the like. In other words, the new trial gives the defendant another opportunity for acquittal. Only in rare circumstances will an appellate court find that the errors in the first trial are so egregious that a second trial would be double jeopardy. (See Historical Highlight: *Commonwealth v. Smith*.)

Trial in Both State and Federal Court for the Same Act

Another exception to the rule against double jeopardy is a second trial in the event a defendant violates the laws of two or more jurisdictions by one act. The double jeopardy clause doesn't prevent both state and federal courts from prosecuting, convicting, and sentencing the same defendant for committing one act that is both a federal and a state crime.

HISTORICAL HIGHLIGHT

Commonwealth v. Smith, *Suppressed Evidence Taken with a Grain of Sand*

Susan Reinert had reason to be happy in the summer of 1979. She was engaged to a fellow teacher, William Bradfield, and was to be married that summer. She also had reason to be afraid. Bradfield and Smith, the assistant principal of the school where Reinert and Bradfield taught, may have planned to murder her and her children. The possible reason was the $730,000 of insurance Bradfield had persuaded her to purchase, naming him as the beneficiary.

Ms. Reinert and her two children left their home on the evening of June 22, and were not seen alive again. Reinert's nude and beaten body was discovered in the trunk of a car parked in a hotel parking lot 100 miles away from her home. Her children's bodies were never found.

According to the prosecution, Bradfield and Smith had planned to kill Reinert and her children for the insurance money. The prosecution also showed that the two had engaged in a criminal conspiracy before. In 1977 Smith had been accused of theft, but Bradfield had provided an alibi for him. Despite Bradfield's testimony, Smith had been convicted. Smith was due to start his sentence on June 26, 1979, the day after Reinert's body was discovered.

The prosecution theorized that it was a doublecross. Bradfield was to kill Reinert, and Smith was to dispose of the children. The bodies were not supposed to be found, and after the seven-year waiting period, the two would share in the insurance money. Smith would have the alibi of being incarcerated at the time of the "disappearance." Perhaps, the prosecution argued, Bradfield realized that Smith would be in jail, and if Reinert's body was discovered, he could collect the money right away and be long gone by the time Smith finished his sentence.

Both men were eventually charged with the murders and they were tried separately. Bradfield was convicted and sentenced to three life terms. He died in prison in 1998. Smith was convicted and sentenced to death.

However, the prosecution had suppressed a piece of evidence at Smith's trial. The State Police had lifted grains of sand from Reinert's feet. Smith had maintained as his defense that Bradfield had taken Reinert to the New Jersey shore and killed her there. Despite the fact that several other key pieces of physical evidence tied Smith to Reinert's death, the Pennsylvania Supreme Court ruled that the suppression of evidence was prosecutorial misconduct. Normally, this would mean a new trial, but the high court went further. They ruled that the conduct was so egregious that to try Smith again would violate the Constitutional prohibition against double jeopardy. The conviction was overturned and Smith was set free.

In 1998, Smith sued prosecutors, policemen, and author Joseph Wambaugh, who wrote a best-seller about the case, *Echoes in the Darkness*, alleging they violated his civil rights. Smith claimed Wambaugh had offered to pay a Pennsylvania State police officer if his book was a success. Attorneys for the prosecutors and policemen argued in the civil trial that the "grains of sand" were quartz that could have come from anywhere. Thus, they were not deemed important at the time of trial. The jury apparently was convinced by this argument, but was skeptical of Smith's explanation of how one of his combs was found under Reinert's body, and how pieces of her clothing were discovered in his car.

Smith is free. This case shows that even in cases where there is strong evidence pointing to a person's guilt, the Constitutional protection against double jeopardy can prevent the state from trying that person again.

For example, if a defendant makes moonshine that violates both a state law against home-brewing and federal laws against producing moonshine for transportation across state lines, he or she can be punished under both laws. That's because each jurisdiction has the right to enforce its criminal laws.[37] If he or she was acquitted of state charges, he or she can also still be convicted on the federal charges.

A number of crimes have both state and federal consequences. For example, both the federal government and the individual states have laws against the sale and distribution of controlled substances. In most cases, the state laws are virtually identical to the federal law. A defendant who sells heroin violates two criminal laws with each sale, and can be prosecuted in both state and federal court. As a practical matter, though, most defendants are prosecuted under either state or local laws, not under both. This is due in part to the Petite policy, a policy developed by the Department of Justice that essentially prohibits federal prosecutors from prosecuting a defendant on state charges if the federal law violated is substantially similar to a state one, and the state has prosecuted the defendant on the state charges.

Only in cases that would create a manifest injustice if the defendant were allowed to go free does the federal government prosecute an individual who has already been tried and convicted or acquitted of an act that is a state crime and also a federal crime. You may recall from Chapter 2 that the police officers who were acquitted of beating Rodney King were later tried and convicted in federal court for violating Mr. King's civil rights. The unique fact situations of the Rodney King beatings and the riots that followed the acquittal of the police officers caught on camera was such a circumstance warranting another prosecution.

Right on Retrial to Ask for and Get the Death Penalty if the Defendant was Originally Sentenced to Life in Prison but Appealed the Conviction and Won a New Trial

What happens if a murder defendant is convicted and sentenced to life in prison, but receives a new trial? Can the prosecution seek the death penalty? The answer was until recently "No." The Supreme Court had ruled that to do so would be double jeopardy.[38] But in 2003, a divided Court concluded the opposite. The case involved a Pennsylvania defendant who was convicted of murder by a jury for killing a restaurant worker during a robbery. The jury was unable to agree on whether the defendant should receive death or life in prison. Because it was deadlocked, Pennsylvania law dictated he be sentenced to life.

He appealed and was granted a new trial based on other defects in the trial. The prosecution again sought death, and this time the jury was willing to order it. The Supreme Court ruled that there was no double jeopardy in this case, but left open the possibility that had the first jury voted for life rather than being unable to agree, the prosecution would be barred from seeking death.[39]

EX POST FACTO LAWS AND BILLS OF ATTAINDER

Two rights granted by the Constitution that are rarely the subject of controversy in criminal law deserve at least a brief mention, if only to illustrate the mind-set of the founding fathers and the tyranny they sought to protect the citizens of their new nation from. These two concepts are the prohibition against the passage of *ex post facto* laws and *bills of attainder*. *Ex post facto* laws are laws that criminalize behavior after the behavior has already taken place. Bills of attainder are criminal statutes passed that make behavior a crime for only some persons and not others.

EX POST FACTO LAWS

The Constitution outlaws *ex post facto* laws. That is, neither the federal government nor a state or local government can pass a law that makes an act a crime that was not a crime when the defendant committed the act. Nor can a legislature pass laws that increase the penalty for a crime that was committed before the law was passed. "The Constitution forbids the application of any new punitive measure to a crime already consummated, to the detriment or material disadvantage of the wrongdoer."[40]

   The reason for the prohibition is rooted in the criminal law concept that holds crimes are intentional acts in disobedience of the law. A person can't disobey a law that does not yet exist. And it would be patently unfair for the justice system to punish people after the fact. There is an exception, though. So-called "three times, you're out" recidivism statutes aren't *ex post facto* even if the first two crimes were committed before the passage of the recidivism law went into effect, as long as the third strike happened after the recidivism law went into effect. In other words, a defendant must be on notice that another conviction will mean a longer sentence than the third conviction ordinarily would carry but for his or her prior record.

   What about a prisoner sentenced to a lengthy term who would have had a parole hearing every year until the law changed the interval between hearings? The Supreme Court has ruled that since the change doesn't affect the original sentence, only his potential early release, the change wasn't an *ex post facto* law.[41]

   A recent Supreme Court opinion clarified how far the legislature can go to punish behavior that occurred a long time ago. The case involved a 70-year-old grandfather who was charged with sexual offenses against minors—something that happened over 50 years earlier. In response to complaints that the state's statute of limitations for sex crimes for minors was too short (it had been three years for some time), the California legislature authorized prosecutors to charge defendants up to one year from the time they were notified by a victim that the assault had taken place. The law was passed in part to help victims of childhood sexual abuse who may have feared coming forward for years.

The Supreme Court ruled that the law violated the prohibition against *ex post facto* laws and threw out the conviction by a 5–4 vote.[42] The decision put in question the arrest and conviction of a number of priests accused of abusing young boys in their charge. In states that have changed their statute of limitations since the abuse occurred, no prosecution seems likely.[43]

BILLS OF ATTAINDER

Bills of attainder are criminal laws passed that only apply to a specific person or specific group of persons. In England, bills of attainder originally singled out individuals for capital punishment without benefit of a trial. The term now refers to any law that targets a specific individual or group for criminal punishment. For example, assume a local city government passed an ordinance that made it a crime for John Smith to smoke in public. Since the law names an individual, it is a bill of attainder. Everyone else can smoke in public, except John Smith. Laws also can't designate an identifiable group as the subject. For example, a law banning all Communist Party members from holding union offices unfairly singled out a specific group for special treatment, and was ruled a bill of attainder.[44] In short, a law is a bill of attainder if it singles out either a specific person or a group of persons for prosecution or other punishment.

RIGHT TO REMAIN SILENT

The Fifth Amendment provides that no person "shall be compelled in any criminal case to be a witness against himself." The right against self-incrimination, or the **right to remain silent,** is fundamental to the American system of justice. It reflects the fundamental belief of the founding fathers that it's the government that has the burden of proof in criminal cases, and that the accused can't be forced to do the prosecutor's job. Simply put, a defendant cannot be compelled to confess to a crime or to provide testimony against himself. He may, of course, do so voluntarily.

Police have an obligation to inform suspects in custody or under arrest of the right to remain silent, among other rights. Since the Supreme Court's decision in *Miranda v. Arizona*,[45] law enforcement officers routinely read suspects their rights. This has become known as "mirandizing" a suspect. *Miranda* is discussed in detail in the next chapter.

There are several exceptions to the rule, however. Defendants can be compelled to provide some forms of physical evidence that can be used against them at trial. The second exception involves compelled testimony under a grant of immunity. The exceptions are discussed in the next chapter.

RIGHT TO REASONABLE BAIL

Another fundamental right enjoyed by Americans is the Eighth Amendment guarantee against excessive bail. Though not without limits, defendants are generally entitled to bail pending trial. Release from prison before trial serves several purposes. First, it serves as an incentive for the government to bring cases to closure. If defendants could be indefinitely

HISTORICAL HIGHLIGHT
Ex Post Facto *and Sex Offender Registration*

Perhaps no crime strikes greater fear in the community than violent offenses against children. Children who are victims of rape or other forms of sexual abuse are understandably sympathetic victims. Likewise, their assailants are almost universally reviled, even among other criminal offenders. So deep does the prohibition against harming defenseless children go that prisons almost always separate child abusers from the rest of the inmate population to protect the abusers from harm.

It should come as no surprise, then, that laws designed to identify criminals who prey on children are popular in many communities. So-called sexual predator laws typically require those convicted of sexual offenses involving children to register their addresses. Usually referred to as *Megan's Laws*, because they were inspired by the tragic death of Megan Kanka at the hands of a sexual predator who lived in her neighborhood, the laws require community notification when a sex offender moves into a neighborhood. Presumably, parents and other adults will be more vigilant when they know their neighbor has a history of violent sexual crimes.

Sexual predator registration laws have been challenged by offenders who argue that having to register as predators is additional punishment inflicted after they have served their sentences, especially for those who committed their crimes before the laws were passed. *Megan's Laws*, they argue, amount to *ex post facto* laws and violate the Constitution.

When Alaska passed a version of *Megan's Law*, two former sex offenders sued. They argued that registering after they had served their sentences was additional punishment for a crime they had committed long before the law was passed. The Alaska Sex Offender Registration Act required that the former offender's name, address, place of employment, conviction and sentence, driver's license information, and photograph be published on the Internet. One offender had been convicted of sexually abusing his daughter from age 9 through 11 and the other had pled no contest to charges he had sexually abused a 14-year-old teen.

The Supreme Court, in a 6–3 decision, upheld the legislation. Although registering might subject the offenders to shame, that was not punishment as contemplated by the *ex post facto* clause, reasoned the majority. The Court wrote that:

> The purpose and the principal effect of notification are to inform the public for its own safety, not to humiliate the offender. Widespread public access is necessary for the efficacy of the scheme, and the attendant humiliation is but a collateral consequence of a valid regulation.

Smith v. Doe, 538 U.S. 1009 (2003)

detained in prison pending trial, there would be little incentive to moving the case forward. Second, the **right to bail** allows the defendant to fully participate in his or her defense, something difficult to do from the inside of a prison cell. Coupled with the right to a speedy trial (discussed in the next chapter), the right to bail helps grease the wheels of justice.

The amount of bail set is intended as a guarantee that the defendant will show up for trial. Bail generally is set in an amount that will guarantee that the defendant doesn't skip town. Since 1987, however, bail can be denied altogether if the defendant poses a danger to the community. Bail can be denied in capital cases, in cases where the defendant may intimidate witnesses, or in cases where the public's safety is at stake. A hearing is required before bail can be denied, and the government must show that the defendant poses a public threat that no conditions of release can change.[46]

CHAPTER SUMMARY

Americans enjoy a long list of protections from police and governmental interference in their lives. These protections naturally extend to persons suspected of criminal activities. Working from the presumption that all persons are innocent until proven guilty, law enforcement officials must go about the task of solving crimes by assembling the evidence to prove beyond a reasonable doubt that a defendant is guilty without interfering with the people's right to liberty.

All persons are accorded the right to be free from unreasonable searches and seizures. The Constitution protects the public's reasonable expectation of privacy, whether at home, at work, or in a closed phone booth along the interstate. Police can only search private places with either consent or a search **warrant.** A search warrant requires that police officers obtain one from a neutral magistrate or judge after presenting probable cause that the place to be searched will yield evidence of a crime or the person to be detained has committed a crime.

Officers can detain, search, and arrest individuals without a warrant, but with probable cause, if certain circumstances mitigate against obtaining a search warrant from a magistrate or judge. These include the searching of an automobile stopped for reasons that amount to probable cause, exigent circumstances like the pursuit of a suspect on foot or in a car, and the temporary detainment, identification, and search of an individual in a stop and frisk.

If a defendant can show that the police violated his or her right to be free of unreasonable searches and seizures, the remedy may be that the evidence obtained cannot be used in court. This is the exclusionary rule.

In the American system of justice, the government has only one opportunity to try a suspect; if a jury acquits him, he is free to go even if later he shouts his guilt from the highest rooftop. Double jeopardy protects him, and all others, from repeated attempts at conviction for the same offense. It does not mean that a defendant who wins an appeal can't be retried. Nor does it prevent another trial if the jury is unable to reach a verdict. Defendants can also be tried in both state or federal court for activities that violate both state and federal laws.

The rule against *ex post facto* laws prevents the government from punishing persons who committed acts that were legal at the time but were made illegal later. The rule against bills of attainder prevent the government from passing laws that apply only to certain individuals or specific groups of people.

Finally, defendants and suspects have the right to legal counsel to represent them at most stages of a criminal prosecution and the right to remain silent throughout the process.

KEY TERMS

Bail: Money or other guarantee posted to assure a defendant who is released from custody pending trial or appeal will appear when called or forfeit the security posted.

Bill of attainder: A law passed that singles out a person or persons as the only individuals affected by a criminal law. Originally, a bill of attainder singled out an individual for capital punishment without benefit of a trial.

Double jeopardy: The rule, based on the Fifth Amendment, that a person can only be tried once for the same offense. The rule has several exceptions.

Ex post facto **law**: The rule that a person cannot be charged with a crime that became a crime after he committed the act made illegal.

Exclusionary rule: The "fruit of the poisonous tree" doctrine that prohibits the admission of evidence obtained illegally at a defendant's criminal trial. The rule does allow the use of evidence obtained with a technically defective warrant, but in good faith.

Exigent circumstances: Situations that require urgent action, sufficient to excuse delay to get a warrant issued.

Probable cause: The amount of proof required before an officer can obtain a search warrant, stop a suspect, or make an arrest. Enough evidence from which a reasonable person could conclude that the facts alleged are probably true.

Right to bail: The limited right to be released from prison pending trial after posting enough security to assure appearance at the time of trial. The right is subject to limitation in cases of murder or where release has been shown to pose a threat to the public.

Right to remain silent: The right of all persons not to testify against their own interests when suspected of or charged with a crime. The right to remain silent is rooted in the belief that it is the government's obligation to prove guilt.

Self–incrimination: The act of giving testimony against one's penal interest. Generally, persons have a right to withhold information that may incriminate and to refuse to answer questions that incriminate. The right does not generally extend to giving DNA samples or submitting to blood-alcohol testing or withholding other physical evidence.

Stop and frisk: Police officers may briefly stop, identify, and frisk persons reasonably believed to have committed a crime during the course of an investigation.

Unreasonable searches and seizures: The rule, based on the Fourth Amendment, that police must obtain a warrant before searching a home or arresting a suspect. The rule has numerous exceptions.

Warrant: A document issued by a magistrate or judge authorizing the search of a place or the arrest of a person.

DISCUSSION QUESTIONS

1. Discuss the right to privacy in one's home and in other places discussed in this chapter. Does the system provide sufficient safeguards against unreasonable searches or does it hamper law enforcement to the detriment of law-abiding citizens' rights to be free from crime?

2. You have been stopped by a police officer because your brake light is out. Your brother, whom you suspect has a drug problem, throws something under your seat. The officer asks if he can look around. What do you do?

3. A trend in recent years has been for state legislatures to pass laws that require sex offenders who have served their sentences to register their address with the police and for the government to notify communities that a convicted sex offender is now their neighbor. What arguments would you make on behalf of a sex offender who committed the offense before the passage of the registration law?

4. How intrusive a search are you willing to undergo in order to fly? Does your tolerance for searches change if instead of flying, you are taking the train? A bus? A taxi? Entering a sporting event?

FOR FURTHER READING

1. Alderman, E., & Kennedy, C. (1997). *The Right to Privacy.* Vintage Books. Examines the origin of the right to privacy and its application in civil and criminal law through case studies such as the story of the routine strip-searching performed on women arrested for minor traffic violations.

2. Alderman, E., & Kennedy, C. (1992). *In Our Defense: The Bill of Rights in Action.* Avon Books. Explores the origin and history of the Bill of Rights using case examples.

3. Amar, A., & Hirsch, A. (1998). *For the People: What the Constitution Really Says About Your Rights.* Free Press. Provides an alternative interpretation of the history of the Constitution and the Bill of Rights that focuses on the rights of the collective "we the people" rather than on the rights of the individual.

4. Katz, L., & Shepard, T. (1994). *Know Your Rights.* Banks-Baldwin. This practical legal guide answers questions like what to do when stopped by a police officer on the road or are arrested.

5. Moore, W. (1996). *Constitutional Rights and Powers of the People.* Princeton University Press. This book examines how the social and political climate of the time affects the interpretation of the Constitution.

QUOTATIONS FOR CHAPTER FOUR

1. *Pain forces even the innocent to lie.*
   Publilius Syrus, first century B.C.

2. *A right is not what someone gives you; it's what no one can take from you*
   Ramsey Clark, former U.S. attorney general, *New York Times* (2 Oct. 1977)

3. *Even an attorney of moderate talent can postpone doomsday year after year, for the system of appeals that pervades American jurisprudence amounts to a legalistic wheel of fortune, a game of chance, somewhat fixed in the favor of the criminal, that the participants play interminably.*
   Truman Capote, *In Cold Blood* (1965)

4. *Those who would give up essential liberty to purchase a little temporary safety deserve neither safety nor liberty.*
   Benjamin Franklin, in the Pennsylvania Assembly (1755)

The right to be let alone is indeed the beginning of all freedoms.
William O. Douglas (1952)

*The Fifth Amendment is an old and a good friend . . .   one of the great landmarks in men's
struggle to be free of tyranny, to be decent and civilized.*
William O. Douglas, *An Almanac of Liberty* (1954)

*For my part I think it less evil that some criminals should escape, than that the government should
play some ignoble part.*
Oliver Wendell Holmes Jr., in *Olmstead v. United States* (1928)

If we are to keep our liberties, there must be one command; Thou shalt not ration justice.
Learned Hand, speech (1951)

*Before going to prison I believed that criticism of the criminal justice system for its treatment of the
poor was so much liberal bleating and bunk. I was wrong.*
G. Gordon Liddy (1977)

ENDNOTES

1. *Olmstead v. United States*, 277 U.S. 438 (1927).
2. *Buck v. Bell*, 274 U.S. 200 (1927).
3. *Skinner v. Oklahoma ex Rel. Williamson, Attorney General*, 316 U.S. 535 (1942).
4. *Griswold et al. v. Connecticut*, 381 U.S. 479 (1965).
5. *Roe v. Wade*, 410 U.S. 113 (1973).
6. *Bowers, Attorney General of Georgia v. Hardwick et al.*, 478 U.S. 186 (1986).
7. *Lawrence v. Texas*, 539 U.S. 558 (2003).
8. *Camara v. Municipal Court*, 387 U.S. 523 (1967).
9. *Mancusi v. De Forte*, 392 U.S. 364 (1968).
10. *Cowles v. Alaska*, 23 P.3d 1168 (2001) cert den. 2002 U.S. Lexis 701.
11. *Minnesota v. Olson*, 495 U.S. 91 (1990).
12. *Katz v. United States*, 389 U.S. 347 (1967).
13. *Kyllo v. United States*, 533 U.S. 27 (2001).
14. *United States v. Drayton et al.*, 536 U.S. 194 (2002).
15. *Chapman v. United States*, 365 U.S. 610 (1961).
16. *Carroll v. Illinois*, 267 U.S. 132 (1925).
17. *United States v. Ross*, 456 U.S. 798 (1982).
18. *Indianapolis v. Edmond*, 531 U.S. 32 (2000).
19. *Illinois v. Lidster*, 540 U.S. 419 (2004).
20. *Thornton v. United States*, 124 S. Ct. 2127 (2004).
21. *Maryland v. Pringle*, 370 Md. 525; 805 A.2d 1016 (2002), affirmed 540 U.S. 366
    (2003).
22. *Maryland v. Pringle*, 540 U.S. 366 (2003).
23. *Terry v. Ohio*, 392 U.S. 1 (1968).
24. *Brignoni-Ponce v. United States*, 422 U.S. 873 (1975).
25. *Hiibel v. Nevada*, 124 S. Ct. 2451 (2004).

26. *United States v. Sokolow*, 490 U.S. 1 (1989).

27. J. Gibeaut, *Marked for Humiliation*, 85 ABA J. 46 (February 1999).

28. F. Bayles, "Shoe-bomb Suspect's Travel Suggests Financial Help," *USA Today* (December 31, 2001) Gannett Company, Inc.

29. *Brinegar v. United States*, 338 U.S. 160 (1949).

30. *United States v. Banks*, 540 U.S. 31 (2003).

31. *Illinois v. Gates*, 462 U.S. 213 (1983).

32. U.S. Constitution, Fourth Amendment.

33. *Illinois v. Krull*, 480 U.S. 340 (1987).

34. *Digest of Justinian*: Digest 48.2.7.2, translated in 11 Scott, The Civil Law.

35. *Ashe v. Swenson*, 397 U.S. 436 (1970).

36. *Benton v. Maryland*, 395 U.S. 784 (1969).

37. *United States v. Lanza*, 260 U.S. 377 (1922).

38. *Bullington v. Missouri*, 451 U.S. 430 (1981).

39. *Sattazahn v. Pennsylvania*, 537 U.S. 101 (2003).

40. *Kring v. Missouri*, 107 U.S. 221 (1883).

41. *California Dept. of Corrections v. Morales*, 513 U.S. 1074 (1995).

42. *Stogner v. California*, 123 S. Ct. 2446 (2003).

43. C. Goodyear and P. Podger, "California Molestation Law Struck Down," *S. F. Chronicle* (June 27, 2003).

44. *United States v. Brown*, 381 U.S. 437 (1965).

45. *Miranda v. Arizona*, 384 U.S. 436 (1966).

46. *United States v. Salerno*, 481 U.S. 739 (1987).

CHAPTER 5
Constitutional Rights After Arrest

CHAPTER OBJECTIVES

After studying this chapter, you should be able to:

- Explain the *Miranda* warning
- Explain when a criminal defendant has a right to counsel
- Explain the rights of indigent defendants to a public defender
- Explain the right against self-incrimination
- List and explain the circumstances under which a person can be compelled to testify against himself
- Explain the attorney-client privilege, husband-wife privilege, and priest-penitent privilege
- Explain when physical evidence can be compelled from defendants without violating the right against self-incrimination
- Explain the right to a speedy trial
- Distinguish statutes of limitations from the Constitutional right to a speedy trial

CHAPTER CONTENTS

> *Every society gets the kind of criminal it deserves. What is equally true is that every community gets the kind of law enforcement it insists on.*
>
> **Robert Kennedy,** *The Pursuit of Justice*

> *If one really wishes to know how justice is administered in a country, one does not question the policemen, the lawyers, the judges, or the protected members of the middle class. One goes to the unprotected, those, precisely, who need the law's protection most! And listens to their testimony.*
>
> **James Baldwin,** *The Price of the Ticket* **(1972)**

INTRODUCTION

As you have learned in the last few chapters, many of the rights we accord persons charged with crimes stem from abuses suffered by the colonists at the hand of the British crown. The Constitution and the Bill of Rights serve as reminders that our forefathers vowed that never again would they be subjected to the whims of a monarch, but that the right to a prompt, fair, public trial and adequate legal representation would be sacrosanct. In this chapter, we will explore the rights of defendants in the crucial time between arrest and trial.

Of primary importance to defendants is the right to have an attorney represent their interests as the case winds its way through the court system. Since many defendants lack financial resources, the right to counsel includes the right to a court-appointed attorney if money is a problem.

Defendants also have the right to remain silent, that is, the right to compel the government to prove the case against him or her. As we will see, that right is limited to testimonial silence. In some circumstances, defendants can also prevent others from providing testimony.

The right to remain silent is not absolute. Some forms of physical evidence can be compelled. A person can also be compelled to testify if he or she has received immunity from prosecution or the statute of limitations has expired.

THE CONSTITUTIONAL RIGHT TO COUNSEL IN CRIMINAL CASES

The Sixth Amendment states that: "In all criminal prosecutions, the accused shall enjoy the right . . . to have the Assistance of Counsel for his defense." Given the complexity of the legal system and the high stakes for a defendant, very few persons accused of a crime elect to represent themselves. Most prefer to have a trained attorney at their side. But the right to assistance of counsel wasn't widespread until this century, at least in "minor" criminal cases.

For many years, the right to be represented by a member of the bar was limited to capital cases (cases where the death penalty was sought by the prosecution). In 1932, the Supreme Court wrote that a layman:

> lacks both the skill and knowledge adequately to prepare his defense, even though he has a perfect one. He requires the guiding hand of counsel at every step . . . without it, though he is innocent, he faces the danger of conviction because he does not know how to establish his innocense.[1]

By 1938, the right was extended to all federal felony cases. By 1963, defendants charged with any felony, state or federal, were entitled to counsel regardless of their ability to pay for one.[2] And by 1964, the Supreme Court had ruled that confessions obtained after police didn't tell the defendant he was entitled to counsel or refused to let him talk to his attorney are not admissible.[3]

The right to counsel isn't limited to having an attorney to represent you at trial. A defendant has a right to counsel at his or her arraignment, preliminary hearing, during most police questioning, during a lineup, at trial, and at sentencing. In addition, he or she has a right to counsel for his or her first appeal.

The right to counsel means little if the defendant is ignorant of his right to counsel. Therefore, the Supreme Court decided in the *Miranda* case that police have an obligation to inform a suspect of his rights under the Constitution.

Police must inform any person put under arrest or held in a custodial interrogation, such as at a police station, that he has the following rights before questioning begins:

1. That he has the right to remain silent,
2. That anything he says can and will be used against him,
3. That he has the right to an attorney during questioning,
4. That if he can't afford one, one will be appointed at no charge before questioning, and
5. That at anytime during the questioning, he can stop and the interrogation will end.

HISTORICAL HIGHLIGHT
The Scottsboro Boys: The Right to Counsel

On March 31, 1931, a train was rolling through the Alabama countryside. As was often the case during the Depression, many drifters were riding in the train's boxcars. This train had a group of young black boys, ages 12 to 19, and a group of white boys along with two white girls. A fight broke out among the boys and all the white boys except for one were thrown from the train. They immediately alerted the authorities and at the next stop the blacks were arrested after the girls accused them of rape.

As a group, these boys had little or no education. All were illiterate, and not one of them was an Alabama native. By the time they were in custody, word had spread of the incident and a large angry crowd awaited them at Scottsboro. The local sheriff called for the state militia to help protect the boys.

The trial was set for a week after the indictment. The local judge appointed all members of the local bar to assist in the boys' defense, but charged no one attorney in particular to represent them. A Tennessee attorney was contacted by the families of one of the defendants, and appeared at the first day of trial offering to assist the court-appointed attorney. Although some members of the local bar had spoken with the defendants, none were prepared to conduct their defense. The Tennessee attorney was given the opportunity to represent them by himself, but explained that he wasn't prepared for trial and was unfamiliar with court practices in Alabama. Eventually, one of the local attorneys was appointed and the Tennessee attorney assisted him.

The defendants were tried as three groups, and with the exception of the 12-year-old defendant, separately sentenced to death. The trials lasted one day each. The convictions were upheld by the appeals court and the Alabama Supreme Court, and only Chief Justice Anderson dissented, stating he did not feel the boys received a fair trial.

The International Labor Defense, a Communist organization, represented the boys when the case was appealed to the U.S. Supreme Court. The case was appealed on three grounds: (1) they were not given a fair, impartial, and deliberate trial; (2) they were denied the right of counsel, and with the accustomed incidents of consultation and opportunity of preparation of trial; and (3) they were tried before juries from which qualified members of their own race were systematically excluded.[4]

The Supreme Court dealt only with the second charge, the denial of right to counsel. The High Court, citing the Sixth Amendment, reaffirmed the right to counsel for all citizens accused of a crime, and described the type of defense afforded the Scottsboro boys as "rather pro forma than zealous and active."[5] The Court noted the lack of time for the defense to prepare for trial, and the lack of time for the defendants, all of whom lived out of state, to secure counsel of their own choice as sufficient to invalidate their defense. The Court reversed the convictions and sent the cases back to be retried with adequate counsel.

At the second trial, the boys were convicted, but the judge found the testimony of the girls unbelievable and set aside the verdict and ordered a new trial. He was defeated in the next election.[6]

The Scottsboro boys' saga dragged on for many years. None of them were ever executed, but all spent time in prison. The last one, Clarence Norris, was finally pardoned by Governor George Wallace in 1976.[7]

Miranda is discussed more fully in the Historical Spotlight: "How *Mirandizing* Became a Verb." In 2000, the Supreme Court had an opportunity to consider *Miranda* again. In 1968, Congress passed a law that essentially intended to gut the *Miranda* decision. This law

(18 U.S.C.S. § 3501) provided that as long as the defendant's confession was voluntary, it needn't be preceded by the *Miranda* warning. Dickerson, the defendant, was indicted for a bank robbery. He confessed to the crime when asked by the FBI, and then moved to strike his confession because he gave it without being warned as required by *Miranda*. The government argued that under 18 U.S.C.S. § 3501, it wasn't required to warn him.

The trial judge suppressed the confession, but the Fourth Circuit Court of Appeals reversed. The defendant appealed to the Supreme Court. The Court, in a strongly worded opinion, ruled that it meant what it said in *Miranda,* and ordered the confession suppressed. The Court found the warning to be a fundamental Constitutional right.[8]

What happens if a police officer deliberately doesn't read a suspect her Miranda rights, gets her to confess, then *Mirandizes* her, and gets the confession the second time? That was the issue before the Court in a 2004 case involving a mother who allegedly conspired to commit arson to cover up a child's natural death. Unfortunately, the cover-up arson went badly and killed another youth. The officer who questioned her claimed to have learned the double confession trick at a training seminar. The Court ruled 5–4 that the tactic was illegal and the second confession was invalid.[9]

The Supreme Court recently heard another case involving double confessions. In that case, the officers came to the defendant's house and asked him if he had been involved in illegal drug use after telling him he had been indicted. He confessed and was taken to the police station, where he was read his *Miranda* rights and again confessed. On appeal, he argued both confessions should be thrown out because he had not been read his rights. A unanimous Supreme Court sent the case back to the lower court, stating that the real question was whether the defendant's Sixth Amendment rights to counsel had been violated in that he had not been offered the opportunity to have his lawyer present.[10]

The issue is one that doesn't seem to want to go away. On the same day it concluded that the arson-setting mother's confession was illegal, the Court also decided that a gun found after a defendant admitted he had one can be used as evidence even though the admission came after the police failed to read the suspect his *Miranda* rights. The case involves a defendant, who, when arrested, stopped the officer from reading the *Miranda* warning because he claimed to know it already. The confession he made was suppressed, but the gun the police seized was allowed into evidence. The Court, in another 5–4 decision, upheld the use of physical evidence found as a result of information gleaned from an illegal confession.[11]

THE POOR AND THE RIGHT TO COUNSEL

A criminal defendant is entitled to more than just an attorney to represent him or her. The defendant has the right to "effective" assistance of counsel. Effective counsel is competent counsel.[12] Obviously, the right to counsel would mean very little if a defendant doesn't have the means to retain an attorney. After all, the government expends a vast amount of money on its police force, district attorneys, judges, and other court personnel. As the Supreme Court pointed out in *Gideon v. Wainwright,* the fact that "[t]he government hires lawyers to prosecute and defendants who have the money hire lawyers to defend are the strongest indications of a widespread belief that lawyers in criminal courts are necessities, not luxuries."[13]

Indigent defendants have the right to court-appointed counsel at no charge. Since 1964, when the Criminal Justice Act of 1964 was passed into law, defendants charged with

---

HISTORICAL HIGHLIGHT
How Mirandizing *Became a Verb*

Watch any police show on television or in a movie theater, and invariably at some point in the plot line, a police officer will read a defendant or suspect his rights. You can probably recite the warning verbatim yourself, so often have you heard it. "You have the right to remain silent and the right to consult an attorney. Anything you say can and will be used against you in a court of law. . . ."

The warning has almost become a police officer's mantra. In fact, almost every police officer carries a copy of the *Miranda* warning with him or her. That's not because he or she is likely to "forget" to inform a defendant of a right. Rather, it reflects an easy way for officers to testify later. Sometime in the future, the officer will be asked whether he or she read the defendant his rights. The officer is unlikely to remember the exact details of an arrest or interrogation that happened months, even years, earlier. Instead, the officer will testify that he did read the suspect his rights, by pulling out the card, and reading it to him word for word. The officer will tell the court how he *Mirandized* the defendant.

Just how did *Mirandizing* become a verb? The term, of course, is derived from the 1966 Supreme Court decision in *Miranda v. Arizona.* The case actually involved not just Ernesto Miranda, the Arizona defendant who lent his name to the legal warning. In the same decision, the Court also decided that Michael Vignera, a New Yorker, Carl Calvin Westover of Kansas City, and Roy Allen Stewart of Los Angeles had confessed without knowing their Constitutional rights.

Together, their cases served to highlight just how common was the police practice of extracting quick confessions from suspects unfamiliar with their rights. All gave confessions after lengthy interrogations. At least one confession declared that the statement was made "with full knowledge of my rights." Another confessed after a series of interrogations that spanned five days. Together, their cases convinced the Court that something as simple as a warning was needed to curb the widespread denial of suspects' right to remain silent. Ever since, police officers *Mirandize* suspects.

---

federal crimes are entitled to a federal public defender. The states have passed similar legislation to assure a supply of experienced criminal law attorneys are available to those who cannot afford an attorney. Most public defender offices also have available professional investigators who can assist in preparing cases for trial.

Judges sometimes appoint and the government pays for experienced private attorneys in complex and serious cases when the local public defender office is short staffed or lacks a staff public defender with expertise in complicated trials. Court-appointed private counsel is generally reserved for high-profile capital cases such as the Oklahoma City bombing cases.

The right to counsel continues after trial through the posttrial appeals and any direct appellate appeals.

HISTORICAL HIGHLIGHT
Susan McDougal: The Price of Silence

In 1996, Special Prosecutor Kenneth Starr was charged with investigating the role of Bill and Hillary Clinton in their Whitewater Real Estate venture. Susan McDougal, the Clinton's former Whitewater business partner, was convicted of mail fraud, misapplications of small business investment company funds, falsifying small business investment company records, and making false statements to a small business investment company. She was sentenced to two years in prison. Citing health problems, the court reduced her sentence to time served plus 90 days of home confinement.

Starr offered McDougal use immunity in return for her testimony. However, McDougal maintained that she would be open to prosecution because testimony that Starr already obtained would conflict with McDougal's testimony. The federal judge in the case cited McDougal for civil contempt and sent her back to prison.

Civil contempt is punishable under federal law with up to 18 months in prison. Under civil contempt, the person is imprisoned until (a) the person agrees to cooperate with the court or grand jury, (b) the court or grand jury expires, or (c) 18 months have passed.

McDougal again refused to testify. As her 18 months neared its end, Starr subpoenaed her again. When she refused to testify again, she was charged with criminal contempt.

Summary criminal contempt can be imposed by a judge with no due process for "charges of misconduct, in open court, in the presence of the judge which disturbs the court's business."[14] However, the sentence cannot exceed six months. Felony contempt would require a trial.

Starr's methods met with widespread criticism, but demonstrated the length to which the state may go to enforce its will. McDougal was released before the end of her term due to her failing health.

A federal law called the Recalcitrant Witness Statute[15] allows for the release of a prisoner if it appears unlikely that additional jail time will change the witness's mind. McDougal's attorneys had attempted to get her released under this statute, but the court would not relent. In a controversial move, President Clinton included Susan McDougal on his list of pardons granted just hours before he left office in January 2001.

THE CONSTITUTIONAL RIGHT TO REMAIN SILENT

So far, we have concentrated on the right to have counsel represent a person during criminal procedures and only touched on the related right not to incriminate oneself. That right is enshrined in the Fifth Amendment to the Constitution as "No person . . . shall be compelled in any criminal case to be a witness against himself." A person who refuses to answer questions about alleged criminal activities is said to "plead the Fifth." No right is fundamentally more representative of the American way of justice. It is always the government's prosecutor and police officers who must prove a person guilty of a crime, not the person's responsibility to prove himself innocent. All men and women are indeed innocent until proven guilty. To protect that fundamental right, no person can be compelled to help the government by being forced to give evidence against himself or herself.

Confessions can only be used against a defendant if the prosecution can show that they followed the procedures laid out in *Miranda* and that they did not coerce or otherwise extract a confession from the defendant. All confessions must be voluntary and have been given after notification of the right to remain silent.

The right to remain silent is not without limits. In some circumstances, there is no risk associated with speaking. In that case, prosecutors and others can compel testimony. That's because the right to remain silent is the **right against self-incrimination.** That is, in order for the right to apply, the act of speaking must be related to the possibility of criminal prosecution. If that possibility doesn't exist, there is no potential self-incrimination. For example, if the statute of limitations has expired, there is no restriction on what can be asked. There is also nothing to prevent police or others from demanding sworn testimony under oath when the defendant's criminal trial has already ended and he or she has been sentenced or acquitted. That's because he or she no longer faces the possibility of the testimony being used against him or her. In addition, if a defendant has been given immunity, testimony can be compelled. Immunity is explored below.

IMMUNITY

It has long been the rule that a person who receives immunity can be compelled to testify, no matter how personally embarrassing or humiliating testifying may be. As long as the prospect of criminal prosecution is absent, there is no right to "plead the Fifth." That's been the rule since 1888.[16]

USE IMMUNITY

Immunity falls into two different categories. The first is **use immunity.** If a defendant is granted use immunity, anything he says to investigators cannot be directly used against him in a later trial. That is, the prosecutor can't use his direct words or anything the prosecution discovers that was related to the testimony. For example, assume that a defendant was granted use immunity in exchange for testimony about a murder. If the defendant testifies that he threw the weapon in the Susquehanna River, police can't dredge the river for the gun and use the weapon as evidence. However, if a bather, independent of the government, stumbles upon the gun and turns it in, the gun can be used against the defendant. The key is that independent evidence gathered by the police or others can be used even if immunity has been granted as long as it can be shown that it wasn't the testimony that led to the discovery of the evidence.

HISTORICAL HIGHLIGHT
Suspected Nazi War Criminal Must Sing

In this chapter you have learned that the right to remain silent protects defendants from having to provide testimony that can be used against themselves in a criminal proceeding. You have also learned that the rule against self-incrimination applies to the states, not just the federal government. Defendants also can't be forced to testify in a federal criminal case if they face the reasonable prospect of having that testimony used against them in a state criminal case. But what happens if the information requested places the defendant in danger of prosecution in a foreign nation? Can the defendant refuse to testify in that situation?

The United States Supreme Court answered that question in 1998 in *United States v. Balsys.* The real and substantial fear of prosecution in a foreign nation does not mean that a defendant can refuse to answer on the ground that his answer may incriminate him.

Balsys involved a resident alien who had been admitted to the United States in 1961 under the Immigration and Nationalization Act. All applicants for resident status under that law must provide sworn information about his or her criminal past, if he or she has one. The application Balsys signed in 1961 provided that if he provided false or misleading information, he would be subject to criminal prosecution in the United States and face deportation. In his application, Balsys swore that he had served in the Lithuanian Army from 1934 through 1940 and had lived in hiding from the start of World War II to 1944.

More than 35 years after his admission to the United States, the Justice Department began an investigation into whether Balsys had participated in Nazi persecution of Jews and other groups during World War II. If he had, he would be subject to deportation. When he was subpoenaed, he refused to answer questions about his alleged Nazi past on the grounds that it would subject him to criminal prosecution in Israel or Lithuania as a war criminal. He didn't claim any fear of prosecution in the United States, because the statute of limitations on falsifying his immigration application had passed. Therefore he had no valid fear of prosecution in this country.

After the Supreme Court ruling, Balsys faced the prospect of being held in criminal contempt if he continued to refuse to answer questions about his alleged Nazi past, or answering and being deported to face a war crimes trial.

TRANSACTIONAL IMMUNITY

Transactional immunity is the preferred form of immunity for defendants. With transactional immunity, the government is forever barred from prosecuting the defendant for the crime from which he or she was granted immunity. No amount of independently gathered evidence can support a prosecution. The defendant, in exchange for testimony, is guaranteed that he or she will never be prosecuted for the crime about which he or she testified.

PRIVILEGE AND THE RIGHT TO KEEP OTHERS SILENT

A concern for the sanctity and privacy of personal conversations and actions is inherent in the Constitution and the Bill of Rights. The focus on privacy can be seen in the reluctance to allow unfettered police access to our homes and possessions and in the recognition of a number of testimonial privileges that prevent the prosecution from compelling attorneys, spouses, and others from testifying about private conversations.

ATTORNEY-CLIENT PRIVILEGE

A privilege has long existed in conversations between counsel and client. The attorney-client privilege is one of the oldest recognized privileges for confidential communications.[17] The privilege is intended to encourage full and frank communication between attorneys and their clients. Without the guarantee that what is said to one's attorney is confidential, few faced with difficult circumstances would avail themselves of the right to counsel. The privilege applies to the attorney and anyone else on his or her staff.

In order for attorney-client privilege to apply, there must be an underlying agreement that the attorney has been retained to represent the defendant. If not, there is no privilege. Attorneys and their office staff should consult their state bar association for specific guidance on what is necessary for the formation of an attorney-client relationship and to learn under what circumstances attorneys are required to withdraw from representation if the client reveals he or she will lie under oath.

The attorney-client privilege does not extend to an attorney's participation in a crime. For example, an attorney can't hold the murder weapon in his or her safe or conceal and destroy records that have been entrusted to his or her care. The attorney-client privilege does protect notes that attorneys make memorializing client discussions and outlining the course of action recommended. The **work product rule** protects from disclosure any material the attorney created to prepare for trial.

SPOUSAL PRIVILEGE

Another well-established privilege available to criminal defendants is the spousal privilege. This privilege is meant to protect private conversations between husband and wife and to protect marriages from the destructive effects of being compelled to testify against a husband or wife. This rule, like so many others, is not without limits.

As with many other Common Law rules, spousal privilege has a long history, springing from medieval society. Two justifications for the **marital privilege** developed over time. First, of course, was the rule that a defendant can't or shouldn't be compelled to testify against himself. Second, because husband and wife were regarded as one, and since a wife had no recognized separate legal existence, if a wife were compelled to testify, it would be the same as if the husband were the one forced to speak. Thus, what was inadmissible from the lips of the defendant's husband was also inadmissible from his wife.

For many years, courts assumed that the marital privilege meant that neither husband or wife could be compelled to testify against each other and that each could prevent the other from testifying against the other. That changed in 1980 when the Supreme Court

---

HISTORICAL HIGHLIGHT
How Ken Starr Got Monica to Talk

In 1998, Special Prosecutor Kenneth Starr was appointed to investigate President and Mrs. Clinton's involvement in the Whitewater Real Estate deal. However, he was given a broad mandate. When no criminal activity was found directly related to Whitewater, Starr looked elsewhere.

Eventually, Starr settled on the president's testimony in the Paula Jones case. Paula Jones was a former Arkansas state employee who claimed to have been invited to then-Governor Clinton's hotel room where Clinton allegedly dropped his pants and requested oral sex. Clinton denied the incident, but was deposed in the case. He was asked about his relationship with Gennifer Flowers. During the election of 1992, he had denied having an affair with her. In the Jones deposition, he admitted that an affair had taken place.

But the Jones lawyers had another trick up their sleeve. They asked the president about a young White House intern named Monica Lewinsky. The president denied he had an affair with her.

Starr, however, had evidence that Lewinsky had an affair with the president. She had spoken with her friend Linda Tripp, who like all good friends, had taped her conversations with Monica.

The key to Starr's case against the president was to get Lewinsky to testify and prosecute the president for perjury. Lewinsky, however, steadfastly denied an affair, swearing in an affidavit that it had not happened. Starr offered her transactional immunity.

Transactional immunity shields the recipients from all prosecution in the case as long as the person tells the truth. This is different from use immunity in that with use immunity the person can be prosecuted if other evidence of criminal activity comes to light.

Lewinsky, however, wanted an even better deal. She held out for transactional immunity for herself, her mother, and her father. She had confided in them during the period, and did not want to risk any criminal liability on their part. She testified, and her answers set off a chain of events that ended with an attempt to impeach Clinton.

---

decided *Trammel v. United States.*[18] Elizabeth Trammel traveled to Thailand where she bought heroin. She then boarded a plane for the United States with several ounces of heroin on her person. During a routine customs stop in Hawaii, she was searched, the heroin was discovered, and she was arrested. She made a deal with the Drug Enforcement Agency in which she received immunity in exchange for her testimony against her husband. He claimed that her testimony violated the marital privilege.

HISTORICAL HIGHLIGHT
Attorney-Client Privilege Survives Death

In 1993, shortly after the beginning of William Clinton's first term as president of the United States, employees who worked for the White House Travel Office were discharged en masse. At the time there was a great deal of speculation in the press about who ordered the firings, and why. The White House conducted its own internal investigation into the firings. Shortly after, several investigations were initiated into whether anyone in the White House involved with the investigation had committed criminal acts. Deputy White House Counsel Vincent W. Foster, Jr., a personal friend and former law partner of the First Lady, was involved in the investigation.

On July 20, 1993, Vince Foster took his own life in a public park in Washington, D.C. Nine days earlier Foster had met with James Hamilton, an attorney at the law firm of Swidler & Berlin in Washington, D.C. Vince Foster sought the firm's representation, and asked whether the conversation would be covered by the attorney-client privilege. James Hamilton took three pages of handwritten notes during the meeting, all under the heading "privileged."

By December 1995, an Independent Counsel, Kenneth Starr, had been appointed to investigate potential wrongdoing by the White House, including the circumstances surrounding the Travel Office firings. At Starr's request, a federal grand jury subpoenaed James Hamilton's handwritten notes. The law firm filed a motion to quash the subpoena. A motion to quash is a request to a court to be excused from complying with a subpoena. The firm argued that the notes were protected by attorney-client privilege. The Special Counsel argued that the privilege dies with the client, and Vince Foster was dead.

The United States Supreme Court took up the novel question, and issued an expedited opinion. On June 25, 1998, the Court issued an opinion that declared that the attorney-client privilege survives death. The Court wrote:

> Knowing that communication will remain confidential even after death encourages the client to communicate fully and frankly with counsel. . . . Clients may be concerned about reputation, civil liability, or possible harm to friends or family. Posthumous disclosure of such communications may be as feared as disclosure during the client's lifetime.

Swidler & Berlin and Hamilton v. United States, 524 U.S. 399 (1998)

The Supreme Court disagreed, and ruled that a spouse who voluntarily chooses to testify against her husband may do so. The privilege belongs to the person speaking, not to the other spouse. The Court reasoned that women are no longer considered an extension of their husbands, but individual human beings. Presumably that means they can use that individuality to decide for themselves whether they will protect their spouse or cut a deal with the prosecutor.

Additionally, in state and local jurisdictions, this rule can have multiple variations. For example, Pennsylvania does not afford spousal privilege in cases "in which one of the charges pending against the defendant includes murder, involuntary deviate sexual intercourse or rape."[19]

PRIEST-PENITENT PRIVILEGE

At Common Law there also existed a **priest-penitent privilege.** Its intent was to keep secret statements made in the confessional. The privilege has been mentioned in passing in several Supreme Court decisions, but the Court has never faced the question of its continued relevance. An attempt to call a priest or other religious figure to the stand to testify would likely be met with opposition. The issue may be raised in criminal prosecutions of Catholic priests accused of molesting boys in their parishes. It remains to be seen if those to whom the priests confessed within the Church hierarchy will be forced to testify later.

PATIENT-COUNSELOR PRIVILEGE

Another privilege recognized by the Supreme Court, the **patient-counselor privilege,** is the right to keep confidential conversations between a patient and his or her psychotherapist. For example, in one case the Supreme Court ruled that a police officer's social worker could not be compelled to testify in a civil suit brought by the family of a man killed by a female police officer responding to a call. She had received extensive counseling after the shooting. The officer had been sued by the family for allegedly violating the dead man's civil rights. The Court concluded that "[t]he psychotherapist privilege serves the public interest by facilitating the provision of appropriate treatment for individuals suffering the effects of a mental or emotional problem. The mental health of our citizenry, no less than its physical health, is a public good of transcendent importance."[20]

COMPELLING THE PRODUCTION OF PHYSICAL EVIDENCE

The right against self-incrimination doesn't apply to physical evidence. That is, the government can make a suspect produce physical evidence of guilt as long as the method used isn't unreasonably intrusive. Defendants can be made to try on items of clothing, such as a shirt or a glove.[21] But taking a suspect to the hospital and making him vomit up evidence by pumping his stomach is unreasonably intrusive.[22]

Defendants can be brought down to the police station and be made to stand in a lineup. That's because the Constitution only protects a defendant against "being compelled to testify against himself, or otherwise provide the State with evidence of a testimonial or communicative nature."[23] A lineup merely serves as a way for the police to determine if the suspect is likely to be the individual sought. The state will still have to show beyond a reasonable doubt that he committed the crime and defendants are entitled to have an attorney present during the lineup.

Defendants can also be compelled to submit to fingerprinting, photographing, and measuring. They can also be forced to provide writing and voice samples, and the results can be introduced in court.

BREATH ANALYSIS, BLOOD, AND DNA EVIDENCE

Physical evidence obtained by reasonable means can be used against a suspect. For example, most state driving under the influence laws provide that motorists stopped on suspicion of driving under the influence of drugs or alcohol must submit to a Breathalyzer test or forfeit their license to operate a motor vehicle. The results of the test can be admitted at a criminal trial. He or she can also be compelled to take a blood test to determine the amount and kind of intoxicant in the body.[24]

Again, the evidence can be used for trial. However, defendants and suspects can't be compelled to take physical tests that seek to measure physiological responses that the examiner can claim indicate guilt or a state of mind. Thus, suspects can't be made to take a lie detector test.

Since the middle of this century, blood evidence compelled from a suspect has been available in court. With the advent of new, more sophisticated analysis of blood, the justice system has increased its use of such evidence. For example, DNA evidence is now routinely used to solve rape and murder cases. DNA analysis can exclude suspects altogether or provide compelling odds that the defendant committed the crime. Defendants in both civil and criminal cases are finding it hard to argue that DNA evidence doesn't prove either beyond a reasonable doubt or by a preponderance of the evidence (the criminal and civil standards of proof) that the defendant left the genetic material in question.[25]

An interesting twist on compelling physical evidence came in a recent Supreme Court case. The City of Charleston, South Carolina, decided something had to be done to combat cocaine use by pregnant women. Working with the local police department, the public hospitals in town drew urine tests on pregnant women without their consent, and without a search warrant, and tested for cocaine use. Positive test results were referred to the police department for prosecution. The case ended up before the Supreme Court, which ruled that nonconsensual urine tests violated the Fifth Amendment's prohibition against unreasonable searches.[26]

THE RIGHT TO A SPEEDY TRIAL

The Sixth Amendment to the Constitution guarantees a defendant the right to a "speedy and public" trial. The Amendment prevents defendants from being left in jail to rot pending trial, or from enjoying years of freedom outside prison if he or she has been able to make bail.

The Supreme Court has ruled that the right to a speedy trial is flexible, with no fixed number of days or weeks dictating whether the right has been denied.[27] Instead, the Court suggested that state and federal legislatures pass laws setting time limits, if they choose. As a result, most states have laws on the books that set strict time limits for bringing defendants to trial, usually within a year of being formally charged and arrested.

The Speedy Trial Act of 1974[28] sets strict time limits for bringing federal defendants to trial. The Act has a built-in mechanism for dealing with requests for continuances and other common delays. The penalty for violating the right to a speedy trial is dismissal of the charges.

Don't confuse the right to a speedy trial with statutes of limitations. Each state and the federal government has set time limits for the initiation of criminal proceedings against persons suspected of committing crimes. These limits range from a few years for minor crimes to indefinitely for murder. In effect, statutes of limitations set a deadline for the commencement of criminal actions, while the right to a speedy trial dictates how soon the trial must begin after a suspect has formally been charged with that crime. For example, a woman who murders her boyfriend at 18 can be charged with that murder at age 80, but is then guaranteed a speedy trial within her state's time limits.

CHAPTER SUMMARY

For a person charged with a crime, one of the most important Constitutional guarantees is the right to counsel. Without counsel, a defendant would be left to navigate a complicated labyrinth without a guide. The right to counsel is so crucial to the legitimacy of the criminal law system that all persons, whether rich or indigent, are entitled to the services of a competent attorney. Those without adequate resources to retain private counsel are entitled to the services of a state or federal public defender or other court-appointed counsel.

A criminal suspect or defendant is also entitled to remain silent. In the American system of justice, all persons are presumed innocent until the state or federal government proves beyond a reasonable doubt that the suspect is guilty. No defendant is required to help the prosecutor prove his case through his own words. The right to remain silent and the exclusionary rule, which prevents prosecutors from using confessions or evidence obtained in violation of Constitutional rights, serve to curb possible police abuses. Confessions beaten out of defendants can't be used to convict them.

The right to remain silent has several significant limitations. First, an individual who faces no possibility of having his or her words used against him or her cannot "plead the Fifth." For example, a person who has already been convicted of a crime no longer faces the possibility that his words will be used to convict. Persons granted immunity can also be forced to testify, since they don't face the possibility of having their words used against them either.

In our legal system, some relationships are regarded as inviolate. Therefore, confidences expressed in private with attorneys, counselors, a spouse, or a spiritual advisor are generally protected by a privilege against compelled revelation.

However, the privilege against self-incrimination doesn't apply to physical characteristics or evidence that is obtained in a reasonable fashion. For example, DNA and fingerprint evidence are standard fare in criminal prosecutions.

The right to remain silent and the right to counsel would mean little if persons charged with crimes were unaware of those rights. Therefore, law enforcement officers are required to tell a suspect or person under arrest that he has those rights and the right to have counsel appointed if indigent. The *Miranda* warning has become the standard method for police to convey those rights.

Defendants are also entitled to a speedy trial. Prisoners are not allowed to linger in prison awaiting trial or remain out on bail indefinitely.

KEY TERMS

Marital privilege: The right of a person to refuse to testify against his or her spouse.

Patient-counselor privilege: The right of confidentiality accorded counselors for conversations held in the course of mental health treatment.

Priest-penitent privilege: The right of confidentiality accorded members of the clergy for conversations held during the ritual of confession.

Right against self-incrimination: The right embodied in the Fifth Amendment that allows an accused person to remain silent. Its corollary is "innocent until proven guilty."

Transactional immunity: A broad form of immunity where the person cannot be prosecuted for any action related to the testimony as long as the person testifies truthfully.

Use immunity: A limited form of immunity where the person's testimony cannot be used as evidence against him or her.

Work product rule: The rule that protects material produced by an attorney in preparation for a trial, or the work product, from discovery.

DISCUSSION QUESTIONS

1. Several states have recently started DNA databases. These are similar to the fingerprint databases kept by the FBI to aid in the solving of crimes. By using DNA taken from prisoners, agencies hope to be able to match prisoners with unsolved crimes still on the books and to be able to match future unsolved crimes to past prisoners. Discuss the legal and ethical implications of this trend.

2. Computer technology has grown by leaps and bounds in the last decade. As the new technologies develop, criminals are using more sophisticated encryption tools to safeguard the contents of their e-mail and the documents on their hard drive. Assuming that police had a valid warrant to seize and search a suspect's hard drive for evidence of criminal activity, can the suspect be compelled to give police the key to his encryption program so that they may have access to his records?

3. Indigent defendants are entitled to a public defender in criminal cases, but not in civil cases. Building on what you have learned in the previous chapters, why do you think this is so?

4. What methods and procedures do you think should be in place in a law firm to protect the confidentiality of information obtained from persons who have an attorney-client relationship with attorneys in the firm?

5. You have learned about the *Miranda* warning. Do you think the warning is sufficient to convey Constitutional rights?

FOR FURTHER READING

1. Lewis, A. (1989). *Gideon's Trumpet.* Vintage Books. This book details the landmark case of *Gideon v. Wainwright* that established the right to legal counsel for everyone.

2. Leo, R. A., Thomas, G. C. III, and Thomas, G. C. (eds.). (1998). *The Miranda Debate: Law, Justice, and Policing.* Northeastern University Press. This is a collection of essays from across the political spectrum about the *Miranda* decision and its impact on law enforcement and society.

3. Horne, G. (1997). *Powell v. Alabama: The Scottsboro Boys and American Justice (Historic Supreme Court Cases).* This book is geared toward young adults, but tells the story of the Scottsboro boys in detail, and explains the importance of the case in legal and historical context.

FOR FURTHER VIEWING

1. *Gideon's Trumpet.* (1980). The story of Clarence Earl Gideon's case as it went to the Supreme Court. Henry Fonda, José Ferrer, John Houseman.

2. *Judge Horton & the Scottsboro Boys.* (1976). A made-for-TV movie about the Scottsboro boys episode. The two women who claimed they were raped by the boys filed suit over this presentation. The suit was dismissed.

QUOTATIONS FOR CHAPTER FIVE

1. *Law enforcement, however, in defeating the criminal, must maintain inviolate the historical liberties of the individual. To turn back the criminal, yet, by so doing, destroy the dignity of the individual, would be a hollow victory.*
   J. Edgar Hoover, *Civil Liberties and Law Enforcement: The Role of the FBI*, 37 Iowa L. Rev. 175 (1952)

2. *The quality of a nation's civilization can be largely measured by the methods it uses in the enforcement of its criminal law.*
   Professor Schaefer, *Federalism and State Criminal Procedure*, 70 Harvard L. Rev. 1 (1956)

3. *The need for counsel in order to protect the privilege [against self-incrimination] exists for the indigent as well as the affluent.*
   Chief Justice Earl Warren, *Miranda v. Arizona* (1969)

4. *If the glove doesn't fit, you must acquit*
   Johnny Cochran, in closing argument to the jury, *California v. O. J. Simpson*

ENDNOTES

1. *Powell v. Alabama,* 287 U.S. 45 (1932).
2. *Gideon v. Wainwright,* 372 U.S. 335 (1963).
3. *Escobedo v. Illinois,* 378 U.S. 478 (1964).
4. *Powell et al. v. State of Alabama,* 287 U.S. 45 (1932).
5. Ibid.
6. *Famous American Trials: The Scottsboro Boys.* http://www.law.umkc.edu/ftrials/scotboro. *Trials 1931–1937.*
7. Ibid.

8. *Dickerson v. United States*, 530 U.S. 428 (2000).

9. *Missouri v. Seibert*, 124 S. Ct. 2601 (2004).

10. *Fellers v. United States*, 124 S. Ct. 1019 (2004).

11. *United States v. Patane*, 124 S. Ct. 2620 (2004).

12. *McMann v. Richardson*, 397 U.S. 759 (1970).

13. *Gideon v. Wainwright*, 372 U.S. 335 (1963).

14. *Pounders v. Watson*, 521 U.S. 982 (1997); quoting *In re Oliver*, 333 U.S. 257 (1948); *Cooke v. United States*, 267 U.S. 517 (1925).

15. Recalcitrant Witness Statute, 28 U.S.C. § 1826.

16. *Hunt v. Blackburn*, 128 U.S. 464 (1888).

17. *Brown v. Walker*, 161 U.S. 591 (1896).

18. *Trammel v. United States*, 445 U.S. 40 (1980).

19. 42 Pa. C. S. § 5914, Act 16 of 1989.

20. *Jaffee v. Redmond*, 516 U.S. 1091 (1996).

21. *Holt v. United States*, 218 U.S. 245 (1910).

22. *Rochin v. California*, 342 U.S. 165 (1952).

23. *Schmerber v. California*, 384 U.S. 757 (1966).

24. Ibid.

25. For example, DNA comparison testing of a stain found on Monica Lewinsky's now-infamous navy blue dress with a blood sample obtained from President Bill Clinton revealed a probability of 1 out of 7.87 trillion that the stain was left by a Caucasian other than the president.

26. *Fergusen v. City of Charleston*, 532 U.S. 67 (2001).

27. *Barker v. Wingo*, 407 U.S. 514 (1972).

28. Speedy Trial Act, 18 U.S.C.S. § 3161.

CHAPTER 6
The Constitutional Right to Trial by Jury

CHAPTER OBJECTIVES

After studying this chapter, you should be able to:

- Explain the history of the right to trial by jury in criminal cases
- Define *jury*
- List and explain the provisions in the U.S. Constitution that require trial by jury in criminal cases
- Explain how the members of a jury pool are selected
- Explain the process of *voir dire*
- List some reasons a potential juror can be excused for cause
- Explain sequestration
- List some reasons for a change of *venue* and change of *venire*
- Explain what "beyond a reasonable doubt" means
- List and explain some differences between federal juries and state juries

CHAPTER CONTENTS

> *In all criminal prosecutions the accused shall enjoy the right to a speedy and public trial, by an impartial jury of the state and district wherein the crime shall have been committed.*
>
> **U.S. Constitution, Eighth Amendment (1791)**

> *The jury is both the most effective way of establishing the people's rule and the most efficient way of teaching them how to rule.*
>
> **Alexis De Tocqueville, *Democracy in America* (1835)**

INTRODUCTION AND HISTORICAL BACKGROUND

Every year, all across the United States, millions of very ordinary citizens are called to **jury** duty. For a brief time, 12 men and women gather together to render judgment on a fellow human being. Once judgment has been passed, they part company as abruptly as they came together. These ordinary men and women perform an extraordinary task that many see as an essential component of American democracy. As jurors, they are the fact finders in both criminal and civil cases. That is, they decide what witness and what evidence is worthy of belief. In this chapter we will explore the origin of the jury system, its modern use, and its role in bringing criminal defendants to justice and judgment.

One of the earliest known uses of ordinary citizens as fact finders is the use of volunteers in ancient Greece. These volunteers were collectively referred to as the dicastery. From this pool of citizens, individual dicasts would be picked to decide the fate of fellow citizens.

The Vikings, whose warriors spread fear and destruction through Europe and the British Isles during the centuries between 900 A.D. and about 1300 A.D., also had a well-developed internal system of justice. The *Thing* (pronounced Ting), a group of Viking citizens, met to mete out justice.

England traces the right to trial by jury as far back as Henry II's Constitutions of Clarendon in 1164 and the **Magna Carta** in 1215. Its usage grew and developed so that by the eighteenth century the great legal commentator, Blackstone, could write:"... the truth of every accusation ... should afterwards be confirmed by ... twelve of his equals and neighbors."[1]

Trial by jury replaced two earlier methods for determining guilt in medieval England, trial by battle and trial by ordeal. In trial by battle, the defendant and his accuser fought to the death. **Trial by battle** was essentially used when a private individual believed himself or his clan wronged by the accused in some way. These cases were generally civil rather than criminal in nature. As early as 1110, Henry I ordered lords who could not settle their

HISTORICAL HIGHLIGHT
Socrates Condemned to Death by Jury for Corrupting Youth

Socrates was a Greek philosopher and teacher who lived in Athens from about 469 B.C. to 399 B.C. Students of the law may be most familiar with him through a teaching method he is credited with inventing. The Socratic Method is a staple of many law school classes. It involves the instructor questioning and challenging students to come up with answers rather than the teacher lecturing on the subject matter. Through the Socratic Method, inductive reasoning is used. Facts particular to the subject being taught are discussed. From the discussion, students draw conclusions that are general or universal, not just pertinent to the particular facts at hand. For example, a student may discuss a case that involves an automobile running a red light, causing an accident. The driver is found to have been negligent. Using the Socratic Method, students applying inductive reasoning may conclude that any person who violates a law and, because of the violation, causes damage to another is negligent. From the specific facts the student generalizes about negligence in any case.

So popular was Socrates among young people, and so unpopular were his views, that he was brought to trial. He was charged with undermining democracy in Athens. He was tried before a jury consisting of volunteers who swore to uphold the laws of Athens much the same way a modern jury is sworn. A jury of citizens of Athens found him guilty and sentenced him to death. He died after drinking a cup of poison made from the bark of the hemlock tree, surrounded by the young people he was charged with corrupting. An account of the trial and Socrates' last days can be found in Plato's *Apology*.

differences to do so by duel. Trial by battle in the form of the duel survived well into the nineteenth century. For example, in 1801 Alexander Hamilton was killed in a duel with Aaron Burr.

Trial by ordeal involved having the accused perform some physical task. If he survived unharmed, he was innocent. For example, the accused was made to carry a red hot piece of iron for a short distance or to dip his hand in a pot of boiling water long enough to pull out a stone. After performing the feat, his hand was bandaged. If after three days there was no sign of infection, the accused was declared innocent.[2] See Chapter 2 for a more complete explanation of trial by ordeal.

The right to a jury trial came to America with the English colonists. The settlers demanded that they be tried in America, not back in England. They also insisted that the jury consist of fellow colonists, not Englishmen.[3]

After the Revolution, the right to a jury trial in a criminal case was specifically provided for in the Constitution, not once, but twice. First, Article III, Section 2 of the

Constitution states that "[t]he Trial of All Crimes, Except in Cases of Impeachment, shall be by Jury; and such Trial shall be held in the State Where the Said Crimes have been committed." Then, the **Sixth Amendment** reiterates the right by providing that "[i]n all criminal prosecutions, the accused shall enjoy the right to a speedy and public trial, by an impartial jury of the State and district wherein the crime shall have been committed."

Over the last two centuries, our courts have refined the right to a jury trial in many important ways. Through judicial interpretation, the right to a jury trial has been expanded and refined. It is now clear that every criminal defendant who is accused of a crime punishable by more than six months in prison can demand a jury trial. Both states and the federal government must provide juries for criminal defendants who want them. And ordinary citizens are finding it more difficult than ever before to avoid jury duty. That's because the Supreme Court has set strict standards for the composition of juries so that they reflect the philosophy that citizens must be tried by a "jury of one's peers" and that the pool from which a jury is picked was assembled in a nondiscriminatory way.

DEFINING THE RIGHT TO TRIAL BY JURY

WHO CAN DEMAND TRIAL BY JURY?

The federal government has always allowed defendants in criminal cases to have their case heard by juries. In addition, every state constitution provides some type of guarantee that criminal defendants may have their case heard by a jury. But until 1968, it was unclear if persons charged with state crimes had the exact same right to a jury trial as a person charged with a federal crime. For example, some state constitutions only provided for the right to a jury trial in cases where the punishment was death or imprisonment at hard labor for a long period of time. One such state was Louisiana.

The case that firmly established that the Sixth Amendment's guarantee of a jury trial applied to the states was *Duncan v. Louisiana.*[4] *Duncan* involved a young man charged with simple battery. He asked for a jury trial, but instead was tried by a judge. The crime carried a possible penalty of up to two years in prison, although young Duncan received a sentence of 60 days. He appealed to the U.S. Supreme Court. The Court wrote that the Sixth Amendment applied to states, too, not just to the federal government. "Our conclusion," wrote the Court, "is that in the American States, as in the federal judicial system, a general grant of jury trial for serious offenses is a fundamental right, essential for preventing miscarriages of justice and for assuring that fair trials are provided for all defendants."[5]

But not every state crime requires a jury trial. Petty, or minor, offenses can be tried before a judge or even a district magistrate or justice of the peace. Generally, if the punishment possible under a criminal law is six months or less in prison, there is no right to a jury trial.[6] If the defendant faces the possibility of more than six months in prison, he or she has the right to demand a jury trial. The choices are: plead guilty, be tried by a judge, or be tried by a jury.

Recently some state legislatures have discussed changing their state constitutions to guarantee the prosecution the right to have criminal cases heard by juries. It remains to be seen if that would be Constitutional. Until now, the right to have a criminal case heard by a jury has been the defendant's.

PLEA BARGAINING AND TRIAL BY JURY

As a practical matter, not every criminal defendant gets a jury trial. According to the Department of Justice 2001 statistics, almost 95 percent of defendants sentenced for a federal crime pled guilty, with only a little over 5 percent of defendants in federal courts going to trial before a judge or jury. Of those who go to trial, 74.06 percent are convicted.[7]

These figures may reflect the prevalence of the practice of plea bargaining. Many courts have crowded dockets, and criminal cases must be moved through the system. Criminal defendants are entitled to a speedy trial (see Chapter 5). Therefore, most courts sanction the practice of plea bargaining. A plea bargain is an agreement between the prosecutor and a criminal defendant that calls for the defendant to plead guilty in exchange for receiving a lighter sentence than he might have received had the case gone to trial or in exchange for a reduction in the type or number of charges.

For example, let's assume that a defendant is charged with 12 counts of forgery. In our example, each count represents one forged check written on a pack of stolen checks. If the defendant were convicted of all 12 counts he would face the sentence for forgery multiplied twelvefold. A two- to five-year sentence could become 24 to 60 years. If he chooses a jury trial, he runs the risk of a substantial sentence. If he makes a **plea bargain** (in street parlance, if he "cops a plea"), he may be able to reduce the possibility of a long sentence. Through his attorney, he may agree to plead guilty to one count, and the prosecutor drops the remaining 11 counts. Now his possible sentence is two to five years. What's in this for the prosecutor and the court? For one thing, jury trials are expensive and time consuming. A jury trial may tie up the court for a week or more; a plea of guilty can take 10 minutes. But perhaps most important, a plea of guilty is final. As long as all the parties fulfill the terms of the plea agreement, the defendant can't appeal his case. Plea bargaining is a common and accepted means of dealing with criminal court backlogs among the members of the legal community. Members of the public frequently criticize the practice as being "easy on crime."

On the federal level, plea bargaining has recently come under attack by the current Attorney General, John Ashcroft. A tough-on-crime lawyer, Mr. Ashcroft has directed the U.S. attorneys who work under his direction to curtail plea bargaining and press for convictions in every case in which they believe there is sufficient evidence to convict. Critics claim the new practice will clog the court system with jury trials.[8]

TRIAL BY JUDGE

Sometimes the defendant and his counsel are unable to reach an agreement that will dispose of the case without trial. That doesn't mean that the case will always be heard by a jury. In a few cases, trial may be by a judge. A defendant may choose **trial by judge** if the case involves facts that might inflame a jury. For example, cases involving child sexual abuse or abuse of elderly citizens may make it difficult for a jury of everyday citizens to be impartial. Judges, however, have heard it all before. A defendant charged with crimes most jurors would find abhorrent may not want to plead guilty, but might want to take a chance on a judge. When a judge hears a case, he or she assumes the role the jury would have fulfilled, by deciding what the facts of the case are and by applying those facts to the law.

Trial by judge has another advantage: Unlike a guilty plea, the decision can be appealed to a higher court.

HOW THE JURY POOL IS SELECTED

GRAND AND PETIT JURIES

There are two types of juries: **grand** and **petit.** Each has distinct features and functions. One serves as a mechanism for bringing criminal charges, and the other decides whether the accused is guilty as charged or innocent of the charges against him.

A grand jury is a group of people selected to decide whether a prosecutor has enough evidence to charge an individual with a crime. The grand jury hears evidence and decides if the accused should be indicted and tried. If the grand jury finds there is **probable cause** to believe the defendant committed a crime, he or she is indicted. To find probable cause, the grand jurors must believe that the alleged facts are probably true. A grand jury usually consists of 23 members, thus, the name "grand." The Fifth Amendment to the U.S. Constitution guarantees that no person can be charged with a serious federal crime unless a grand jury authorizes a federal prosecutor to charge him or her.[9] Grand juries may meet over the course of many weeks or months on a complex case. For example, some federal grand jurors are required to meet once a week for a year to hear evidence in one or more cases that a federal prosecutor is investigating.

A petit jury is the trial jury. In a criminal case, the petit jury decides whether the government has proven beyond a reasonable doubt that the accused is guilty of the crime with which he was charged. Essentially, petit juries are fact finders; they decide collectively what the facts are in a case. Petit juries usually consist of 12 or fewer members, thus the term *petit*.

Grand juries hear requests for permission to file serious criminal charges from federal prosecutors. Some states also use their own versions of grand juries to bring charges in criminal cases or as investigative bodies. Other states give their district attorneys or attorneys general the authority to bring charges without the use of a grand jury. There is no requirement that states use grand juries to authorize serious criminal prosecutions. For more information on the criminal trial process, see Chapter 1.

HOW JURORS ARE CALLED

The group of people from which a jury is selected is referred to by many names. The group is variously known as the jury pool, array, panel, or *venire*. The pool from which jurors are to be picked is drawn from the local population. The U.S. Constitution requires that jurors be selected from "the State and district wherein the crime shall have been committed," and that "such Trial shall be held in the State where the said Crimes shall have been committed."[10] In other words, the *venire* members must at the very least come from the state where the crime was committed. This guarantees that a Virginian will not be judged by jurors from Alaska or another distant community whose mores and standards of conduct may differ considerably. For a discussion on change of *venue* and change of *venire*, see the discussion later in this chapter.

The jury pool must be varied enough to allow the jury selected from the pool to be a "representative cross section of the community."[11] Selection for a federal jury is governed by the *Federal Jury Selection and Service Act of 1968,* which requires that both grand juries and petit juries be selected at random from a fair cross section of the community.[12]

States differ in the ways that they select community members to serve on jury duty. Most jurisdictions use a combination of methods to secure jurors for the pool. These include using voter registration lists, tax records, and driver's license records. At Common Law, the sheriff was authorized to conscript jurors from those passing by. States can use any method that does not exclude from selection an identifiable group or class such as women or minorities.

The Supreme Court has consistently upheld the right of all groups or classes of citizens to serve on juries. For example, in 1998 the Court decided that the apparent systematic exclusion of blacks as grand jury forepersons violated the due process clause of the Fourteenth Amendment. In that case, a white defendant challenged the Louisiana method of choosing the foreperson. The selection was made by the judge, and in the last 20 years there had never been an African American selected even though more than 20 percent of the registered voters in the district were African American. The Court

---

HISTORICAL HIGHLIGHT
Don't Venture Near the Courthouse,
You May End Up on a Jury!

A little-known power of county sheriffs is the right to literally "pull people off the street" to empanel a jury. This power dates back to medieval England. Modern-day usage is rare, and it often meets with an angry response.

In Pennsylvania, a retrial of a murder case exhausted the pool of potential jurors for that month. The judge ordered the sheriffs to go out in the night and bring in people scheduled for the following month's pool. When they knocked on the door of one of the potential jurors, his wife slammed the door in the sheriff's face. After some persistent knocking and cajoling, the door opened and the sheriff took the man to court.[13]

A Texas couple was at a grocery store when they observed constables roaming through the parking lot talking to people. When they were approached, they were informed that the night court needed one more juror to try a misdemeanor speeding case, and one of them would have to go. She went and was elected jury foreperson.

The constables reported that not everyone was quite as amiable. Some people had to be shown the writ issued by the judge. Others were simply incredulous that people were being brought in to try a speeding case. When the judge needed a jury for a second case, he suggested sending the constables out "shopping" again. The deputy sheriff spoke with the judge, and it was decided the trial could wait another day.

Dragging in jurors off the streets is one of the long-held powers of local sheriffs. In colonial New England sheriffs could draft townsmen to help in any emergency, and they could be fined if they refused. Although modern methods of jury pool selection make these sheriffs' surprise visits rare, it might be a good idea to avoid the courthouse area if you have plans for the evening.

concluded that if the selection "process is infected with racial discrimination, doubt is cast over the fairness of all subsequent decisions."[14] The decision is the latest in a long line of cases that have held African Americans cannot be excluded from the jury pool because the Fourteenth Amendment prohibits unequal treatment and discrimination on the basis of race. As early as 1880, the Supreme Court ruled that a fair trial demanded that all racial groups be included in the pool of potential jurors and that all groups have the opportunity to serve on juries.[15]

EMPANELING THE JURY

EXCUSING JURORS FOR HARDSHIP

The next step in the jury selection process is excluding potential jurors who can't serve for business, personal, or some other reason. Some jurisdictions allow potential jurors to request exemptions as soon as they receive written notice to appear for jury duty. Others require all jurors to appear before the trial judge to request an exemption.

Common reasons cited by potential jurors include health conditions, running a small business, being the caregiver for young children, farming during planting season or the harvest, and being in a profession that requires long and irregular hours such as medicine. Note that these reasons have nothing to do with the particular case being tried. Jurors excused from service for these personal reasons claim they can't serve on any jury because of competing obligations. Granting every request tends to concentrate those with "free time" on juries, usually the retired, the unemployed, and students. In recent years, judges have grown less tolerant of requests to be excused.

VOIR DIRE

Those accused of committing crimes are entitled to an impartial jury selected from a jury pool that is representative of the community. Note that the actual jury need not be representative of the community, only that the pool from which they are selected is representative. One reason for that is that it is difficult, if not impossible, to find 12 jurors who are impartial, and who also mirror the racial, ethnic, sexual, and religious composition of the community for every case.

When the court or attorneys involved in a case question potential jurors about their ability to serve as impartial jurors, the process is called *voir dire*. *Voir dire* literally means "to speak the truth." Jurors are asked a series of questions about their ability to decide the case based on what they hear as evidence in the case, and not based on what they read in the paper or saw on the six o'clock news. *Voir dire* also helps weed out those who may be prejudiced against the defendant because of his race, religion, or national origin.

If, during *voir dire*, attorneys for either the state or the defense find that the answers a juror gives indicates that he or she may not be able to render an impartial verdict, the attorney will ask the trial judge to strike the juror from consideration. This can be done through either a challenge for cause or the use of a peremptory challenge.

HISTORICAL HIGHLIGHT
The Right of Women to Serve on Juries

As a group, women have only recently begun to secure equal rights and privileges on a par with those accorded men. Women saw African American males given equal protection of the laws long before females were granted the right to vote. It wasn't until 1920 that Congress saw fit to give all citizens a say in choosing their government. The Nineteenth Amendment to the U.S. Constitution provides that "[t]he right of citizens of the United States to vote shall not be denied by the United States or by a State on account of sex." It would be another 55 years before jury service by women was recognized as a fundamental privilege of citizenship. Women's quest for equal political status has met with considerable opposition over the years.

Consider the Equal Rights Amendment. The Equal Rights Amendment would have extended equal rights to women on the same basis as the Fourteenth Amendment did for African Americans in 1868. It was passed by Congress in 1972, but never ratified by the required 38 states (3/4) to become effective. It expired in 1982, just two states short of ratification. Women have had to rely on state legislatures and the U.S. Congress to provide equal rights in the workplace. Some federal statutes that protect women include the Equal Pay Act, the Civil Rights Act of 1963, and the Pregnancy Discrimination Act. The Supreme Court's interpretation of the Fourteenth Amendment's equal protection clause has also helped broaden women's rights.

Fifty-five years after women were granted the right to vote, a Sixth Amendment case provided the Supreme Court with an opportunity to address the right of women to fully participate in the nation's political life through jury service. The case was *Taylor v. Louisiana,* 419 U.S. 522 (1975). Ironically, it was a male who secured a woman's right to jury duty. He argued that Louisiana's exclusion of women from petit (trial) juries violated his right to be tried by citizens representing a cross section of the community. Until *Taylor,* female jurors were often the exception rather than the rule. Women's right to jury service evolved slowly.

In 1789, Congress passed the first law regulating the selection of juries for federal trials. Jurors were to be picked based on the rules in the state where the federal court was located. Since no state allowed women as jurors, federal jurors were also all male. As states added women to the list of eligible jurors, more federal courts also did. The first state to allow women jurors was Utah, in 1898. By mid-century, Congress changed the 1789 law. The Civil Rights Act of 1957 finally allowed women to serve on all federal juries. But many states still excluded women well into the later part of this century.

Taylor involved a male who was charged with kidnaping in a Louisiana state court. At that time, women were called to jury duty only if they asked to serve, while men were simply ordered to serve. The Supreme Court ruled that by systematically excluding a group that made up 53 percent of the population, Louisiana had violated the defendant's right to a jury drawn from a fair cross section of the community.

HISTORICAL HIGHLIGHT
Oklahoma City Jurors Make Excuses

THE SEARCH FOR UNBIASED JURORS

Few events in the last decade shocked Americans more than the events of April 19, 1995. At 9:03 A.M., as federal workers grabbed the first cup of coffee of the day and children settled into their daily routine at the on-site child care center in the Alfred P. Murrah Federal Building in Oklahoma City, Oklahoma, a powerful explosion shattered the morning calm. Before nightfall, the death toll was staggering. In all, 168 people were dead and over 500 more were injured. Like the John F. Kennedy assassination in 1963, the *Challenger* accident in 1986, and September 11, 2001, almost every American old enough to remember vividly recalls where he was and how he felt when the news broke.

How the judicial system found jurors to serve in the Oklahoma City bombing cases is a classic example of how difficult it is to guarantee all criminal defendants a trial by an unbiased jury of peers. Both Timothy McVeigh and Terry Nichols chose trial by jury. Finding willing jurors was a daunting task.

The problem became particularly acute in Terry Nichols' trial after the national publicity McVeigh's conviction and death sentence received. Over 500 potential jurors were summoned to a state fairground for the first round of selection. There they filled out detailed questionnaires about their background, exposure to pretrial publicity, and attitudes. Apparently many of the potential jurors called for the jury pool concluded that they could avoid jury duty by providing the "wrong" answers on *voir dire*.

One potential juror announced that she was psychic and heard messages from time to time. Nichols' attorney asked that she be excused even though she had promised to tell the court if she received any messages from the hereafter. His request was granted.

Another juror expressed faith of another kind, in technology. He proclaimed that all he had to do to arrive at the "correct" decision on guilt or innocence was to put the "facts" into his laptop computer, which he conveniently carried with him. The following exchange took place between the potential juror and the court:

THE COURT: Now, you know, this isn't like computers. This isn't like feeding a lot of stuff into a database and pulling it up. This involves human judgment. That's what being on a jury is. Human judgment. That's why we don't have computers deciding cases. There's quite a difference. Do you agree?

A. Maybe we should look into computers. I would agree, yes, sir.

THE COURT: Would you like to be judged by a computer?

A. Depending on the given parameters.

THE COURT: Parameters of judgment as to whether what a witness says is true? Do you think that's a human function, to judge the truth of what another person says?

A. It would be impartial and unbiased.

Another was convinced that Nichols was hiding something, because of a particular look in his eyes. She couldn't be persuaded to set aside her belief. She was also removed from the pool.

A jury of seven women and five men was finally chosen. They spent two months together considering the evidence against Nichols before convicting him of conspiracy to bomb the Murrah building and manslaughter in the death of the federal agents killed in the blast. After the verdict, the foreperson received death threats. She explained that if she had it to do over again, she would try to avoid jury duty.[16]

THE CHALLENGE FOR CAUSE

When making a **challenge for cause,** the attorney states his or her reasons for believing that the jury pool member is unable to be an impartial judge of the facts of the case. That belief may be based on the juror's religion, nation of origin, race, gender, or relationship to the defendant, the judge, the attorneys, or the victim in the case. For example, if the potential juror is married to a police officer, and the case involves the brutal murder of a police officer, the spouse may not be impartial. The judge in a case may strike as many jurors from consideration for cause as is necessary. That's because every defendant is guaranteed an impartial jury.

THE PEREMPTORY CHALLENGE

A **peremptory challenge** involves striking a juror from consideration as a juror for any reason, or no reason at all. In most courts, only a few peremptory challenges are allowed for each side. Peremptory challenges allow attorneys to help mold a jury into a group each presumes will be inclined to convict or acquit. It was designed, in the words of the Supreme Court, " . . . to eliminate persons thought to be inclined against their interests. . . . "[17] Since no reason needs to be given, an attorney defending someone charged with the rape of a young girl may try to exclude potential jurors with daughters or granddaughters the age of the victim.

A word of caution is due here, though. The courts have warned attorneys, especially prosecutors, against using peremptory challenges to strike potential jurors of one race or another in order to get a racially pure jury. For example, prosecutors can't strike all black jurors to get an all white jury or all women to get a male jury. That would be a violation of the juror's Fourteenth Amendment right to equal protection and equal participation in civic life, and would taint the perception of the justice system as fair and impartial. It doesn't matter whether the defendant is black or white.[18]

Recently the Supreme Court considered just such a case. In a case involving a black defendant who faced death, Texas prosecutors allegedly followed an informal practice of striking potential jurors who were black on the assumption they were less willing to punish a black defendant. The 8–1 decision overturned the death sentence based in part on the Court's perception that Dallas prosecutors historically discriminated against black jurors and that in this case, they struck almost every black juror in the pool. The lone dissenter was Clarence Thomas, the only African American justice.[19]

DEATH QUALIFYING JURORS

There are special rules for selecting members of a jury who will hear a capital case. A capital case is a case in which the possible penalty is death. A jury that will hear a death penalty case must be *Witherspoon* qualified. The term comes from the Supreme Court case *Witherspoon v. Illinois.*[20] In that case, the Court ruled that members of the jury pool can't be automatically excluded from a jury because they are conscientiously opposed to the death penalty. They must be asked whether they are able to follow the court's instructions on the law and can vote for death if the facts are appropriate. If they answer "yes," they are **"*Witherspoon* qualified."** Similarly, jurors who say they don't have a conscienstious objection to the death penalty must assure the court that they won't automatically impose the death penalty.[21] (See Chapter 7 for more information about the death penalty.)

HOW MANY JURORS DOES A JURY MAKE?

In federal criminal cases, a jury must have 12 members. That's been the law of the land since 1898, when the Supreme Court decided *Thompson v. Utah.*[22] *Thompson* involved a livestock thief who was tried twice. Utah was still a federal territory at the time of the first trial. The first jury consisted of 12 men. He won an appeal that gave him a new trial. Meanwhile, Utah became a state. Under Utah's new constitution, he was allowed only eight jurors. When he was again found guilty, he claimed he had been denied his Sixth Amendment rights to a jury of 12.

When the case was heard by the Supreme Court, he argued that the theft happened when Utah was still a territory under the federal government's control. The case was therefore a federal, not a state, matter. The Supreme Court agreed. The Sixth Amendment right to trial by jury was a part of the common law as brought to America by the colonists. Since according to English common law, a jury contained 12 members, so must a federal jury.

Criminal trials in state court can use a lesser number of jurors, however. In 1970 the Supreme Court held that six jurors were a sufficient number. By the time of the decision in *Williams v. Florida,* the Court concluded that " . . . the fact that the jury at common law was composed of precisely 12 is a historical accident, unnecessary to effect the purposes of the jury system and wholly without significance except to mystics."[23]

Five jurors are too few. That's what the Supreme Court concluded a few years later in *Ballew v. Georgia.*[24] The case involved the Paris Adult Theatre in Atlanta. In 1973 two county investigators saw the film *Behind the Green Door* at the theater. The film was an "adult" picture featuring Marilyn Chambers, a former mainstream model. After getting a warrant, they saw the movie again and then promptly seized it as evidence. The owner was charged with violating the Georgia obscenity laws, which were misdemeanor criminal offenses. Under Georgia law, defendants charged with misdemeanors were entitled to a jury of five. Ballew argued that a jury of five couldn't be expected to assess what were the contemporary standards of the community, which is required in order to convict on an obscenity charge. He was convicted and appealed the use of a five-person jury.

The Supreme Court relied on a number of studies on jury deliberations and group dynamics. These studies concluded that as the size of the jury shrinks from twelve to fewer than six jurors, the dynamics change. In fact, one study cited by the Court found that the likelihood of convicting an innocent person rises as the size of the jury shrinks, while the risk of not convicting a guilty person rises as the size of the jury gets larger. Based upon the studies, and the arguments of the attorneys in the case, the Supreme Court held that six is the minimum number of jurors allowed on a criminal petit jury.

PRETRIAL PUBLICITY, CHANGE OF VENUE OR VENIRE, AND SEQUESTRATION

THE MEDIA AND FINDING IMPARTIAL JURORS

As we have learned in this chapter, the Constitution requires that an impartial jury decide whether the government has proven beyond a reasonable doubt that the defendant is guilty of the crime he was charged with. A century ago finding a jury that hadn't heard the details about a criminal case was relatively easy. There was no television news, no Internet news reports delivered worldwide in an instant, and no satellite communications. Today the details of crimes are known to millions of people almost as soon as they happen. If you have any doubt about the speed and distance news travels, ask yourself if you would have known the details of the following crimes and news events had you lived in the 1800s:

- O. J. Simpson's Bronco ride down the L.A. Freeway
- The disappearance of Washington D.C. intern Chandra Levy
- JonBenet Ramsey's murder in Denver
- The Unabomber
- The Laci Peterson murder case in California

Juries are obligated to judge defendants impartially. Jurors can only consider the evidence presented at trial. They can't consider what they may have learned about the case from the newspaper or television reports. The more publicity a case has received before trial, the more likely a potential juror may have prejudged the case. The ideal juror knows absolutely nothing about the defendant, the victim, or the case. But the ideal juror doesn't exist in the age of electronic communications. Few hermits are called to jury service.

The courts have come up with several ways to minimize the impact of pretrial publicity on potential jurors, to judge whether pretrial publicity will affect a juror's ability to be impartial, and to assure that jurors decide the case only on the evidence they hear and see in the courtroom. These methods include change of venue, change of *venire,* and sequestration.

CHANGE OF VENUE AND *VENIRE*

Many crimes receive intense media coverage locally, but little mention statewide or nationally. The victim or the accused may be well known in their community, but unknown in other geographic areas. If a defendant claims he or she can't get an impartial jury, the case can be moved to another location for trial if the court agrees. This usually involves trying the case in another county if it is a state case or another federal courthouse in the same judicial district if it's a federal case. For example, the Oklahoma City bombing trials were moved to Denver from Oklahoma City. Moving the case to another geographic area is called a change of **venue.** Depending on the complexity of the case, the number of witnesses, and how long the trial will last, a change of venue can be expensive. A request for change of venue is seldom granted.

Another way of finding impartial jurors is through a change of *venire.* Sometimes the court concludes that impartial local jurors are hard to come by because of extensive pretrial publicity, but doesn't want to require witnesses, prosecutors, and defense attorneys to travel to another location. In that case, the simplest solution may be to bring the jurors in from another location. In other words, the jury pool or *venire,* is brought in from out of town. This solution may be attractive when trial publicity will be extensive and the court anticipates sequestering the jury anyway. (See discussion below.)

SEQUESTRATION

Once a trial starts, jurors are told to disregard anything they hear about the case other than in the courtroom. Jurors are told not to read about the case, not to listen to news reports about the case, and not to discuss the case with anyone until it's time to deliberate. They are also told not to discuss the case among themselves until they retire to the jury room to decide the defendant's fate. Since most trials last only a day or two, jurors generally don't have too much trouble following the court's directions. But in cases heavily covered by the media or that will take a long time to try, it may be impossible to avoid hearing about the case from other sources.

To minimize the possibility of exposure to facts outside the courtroom, juries can be sequestered. **Sequester** means to separate. When jurors are sequestered, they are housed and fed, at government expense, until the case is over. Usually sequestered jurors have only very limited contact with their families and are guarded by the local sheriff and deputies. Their mail, telephone calls, and reading materials are censored.

Sequestration is used very rarely because it is expensive and very disruptive. But some jurors have been sequestered for months or longer. For example, the jurors in the O. J. Simpson murder case were sequestered for over a year. For many, sequestration represents a real hardship, both financial and personal. Consider how hard it would be to be away from your family, friends, school, or job for months.

CHART: WHAT PRICE, DUTY? FEES PAID FOR JURY SERVICE NATIONWIDE

Jurisdiction	Juror Fees Per Day	Jurisdiction	Juror Fees Per Day
Federal	$40.00[a]	Missouri	$6.00
Alabama	10.00	Montana	12.00[o]
Alaska	12.50[b,c]	Nebraska	20.00
Arizona	12.00[d]	Nevada	(p)
Arkansas	5.00[e]	New Hampshire	10.00[h]
California	5.00[f]	New Jersey	5.00
Colorado	(g)	New Mexico	(q)
Connecticut	(h)	New York	(r)
Delaware	15.00	North Carolina	12.00[s]
District of Columbia	30.00[i]	North Dakota	25.00
Florida	(j)	Ohio	10.00[k,t]
Georgia	5.00[k]	Oklahoma	12.50
Hawaii	30.00	Oregon	10.00
Idaho	10.00[b]	Pennsylvania	(u)
Illinois	4.00[k]	Rhode Island	15.00
Indiana	7.50[l]	South Carolina	10.00
Iowa	10.00	South Dakota	10.00[k,v]
Kansas	10.00	Tennessee	10.00
Kentucky	12.50	Texas	6.00[k,w]
Louisiana	12.00	Utah	17.00
Maine	10.00	Vermont	30.00
Maryland	15.00[k,m]	Virginia	30.00
Massachusetts	(g)	Washington	10.00[k]
Michigan	7.50[b]	West Virginia	15.00
Minnesota	30.00[n]	Wisconsin	8.00[b,k]
Mississippi	15.00	Wyoming	30.00

Note: Daily juror fees are set by State statutes and do not include any mileage payments to jurors.

[a]May be raised to $50.00 per day after 30 days of service upon discretion of the judge.

[b]Half-day rate.

[c]Anchorage provides $5.00 half-day rates for the first day, then $12.50 per half-day after the first day.

[d]No fee for the first day (discretionary); $12.00 per day thereafter.

[e]$20.00 per day while actually serving (sworn).

[f]Fees vary among counties; $20.00 maximum per day.

[g]No fee for the first 3 days; $50.00 per day thereafter. Expenses for unemployed available. Employers must pay employees for first 3 days while serving.

[h]No fee for first 5 days; $50.00 per day thereafter. Expenses for unemployed available. Employers must pay employees for first 5 days while serving.

[i]No fee for first day; $30.00 per day thereafter.

[j]If employer pays salary or wages of person on jury duty, then there is no fee paid for 3 days; then $30.00 per day thereafter. If individual is not employed or employer does not pay salary, then fee is $15.00 per day for first 3 days; then $30.00 per day thereafter.

[k]Fees vary among counties.

[l]$17.50 per day while actually serving (sworn).

[m]Provided as an expense; not reported as income or remitted to employer.

[n]Child care expenses available.

[o]$25.00 per day while actually serving (sworn).

[p]$15.00 per day while actually serving (sworn). $30.00 per day after 5 days of service. $9.00 per day if not sworn.

[q]$4.25 per hour.

[r]If employer has more than 10 employees, must pay at least $40.00 per day for the first 3 days. After 3 days, the court must pay $40.00 per day. If juror is not employed or if employer has less than 10 employees, then court must pay $40.00 per day from day 1.

[s]$30.00 per day after 5 days of service.

[t]$15.00 maximum per day.

[u]$9.00 for first 3 days; $25.00 per day thereafter.

[v]$40.00 maximum per day while actually serving (sworn).

[w]$30.00 maximum per day while actually serving (sworn).

[x]May be raised to $50.00 per day after 4 days of service upon the discretion of the judge.

Source: Sourcebook of Criminal Justice Statistics Online

RENDERING THE VERDICT BEYOND A REASONABLE DOUBT ═══════

WHAT IS REASONABLE DOUBT?

Chapter 1 covered the essential differences between civil law and criminal law. One of those differences is the burden of proof that the prosecutor or the plaintiff must meet in order to prevail. Recall that in a civil case, the plaintiff must prove his or her case by a preponderance of the evidence. In a criminal case, the burden of proof is considerably higher. The state must prove that the defendant is guilty of a crime **beyond a reasonable doubt.** If the legal scales of justice must tip ever so slightly in favor of the plaintiff in a civil case, in a criminal case they must tip heavily in favor of guilt.

When a jury hears a criminal case, the jury must decide if there is enough evidence to prove beyond a reasonable doubt that a crime was committed, and the defendant did it. The court defines *reasonable doubt* for the jury before it begins deliberations. Reasonable doubt is perhaps best defined by what it is not. It is not without any doubt. If that were the case, few convictions would be possible. Jurors are only required to decide that they are convinced that the defendant did it. Reasonable doubt is somewhere between more likely than not that the defendant did it and absolute certainty that he did. A reasonable doubt is a fair doubt based upon common sense.

Juries are told before they begin deliberation that their function is to decide what the facts are and then to apply the law to those facts. These are the **jury instructions.** The court tells the jury what the law is. Juries are also told that they must apply the law as it is, even if they think it's an unjust, unfair, or stupid law. In other words, the jury only decides the facts, not what is the law. There have been many cases, however, where juries have seemingly ignored the law and refused to convict a defendant. This is referred to as jury nullification.

JURY UNANIMITY, HUNG JURIES, AND REASONABLE DOUBT

In federal criminal trials, the jury must reach a unanimous decision. That is, all 12 jurors must agree that the defendant is guilty beyond a reasonable doubt. But just as state criminal juries don't need to have more than six jurors, neither do state juries have to reach a unanimous verdict. The Supreme Court has upheld a state law that required only 9 out of 12 jurors to agree on conviction or acquittal.[25] The fewer members there are on a jury, the more likely it is that the members must make a unanimous decision. In 1979 the Supreme Court ruled that juries of six (the smallest criminal jury allowed) must reach a unanimous decision.[26]

Most states do require a unanimous jury decision. In those states, if all jurors don't agree on the defendant's guilt or acquittal, the jury is said to be a **hung jury.** A defendant can be retried if the jury is unable to convict or acquit him or her. (See Chapter 4 for a discussion of why a retrial isn't double jeopardy.)

The role of the jury and the role of the judge

It is important to understand how the responsibilities of the judge differ from the responsibilities of the juror, as their roles are distinctly separate. The judge is charged with the task of interpreting and determining what is law. The jury is given the role of finding the facts in a case.

HISTORICAL HIGHLIGHT
William Penn and Jury Nullification

One of the most famous jury trials in history involved William Penn, the founder of the Colony of Pennsylvania. William Penn was a Quaker at a time when England was intolerant of religious beliefs other than the Church of England's. Quakers were seen as dangerous radicals. Their religious services, held in "meeting houses," were closed by the government. They were forbidden to meet or to preach in the streets. In 1670 William Penn and a fellow Quaker, William Mead, defied the king of England and were arrested. They were accused of trying to incite a riot.

A jury of 12 men was selected to hear the case. Four of the 12 refused to find Penn and Mead guilty. The judge ordered them all to continue deliberating until they reached the proper and correct verdict. What happened next illustrates the idea of jury nullification. Jurors are generally told by the judge before they begin deliberations that they must follow the law. For example, jurors are instructed that they cannot refuse to find a defendant guilty because they believe the law they are applying to the facts is an unjust or immoral law. **Jury nullification** occurs when a jury deliberately ignores the court's instructions to apply the law, however unjust, to the facts.

In William Penn's case, the jurors were denied food, drink, and tobacco until they reconsidered. After a few days, the 12 jurors united. Now the vote was unanimous. Penn and Mead were not guilty! The judge finally accepted their verdict, but jailed the jurors for rendering an improper verdict. They won on appeal. The case helped establish the sanctity of jury verdicts, even when that verdict seems contrary to law or common sense. A jury has the last word since defendants can't be tried again. A second trial would be double jeopardy.

Apprendi v. New Jersey[27] illustrates this distinction. During the sentencing phase of this case, the prosecution presented evidence to the judge that Apprendi's crime had been racially motivated. Under New Jersey law, a judge was given the ability to increase the maximum sentence for a crime that is motivated by racial biases. However, when the case reached the Supreme Court, it was decided that "The Constitution requires that any fact that increases the penalty for a crime beyond the prescribed statutory maximum, other than the fact of a prior conviction, must be submitted to a jury and proved beyond a reasonable doubt."

In *Ring v. Arizona,*[28] the Supreme Court affirmed their previous decision in *Apprendi.* Timothy Stuart Ring had been convicted of felony murder, which had taken place in the course of an armed robbery. After being convicted by a jury, the judge held a separate sentencing hearing and reviewed evidence of aggravating circumstances.[29] The judge then increased Ring's possible maximum sentence, giving him the death penalty. Upon appeal, the Supreme Court ruled that allowing a judge to determine aggravating circumstances, which would increase the defendant's possible sentence beyond the maximum, would violate the defendant's Sixth Amendment right to a jury trial. The Court, however, refused to apply the rule in *Ring* retroactively to others on death row sentenced under the procedure the Court found deficient in its earlier decision.[30]

CHAPTER SUMMARY

Juries are an old legal tradition going back at least to the ancient Greeks. In England, the jury traces its roots to the time of Henry II and King John. When King John signed the Magna Carta in 1215, he agreed that his subjects would be judged by their peers and the law of the land rather than simply by royal command. The jury grew to be an important buffer between the people and the will of the government.

The colonists took English common law with them when they colonized North America. One of these traditions was the right to trial by jury. Every state constitution contains a provision for trial by jury. The U.S. Constitution guarantees the right to trial by jury in federal criminal cases in Article III and in the Sixth Amendment. This protection also extends to the states through the Fourteenth Amendment. In every criminal case where the defendant faces the possibility of imprisonment for more than six months, he or she is guaranteed trial by jury.

The right to request trial by jury rests with the accused. When charged with a crime, a defendant faces several choices. He or she can demand trial by jury, can plead guilty, or can request trial by judge. Few cases are actually tried by juries. Most defendants plead guilty, usually after making a plea bargain. Plea bargains are agreements between the government and the defendant that usually involve a reduction in the kind or number of charges or the length of the sentence in exchange for a plea of guilty. One advantage of plea bargaining is finality. A defendant who voluntarily pleads guilty can't appeal his conviction to a higher court. Another advantage is cost. Jury trials are very expensive, especially if the members of the jury have to be sequestered.

There are two types of juries, petit and grand. A grand jury hears evidence and decides if there is enough evidence to charge someone with a crime. A grand jury may have 23 members. A petit jury is a trial jury. It usually has 12 members, but some states allow petit juries to have as few as six members. A petit jury actually hears the criminal case and decides if the defendant is guilty beyond a reasonable doubt.

The group from which a petit jury is selected is known as the jury pool, array, panel, or *venire*. The members of the pool must be selected in a way that creates a pool that is representative of the community where the defendant allegedly committed the crime. Therefore, methods of calling potential jurors that eliminate segments of the community from the pool are illegal. Many jurisdictions use methods to locate jurors that are race, sex, color, and national origin blind. Some common techniques are to use voter registration records, tax records, license records, and the like in order to create a representative jury pool.

Defendants are guaranteed that the jury pool is representative of the community, but have no constitutional right to a jury that is representative of the community. That is, it's enough that the jury pool is representative, but the actual jury picked doesn't have to mirror the community. Attorneys must be careful, though, in how they exclude potential members of the jury. A prosecutor can't, for example, strike all African Americans from the jury through the use of his or her peremptory strikes.

Jurors can be removed from the jury pool for hardship, for cause, or through the use of a peremptory strike. Courts sometimes excuse jurors for hardships like illness, financial need, family obligations, and business obligations. Courts will eliminate jurors for cause if there is a reason that the juror can't be impartial. Reasons include being acquainted with the parties or victim, having independent knowledge of the case or the evidence, and having prejudged the defendant's guilt or innocence. Peremptory challenges, in contrast, are challenges that the attorneys don't have to provide a specific reason for. Most courts limit the number of peremptory charges to a handful. Challenges for cause are unlimited in number. A process called *voir dire* is used to select those potential jurors who will serve. During *voir dire,* potential jurors are asked questions by the court or the attorneys that are intended to identify jurors who can't be impartial.

In federal criminal cases, the jury must have 12 members, and the jury must reach a unanimous verdict. In some state courts, the jury may have as few as six members. In addition, state juries don't have to make unanimous decisions unless the jury has only six members.

Defendants are guaranteed an impartial jury. Pretrial publicity can make it difficult to find jurors who haven't prejudged the case. If the publicity has been intense, the court may change the venue, or move the case to another geographic location. Another solution is to bring in a jury pool from another location. This is a change of *venire*. To prevent jurors from receiving outside information about the case, the court can also sequester the jury away until the case is over.

Juries are obligated to convict a defendant when they conclude that he or she is guilty beyond a reasonable doubt. Beyond a reasonable doubt is a heavy burden, but doesn't require that the jury be absolutely certain that the defendant did it.

KEY TERMS

Beyond a reasonable doubt: The standard of proof in criminal cases. The prosecutor is required to prove beyond a reasonable doubt that the defendant committed the crime he or she was charged with. A reasonable doubt is a fair doubt based upon common sense.
Challenge for cause: If a juror can't be impartial because he or she knows about the case, knows the defendant's family, knows the victim or any of the people involved in the case, has already made a decision about the defendant's guilt or innocence, or admits to prejudice, he or she can be challenged for cause. There are an unlimited number of challenges for cause available. Any potential juror who can't be impartial can be stricken for cause.
Grand jury: A body of members of the community, usually 23, who decide whether there is enough information to indict an individual. The standard used is "probable cause." Probable cause is a reasonable belief that the alleged facts are probably true. The right to a grand jury indictment is guaranteed in all federal criminal cases by the Fifth Amendment.
Hung jury: A jury that is unable to reach a verdict.
Jury: A group of men and women from the community selected to determine the truth. *While the judge is responsible for interpreting the law, the jury is charged with the task of finding the facts of the case.* The right to trial by jury is guaranteed by the Constitution in all serious criminal cases. A jury decides what the facts of the case are, and applies those facts to the law. Juries must be convinced beyond a reasonable doubt that the defendant broke the law.
Jury instructions: The directions the judge gives jurors about how they are to come to a verdict. Jury instructions typically include an explanation of the law and what must be proven to convict the defendant.

Jury nullification: A decision by a jury to ignore the law or the judge's instructions when deliberating. For example, jurors who believe the law is unjust may refuse to convict the defendant even if it is clear that he broke the law.

Magna Carta: The "Great Charter," a document that was signed by King John of England in 1215. It guaranteed the noblemen under the King's jurisdiction life, liberty, and property. Many of the promises made in the Magna Carta became the basis of the guarantees found in the U.S. Constitution and the constitutions of the states.

Peremptory challenge: Attorneys are allowed a number of peremptory challenges when selecting jurors. The number varies from court to court. Peremptory challenges are without cause; that is, the attorney making the challenge need not state the reason for eliminating the potential juror. Caution must be used when peremptory challenges follow a pattern that seems race or gender based.

Petit jury: A trial jury. In criminal cases, the petit jury determines the facts of the case, applies those facts to the law as given them by the judge, and decides if the state has proven beyond a reasonable doubt that the defendant committed the crime he or she was charged with. Federal juries consist of 12 jurors; state juries can consist of as few as six jurors.

Plea bargain: In a criminal case, an agreement between the prosecuting attorney and the defendant for the defendant to plead guilty in exchange for some benefit or advantage such as a reduction in the kind or number of charges or a reduced sentence. Most criminal cases are settled with some form of a plea bargain.

Probable cause: A standard of proof used to issue search warrants, and to determine if a person should be charged with a crime. Probable cause is a reasonable belief that the alleged facts are true.

Sequester: To separate jurors in order to assure that they will remain impartial during the trial and deliberations.

Sixth Amendment: The provision of the Bill of Rights that originally guaranteed all federal criminal defendants the right to trial by jury. It has since been applied to the states through the Fourteenth Amendment, which guarantees all citizens equal protection of the laws of the United States.

Trial by battle: A method of determining guilt in medieval England. Usually reserved for civil cases, in trial by battle the winner of the battle won the lawsuit.

Trial by judge: A defendant may choose to be tried by a judge rather than by a jury or rather than pleading guilty. When a judge tries a case, he or she decides both the facts and the law.

Trial by ordeal: A method of determining guilt in medieval England. In trial by ordeal, the defendant was made to perform a physical task, like holding a hot piece of iron. If the wound healed without becoming infected, the accused was innocent; if it became infected, he was guilty (and ill).

Venire: A group of individuals from the community from whom the petit jury that will hear a criminal case is drawn. Also referred to as the jury panel, pool, or array.

Venue: The county or judicial district in which a case is tried. In criminal cases, the venue is usually where the crime was committed.

Verdict: The final decision of a jury.

Voir dire: Literally, "to speak the truth." During the *voir dire* phase of a criminal trial, the attorneys or the judge ask questions of the jury pool. These are designed to ferret out those jurors who can't be impartial, who can't serve on the jury because of illness or other obligations, and to help the attorneys in the case decide where and when to use available peremptory challenges.

Witherspoon **qualified:** A jury in a capital case who have stated they will consider imposing the death penalty even if they are opposed to the death penalty.

DISCUSSION QUESTIONS

1. What are the provisions in the U.S. Constitution that require trial by jury in criminal cases?
2. How are the members of a jury pool selected?
3. What information would you like to get from a potential juror during *voir dire*?
4. What are some reasons a potential juror can be excused for cause?
5. What are the advantages and disadvantages of sequestration for the prosecution? the defense?
6. Why would a defense attorney want a change of *venue* or change of *venire*?
7. Explain what "beyond a reasonable doubt" means.
8. List and explain some differences between federal juries and state juries.

FOR FURTHER READING

1. Grisham, J. *The Runaway Jury.* Legal thriller recounting what happens when a man with a vendetta wants to be on a jury to hear a landmark tobacco liability case.

FOR FURTHER VIEWING

1. *To Kill a Mockingbird.* (1962). Adaptation of the novel by Harper Lee. A small-town lawyer in the South defends a black man accused of raping a white woman. Starring Gregory Peck.
2. *My Cousin Vinny.* (1992). New York lawyer goes to Wahzoo, Alabama, to defend his cousin and his friend on murder charges. Starring Marisa Tomei, Joe Pesci.
3. *Inherit the Wind.* (1960). Midwestern school teacher is put on trial for teaching Darwin's theory of evolution. Starring Gene Kelly, Dick York, Spencer Tracey.
4. *Class Action.* (1991). Father and daughter, both lawyers, serve on opposite sides of a case. Starring Gene Hackman.
5. *Judgement at Nuremberg.* (1961). Four German judges are put on trial for compromising their integrity for the Nazis. Starring Judy Garland, Montgomery Clift, Marlene Dietrich, Burt Lancaster, Spencer Tracey, and Maximilian Schell.
6. *The Verdict.* (1982). A drunkard attorney sobers up long enough to seek justice for comatose victim of a hospital's carelessness. Starring Paul Newman.
7. *Twelve Angry Men.* (1957). A courtroom drama in which one jury member holds out against the rest of the jury's desire for a quick conviction. Starring Henry Fonda and Jack Klugman. If you see no other film on the jury system, see this one.
8. *The Runaway Jury.* (2003). John Cusack stars in this adaptation of the Grisham book. The movie version changes the case from one about tobacco to one about guns.

QUOTATIONS FOR CHAPTER SIX

1. *Jury service is an exercise in responsible citizenship by all members of the community, including those who might not have the opportunity to contribute to our civic life.* Justice Antonin Kennedy in *Powers v. Ohio*, 499 U.S. 400 (1991)

2. *For as Christ and his twelve apostles were finally to judge the world, so human tribunals should be composed of the King and twelve wise men.*
Credited to Morgan of Gla-Morgan, king of Wales (725 A.D)

3. *The judicial system is the most expensive machine ever invented for finding out what happened and what to do about it.*
Irvin R. Kaufman quoted in *The San Francisco Chronicle* (4/17/77)

4. *"No, no!" said the Queen, "Sentence first, verdict afterwards."*
Lewis Carroll, *Alice in Wonderland* (1865)

5. *No freeman shall be taken, or imprisoned, or outlawed, or exiled, . . . except by the legal judgment of his peers or by the law of the land.*
Magna Carta, Clause 39 (1215)

6. *It is better that ten guilty persons escape than that one innocent suffer.*
Blackstone, *Commentaries on the Laws of England* (1899 ed.)

ENDNOTES

1. W. Blackstone, *Commentaries on the Laws of England,* ed. Cooley (1899).

2. V. P. Hans and L. Vidmar, *Judging the Jury* (New York: Plenum Press, 1986).

3. R. Perry, ed., *Sources of Our Liberties* (1959).

4. *Duncan v. Louisiana,* 391 U.S. 145 (1968).

5. Ibid.

6. *Blanton v. North Las Vegas,* 489 U.S. 538 (1989).

7. Department of Justice, Bureau of Crime Statistics, *Sourcebook of Criminal Justice Statistics 1993.*

8. A. Liptak and E. Lichtblau, "New Plea Bargain Limits Could Swamp Courts, Experts Say," *New York Times* (September 24, 2003).

9. U.S. Constitution, Fifth Amendment.

10. U.S. Constitution, Sixth Amendment and U.S. Constitution, Article 3.

11. *Taylor v. Louisiana,* 419 U.S. 522 (1975).

12. *Federal Jury Selection and Service Act of 1968,* 28 U.S.C. § 1861.

13. As recounted by the author's husband, who served on the sequestered jury. The gentleman in question became an alternate juror.

14. *Campbell v. Louisiana,* 523 U.S. 392 (1998).

15. *Strauder v. West Virginia,* 100 U.S. 303 (1880).

16. However, the author would welcome the opportunity to serve on a jury. She was once sent a selection notice that asked for her occupation and responded that she was a Pennsylvania licensed attorney who had served as an assistant attorney in another county at the beginning of her career. She was never called for the jury pool. Recently she received another selection notice. This time she put her occupation as "writer." It remains to be seen if she will called to a jury pool this time, and if so, whether *voir dire* questioning will eliminate her.

17. *Holland v. Illinois,* 493 U.S. 473 (1990).

18. *Powers v. Ohio,* 499 U.S. 400 (1991).

19. *Miller-El v. Cockrell,* 537 U.S. 322 (2003).

20. *Witherspoon v. Illinois,* 391 U.S. 510 (1968).

21. *Morgan v. Illinois,* 504 U.S. 719 (1992).

22. *Thompson v. Utah,* 170 U.S. 343 (1898).

23. *Williams v. Florida,* 399 U.S. 78 (1970).

24. *Ballew v. Georgia,* 435 U.S. 223 (1978).

25. *Johnson v. Louisiana,* 406 U.S. 356 (1972) and *Apodaca v. Oregon,* 406 U.S. 404 (1972).

26. *Burch v. Louisiana,* 441 U.S. 130 (1979).

27. *Apprendi v. New Jersey,* 530 U.S. 466 (2000).

28. *Ring v. Arizona,* 122 S. Ct. 2428 (2002).

29. An aggravating circumstance is a fact in a case that may make sentencing more severe. Examples of aggravating circumstances may include the commission of a crime in conjunction with another crime, murder in the course of an armed robbery, past criminal record, or likelihood to present future danger to society.

30. *Schriro v. Summerlin,* 124 S. Ct. 2519 (2004).

CHAPTER 7
Constitutional Rights Post-Conviction

CHAPTER OBJECTIVES

After studying this chapter, you should be able to:

- Explain the history of the Eighth Amendment to the U.S. Constitution
- Define criminal punishment
- List and explain the two requirements that must be satisfied before a punishment is "cruel and unusual"
- Explain why capital punishment is not unconstitutional as "cruel and unusual" punishment
- Explain what procedural protection is required before the death penalty can be carried out
- Define aggravating and mitigating circumstances
- List the classifications of persons who can be executed
- List the crimes that are punishable by death
- Explain the Supreme Court's position on life in prison for repeat offenders
- List and describe two current trends in punishment

CHAPTER CONTENTS

Thou shalt give life for life, eye for eye, tooth for tooth, hand for hand, foot for foot, burning for burning, wound for wound.

The Bible, King James Version, Exodus 21:23–25

Excessive bail shall not be required nor excessive fines imposed, nor cruel and unusual punishments inflicted.

U.S. Constitution, Eighth Amendment (1791)

INTRODUCTION AND HISTORICAL BACKGROUND

Throughout history men have experimented with various forms of punishment for those who fail to conform to society's expectations. Law breakers have been punished in many ways. In ancient Rome condemned prisoners did battle with wild beasts in arenas while the public watched from the stands.[1]

Punishment in England was often equally harsh and public. During the seventeenth through the early nineteenth century criminals in England were frequently punished harshly, sometimes for what are today considered minor offenses. Dozens of prisoners were hung at a time for offenses ranging from murder to horse thievery and house breaking. In light of the penal practices of the day, it was little wonder that the criminal law was popularly known as the **"Bloody Code."**[2]

Executions were often great public spectacles. Such a scene was recorded by Samuel Pepys (1633–1703), who served as the English secretary of the Admiralty. He kept a diary covering his life from 1660 through 1669. His entry for October 13, 1660 reads:

> . . . I went out to Charing Cross to see Maj.-Gen. Harrison hanged, drawn and quartered—which was done there—he looked as cheerful as any man could in that condition. He was presently cast down and his head and his heart shown to the people, at which there was great shouts of joy.[3]

Prisons were reserved for very minor offenses, and stays there were short.

An alternative to hanging or a short prison stay was the practice of "transportation."[4] **Transportation** was a form of banishment or exile. Criminals were shipped to the American Colonies, often for life. The practice did not end until the American Revolution, when the colonies were no longer a practical dumping ground for prisoners. England's temporary solution was to turn abandoned ships into floating prisons moored on the Thames.[5] It is against this background that we examine the meaning and application of the Constitution's prohibition against **"cruel and unusual" punishment.**

The Eighth Amendment's language was taken from a provision of the *Virginia Declaration of Rights of 1776*. And Virginia borrowed the provision from the English *Bill of Rights of 1689*, which was passed by Parliament upon the ascent of William and Mary. The English Bill of Rights was an attempt to curb the royal misuse of punishment in criminal cases during the reign of King James II. It provided that "excessive Baile ought not be required nor excessive Fines imposed nor cruel and unusual Punishments inflicted."[6] The law was based on an earlier document, the *Magna Carta of 1215*, in which the noblemen forced King John to agree that "amercements" would not be excessive.[7]

The Eighth Amendment was not a part of the original Constitution as ratified in 1789. Rather, it is a part of the Bill of Rights, added in response to concerns that the new Constitution provided few protections for accused criminals. The Bill of Rights was added to the Constitution in 1791.

As we explore the meaning of "cruel and unusual punishment" you may want to keep three questions in mind. They are:

1. What types of penalties are considered "punishments" within the meaning of the Eighth Amendment?
2. What punishments are outlawed because they are "cruel and unusual"?
3. Who is protected from "cruel and unusual punishment"?

DEFINING PUNISHMENT

Is a junior high student who is paddled by his teacher so hard that a hematoma[8] develops on his buttocks, causing him to miss school for several days, protected by the Eighth Amendment? The U.S. Supreme Court has said no. **Corporal punishment** of children is not the sort of punishment protected by the Eighth Amendment.[9]

The Eighth Amendment only applies to punishment for criminal behavior. Ask yourself: Is this punishment for the commission of a crime? If the punishment is not for the commission of a crime, the individual punished is not protected by the Eighth Amendment.[10] (That is not to say that corporal punishment may not be a crime. A teacher who paddles a child may face criminal charges of assault, child abuse, or reckless endangerment, among other possibilities.)

Therefore, we must first determine if the individual being punished has committed a crime. A **crime** is defined as a breach of a law made for the public good that is punishable by public law, or simply, an offense against society.[11] Most of the time the question is answered by looking at the law the defendant is accused of breaking. If the government has classified the offense as a crime, the punishment the statute imposes must meet Eighth Amendment standards.

Sometimes a criminal statute is challenged because the statute makes a crime of an action that is not properly a crime. If the act or behavior being punished is not properly a crime, its criminalization is in and of itself cruel and unusual and therefore improper. For example, a California law that made being a drug addict a crime punishable by imprisonment was a violation of the ban on cruel and unusual punishment because it criminalized a status or condition, not behavior.[12] As Justice Stewart wrote in that case, "Even one day in prison would be cruel and unusual punishment for the 'crime' of having a common cold."[13] Legislatures cannot create crimes of conditions such as being HIV positive or being an alcoholic. It is not a crime to be sick or to have an addiction.

CRUEL AND UNUSUAL PUNISHMENTS

We now turn to determining what criminal punishments are cruel and unusual. The Supreme Court has held that the Eighth Amendment outlaws a punishment as cruel and unusual if the punishment itself involves unnecessary infliction of pain or if the punishment is grossly disproportionate to the nature or severity of the crime. To be excluded, a punishment must have been considered cruel and unusual at the time the Bill of Rights was adopted (1791)[14] or be contrary to the "evolving standards of decency that mark the progress of a maturing society."[15]

We will first consider capital punishment; second, life imprisonment; third, prison conditions; and finally, chemical castration and sex offender registration.

THE DEATH PENALTY

Capital punishment is not **per se** cruel and unusual punishment. The Constitution implicitly assumes executions are an allowable punishment. It provides that "No person shall be held to answer for a capital or otherwise infamous crime unless on a presentment or indictment of a Grand Jury. . . ."[16] Therefore, we can assume that the Founding Fathers accepted capital punishment.

Thirty-eight states and the federal government currently authorize the death penalty, while 12 states plus the District of Columbia do not.[17] Generally, the death penalty only applies to cases where the defendant deliberately killed another human being,[18] or where the defendant was a major participant in a felony-murder.[19] In addition, federal law authorized death for certain federal offenses such as espionage and treason. At the end of 2000, the latest year for which national figures are available, there were 3,593 individuals on Death Row, including 54 women.[20]

Death is an accepted and acceptable sanction under the Constitution. It is the way that the death penalty is carried out that is subject to scrutiny under the Eighth Amendment. As the Supreme Court wrote in *Louisiana ex rel. Francis vs. Resweber,*

> The cruelty against which the Constitution protects a convicted man is cruelty in the method of punishment, not the necessary suffering involved in any method employed to extinguish life humanely.[21]

We will consider the procedural safeguards required before an execution can take place and what methods can be used to "extinguish life humanely."

PROCEDURAL SAFEGUARDS REQUIRED BY THE EIGHTH AMENDMENT

In recent years the Court has focused on the procedures used by states to arrive at death as the sanction for criminal behavior rather than on the continued use of the death penalty by the criminal justice system. This is despite the fact that Amnesty International, the Roman Catholic Church, and various other human rights groups condemn death as a sanction and many modern nations have abolished it altogether.[22] For example, the European Union makes it a condition of membership that nations abolish the death penalty.

The Supreme Court has never ruled that the death penalty is always unconstitutional. The Court will, however, invalidate state statutes that do not provide enough procedural safeguards for defendants facing death. For example, in the 1972 case of *Furman v. Georgia,*[23] the Supreme Court effectively halted the death penalty, temporarily. The Court ruled that Georgia's statute was so procedurally flawed that the penalty was arbitrarily and capriciously imposed. As a practical matter, no executions were carried out between 1972 and 1976, when the Supreme Court again considered the issue.

As a result of the Supreme Court's decision in *Furman,* many states revamped their death penalty laws. In 1976 the Supreme Court again considered the death penalty, this time reviewing new state statutes designed to overcome the Court's earlier objections. The Court concluded in *Gregg v. Georgia*[24] that execution remains a Constitutionally sanctioned punishment, given the existence of certain procedural safeguards. These can include:

1. A bifurcated trial, in which the jury first decides whether the defendant is guilty, and a sentencing stage, at which the jury determines punishment after hearing evidence of **aggravating** or **mitigating circumstances.** The condemned prisoner must be given an opportunity to present mitigating factors in his defense, no matter how heinous his crime. The sentence of death cannot be automatic.[25]
2. An automatic appeal to the state supreme court of all sentences of death, at least if an appeal is requested by the condemned prisoner.

The Supreme Court recently considered what information jurors are entitled to receive when weighing whether a defendant should be put to death. In *Kelly v. South Carolina,* 534 U.S. 246 (2002), the Court ruled that in the penalty phase of a death penalty case where the choice is between life in prison with no possibility of parole or death, the jury must be told that life in prison means just that. That way, those concerned about recidivism won't feel compelled to choose death because they fear the defendant will be freed at some point, possibly to kill again.

Since the Supreme Court's decision in *Gregg* on September 15, 2003, there have been 875 executions carried out. The annual number has risen sharply, from one in 1977 to a high of 98 in 1999. In 2001, 66 death sentences were carried out. In 2002, 71 prisoners were executed. The number of executed prisoners fell to 65 in 2003.

APPROPRIATE METHODS OF DEATH

Generally, the sanction of death may be imposed in any way that is not unnecessarily cruel. The Supreme Court held in *In re Kimmler*[26] that "[p]unishments are cruel when they involve torture or a lingering death." Thus, firing squads are permissible,[27] as are electrocutions, lethal gas, and lethal injections. In one case the Supreme Court ruled that it was not cruel and unusual punishment to attempt to execute the same person twice. Willie Francis was convicted of murder and sentenced to death by electrocution in September, 1945. On May 3, 1946, Francis was placed in the electric chair. The executioner threw the switch, but the apparatus failed. Francis was returned to his cell and a new death warrant was signed, setting his execution for May 9, 1946. He appealed this second attempt to kill him, alleging that two attempts at electrocution was cruel and unusual punishment. The Supreme Court disagreed, writing that "[t]he fact that an unforeseeable accident prevented the prompt consummation of the sentence cannot, it seems to us, add an element of cruelty to a subsequent execution."[28]

Equipment malfunctions still occasionally happen. For example, on March 25, 1997, during the successful execution of convicted killer Pedro Medina in Florida, witnesses reported that a six-inch flame erupted from the head of the prisoner, filling the execution

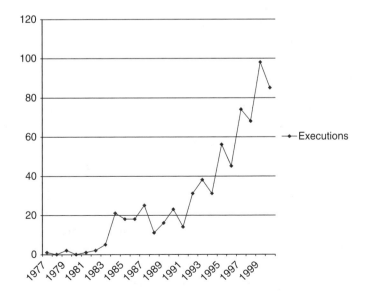

Number of Persons Executed by Year Since 1977

chamber with smoke and the smell of burning flesh.[29] The Florida State Attorney General commented that "[p]eople who wish to commit murder, they better not do it in the state of Florida because we may have a problem with our electric chair."[30]

Of the 358 prisoners executed between 1977 and 1995, there were 216 killed by lethal injection, 128 by electrocution, 9 by lethal gas, 3 by hanging, and 2 by firing squad.[31] Since then, the trend has been away from electrocution and to lethal injection. In 2000, of the 85 executions carried out, 80 were by lethal injection, and 5 were by electrocution. By 2002, the almost universal choice of executioners was lethal injection. Only one of 71 condemned prisoners died from electrocution. Most states that use capital punishment either mandate the use of lethal injection or give the condemned inmate a choice.

PERSONS WHO CAN BE EXECUTED

Although death itself may not be cruel and unusual punishment, it has been argued that it may be cruel and unusual to impose death on particular classes of individuals. These include the mentally ill, the mentally retarded, and those who were minors at the time of the commission of the offense for which death is the sentence.

MENTALLY ILL AND MENTALLY RETARDED

The Supreme Court has ruled that a state may not execute a prisoner who is mentally incompetent at the time of execution.[32] The Court concluded that the execution of an individual who is insane violates the Eighth Amendment because the defendant is either unaware of his impending execution or the reason for it. The defendant did not believe he would be executed because he had delusions that he owned the prison and could communicate with the warden via telepathy. The Supreme Court wrote: ". . . the Eighth Amendment prohibits a State from carrying out a sentence of death upon a prisoner who is insane. Whether its aim is to protect the condemned from fear and pain without comfort of understanding, or to protect the dignity of society itself from the barbarity of exacting mindless vengeance, the restriction finds enforcement in the Eighth Amendment."[33]

However, prison officials can force an otherwise mentally incompetent individual to receive medication to restore his competence even if the prisoner objects.[34] The question the Supreme Court has not addressed is whether a prisoner facing execution can be forced to take medication to restore his competence long enough to be executed. In another case, the Court refused to hear arguments that forcing a prisoner to take antipsychotic medication violated the Constitution. That case was *Perry v. Louisiana,* in which the State of Louisiana argued that a defendant could be forced to receive medication to restore his mental state to normal long enough to carry out the sentence of death.[35] The Supreme Court of Louisiana later rejected that notion and concluded it was a clear violation of the Constitution to force someone to take drugs long enough to be executed.[36]

The Supreme Court seems ready to consider the issue again. On February 20, 2002, the Georgia parole board stayed the execution of a killer who was allegedly so psychotic he believed that Sigourney Weaver was God. The prisoner, Alexander Williams, claimed that he had been forcibly medicated to make him eligible for execution. His attorneys had appealed to the Supreme Court, but his sentence was commuted to life in prison without the possibility of parole by the state's parole board before the Supreme Court could make any decisions.[37]

The following year, the Court did hear a case involving a man charged with less serious crimes who did not want to be medicated. The state wanted to medicate him so that he could become competent to stand trial. In a 6–3 decision, the Court ruled that the state cannot medicate a prisoner solely to stand trial, but can do so "if the treatment is medically appropriate, is substantially unlikely to have side effects that may undermine the trial's fairness, and, taking account of less intrusive alternatives, is necessary significantly to further important governmental trial-related interests." In this case, the government had not met its burden of showing that the medication would not interfere with the defendant's ability to prepare his defense.[38]

At one time, many states allowed the execution of the mentally retarded. Some states, including Colorado, Indiana, Kansas, and New York, prohibited the execution of defendants shown to be mentally retarded.[39] The Supreme Court had ruled in *Penry v. Lynaugh* that the Eighth Amendment did not bar a retarded individual from death, but requires that he be treated like any other defendant. He could only attempt to use his retardation as mitigating evidence.[40]

Interestingly, the same case resurfaced in the Supreme Court in 2001. The defendant, John Paul Penry, was retried and again convicted. This time, he argued that the jury that decided whether he would live or die wasn't given enough information about his disability. The Supreme Court agreed, and reversed his sentence. He will now face another sentencing hearing, at which the jury will hear and consider evidence of his mental handicap as mitigating evidence. The case is *Penry v. Johnson,* 532 U.S. 782 (2001).

Finally, in 2002, the Supreme Court ruled in *Atkins v. Virginia* that executing the mentally retarded does violate the prohibition against cruel and unusual punishment. The Court found that contemporary standards of what is appropriate have changed and that the mentally retarded, with limited ability to understand the consequences of the punishment they face, should not be subjected to execution.

HISTORICAL HIGHLIGHT
Executing the Mentally Retarded—Cruel or Unusual?

Terry Washington had organic brain damage. He had the mind of a 6-year-old, but managed to work in a restaurant as a dishwasher. This was no easy task, for his condition would sometimes cause him to have violent seizures, and foam at the mouth. Unfortunately, one night after an argument with his supervisor, Terry murdered him.

Little doubt exists that Terry Washington killed the man. The trial was an open-and-shut case, and the jury voted to give Washington the death penalty. However, the jurors were never told that Washington was severely retarded.

Washington invoked his Fifth Amendment right not to testify during the trial. His attorneys never raised the issue, either, during the determination of guilt phase of the trial or the sentencing phase. On May 6, 1998, Washington became one of the approximately 25 mentally retarded people to be executed since the death penalty was reinstated in 1976.

The Supreme Court had ruled previously that the execution of mentally retarded convicts was not cruel and unusual punishment per se. But the decision left the door open when it said "a national consensus against execution of the mentally retarded may someday emerge reflecting the evolving standards of decency that mark the progress of a maturing society."[41]

The landscape of the death penalty has changed dramatically since then with the Supreme Court's ruling that execution of the mentally retarded violates the Eighth Amendment protection against cruel and unusual punishment. Daryl Atkins, who was convicted of murder and sentenced to death, had an IQ estimated at 59. He appealed his death sentence. The Supreme Court found that a national consensus against execution of the mentally retarded had finally emerged based upon a majority of states having laws prohibiting such executions. The Court relied on information about changes to some state laws since it last reviewed a similar case. Using that information, the Court concluded that the nation's mood had changed and what was acceptable just a few years earlier was no longer acceptable.[42]

More recently, the Court rejected a Texas scheme that made low intelligence an aggravating rather than a mitigating factor in a jury's decision whether to order the death penalty or life in prison. The Court ruled that low intelligence may only be considered a mitigating factor, not a ground to execute a defendant.[43]

MINORS

According to Amnesty International, a group dedicated to eliminating human rights violations worldwide, nine persons who were under the age of 18 at the time of their offense were executed worldwide between 1990 and 1994.[44] The United States led the way with six of the nine executions, while Saudi Arabia, Pakistan, and Yemen each executed one.

Not every **minor** can be executed. In 1988 the Supreme Court ruled that it is cruel and unusual punishment to impose the death penalty on persons who committed their offense while 15 years of age or younger. However, the next year the same Court concluded, in *Thompson v. Oklahoma,* that a youth 16 or 17 at the time of the offense can be sentenced to death.[45]

Of the 2,849 individuals on death row as of the end of 1996, there were 2.2 percent, or 64, who were age 17 or younger at the time of the commission of the offense.[46] Two states set 14 as the statutory age limit,[47] while 8 set no lower limit.[48] However, in light of the Supreme Court decision in *Thompson,* an age of 16 is the Constitutional limit. A total of 19 states allow the execution of those who were minors when they committed their crimes, down four states from 23 in just the last three years.

The execution of those who were minors when they committed their crime puts the United States in the international spotlight. In fact, the United Nations Convention on the Rights of the Child forbids countries from killing those who commit crimes as juveniles. The treaty has not been ratified by Congress. Today, the United States is definitely in the minority. Other than the United States, only Iran and the Democratic Republic of the Congo have held such executions in the past three years. Both have pledged that they won't carry out any more juvenile executions, leaving the United States the sole holdout.[49]

The Supreme Court recently had many opportunities to review a case involving a defendant who was 17 when he committed murder. In the first case, a youth, Napoleon Beazley, was convicted of murdering the father of a federal judge and sentenced to death. Beazley, who had been president of his senior class at the time of the murder, allegedly shot John Luttig as part of a car-jacking attempt. The victim's son is an acquaintance of three Supreme Court justices, Antonin Scalia, Clarence Thomas, and David Souter. When the case came before the Court, the three recused themselves, leaving six justices to consider whether to take the case. They didn't, and Beazley was executed.

Within weeks of the Court's October 1, 2001, refusal to hear the Beazley case, the Court was asked to stay the execution of another man who was 17 when he killed a buyer in a drug deal. Gerald Mitchell's attorneys argued that the United States should accept international standards for the treatment of juvenile offenders even if Congress hadn't ratified the United Nations Convention on the Rights of the Child. The Court rejected the appeal and Texas executed Mitchell on October 22, 2001. In late 2002, the Court turned down another opportunity to rule on the issue, with four justices concluding they should consider outlawing the practice.[50]

The death penalty is a good example of evolving standards of law. After allowing the execution of Beazley and Mitchell, the Supreme Court agreed on January 26, 2004, to hear another juvenile challenge to the Eighth Amendment. The case is *Roper v. Simmons* and came to the Court from Missouri. The Missouri Supreme Court had concluded that there is a national consensus against the execution of those who were under age 18 at the time of the crime. The state appealed and the Supreme Court will hear arguments on October 13, 2004.[51] A wide range of organizations and individuals have filed amicus briefs with the Court, arguing that evolving standards of decency require that we no longer execute those who were children when they committed their crimes. These include former president Jimmy Carter and other Nobel Peace Prize winners and the American Medical Association.

OFFENSES PUNISHABLE BY DEATH

Generally, most states reserve the death penalty for murder or felony murder, at least where the defendant was substantially involved in the victim's death.[52] Whether someone is substantially involved in a murder depends on the facts of the case. For example, substantial involvement was not found in a case where the defendant did not intend to kill anyone, did not know that his codefendant would do so, and only drove the getaway car.[53] However, when another defendant, along with other family members, planned his father's escape from prison, and watched his father kill and rob a family of four during the getaway, the defendant was sentenced to death. The father was serving a life sentence because he had killed a guard in a previous, unsuccessful escape attempt. The son's sentence was upheld by the Supreme Court in *Tison vs. Arizona*.[54]

A few states add **treason** as a capital offense. One state, Louisiana, specifies death for the aggravated rape of a victim under age 12. If the rape involves an adult the death penalty is improper. In *Coker v. Georgia*, the Supreme Court ruled that death for rape is

HISTORICAL HIGHLIGHT
Death for Corruption?

For as long as the debate about capital punishment has raged, the question of when to use it has been at the forefront. In the days of segregation, crimes committed by African Americans were capital crimes, while the same crime committed by a Caucasian only brought a jail sentence. This clearly unfair application of capital punishment fed the movement against capital punishment in the late 1960s and early 1970s.

There are some who believe in the death penalty, but don't like the way it is applied. Some believe that chronic sex offenders should receive the death penalty, while teenagers who commit violent crimes should not. They reason that the violent teenagers are more likely to be rehabilitated than the sex offenders.

In an interesting twist in the debate, Pennsylvania Supreme Court nominee John A. Maher advocated the death penalty for corrupt politicians during his confirmation hearings in 1997. Understandably, the Pennsylvania State Senators who had to confirm Maher in order for him to take a seat on the high court were less than enthusiastic about his views.

Maher was quoted by the *Philadelphia Inquirer* as saying, "I think the highest crime is the sale of office, and I am always offended as a citizen when I read the sale of office accompanied by a two-year probation. I'm not against capital punishment. I just think we should be more careful about what we give it for. The sale of office is an offense against the very existence of society."[55]

Maher's position was seen as too extreme, certainly for the politicians passing judgment on him, and he was not confirmed. At Maher's request, then Pennsylvania Governor Tom Ridge withdrew his name from consideration.

---

unconstitutional.[56] The defendant, while serving a life sentence for murder, rape, kidnapping and aggravated assault, escaped from a Georgia prison and raped an adult woman. In *Coker,* the Supreme Court ruled that the Eighth Amendment bars punishments that are "excessive." The Court wrote:

> [a] punishment is "excessive" and unconstitutional if it makes no measurable contribution to acceptable goals of punishment and hence is nothing more than purposeless and needless imposition of pain and suffering or is grossly out of proportion to the severity of the crime.[57]

Under federal law, death is an allowable sanction for a number of offenses, including the taking of a human life, **espionage,** terrorist acts, and treason.[58] The Supreme Court has upheld death for espionage.[59]

HISTORICAL HIGHLIGHT
Julius and Ethel Rosenberg Executed for Espionage

Julius and Ethel Rosenberg are the only Americans to receive the death penalty during peacetime for the crime of espionage. They were executed in New York's electric chair at Sing Sing Prison on June 19, 1953, after last-minute appeals to the Supreme Court were turned down and President Dwight Eisenhower denied a plea for executive clemency. They left behind two young sons, Robert, aged 6, and Michael, aged 10. Both boys were later relocated and placed in an adoptive home.

The Rosenbergs were accused of giving the Soviet Union top secret information about the United States' development of an atomic bomb during World War II. The program, code-named the Manhattan Project, led to the end of the war with Japan after the atomic bomb was dropped on Japanese civilians in the cities of Nagasaki and Hiroshima. Many of the scientists working on the project were refugees from wartime Europe. One of them, German born and lifelong Communist Klaus Fuchs, provided secret data to the Russians.

Klaus Fuchs was arrested and convicted of espionage in Great Britain in 1949. He received a 15-year jail term in exchange for providing information about other spies. He provided authorities the name of American Harry Gold. Gold, in turn, implicated David Greenglass as another spy for the Soviets. Greenglass was Ethel's brother. In exchange for a guarantee that his wife would not be prosecuted and no prison sentence for himself, he implicated his sister and her husband, Julius. He claimed they had recruited him for the Soviets. He testified against them at their trial.

Both Ethel and Julius insisted that they were innocent, but were convicted of espionage by a jury. Although urged to do so, they would not cooperate and name others as spies. They were sentenced to death. Up until the hour of their executions they were offered clemency if they would name others in their alleged spy ring. Recently declassified information in both the United States and the former Soviet Union indicate that Julius, but not Ethel, may have been involved in low-level espionage, but does not implicate them in passing atomic secrets.

LIFE IN PRISON

According to the FBI there were 11.6 million crimes reported to law enforcement officials in 2000. These included 15,517 murders, 90,186 forcible rapes, and about 2 million burglaries.[60] In 1996 that rate was 13.5 million crimes.[61] Although these figures actually represent a decline in the crime rate, numbers such as these have resulted in a public call for longer prison sentences. In response, many legislatures have passed laws requiring long

Rising Crime Rate?

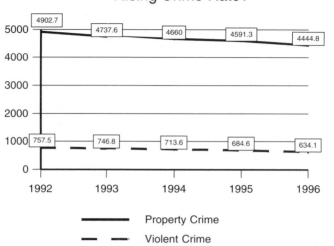

Note: Figures shown are crime rates per 100,000 population. Source: *FBI Uniform Crime Report.*

sentences for recidivists. So-called "three strikes and you're out" legislation has been popular with many state lawmakers. These laws punish recidivists by providing that repeat offenders be imprisoned for life, thus eliminating recidivism.

The Supreme Court has upheld some forms of repeat offender legislation as a legitimate use of state police powers, writing that states have an "interest expressed in all recidivism statutes, in dealing in a harsher manner with those who by repeated criminal acts have shown that they are simply incapable of conforming to the norms of society. . . ."[62]

Prisoners have argued that mandatory life in prison for repeat offenders is cruel and unusual punishment, especially when applied to relatively minor crimes. Two such cases have reached the Supreme Court. In 1980, the Court concluded that life in prison for three nonviolent crimes was not unconstitutional as long as the prisoner was at some point eligible for parole. The case involved the following three convictions:

1. Credit card theft, $80.00
2. Forged check, $28
3. False pretenses, $120

Defendant was therefore given a life sentence as a recidivist for the theft of $228 over a nine-year period.[63]

However, in 1983, the Supreme Court struck down a similar law in a case where a defendant was sentenced to life in prison with no chance of parole for writing a bad check for $100, his third petty offense. Because he was never eligible for parole, the Court ruled the punishment cruel and unusual.[64]

HISTORICAL HIGHLIGHT
That's the Way the Cookie Crumbles

A parolee, Kevin Weber, broke into a restaurant to steal chocolate chip cookies and was sentenced to 25 years to life. The sentence may seem a little stiff, but the judge had no choice. Under California's "three strikes, you're out" law, any third felony conviction sends the felon away for a long time. Weber's intention was to rob the restaurant's safe, but he was unable to open it before he set off the burglar alarm. Apparently somewhere along the way he decided he needed a snack, and picked up some chocolate chip cookies. When police arrested him, he had the cookies in his pockets.[65]

Critics of the "three strikes, you're out" law argue that it ties judges' hands when sentencing offenders, and makes no distinction between violent felons and nonviolent cookie snatchers. Supporters of the law, however, feel that anyone who is convicted of a third felony is a career criminal and should be locked away.

This case and others like it received much publicity. In fact, California has sentenced over 300 petty criminals to life in prison under the three strikes law. When the Ninth Circuit Court of Appeals got a case testing the constitutionality of California's three strike law, it concluded the law was unconstitutional as applied to convictions for shoplifting that resulted in a term of life in prison. The February 7, 2002, decision affects only those whose third convictions are for shoplifting. The same Court ruled earlier that the law applied to the theft of videotapes was unconstitutional as cruel and unusual punishment. California appealed both cases to the U.S. Supreme Court.[66] The Court agreed to hear arguments on both cases in the 2002–2003 term.[67] On March 5, 2003, the Court by a 5–4 vote upheld the sentences.

PRISON CONDITIONS

Generally, the punishments prohibited by the Eighth Amendment are those considered to be torture or otherwise barbarous. The Constitution prohibits the "wanton and unnecessary infliction of pain."[68] Imprisonment itself obviously carries with it some control over the day-to-day lives of the inmates, including confinement and physical coercion when necessary. These are not constitutionally prohibited unless they rise to a level that can cause serious illness or injury. Thus, double bunking in prison is allowable.[69] However, conditions cannot be so poor that inmates are allowed to prey on each other and prisoners suffer malnutrition.[70] In addition, adequate medical care must be provided for inmates.[71]

HISTORICAL HIGHLIGHT
The Hitching Post Meets the Eighth Amendment

In June of 1995, Larry Hope, an inmate at the Limestone Prison in Alabama, received the usual punishment for disruptive behavior. He was confined to a hitching post, a bar placed approximately 57 inches above the ground.

While being taken to his chain gang's work site, Hope made vulgar remarks and wrestled with a prison guard. The guards transported him back to the prison in handcuffs and shackles. Upon arrival, they removed Hope's shirt and handcuffed him to the hitching post. He remained shirtless, in a standing position with his hands above his shoulders, for seven hours in the hot Alabama sun. During his time on the hitching post, Hope was offered water only once or twice and was given no bathroom breaks. One guard even taunted him about being thirsty.

In 2002, the U.S. Supreme Court ruled in Hope's favor in a civil suit against the three guards who participated in his punishment. Citing precedence from *Ort v. White,*[72] the justices held that "physical abuse directed at [a] prisoner after he terminates his resistance to authority would constitute an actionable Eighth Amendment violation." The Court also ruled that the guards were not entitled to qualified immunity—they could be held liable in Hope's suit against them—because any reasonable person could have determined that this type of punishment is cruel and unusual.

EMERGING TRENDS

Two trends in punishment have recently received widespread press coverage and attention from state and federal legislators. Both attempt to deal with repeat offenders.

PREDATORY SEX OFFENDER REGISTRATION

Forty-eight states currently have predatory sex offender registration laws mandating that prisoners who are released from prison after violent sexual offenses or those involving children must register their address and make public their presence in the community where they live after release. These laws are generally referred to as "Megan's Laws." Named for Megan Kanka, a young girl who was raped and murdered by a repeat sexual offender, these new laws are causing controversy. Federal law establishes a national database at the Federal Bureau of Investigation designed to track every person who has been convicted of a criminal offense against a minor, a sexually violent offense, or who is a sexually violent "predator." The database is maintained for 10 years after release of the defendant or for his or her lifetime if there have been two or more convictions. In addition, federal law requires that state and local governmental officials release relevant information deemed necessary to protect the public from

HISTORICAL HIGHLIGHT
Prisoners Are Covered by the Americans with Disabilities Act

Ronald Yeskey was a prisoner in a state prison in Pennsylvania when he heard about a program the state offered first-time offenders like himself. It was a motivational boot camp that allowed qualified prisoners to have their sentences reduced upon completion. Yeskey applied for the program, but was rejected because of his history of high blood pressure.

Yeskey claimed that he was being discriminated against because of his disability. In effect, he said he would have to stay in prison longer because of his disability. He filed suit against the Commonwealth of Pennsylvania under the Americans with Disabilities Act (ADA).

The ADA prohibits discrimination against "qualified persons with disabilities" by any "public entity." The case went all the way to the Supreme Court, who ruled in Yeskey's favor. In their ruling they stated that the ADA's wording was very clear that "all public entities" were covered by the ADA.

Attorneys for the Commonwealth of Pennsylvania belatedly attempted to argue that the ADA did not apply to the states on constitutional grounds. The Supreme Court did not rule on that because the issue had not been raised at the district level. Legislation has since been introduced to exempt state and local prisons from the ADA, but it has not passed. For the time being, the ADA covers prisoners.[73]

predators.[74] Many states have their own requirements for registration. Florida has even set up a searchable site on the World Wide Web, complete with pictures, names, and addresses.[75]

"Megan's Laws" have been controversial. Delaware's version of the law provides for the letter "Y" to be imprinted on the driver's license of all monitored sex offenders. Legislatures in New York and California are looking into adopting similar measures.[76] In New Jersey, after neighbors had been notified of a sex offender in their neighborhood, shots were fired through his window.[77]

The Supreme Court has twice in the last few years addressed whether convicted sex offenders who have served their sentences can be further confined. In *Kansas v. Hendricks*, 521 U.S. 346 (1997), the Court concluded that the Kansas Sexually Violent Predator Act was Constitutional. The Act allowed involuntary confinement of persons with a mental abnormality or personality disorder who were found to be dangerous by a jury. The Court also ruled that confinement after serving a sentence for sex offenses wasn't double jeopardy. Nor was the law an *ex post facto* law, since it was not criminal, but civil in nature. In *Kansas v. Crane,* 534 U.S. 407 (2002), the Court clarified that the state must show at a minimum that the person they want to confine must have at least some difficulty controlling his urges, but wasn't required to show that it would be impossible to control those urges.

HISTORICAL HIGHLIGHT
Convicted Sex Offender Programs and Self-Incrimination

The state of Kansas offers convicted sex offenders an opportunity to participate in a Sexual Abuse Treatment Program (SATP), which requires participating inmates to complete a sexual history form revealing all of their prior sexual activities. This list of activities could include any activities that may constitute a criminal offense for which an inmate has never been charged. Kansas makes no promise that the information will never be used against them. Inmates who refuse to participate in the program may have a reduction in their prison privileges and could be transferred to a potentially more dangerous maximum-security area.

Robert G. Lile, a Kansas prisoner, was facing the dilemma of choosing between improved prison privileges and disclosing potentially incriminating information about his past that could lead to further criminal charges. He filed an action for injunctive relief on the grounds that participating in Kansas's SATP would violate his Fifth Amendment protection against compelled self-incrimination.

The Tenth Circuit decided that because refusing to participate in the program would result in an automatic reduction of Mr. Lile's privileges and housing accommodations, the penalty would have a sufficiently substantial impact on him that it would constitute a compelling reason to release information that could create a risk of further prosecution. However, the U.S. Supreme Court overturned this decision on appeal, stating that the consequences for refusing to participate were not great enough to compel a prisoner to abandon his/her right against self-incrimination.[78]

The question still remains of how broadly Megan's Law may be applied. Louis Rocco of Scranton, Pennsylvania, never actually had any physical contact with any of his victims. He admitted to making numerous phone calls and leaving notes threatening violent sexual acts. Although Rocco's case is pending, prosecutors have expressed their intent to try to have Megan's Law applied to his case. Dana Oxley, Assistant District Attorney for Lackawanna County, said "To me, if there was ever a case for Megan's Law, this is it, despite the lack of physical contact. The psychological terror he inflicted on his victims matches or possibly exceeds physical terror."[79]

In a further sign that the Supreme Court continues to consider the impact of sex offender registration laws on Constitutional law, the Court has decided two sex offender registration cases in the 2002–2003 term. The defendants argued that the registration laws are in effect *ex post facto* laws.[80] In 2003, the Supreme Court concluded the registration schemes are not.[81]

CHEMICAL CASTRATION

Chemical castration of sex offenders is also gaining in popularity. Both surgical castration and chemical castration have been used in Norway, Sweden, Denmark, and Switzerland for a number of years. Now several states here have followed suit. California[82] and Georgia[83] have passed laws making chemical castration a condition of parole for sex offenses, especially those involving a child victim. Chemical castration is accomplished by the injection of the chemical medroxyprogesterone acetate, commonly referred to by its trade name, Depo-Provera. The drug reduces the level of testosterone and decreases the male sex drive.

HISTORICAL HIGHLIGHT
Not All Predators Are Male

A Tacoma, Washington, woman is listed as a sexual predator under the provisions of that state's "Megan's Law." The lady, Laura Faye McCollum, was convicted in 1990 of raping a 3-year-old girl. She completed her 5½-year sentence in 1995 and has been housed at a treatment center ever since. She remains confined voluntarily.

McCollum is aware of her condition, but is almost helpless to stop her own actions if left unsupervised. One of her counselors described her as "an obsessive and compulsive child molester who is particularly attracted to preverbal and barely verbal children ages 2 to 4."

This type of obsessive behavior is more commonly found in males, but at least one other woman has made the sexual predator list. Minnesota also has a woman sex offender on that state's list.[84]

HISTORICAL HIGHLIGHT:
Study Blasts Death Penalty

There has been a real resurgence in the past few years in popular opposition to the imposition of the death penalty. A rash of cases in which death row inmates have been proven not guilty through DNA analysis of evidence has shaken some in the legal community. As yet, there has been no definitive cases clearing a defendant who has already been executed. However, there have been enough cases of wrongful conviction to worry even staunch supporters of the death penalty.

Adding to the public discourse is a recently released study by Columbia Law School faculty and researchers. The study, released February 11, 2002, reports that of all capital cases analyzed between 1973 and 1995, there were 68 percent that were reversed on appeal due to serious, reversible error. The study concludes that the "U.S. legal system is collapsing under the weight of error-filled death penalty cases," and recommends the imposition of a new standard of evidence in capital cases. Instead of finding a defendant guilty beyond a reasonable doubt, the researchers call for finding guilt beyond any doubt. The study is *A Broken System, Part II: Why There Is So Much Error in Capital Cases and What Can Be Done About It.*

HISTORICAL HIGHLIGHT
Governor Ryan Has Death Penalty Doubts

Following the release of a thirteenth exonerated death row inmate since the re-instatement of the death penalty in 1977, Illinois governor George Ryan declared a statewide moratorium on executions on January 31, 2002. Ryan appointed a commission to study Illinois's death penalty administration. In April 2002, the Commission of Capital Punishment presented a report suggesting over 80 changes that Illinois could implement to make their death penalty system less likely to convict and execute innocent suspects. These suggestions included establishing a panel to review prosecutorial decisions to seek the death penalty before the case goes to trial, having the police videotape all interrogations of homicide suspects rather than solely the confession, and giving judges the ability to reverse a jury's death sentence if the verdict seems improper. Best-selling author Scott Turow was a member of the commission and the work he did served as a catalyst for his latest legal thriller, *Reversible Errors.* He has also written a short book, *Ultimate Punishment: A Lawyer's Reflections on Dealing with the Death Penalty.*

In a similar situation, Maryland's release of their hundredth innocent death row inmate prompted Governor Paris N. Glendening to declare a moratorium and order a study done on racial bias in the Maryland capital punishment administration. As death penalty activists see that the Supreme Court is susceptible to arguments that evolving community standards may require it to shift its stand on capital punishment, calls for moratoriums are gaining ground.

Chemical castration is likely to be challenged on Eighth Amendment grounds as cruel and unusual punishment.

CHAPTER SUMMARY

The Eighth Amendment has historical roots reaching back at least as far as the Magna Carta of 1215. Transplanted to the United States by English colonists, it serves as the minimum standard by which criminal punishments are measured.

Capital punishment has provided a fertile ground for interpretation of the ban on cruel and unusual punishment. For a brief period of time it seemed as if the death penalty would expire, beginning with the 1972 Supreme Court decision in *Fuhrman v. Georgia.* But rather than signaling its death rattle, proponents came back with new and improved legislation. In 1976 the Supreme Court revisited its 1972 decision and upheld a death penalty statute that provided procedural safeguards against arbitrary and capricious imposition of the penalty.

Life in prison is not cruel and unusual punishment for numerous offenses, including those committed by both violent and nonviolent offenders. For nonviolent offenders, a recidivism statute may not forever foreclose the possibility of parole.

Generally, prison conditions are not cruel and unusual punishment unless they reach the level of wanton and unnecessary infliction of pain.

Two areas of punishment likely to receive review under the Eighth Amendment are lifetime sex offender registration and castration of sex offenders.

KEY TERMS

Aggravating circumstance: Act or conduct that increases the seriousness of an act, often resulting in a harsher punishment.

Bloody Code: Popular name for England's criminal laws because of their harshness and the long list of crimes classified as capital offenses.

Corporal punishment: Punishment inflicted on the body, such as paddling, whipping, or caning.

Crime: An offense against society.

Cruel and unusual punishment: Punishment which violates the Eighth Amendment and which violates evolving standards of decency.

Espionage: Spying; selling or giving secrets to another government.

Magna Carta: Document signed by King John of England in 1215 at Runnymede in which he was compelled to grant noblemen limited civil and political liberties.

Minor: A person who has not yet reached legal age, typically 18.

Mitigating circumstance: Act or conduct that lessens or reduces the punishment for a crime, such as lack of a criminal record, state of mind, or youth.

Per se: Latin; by itself, in and of itself.

Transportation: The practice of exiling or expelling a prisoner from his homeland as punishment.

Treason: Transferring loyalty or allegiance to the enemy.

DISCUSSION QUESTIONS

1. Explain the history of the Eighth Amendment to the U.S. Constitution.
2. Define criminal punishment.
3. List and explain the two requirements that must be satisfied before a punishment is "cruel and unusual."
4. Explain why capital punishment is not unconstitutional as "cruel and unusual" punishment.
5. Explain what procedural protection is required before the death penalty can be carried out.
6. Define aggravating and mitigating circumstances.
7. List the classifications of persons who can be executed.
8. List the crimes that are punishable by death.
9. Explain the Supreme Court's position on life in prison for repeat offenders.
10. List and describe two current trends in punishment.

FOR FURTHER READING AND VIEWING

1. Meeropol, R., and Meeropol, M. (1975). *We Are Your Sons: The Legacy of Ethel and Julius Rosenberg*. Houghton Miffllin. Written by the sons of Ethel and Julius

Rosenberg, who were made orphans by the execution of their parents. This book tells the story of the trial, conviction, and execution of the Rosenbergs through the eyes of 6- and 9-year-old Robert and Michael. It includes death row correspondence from their parents.

2. Prejean, H. (1993). *Dead Man Walking*. Random House. Recounts a Roman Catholic nun's work with Louisiana death row inmates. The book has been made into a major movie starring Susan Sarandon and Sean Penn.

3. Radelet, M. L., Hugo, A. B., and Putnam, C. (1992). *In Spite of Innocence: Erroneous Convictions in Capital Cases*. Northeastern UP. Studies the cases of 400 Americans who have been convicted of capital crimes and either were executed or incarcerated. The authors argue all were innocent of the crimes charged.

4. Roberts, S. (2001). *The Brother: The Untold Story of Atomic Spy David Greenglass and How He Sent His Sister, Ethel Rosenberg, to the Electric Chair*. Random House. After years of silence, a *New York Times* reporter gets Ethel's brother to confess his involvement in the Rosenberg case.

5. Turow, S. (2002). *Reversible Errors*. Farrar Straus Giroux. Tells the fictional story of a corporate attorney appointed to represent a death row inmate who just possibly might be innocent of the triple murder he was sentenced to die for committing.

6. Turow, S. (2003). *Ultimate Punishment: A Lawyer's Reflections on Dealing with the Death Penalty*. Farrar Straus Giroux. Tells of Turow's involvement with the Illinois Commission of Capital Punishment.

7. *The Green Mile*. (2000). Warner. A film starring Tom Hanks and featuring life on death row.

8. *Monster*. (2003). The role of Aileen Wuornos, a prostitute executed in 2002 for a series of murders in Florida, won actress Charlize Theron the 2003 Best Actress Academy Award. The film attempts to explain Aileen's horrific childhood and gradual transformation into a serial killer.

QUOTATIONS FOR CHAPTER SEVEN

1. *Can any of you seriously say the Bill of Rights could get through Congress today? It wouldn't even get out of committee.*
   F. Lee Bailey, *Newsweek* (April 17, 1967)

2. *We do not reprove it because it is a crime, but it is a crime, because we reprove it.*
   Emil Durkheim, *The Division of Labor in Society* (1933)

3. *Death is . . . different. Death is irremedial. Death is unknowable; it goes beyond this world. It is a legislative decision to do something, and we know not what we do.*
   Anthony Amsterdam, oral argument before the U.S. Supreme Court in *Gregg vs. Georgia* (30 March 1976)

ENDNOTES

1. L. O. Pike, *A History of Crime in England* (London: Elder & Co., 1973).

2. M. Ignatieff, *A Just Measure of Pain; the Penitentiary in the Industrial Revolution, 1750–1850* (New York: Pantheon, 1978).

3. M. R. Latham and W. Matthews, eds., *The Diary of Samuel Pepys, A New and Complete Transcription* (Berkeley: University of California Press, 1978).

4. Ignatieff, *A Just Measure of Pain.*

5. Ibid.

6. 1 Wm. & Mary, sess. 2, ch. 2 (1689).

7. *Magna Carta* (1215).

8. *Webster's New World/Stedman's Medical Dictionary,* 1st ed., 1987, defines hematoma as "a localized mass of extravasated, usually clotted, blood confined within an organ, tissue or space."

9. *Ingraham v. Wright,* 430 U.S. 651 (1977).

10. There are other remedies available under the law. For example, school children who are paddled or slapped may be able to recover damages for the torts of assault and battery and the punishment may constitute criminal assault or child abuse.

11. *Black's Law Dictionary.*

12. *Robinson v. California,* 370 U.S. 660 (1962).

13. *Robinson v. California,* 370 U.S. 660, 668 (1962).

14. *Ford v. Wainwright,* 477 U.S. 399 (1986).

15. *Trop v. Dulles,* 356 U.S. 86 (1958).

16. U.S. Constitution, Fifth Amendment.

17. Alaska, District of Columbia, Hawaii, Iowa, Maine, Massachusetts, Michigan, Minnesota, North Dakota, Rhode Island, Vermont, West Virginia, and Wisconsin.

18. *Edmund v. Florida,* 458 U.S. 782 (1982).

19. *Tison v. Arizona,* 481 U.S. 137 (1987). See Chapter 14 for an explanation of the felony murder rule.

20. Bureau of Justice Statistics, U.S. Department of Justice, *Capital Punishment 2000,* 31 December 2000.

21. *Louisiana ex rel. Francis v. Resweber,* 329 U.S. 459 (1947).

22. R. Hood, *The Death Penalty, A World Wide Perspective,* 2nd ed. (Oxford: Clarendon Press, 1996).

23. *Furman v. Georgia,* 408 U.S. 238 (1972).

24. *Gregg v. Georgia,* 428 U.S. 153 (1976).

25. *Roberts v. Louisiana,* 431 U.S. 633 (1977) and *Roberts v. Louisiana,* 428 U.S. 325 (1976). Although both cases involve an automatic death sentence for cop-killers, the two defendants are not related. They only share the same name, crime, and sentence.

26. *In re Kimmler,* 136 U.S. 436 (1890).

27. *Wilkerson v. Utah,* 99 U.S. 1130 (1879).

28. *Louisiana ex rel. Francis v. Resweber,* 329 U.S. 459, 465 (1947).

29. D. P. Baker, *Washington Post* (26 March 1997), p. A01.

30. M. Clay, "Flames leap from inmate's head at execution," *Los Angeles Times* (26 March 1997).

31. Ibid.

32. *Ford v. Wainwright,* 477 U.S. 399 (1986).

33. Ibid.

34. *Washington v. Harper,* 494 U.S. 210 (1990).

35. *Perry v. Louisiana,* 498 U.S. 38 (1990).

36. *State v. Perry,* 610 So. 2nd 757 (1992).

37. "Death sentence commuted for mentally ill man," CNN Online (February 26, 2002).

38. *Sell v. United States,* 539 U.S. 166 (2003).

39. Bureau of Justice Statistics, U.S. Department of Justice, *Capital Punishment 1996.*

40. *Penry v. Lynaugh,* 492 U.S. 302 (1989).

41. Ibid.

42. *Atkins v. Virginia,* 536 U.S. 304 (2002).

43. *Tennard v. Dretke,* 124 S. Ct. 2562 (2004).

44. Amnesty International, *United States of America, Follow Up to Amnesty International's Open Letter to the President on the Death Penalty* (April 7, 1995).

45. *Thompson v. Oklahoma,* 487 U.S. 815 (1988).

46. *Capital Punishment 1996.*

47. Arkansas and Virginia.

48. Arizona, Idaho, Missouri, Louisiana, Pennsylvania, South Carolina, South Dakota, and Utah.

49. K. Axtman, *Teen Murderer Searches for Fairness in Court,* Christian Science Monitor (October 22, 2001).

50. *In re Kevin Nigel Stanford,* 537 U.S. 968 (2002). Justices Stevens, Souter, Ginsburg, and Breyer wanted to hear the case.

51. *Roper v. Simmons,* 124 S. Ct. 1171 (2004) cert. granted.

52. Murder committed during the commission of a felony, such as rape or armed robbery, even if not personally committed by the defendant. See Chapter 14 for a more complete discussion.

53. *Edmund v. Florida,* 458 U.S. 782 (1982).

54. *Tison v. Arizona,* 481 U.S. 137 (1987).

55. "Professor withdraws as high-court nominee: Supreme Court nominee John Maher had said corrupt politicians deserve to die," *Philadelphia Inquirer* (March 19,1997). Professor Maher taught the author everything she knows about corporate and antitrust law while she was a student at the Dickinson School of Law.

56. *Coker v. Georgia,* 433 U.S. 584 (1977).

57. *Coker,* at 593.

58. 18 U.S.C.§ 7794; 18 U.S.C. § 2381.

59. *Rosenberg v. United States,* 346 U.S. 273 (1953).

60. U.S. Department of Justice, Federal Bureau of Investigation, *Crime in America* (October 22, 2001).

61. U.S. Department of Justice, Federal Bureau of Investigation, *Crime in the United States; 1996 Preliminary Release* (June 1, 1997).

62. *Rummel v. Estelle,* 445 U.S. 263 (1980).

63. "Cookie burglar gets at least 25 years," CNN Online (October 27, 1995).

64. *Rummel v. Estelle,* 445 U.S. 263 (1980).

65. *Solem v. Helm,* 463 U.S. 277 (1983).

66. B. Egelko, "Three strikes ruled unjust in shoplifting convictions," *San Francisco Chronicle* (February 8, 2002).

67. *California v. Andrade,* 538 U.S. 63 (2002) and *Ewing v. California,* 538 U.S. 11 (2003).

68. *Hutto v. Finney,* 437 U.S. 678 (1978).

69. *Bell v. Wollfish,* 441 U.S. 520 (1979).

70. *Hutto v. Finney,* 437 U.S. 678 (1978).

71. *Estelle v. Gamble,* 429 U.S. 97 (1976).

72. *Ort v. White,* 813 F. 2d 318 (1987).

73. *Pennsylvania Department of Corrections v. Yeskey,* 524 U.S. 206 (1998).

74. Public Law, 104–105 (April 17, 1996) and 104–236 (October 3, 1996).

75. *http://www.fdla.state.fl.us/Sexual_Predators/*

76. "Will Scarlet Letter 'Y' go nationwide?" *The National Law Journal* (May 4, 1998).

77. "Shooting at ex-sex offender," The National Law Journal (June 29, 1998).

78. *McKune et al. v. Lile,* 536 U.S. 24 (2002).

79. "Megan's Law labels stalker: Man only used frightful words," *The Patriot News* (Harrisburg, PA) (July 30, 2002).

80. *Otte v. Doe,* 534 U.S. 1126 (2002).

81. *Smith v. Doe,* 538 U.S. 84 (2003).

82. "D. Norton, Wilson to sign Castration Bill," *San Francisco Chronicle* (September 17, 1996).

83. "G. Lucas, Chemical Castration Bill Passes," *Augusta Chronicle* (February 12, 1997).

84. "Bill Savitsky, Jr., and Pete Shellem, Woman held as a sex predator: Designation is state's first," *Seattle Times* (January 22, 1997).

Chapter 8
Murder

CHAPTER OBJECTIVES

After studying this chapter you should be able to:

- Define murder
- Distinguish between degrees of murder
- Define conspiracy
- Explain the felony murder rule as it applies to criminal conspiracies to commit a felony
- Define infanticide
- Distinguish between voluntary and involuntary manslaughter
- Explain when killings are not crimes and when they are
- Explain the assisted suicide movement

CHAPTER CONTENTS

> *And it came about when they were in the field, that Cain rose up against Abel his brother and killed him.*
>
> **Genesis 4:8**

INTRODUCTION

The biblical story of Cain and Abel illustrates a second fall of humans from grace following expulsion from the Garden of Eden. Cain was sent to cultivate the ground and be a "vagrant and wanderer on the earth."[1] Cultivating the land is generally regarded as the beginning of modern civilization. Cain's exile at hard labor was both the first punishment for murder and symbolically the start of civilized society's struggle with violence.

As civilized populations increased, so did the number of murders or **homicides.** Traditions arose in each society as to how to treat those who took another's life. Under English Common Law, homicides were divided into three categories, criminal (or felonious), justifiable, and excusable. Attorneys most often deal with **criminal homicide,** which is when a person unlawfully and knowingly, recklessly, or negligently causes the death of another human being.[2] Depending on the circumstances, criminal homicide can be one of several crimes. Most commonly, homicides are categorized as murders, or manslaughter. Murder may be premeditated, or felony murder. Some states have distinctions such as first or second degree murder. Check the laws in your state to understand the distinctions. Manslaughter is a lesser crime usually classified as voluntary or involuntary.

MURDER

The first job of a prosecutor in a murder case is to prove a crime was committed. Proving a crime is committed is called establishing **corpus delicti,** or the body of the crime. Corpus delicti must be established beyond a reasonable doubt. If the state cannot prove a crime was committed, they may not prosecute anyone for its commission. Don't confuse corpus delicti with the actual body in a homicide, though. As you will see below, a body may make murder easier to prove, but isn't essential to a successful murder prosecution.

Cases where the victim's body cannot be found present problems for prosecutors. Evidence of violence, witnesses to a struggle, and various forensic evidence can be pieced together to provide evidence of a crime. Although evidence like this is circumstantial, it still may be used as evidence of a crime, if the whole body of evidence establishes beyond a reasonable doubt that a crime was committed.

PREMEDITATED MURDER

The first-recorded murder in Colonial America was committed by one of the original Pilgrims from the *Mayflower.* Ten years after the Pilgrims landed, John Billington shot his neighbor with a blunderbuss. The punishment for murder was hanging. Billington was convicted and hanged.[3]

At the time, English common law made no distinction between the types of murder. But this one-punishment-fits-all approach was soon to change. After the Revolution, state legislatures created various classifications of murders by statute. It probably occurred to them that it wasn't practical to kill every murderer. Clearly, different circumstances dictated different responses.

Premeditated murder is virtually always classified as **first-degree murder.** Second-degree murder is always a lesser charge, but the elements that comprise second-degree murder vary widely from state to state.

By definition, a person committing first-degree murder must form the **intent to kill** his victim. The law requires the person to have "**malice aforethought.**" In other words, the defendant must have an angry mental state toward the victim that allowed him to plan the victim's murder. This malice need not be of long duration. Even if the intent to kill was formed just prior to the act, the person can be convicted of first-degree murder.[4]

Since we cannot read a killer's mind, intent is very hard to prove. However, there are some common law doctrines that have traditionally been held to establish intent.

First is the **deadly weapon doctrine.** Under this doctrine, if the defendant points a loaded gun at the victim and pulls the trigger, he intended to kill the person. In other words, the defendant believed that the natural and probable consequences of his action would occur.

Deadly weapons do not have to be guns or knives. Fists, scarves, handkerchiefs, rocks, and other common items used as weapons have been held to be deadly weapons in murder trials. Juries must determine the presence of a deadly weapon on a case-by-case basis.

Intent can be transferred to a party to whom the defendant bore no malice. **Transferred intent** can occur when the victim is not the one the defendant meant to kill. A person shooting at one person and accidentally hitting another is guilty of both the crime of murder and bad aim. Once the shot is fired with intent to kill and kills someone, the shooter is guilty regardless of who is killed.

LESSER DEGREES OF MURDER

Defendants who only intended to "rough someone up," but killed him or her by mistake may lack the intent to kill necessary for first-degree murder. Nevertheless, they are responsible for the person's death. In cases like this, defendants are said to possess an "**intent to do serious bodily harm.**" These murders may result in a conviction of second-degree murder, or even manslaughter depending on the definitions in the state.

Some cases involve people who have no intent to cause bodily harm, but are reckless in their behavior. Drunk driving is the most common example. When people behave in a way that endangers others resulting in the death of another person, the person may be charged with a lesser degree of murder or manslaughter depending on the fact situation.

FELONY MURDER

A person can be held responsible for murder even if that person wasn't directly involved in the killing. This is known as the **felony murder rule.** Generally, the rule applies to those who agree to act with others to commit a criminal act. If one of the parties to the

HISTORICAL HIGHLIGHT
Vietnamese Woman Claims Cultural Defense in Shooting of Husband and Stepdaughter

Should a person's culture of origin be used as a defense in a murder case? Vietnamese-born Thu Ha Nguyen came to the United States when she was 23 years old. She married an older Vietnamese man who had two children from a previous marriage. Things did not go well from the beginning. The children were a source of controversy, and Thu felt her husband was verbally abusive to her. As the children got older, Thu feared they would attack her as well.

Despite her fears, Thu never produced evidence she had been beaten. However, the marriage was going badly enough that her husband filed for divorce. Despite the filing, Thu continued to live in the same household.

One day the abuse simply became intolerable. Thu began packing her bags to leave when her stepdaughter began harassing her. The stepdaughter threatened to hit her when Thu's husband intervened. At about the same time, Thu produced a gun and told the husband to tie up his daughter so that she posed no threat. The husband did so, but the stepdaughter became enraged and lunged at Thu. Thu fired, killing her. Thu's husband attempted to get the gun away from her and it went off, killing him.

In court, Thu argued that her fear of being divorced led her to kill her husband. In Vietnamese society, divorced people are ostracized. Thu feared she would have no friends or family.

The judge in the case would not allow the cultural defense to be introduced. Thu appealed, but both the Georgia Appeals Court and the Georgia Supreme Court refused to overturn the decision.

This case was not necessarily the death knell of the cultural defense. It has been used in a number of cases. For instance, an African-born father carried on his culture's custom of celebrating the birth of a son by kissing the newborn's penis. However, a neighbor reported the man for sexual abuse. Is there a place for cultural defenses? You decide.

criminal enterprise commits the murder, all are held to be equally culpable under the felony murder rule. For example, assume two defendants conspire to commit a bank robbery. One defendant drives the getaway car while the other robs the bank and shoots a security guard in the process. The security guard dies. Both can be charged with murder, regardless of who pulled the trigger. In fact, under some circumstances the driver can even be executed.[5]

"Felony murder is committed when a person, acting alone or in concert with others, commits or attempts to commit one of nine predicate felonies, . . . " and "in the furtherance of such crime or of immediate flight therefrom, he, or another participant, if there be any, causes the death of a person other than one of the participants."[6] But, exactly what does "in furtherance of a crime or . . . flight therefrom" mean? Most jurisdictions follow the **res gestae theory,** that if the "killing was committed in, about or as part of the underlying transaction," all conspirators were guilty of the murder.

Clearly, the felony murder rule can be very broad in its application. A person who conspires to commit a felony may be charged with felony murder if his accomplice committed the murder. A **conspiracy** is an agreement between two or more persons to engage in a criminal act. It is one of a class of criminal offenses referred to as **inchoate** or incomplete crime. Other inchoate crimes are criminal solicitation and criminal intent. Conspiracy requires that at least one of the participants takes a step towards the commission of the crime the parties agreed to commit, whether they actually manage to commit the crime. In other words, one of the conspirators must take an overt action towards the accomplishment of the criminal goal. Inchoate crimes like conspiracy are punished as if the crime had been completed. For example, if two conspire to commit armed robbery, and they are stopped before they can rob the target bank, they can be sentenced as if they actually robbed the bank.

Some courts have moved to limit the felony murder rule. For instance, England abolished the felony murder rule in 1957. It is not universally recognized in the United States.[7]

However, in jurisdictions who still have felony murder laws, defendants can possibly face the death penalty. In *Tison v. Arizona*, the Supreme Court ruled that defendants may be executed even if they never "intended to kill the victims nor inflicted the fatal wounds" as long as they "had the culpable mental state of reckless indifference to human life."[8] However, the same set of facts in a jurisdiction lacking a felony murder law will only yield a conviction for the underlying felony.

Many states have limited felony murder laws. Limitations may include one or more of the following:

- The felony that was attempted or committed must be one that is dangerous to life.
- There must be a direct causal connection between the felony and the death that occurred.
- The act that caused the death must have occurred while the felony was in progress.
- The felony must be *mala in se.*
- The act must be a common law felony.

MANSLAUGHTER

Manslaughter is a classification of criminal homicide that is less than murder. Manslaughter can either be voluntary or involuntary. The main difference between murder and manslaughter is that often manslaughter is the result of conflict between the defendant and the victim where the victim contributed to the conflict. Manslaughter can also be a "catchall" type of homicide where mitigating circumstances make the defendant's behavior understandable, but not excusable.

Voluntary manslaughter is where the defendant acted willfully, but was somewhat justified in his actions. For instance, a child who kills an abusive parent when he feels no other avenue is open to him would be an example of voluntary manslaughter. Sentences for manslaughter are far less than those for murder.

Manslaughter also comes into play in plea bargaining arrangements. Defendants may agree take a manslaughter conviction instead of going to trial and risking a murder conviction.

Murder charges may be reduced to manslaughter charges if the court believes the crime occurred in the **heat of passion** as long as other elements are present. In addition to heat of passion,

- There must be adequate provocation;
- There must have been no opportunity to cool off;
- There must be a causal connection between the provocation, the rage, anger, and the fatal act.

Adequate provocation is weighed on a case-by-case basis, but there are some absolutes. Words and gestures are insufficient provocation to reduce charges from murder to manslaughter.[9] Generally, a person who kills in response to physical attack or fear for the safety of his family will be charged with manslaughter. A person catching a spouse committing adultery will probably get manslaughter, but that rule does not necessarily apply to unmarried partners.

Often the homicide investigation will explore whether the defendant had time to "cool off" between the provocation and the crime. Generally, if there was time to cool off and the defendant killed anyway, the conviction will more likely be for murder than manslaughter.

The killing must be in reaction to the provocation. This deals with both the reason and the time frame of the act. A defendant cannot kill someone for an act that occurred several years ago and argue manslaughter.

Juries must decide heat of passion issues in light of the reasonable person test. How much provocation could a reasonable person withstand without retaliating? The defendant's tolerance threshold is not an issue. If the defendant was less restrained than the jury believes a reasonable person would be, then the verdict will be murder, not manslaughter.

In many manslaughter trials, defendants claim they acted in self-defense. If the jury finds the defendant's actions reasonable in light of the circumstances, the defendant may be acquitted.

Involuntary manslaughter refers to two types of homicides, **criminal negligence manslaughter** and **unlawful act manslaughter.** Criminal negligence manslaughter is the crime of causing the death of a person by negligent or reckless conduct. For instance, the crime of a person who leaves a campfire burning that later burns down a home killing the occupant would be considered criminally negligent manslaughter. Unlawful act manslaughter is where the defendant committed a crime that resulted in the death of a person. Many traffic deaths fall into this category, although some states have a special category of homicide entitled **homicide by vehicle.** Homicides by vehicle are not considered to be premeditated, but often the defendant broke one or more traffic ordinances in the process of causing the fatal accident.

EUTHANASIA

An irony of advances in medicine is that many terminally ill people are alive today who would not have been decades ago. As a result, a **euthanasia,** or mercy killing movement has grown steadily since the 1970s. Advocates of euthanasia claim it gives people the right to end their life on their own terms. They say this gives the individual death with dignity.

HISTORICAL HIGHLIGHT
Oregon's Assisted Suicide Law—Death with Dignity or Murder?

In 1997, Oregon's *Death with Dignity Act* took effect. It allows doctors to provide a terminally ill patient with the means to end his or her life. Under the law, two Oregon doctors must agree that the patient has less than six months to live, has freely chosen to die, and is able to make critical health decisions. The law only applies to Oregon residents.

The law was enacted through a statewide referendum. Another referendum seeking to repeal the law failed. The question of whether the law is Constitutional has never been brought before the Supreme Court; however, the High Court has ruled that bans on assisted suicide on the books in New York and Washington state are Constitutional. More to the point, in each of those cases, the Court ruled that states had the right to decide the issue themselves.

In November of 2002, Attorney General John Ashcroft authorized federal drug enforcement agents to revoke the licenses of doctors who assist patients in committing suicide using federally regulated medications under the federal Controlled Substances Act. However, by April of 2002, U.S. District Judge Robert Jones ruled that states' rights to determine what constitutes legitimate medical practices cannot be overridden by the CSA. Recently a federal appeals court agreed with Oregon and the case may be headed for the Supreme Court.[10]

Feelings run strong on both sides of the issue. Pro-life conservatives fear that assisted suicide laws erode legal safeguards protecting life. They see assisted suicide as tied closely to the abortion issue. Pro-choice activists claim to be protecting the right of the individual to choose the time and manner of his or her own death. They view assisted suicide as a reprieve from months of unwanted suffering. Like the abortion issue, assisted suicide is an issue that will be with us for many years to come.

Often, however, seriously ill patients are unable to end their own life. They must be assisted to do so. When someone assists another person to commit suicide, it is sometimes hard to distinguish this act from murder.

The debate rages within the medical community as well. Doctors are pledged to provide care as long as there is any hope of recovery. Even when the patient is terminal, doctors are sworn to make the patient as comfortable as possible. Some have argued that patients who request their doctors provide them with drugs to end their life should have their wish granted under certain conditions. Some states have even passed "doctor-assisted suicide" laws.

How far can doctors and family members go to assist a suicide? The answer obviously varies from state to state. Generally speaking, without assisted suicide laws in place, it is criminal to aid in someone's suicide.

Doctors also confront the problem of how long to leave someone on artificial life support systems. Some patients leave doctors **living wills** that spell out clearly what steps should be taken to revive them and under what circumstances. Living wills should be notarized documents signed freely by an individual of sound mind. Unfortunately, often older people are pressured by family members and doctors to sign documents they might not normally sign. A living will signed under duress is not a valid document.

INFANTICIDE

Infanticide is the murder of a newborn or very young child. Although some cultures condone or at least tacitly permit infanticide, Anglo–American jurisprudence has traditionally held it to be a crime.

Infanticide is different from abortion in that the child has been born. In fact, the live birth of the child is one element the prosecution must prove in an infanticide case. Many infanticides are accomplished by simply abandoning the baby in an area where it would die from exposure and dehydration. Often when children are found still alive, the charge of reckless endangerment or attempted murder is brought against the mother, if she can be located.

KILLINGS THAT ARE NOT CRIMES

Justifiable homicides are those killings committed out of duty with no criminal intent. When the state executes a person who has been duly convicted, the killing is not a murder. In fact, even if evidence that the person was denied due process comes to light later, the state operates under the color of **sovereign immunity.** Sovereign immunity is a holdover from the English legal system. The king could do no wrong, and to a large extent was above the law.

Military actions are not murders. The need for the state to protect itself supersedes criminal law. For the most part, members of the military on active duty operate under the Uniform Code of Military Justice (UCMJ). The UCMJ proscribes appropriate behavior for active duty personnel. The UCMJ must conform to the Constitution. Of course, the military must be subject to the civilian authorities.

Killings done in self-defense are not murders. For a full discussion of self-defense see Chapter 14, "Defenses."

PRACTICE POINTERS

The consequences for those convicted of murder or any of the related offenses are so serious that these cases deserve great attention, regardless of what side of the case you are working for. Capital cases in particular have been in the spotlight and will continue to receive media and academic attention. Sloppy handling of these cases can result in grave injustices, destroyed careers, and contributes to the potential breakdown of the justice system. Representation of a capital defendant should not be taken lightly. It is an awesome responsibility, whether you are part of the prosecution team or the defense.

HISTORICAL HIGHLIGHT
Dr. Death Gets "Life"

Dr. Jack Kevorkian earned the nickname Dr. Death for his role in 130 assisted suicides. Kevorkian was the most outspoken and flamboyant advocate of assisted suicide during the late 80s and early 1990s. He developed a "death machine" that allowed terminally ill patients or a family member to easily administer a lethal injection.

Kevorkian was charged with murder five times, but was acquitted the first four times. He was known for his moving testimony that persuaded jurors not to convict. In each of the first four cases, Kevorkian had merely been present when the patient had committed suicide. But the fifth trial was different.

By now, Kevorkian was no longer licensed to practice medicine. His license had been revoked after he botched a surgical procedure on a recently deceased patient. Kevorkian attempted to remove organs for transplant while performing surgery on a kitchen table. Surgeons noted that the organs were so poorly handled that they were useless for transplants.

In this case, Kevorkian went further than just assisting a patient. He gave Thomas Youk, a man suffering from Lou Gehrig's disease, a lethal injection. And to erase any doubt, he videotaped the procedure. Kevorkian gave the tape to the popular television magazine *60 Minutes*, which broadcast it.

The tape was used as evidence at trial. This time the jury convicted Kevorkian of second-degree murder and sentenced him to 10 to 25 years in prison. In September of 2000, at age 72, Kevorkian requested to be released on bail while he appeals his conviction. The request was denied. He asked again in 2003, but the request was again rejected. Considering his age, his 10- to 25-year sentence may in reality be a life sentence.

There are resources available today that were not available a few years ago. These include national and state bar associations, and professional associations like the following:

- National Association of Legal Investigators at *www.nali.com*
- The National Legal Aid and Defender Association at *www.nlada.org*
- The National District Attorneys' Association at *www.ndaa.org/*
- The National Association of Attorneys General at *www.naag.org/*
- The National Association of Criminal Defense Lawyers at *www.criminaljustice.org*
- The American Bar Association's Criminal Justice Section at *www.abanet.org/crimjust/*
- The National Criminal Justice Reference Service at *www.ncjrs.org/*

Resources, especially research, at local colleges and universities with criminal justice programs or journalism programs are also available. In addition, many law schools operate law clinics that may be of assistance for research, investigation, and planning for a murder trial.

HISTORICAL HIGHLIGHT
Infanticide in the Suburbs: The Peterson/Grossberg Case

Brian Peterson and Amy Grossberg were high school sweethearts from the affluent New York suburb of Wyckoff, New Jersey. They attended different colleges— he at Gettysburg College in Pennsylvania, and she at the University of Delaware—but they continued to see each other.

Amy became pregnant in early 1996. Amy claimed not to know she was pregnant, and even a doctor who treated her in July 1996 noted in his medical records that she did not appear to be pregnant. Nevertheless, in November she delivered a full-term baby boy.

Amy's boyfriend Brian delivered the baby in a Newark, Delaware, motel room. Brian threw the child into a nearby dumpster. The child died from multiple skull fractures and trauma from shaking. Police soon identified the child as belonging to Brian and Amy. Delaware prosecutors at first stated that they would seek the death penalty in the case.

The prosecutors played Brian against Amy. At first, neither would talk about the incident. However, once Brian's attorneys negotiated a manslaughter charge for him, he agreed to testify against Amy. Amy then negotiated a manslaughter plea, and was sentenced to two and a half years. A first-degree murder conviction for either of the two could have carried the death penalty or a life imprisonment sentence. Both were released early for good behavior, after serving half their sentence. Amy went on to counsel pregnant women as part of her parole.[11]

The case raised disturbing questions. First, how could two seemingly affluent, "all-American" kids murder their child? Second, several questions arose concerning fairness:

- Did these two get lighter sentences because they were affluent and could afford top-flight lawyers?
- Amy claimed not to know she had delivered a baby. If that is true, was she forced to plea to a manslaughter charge because her boyfriend lied to avoid a first degree murder charge?
- Does this case illustrate the way that plea bargaining skews justice? Does the first one to enter a plea get the better deal? If so, doesn't that encourage the most culpable person to cooperate resulting in a harsher sentence for others involved?

CHAPTER SUMMARY

Prosecutors in murder cases must prove that a crime was committed or establish a corpus delicti beyond a reasonable doubt. Where investigators cannot produce a body, circumstantial evidence such as evidence of violence, witnesses to a struggle, and various forensic evidence can be pieced together to provide evidence of a crime.

A person committing first-degree murder must form the intent to kill his victim. The law requires the person to have "malice aforethought." The deadly weapon doctrine is used to establish intent to kill. If the defendant uses a deadly weapon to kill a person, it is assumed the requisite intent was present. Transferred intent can occur when the victim is not the one the defendant meant to kill.

Defendants who possess an "intent to do serious bodily harm" are frequently convicted of second-degree murder. Cases involving people who have no intent to cause bodily harm, but are reckless in their behavior, generally result in manslaughter charges.

The felony murder rule states "Felony murder is committed when a person, acting alone or in concert with others, commits or attempts to commit one of nine predicate felonies, . . ." and "in the furtherance of such crime or of immediate flight therefrom, he or another participant, if there be any, causes the death of a person other than one of the participants." In jurisdictions who still have felony murder laws, defendants can possibly face the death penalty if they "had the culpable mental state of reckless indifference to human life."

Manslaughter is a classification of criminal homicide that is less than murder. Manslaughter can either be voluntary or involuntary. Voluntary manslaughter is where the defendant acted willfully, but was somewhat justified in his actions. Sentences for manslaughter are far less than those for murder.

Murder charges may be reduced to manslaughter charges if the court believes the crime occurred in the heat of passion as long as other elements are present.

Involuntary manslaughter refers to two types of homicides—criminal negligence manslaughter, which is the crime of causing the death of a person by negligent or reckless conduct; and unlawful act manslaughter, which is when the defendant committed a crime that resulted in the death of a person.

Euthanasia is mercy killing. When someone assists another person to commit suicide, it is sometimes hard to distinguish this act from murder. Some states have even passed "doctor-assisted suicide" laws.

Infanticide is the murder of a newborn or very young child. Prosecutors must establish that the child was born alive to prosecute an infanticide case.

Justifiable homicides are those killings committed out of duty with no criminal intent. Executions are killings that are not murders, as are military actions. Killings done in self-defense are not murders.

KEY TERMS

Conspiracy: An agreement between two or more persons to engage in a criminal act. It requires at least one overt act and is punished as if the parties accomplished the objective of their agreement.

Corpus delicti: Literally "the body of the crime," the fact that a crime has been committed.

Criminal homicide: A killing that breaks the law, designated as either murder or manslaughter.

Criminal negligence manslaughter: The crime of causing the death of a person by negligent or reckless conduct.

Deadly weapon doctrine: Use of a deadly weapon is proof of intent to kill.

Euthanasia: The act of causing death to end pain and distress. Also called mercy killing.

Felony murder rule: The rule that a death occuring by accident or chance during the course of the commission of a felony is first-degree murder.

First-degree murder: Murder committed deliberately with malice aforethought, that is, with premeditation.

Heat of passion: The expression for a mental state on the part of a criminal defendant adequate in law to reduce the crime from murder to manslaughter.

Homicide: The killing of a human being.

Homicide by vehicle: A form of criminal negligence manslaughter reserved for a person operating a motor vehicle.

Infanticide: The murder of a newborn or very young child.

Intent to do serious bodily harm: A defendant's plan to injure another.

Intent to kill: The plan, course, or means a person conceives to take another life.

Involuntary manslaughter: The unintentional killing of a human being by a person engaged in doing some unlawful act not amounting to a felony, or in doing some lawful act in a manner tending to cause death or great bodily injury.

Justifiable homicides: Those killings committed out of duty with no criminal intent.

Living will: A document in which a person sets forth directions regarding medical treatment to be given if she becomes unable to participate in decisions regarding her health care.

Malice aforethought: An intent to kill or injure, or the deliberate commission of a dangerous or deadly act.

Military actions: Actions carried by members of the armed services under the direction of appropriate civilian authorities.

Res gestae theory: Literally "the acts of the thing," the acts or words through which an event speaks.

Sovereign immunity: The protection from lawsuits government agencies enjoy.

Transferred intent: The doctrine that if a defendant who intends to injure one person unintentionally harms another, the intent is transferred to the person who is unintentionally harmed.

Unlawful act manslaughter: Where the defendant committed a crime that resulted in the death of a person.

Voluntary manslaughter: A homicide committed with the intent to kill, but without deliberation, premeditation, or malice.

DISCUSSION QUESTIONS

1. In your opinion, when is the killing of a human being justified?
2. Should states outlaw assisted suicide?
3. Research the felony murder rule in your jurisdiction. If it has one, what underlying felonies are included?
4. Should drivers who drive drunk and kill be charged with murder?
5. Under what circumstances should heat of passion be a defense to murder?

FOR FURTHER READING

1. Scottoline, L. (2001). *The Vendetta Defense*. HarperCollins. This legal thriller by a former Philadelphia attorney explores a very delayed vendetta as defense to a murder committed by a senior citizen for wrongs long ago.

2. Berendt, J. (1994). *Midnight in the Garden of Good and Evil.* Random House. Nonfiction account of a Savannah, Georgia, murder trial; later made into a movie starring Kevin Spacey.
3. Capote, T. (1994 ed.). *In Cold Blood: A True Account of Multiple Murder and Its Consequences.* Vintage Books. Classic true crime nonfiction, made into an award-winning movie.

QUOTES FOR CHAPTER EIGHT

1. *In films, murders are always very clean. I show how difficult it is and what a messy thing it is to kill a man.*
Alfred Hitchcock
2. *. . . if we believe that murder is wrong and not admissible in our society, then it has to be wrong for everyone, not just individuals but governments as well.*
Helen Prejean
3. *O, my offence is rank, it smells to heaven;*
It hath the primal eldest curse upon 't,
A brother's murder.
Shakespeare, *Hamlet*, Act 3, Scene 3
4. *Murder begins where self-defense ends.*
Georg Buchner
5. *To my mind to kill in war is not a whit better than to commit ordinary murder.*
Albert Einstein

ENDNOTES

1. Genesis 4:12.
2. T. J. Gardner, *Criminal Law: Principles and Cases*, 3rd ed. (West Publishing Co., 1985).
3. J. R. Nash, *Bloodletters and Badmen: A Narrative Encyclopedia of the American Criminals from the Pilgrims to the Present* (New York: M. Evans & Co, 1974).
4. *State v. Neumann*, 262 N.W. 2d 426 (1978).
5. *Hopkins v. Reeves*, 525 U.S. 88 (1998).
6. *New York v. Gladman*, 41 N.Y. 2d 123 (1976).
7. *Commonwealth v. Matchett*, 436 N. E. 2d 400 (1982).
8. *Tison v. Arizona*, 481 U.S. 137 at 146 (1987).
9. *Allen v. United States*, 157 U.S. 675 (1895).
10. *Oregon v. Ashcroft*, 368 F. 3d 1118 (9th Cir. 2004).
11. "Baby-slay mom returns to N.J.," *Daily News* (New York) (May 11, 2000).

CHAPTER 9
Crimes Against the Person: Violence

CHAPTER OBJECTIVES

After studying this chapter, you should be able to:

- Explain the common law concepts of assault and battery
- Explain the modern criminal law concept of assault and list some common variations of assault
- Define common law rape and explain how modern rape statutes differ from the common law definition
- Understand rape shield laws and the type of evidence they exclude and allow
- Define domestic violence and describe federal efforts to reduce its occurrence
- Define hate crime and explain the Supreme Court's major hate crime decisions
- Define kidnapping and abduction
- Explain the tension between the right of parents to raise their children and the right of the state to punish parent behavior it deems to be child abuse

CHAPTER CONTENTS

> *Women have got to make the world safe for men since men have made it so darned unsafe for women.*
>
> **Lady Nancy Astor**

INTRODUCTION

In this chapter we consider crimes of violence against the person that do not necessarily result in loss of life. As you will see, a great many of these crimes are directed against women and children. Rape, indecent assault, domestic violence, abduction, and child abuse strike women and children with greater frequency than men. Old attitudes die hard, and in the Common Law system, women and children were frequently regarded as nothing more than chattel. Domestic violence and child abuse are remnants of the old system of laws that gave women little power over their lives and vested responsibility for the family in the male head.

Violence against women is a major problem in the United States today. Some estimates set the probability that a woman will be the victim of a violent crime during her lifetime at 75 percent.[1] Other studies suggest that violence is the leading cause of injuries to women ages 15 to 44.[2] Clearly, violent crime strikes women early and often.

RAPE AND OTHER SEX CRIMES

Rape was traditionally defined as forced sexual intercourse with a woman, not one's wife. Rape was a serious offense at Common Law, often punished harshly if the victim were high-born. Remedies included payment of wergild (see Chapter 2) to the family of the victim, presumably because the victim's value on the marriage market was decreased by the loss of her virtue.

Today, every state has amended its rape laws to reflect that both males and females can be victims of rape. Most have also amended the law to allow at least limited claims of marital rape. For example, Virginia was one of 32 states that exempted spouses from prosecution for rape under some circumstances. A married woman in Virginia could only have her husband charged with rape if the two were not living together or if she was physically harmed. However, in 2002 a proposed amendment was finally passed that now allows prosecution for rape regardless of whether the couple were cohabitating or the spouse who was raped suffered physical harm.[3]

Rape is not the only sexual offense on the books in most states. They generally have a hierarchy of sex crimes in their crime codes. These include rape as the most serious of sexual offenses and include sexual assault short of rape (cases in which intercourse isn't successful), indecent assault or indecent touching (in which there is groping or other offensive touching, but no sexual act is performed or forced), incest (sexual activity between relatives within a prescribed degree of sanguinity), and offenses such as public exposure. Because each state had a different set of sexual offenses on its books, practitioners must review the offenses in their jurisdiction. The elements required to be proven by the state vary greatly, as do the specific definitions of sexual acts covered.

Most rape statutes require that three elements be proven in a rape case. These are:

- Proof that a sex act took place, with the particular statute-defining sex act. Generally, the sex act that constitutes rape is vaginal intercourse, but it can also include anal intercourse for both male and female victims as well as oral sex acts. Many state statutes require proof that there was penetration of the vagina or anus by the defendant's penis. Ejaculation is not required to prove rape.
- Proof that the charged sex act took place by force or threat of force. Most modern rape statutes don't require that there be physical evidence of force. The victim's testimony that she was forced or was afraid is enough. She need not risk physical harm by fighting back.
- Proof that the sex act performed by force or threat of force was without consent or under circumstances that made consent either invalid (as in statutory rape) or impossible to get (as when the victim is too intoxicated to validly consent or is incapacitated in some way that impairs the victim's ability to freely consent).

THE ROLE OF PHYSICAL EVIDENCE IN RAPE CASES

Physical evidence plays a major role in rape cases. In particular, the presence of semen and saliva can be powerful evidence that, at the very least, sexual activity took place. With the advances made in DNA analysis, identifying whose semen or saliva is present on the victim has become a routine matter. Experts can now state with almost absolute certainty who left biological material at the scene or on the victim.

In a sexual assault case, it's crucial that evidence be promptly gathered and preserved. Unfortunately, far too few rape victims report the crime immediately. Many feel angry and upset or are in a state of shock after the attack. However, prompt reporting and immediate medical attention are crucial to a successful prosecution. Today, most police departments have available specially trained counselors who can work with rape victims and help gather the necessary evidence as soon as possible. Special rape kits are generally used to gather evidence and assure that the appropriate chain of custody for the evidence is followed. Most local governments also have a victim assistance program to help victims through the many stages of a criminal prosecution.

DEFENSE TO RAPE

The most common defense to a rape charge is that the victim consented to sexual activity. Consent is a valid defense as long as the case is not one of statutory rape in which consent is not legally possible due to the age of the victim or in which consent was obtained through trickery or coercion.

In a rape case, the prosecution must prove as an essential element of the crime that a sexual act took place and that the victim did not consent. This is part of the state's case in chief. Sexual activity and lack of consent can be proven directly by the victim's testimony and indirectly through evidence such as bruises, medical damage, ripped clothing, and other signs of a struggle or that physical force had been used. The defense may question the victim about the physical aspects of the attack and ask her if she consented.

Once the prosecution has rested its case, the defense may again raise consent by having the defendant testify. He can also present circumstantial evidence to bolster his claim, such as evidence that the victim freely entered his apartment or bedroom or that the two had sexual relations in the past. This tactic is very likely when the victim and the defendant have known each other for a time.

If the rape case involves a stranger and there was no biological evidence obtained from the victim (as could happen if there is a delay in reporting the crime, or the assailant used a condom, or the act was not completed, or the victim showered before reporting the crime), a common tactic is to claim the victim has misidentified her assailant. This defense typically involves casting doubt on the victim's state of mind and ability to make a positive identification. Given the trauma associated with an attack and that most attacks aren't witnessed, a claim of mistaken identity can be an effective defense.

RAPE SHIELD LAWS

Before the enactment of rape shield laws, defendants frequently attempted to show that their victims were less than chaste. Defendants tried to cast doubt on their victims' credibility by showing that the victims were sexually experienced. The tactic was also used as a way to discourage victims from coming forward. Many were reluctant to discuss their sexual encounters with strangers and on the public record. As a result, many rapes went unreported or unprosecuted.

As women began pressuring for fair treatment in sexual assault cases, states began passing rape shield laws. **Rape shield laws** are a codified rule of evidence that provide for the exclusion of a rape victim's sexual history unless it is directly relevant to his or her consent or other evidence in the case. Most rape shield laws provide that evidence of past sexual conduct is inadmissible in a rape trial. The laws are based on the premise that evidence of past sexual conduct with others other than the defendant simply aren't relevant to the question of whether the victim consented to sex with the defendant in this case. Rape shield laws codify and reiterate that such evidence simply isn't relevant.

A typical rape shield law from Virginia provides that:

> evidence of the complaining witness's unchaste character or prior sexual conduct shall not be admitted. Unless the complaining witness voluntarily agrees otherwise, evidence of specific instances of his or her prior sexual conduct shall be admitted only if it is relevant and is:

HISTORICAL HIGHLIGHT
Date Rape Drugs Are Rapists' Dream and Victims' Nightmare

What if a rapist could pick his victim, sedate her without her knowledge, violate her sexually, and walk away safe knowing she won't remember a thing? Far from being the fantasy of a sociopath, the scenario plays out every day, especially on college campuses. A woman whose new acquaintance hands her a drink may very well wake hours later, not realizing she has been raped thanks to a drug known chemically as flunitrazapam and by the brand name Rohypnol. The drug is manufactured by Hoffman-LaRoche as a sleeping aid for insomnia and to quiet psychotic patients, but hasn't been approved in the United States. The drug reduces inhibitions. But it does more. Those who take it have no memory of what happens while they are under its influence. The drug is popularly known as the date rape drug and can be combined with other drugs common on the college scene such as GHB, or gamma hydroxybutyrate, another unapproved drug. Both drugs are colorless and odorless when slipped into a drink, although they may have a salty flavor.[4]

How do rapists get drugs not on any FDA-approved list? At least some order them over the Internet, if a recent prosecution is any indication. Two South Carolina brothers sold kits over the Internet from which purchasers could produce GHB. The kits provided some of the basic ingredients needed to produce the drug along with instructions on how to get the remainder of the ingredients locally. They were arrested after law enforcement officers came across their website and ordered some of the kits.[5]

1. Evidence offered to provide an alternative explanation for physical evidence of the offense charged which is introduced by the prosecution, limited to evidence designed to explain the presence of semen, pregnancy, disease, or physical injury to the complaining witness's intimate parts. . . .[6]

Some evidence can still be admitted. Evidence that the victim had consensual sex with the defendant before is admissible if the court finds it relevant to the question of whether the victim consented this time. Evidence that the victim had sex with someone else in the hours or days preceding the alleged rape if there is physical evidence of sexual activity (such as evidence of injury, but no biological evidence tying the victim to the defendant). In that case, prior sexual contact that could have caused the injury is relevant to showing that it was someone else other than the defendant who did the damage.

Evidence that the victim discussed wishing to have a sexual relationship with the defendant before the alleged rape, even if that evidence reveals prior sex acts with others, may also be admissible. In general, the evidence that rape shield laws exclude is evidence of unchaste character. A prostitute's sexual history would be excluded in most cases, although evidence that she had sex for money with the defendant before may be admitted to show that she consented this time also.

HISTORICAL HIGHLIGHT
Rape Shield Law Can't Exclude Victim's Sexually Explicit E-mail Addressed to Alleged Assailant

It began with a dinner date in November 1996. Oliver Jovanovic was a Columbia University doctoral student close to completing a Ph.D. in molecular biology when he arranged a dinner date with a Barnard College coed he had met in an Internet chat room. The two had exchanged a series of e-mail messages with heavy sexual content. In some of the messages she identified herself as a sadomasochist. In another she described herself as a submissive partner and told Jovanovic that she was dating a sadomasochist.

After dinner the two went to Jovanovic's apartment. What happened next is unclear. The Barnard student claimed that Jovanovic tied her up, bit her, molested her with a baton, dripped hot wax on her, and held her captive for 20 hours, all against her will. Jovanovic claimed the activities were consensual.[7] At the trial that followed, the defense sought to introduce the e-mail messages from the alleged victim and to question her about any prior sadomasochistic sexual activity. The trial judge ruled the evidence inadmissible under New York state's rape shield laws, and a jury convicted him. He was sentenced to at least 15 years.[8]

The case was appealed and the conviction overturned. The appeals court ruled that New York's Rape Shield Law wasn't meant to exclude evidence of the victim's interest in sadomasochistic sexual activity when her consent to such activity was at the heart of the case. The e-mail can be used to show the victim's state of mind about consent as well as the defendant's reasonable belief about the victim's intentions. The case was scheduled for a second trial in November 2001, but was dismissed when the victim declined to testify a second time.[9]

ASSAULT

Assault is an act of force or threat of force intended to inflict harm upon a person or to put the person in fear that such harm is imminent. Rape and the related offenses discussed earlier are specific forms of assault. At Common Law, assault did not involve the infliction of physical force. Rather, it was an act by the perpetrator that placed the victim in fear that bodily harm was imminent. Battery was the actual physical harm. Today, most crime codes combine the two into the crime of assault. States often create categories of assault, grading the crime in accordance with its seriousness. Possible criminal charges stemming from a bar brawl, for example, could include simple assault, aggravated assault, assault with a deadly weapon (if one is used) and assault with intent to kill, depending on the seriousness of the harm inflicted.

Other modern offenses more akin to the Common Law concept of assault as an act placing the victim in fear of imminent harm include ethnic intimidation, making terroristic threats, harassment, stalking, and making bomb threats. Each has its own set of unique elements that the prosecution must prove beyond a reasonable doubt. For example, in Pennsylvania the Commonwealth must prove that someone it charges with stalking engaged in "*. . . a course of conduct or repeatedly commits acts toward another person, including following the person without proper authority, under circumstances which demonstrate . . . an intent to place the person in reasonable fear of bodily injury or an intent to cause substantial emotional distress to the person.*"[10] Always check the law in your jurisdiction for guidance on the specific elements required to be proven in a particular case.

Some states have enacted statutes that create a special class of assault for the unauthorized administration of an intoxicant. These are generally meant to punish drugging a victim, particularly when the intent is to get the victim in a vulnerable position in order to do him or her harm. For example, in Pennsylvania it is a third-degree felony to "*substantially impair [the victim's] power to appraise or control his or her conduct by administering, without the knowledge of the complainant, drugs or other intoxicants,*" when the defendant does so in order to facilitate a sexual assault. The law is meant to punish those who slip their victims drugs such as Rohypnol and other "date rape" drugs. Doing so can result in the imposition of an additional 10-year sentence on top of the sentence for the underlying sexual assault.[11]

ESSENTIAL ELEMENTS OF ASSAULT

As you have seen in the previous discussion, each type of assault has its own specific proof requirements. It is impossible to provide a general list of elements of assault that would cover the wide variety of crimes that fall under the umbrella of "assault." However, the following example of a state assault statute serves as a starting point for analyzing the essential elements of assault:

The defendant commits assault if he or she:

- attempts to cause or knowingly, recklessly, or intentionally causes bodily injury to another; or
- negligently causes bodily injury to another with a deadly weapon; or
- attempts by physical menace to place another in fear of imminent serious bodily injury.[12]

The statute defines bodily injury as "*impairment of physical condition or substantial pain*" and serious bodily injury as "*Bodily injury which creates a substantial risk of death or which causes serious, permanent disfigurement, or protracted loss or impairment of the function of any bodily member or organ.*" Deadly weapon is defined as "*Any firearm, whether loaded or unloaded, or any device designed as a weapon and capable of producing death or serious bodily injury, or any other device or instrumentality which, in the manner in which it is used or intended to be used, is calculated or likely to produce death or serious bodily injury.*"[13]

As you can see, the simple assault statute above allows room for charging a defendant with assault for a number of acts, including injuring someone in an automobile accident, leaving a gun unlocked and unattended so that as a consequence someone is injured by it, or threatening people in such a way that they fear for their life. Depending on which subsection the defendant is charged with, the prosecution must prove that there was bodily injury or serious bodily injury as that term is defined in the statute. Because there are so many acts that can constitute assault and so many definitions to consider, proving assault can be challenging. Many prosecutors use a simple checklist during the presentation to make sure each element has been proven.

Generally, aggravated assault can be charged if the state can prove that the defendant attempted to cause or caused serious bodily injury to the victim under circumstances manifesting extreme indifference to the value of human life. In some jurisdictions, simple assault is charged as aggravated assault if the victim belongs to a class of persons designated by the legislature as being owed additional protection under the criminal law. These categories commonly involve police and firefighting personnel, teachers, and public officials.[14] Simple assault is often graded as a misdemeanor, while aggravated assault is generally graded as a felony of the first or second degree.

DOMESTIC VIOLENCE

Domestic violence in this country is overwhelmingly directed at women by men. According to the Department of Justice, 92 percent of all domestic violence incidents involve men directing violence at women.[15] The death toll is high. In 1996, 30 percent of all female murder victims in the United States were killed by their husbands or boyfriends.[16] For the 20-year period from 1976 to 1996, the total toll of women murdered by their husbands or boyfriends stood at over 31,000 women.[17]

Most states do not make domestic violence a specific crime. Rather, battery, assault, aggravated assault, harassment, stalking, and other crimes involving physical or mental injury to a victim when perpetrated by the victim's partner are characterized as domestic violence. The best way to look at domestic violence may be to view it as a syndrome, consisting of a series of criminal acts perpetrated against a spouse or paramour rather than as a specific crime.

Until recently, enforcement of criminal laws when the victim was the perpetrator's partner was spotty. Many in law enforcement viewed cases of domestic violence as nuisance cases, and sometimes even refused to respond to calls or arrest the perpetrator. In cases where law enforcement did respond, often the matter was dropped when the victim refused to press charges or to cooperate with police. It has only been in the last few decades that the psychological forces at play in domestic violence have begun to be understood. A victim with no or few economic resources, no place to go, and fear of the perpetrator often saw no way out but to reconcile and drop the charges.

With the advent of more shelters for victims and their families, the availability of educational and job opportunities, and the increasing recognition that acts of violence, no matter who the victim is, should be punished, more victims are cooperating with law enforcement. As a result, today there are far more successful prosecutions than in decades past.

FEDERAL EFFORTS TO COMBAT DOMESTIC VIOLENCE

Recent years have seen an increase in federal involvement in domestic violence issues. Because it saw domestic violence as a problem affecting not just families and communities, but the economy as a whole, Congress passed the Violence Against Women Act **(VAWA)** in 1994, and declared that "all persons within the United States shall have the right to be free from crimes of violence motivated by gender."[18]

VAWA was enacted under the authority of the Commerce Clause of the U.S. Constitution, and sought to end the cycle of violence and draw more women into the workplace and economy by strengthening state efforts to control domestic violence and by enacting federal crimes related to domestic violence.

One provision that received widespread attention was Section 13981(c), which declared that:

> A person (including a person who acts under color of any statute, ordinance, regulation, custom, or usage of any State) who commits a crime of violence motivated by gender and thus deprives another of the right declared in subsection (b) of this section [to be free of crimes of violence motivated by gender] shall be liable to the party injured, in an action for the recovery of compensatory and punitive damages, injunctive and declaratory relief, and such other relief as a court may deem appropriate.

Essentially, VAWA gave victims of domestic or sexual violence a federal private right of action against the assailant for damages. The first test of the statute came when a student at Virginia Tech claimed she had been forcibly raped by two members of the varsity football team. She was unsatisfied with the administrative punishments meted out by the university, and sued the university and the students in federal court for damages, as provided for in VAWA. The defendants raised the Constitution as a bar to the lawsuit, claiming that Congress exceeded its authority under the Commerce Clause when it enacted the law. The U.S. Supreme Court heard the case, *United States v. Morrison*, and concluded Congress didn't have the authority to ". . . regulate non-economic, violent criminal conduct based solely on that conduct's aggregate effect on interstate commerce."[19]

The Supreme Court decision has wider implications for Congressional efforts to enact civil and criminal penalties for crimes that occur within state boundaries, and most likely will mean Congress will not set up a parallel federal criminal and tort law system.

In response to the *Morrison* decision, VAWA was amended in 2000. Rather than relying on the economic impact domestic and sexual violence had on women, Congress focused on providing criminal penalties that punish behavior that crosses state lines, a traditional authority used to enact federal criminal laws. The major criminal provisions that survived in the original VAWA and were added in VAWA II are:

- *18 U.S.C. § 2261 (a): Interstate Domestic Violence:* Makes it a federal crime for anyone to cross a state line with the intent to injure, harass, or intimidate an intimate partner if, in the course of or as a result of such travel, the perpetrator intentionally commits a violent crime that causes bodily harm to his or her partner.
- *18 U.S.C. § 2261 (a) (2): Coercing Across State Lines:* Makes it a federal crime to cause an intimate partner to cross a state line by force, coercion, duress, or fraud and, in the course or as a result of that conduct, intentionally committing a crime of violence and thereby causes bodily injury to the intimate partner.
- *18 U.S.C. 2262 § (a) (1) and (2): Interstate Violation of a Protective Order:* Makes it a federal crime for anyone to cross a state line or force an intimate partner to cross a state line with the intent to engage in conduct that violates a state protection from abuse order already in place.
- *18 U.S.C. § 2261A: Interstate Stalking:* Makes it a federal crime to cross a state line intending to injure or harass another person and then placing that person in

reasonable fear of death or serious bodily injury or reasonable fear of death or serious bodily injury to his or her immediate family.

● *18 U.S.C. § 922 (g) (1), (8), and (9): Possession of Firearm:* Makes it a federal crime for anyone who is subject to a state protection from abuse order, or has been convicted of a misdemeanor crime of domestic violence, or who has been convicted of a crime punishable by a year or more in prison to possess, transport, or receive a firearm or ammunition that has been in interstate or foreign commerce.

HATE CRIMES

In recent years there has been an increase in the number of state and local governments that have enacted what are popularly known as **hate crimes.** The U.S. Department of Justice defines hate or bias motivated crimes as "offenses motivated by hatred against a victim based on his or her race, religion, sexual orientation, handicap, ethnicity or national origin."[20]

Generally, hate crimes consist of enhanced punishment for crimes that are motivated by hate or bias against a group, ethnicity, or religion. The Department of Justice, in accordance with a federal law requiring collecting data nationwide on the prevalence of hate crimes, conducted a pilot study of hate crimes in a dozen states in the years 1997–1999. The agency analyzed over 3,000 reported hate crimes and found that of those victims, 3 were murdered, 4 abducted or kidnapped, 17 sexually assaulted, 42 robbed, and 2,138 assaulted. The most prevalent motivation was racial bias (61 percent), religious bigotry (14 percent), sexual orientation (13 percent), ethnicity (11 percent), and mental or physical disability (less than 1 percent).[21]

Today, there is hate crime legislation covering a wide range of bias, including:

● Race, ethnicity, and religion
● Sexual orientation
● Gender
● Institutional vandalism and interference with religious practices
● Mental and physical disability
● Age
● Political affiliation

The first model hate crime statute was developed by the Anti-Defamation League. The model language provides that: *"A person commits a Bias-Motivated Crime if, by reason of the actual or perceived race, color, religion, national origin, sexual orientation or gender of another individual or group of individuals . . ."* he violated the state's criminal laws such as murder, assault, battery, or the like. The model provision calls for bias-motivated crimes to be punished at least one degree greater than the underlying offense.

ESSENTIAL ELEMENTS OF A HATE CRIME

To obtain a conviction for a hate crime, the prosecution must prove the underlying criminal offense such as murder, rape, assault, battery, or harassment and also prove that the defendant was motivated to commit the crime by bias against a group or category covered by the specific hate crime law in the jurisdiction. That bias is an additional essential element of the offense. The Supreme Court has upheld enhanced penalties for hate crimes in face

HISTORICAL HIGHLIGHT
Victims of Domestic Violence Win Right to New Identity

One of the most pressing concerns victims of domestic violence may have when leaving their abusers is that the abuser will simply follow them. Moving to another address, finding a new job, and starting a new life is difficult for anyone, especially someone fleeing physical danger. Disappearing isn't easy, especially in a time when access to public and private databases has become relatively available and inexpensive.

Consider how easy it would be to track a victim's whereabouts with just one piece of information—the victim's Social Security number. If the victim was married to her abuser, he certainly had access to her Social Security number since it appears on their joint tax return. Social Security numbers, because they are unique to each holder, are commonly used on credit reports, and on medical, insurance, and school records. Today, anyone who can provide basic information such as a Social Security number and a credit card account number can get a credit report online in minutes. That credit report contains current addresses, phone numbers, and name of employer. Although it is a violation of federal law to access credit information for someone else without that person's permission, that's unlikely to stop an abuser who is intent on locating the victim.

To help domestic abuse victims establish new identities and avoid being tracked, the Social Security Administration now will issue new Social Security numbers to victims of domestic abuse and harassment. The policy went into effect in 1998, and allows victims to start new lives in relative anonymity. The Social Security Administration will cross-reference the numbers on earnings records to assure that victims later receive the retirement or disability payments to which they are entitled.

of a challenge that such laws violate the First Amendment because they punish speech in the form of intent to commit a crime based on prejudice, and not just the underlying crime.

Proving bias may be difficult in some cases. For example, belonging to a hate group or espousing racist or religiously bigoted views are generally considered free speech and free association privileges protected by the First Amendment. But even though expression of unpopular views may be protected, acting on those views is not. Thus, if a prosecutor has evidence that a defendant declared his intent to commit a crime against a member of a class protected by a hate law, and then took action, that is not protected. The closer in time to the crime statements showing the defendant's state of mind occur, the more likely that the evidence can be introduced to show intent.

In *Wisconsin v. Mitchell*, 508 U.S. 476 (1993), the Supreme Court considered Wisconsin's hate crime statute. The case involved a young black defendant who was convicted of selecting a white youth as target for a beating. A group of young black men had gathered at an apartment complex and talk turned to a scene in the film *Mississippi Burning* in which a white youth beat a black youth praying. Mitchell suggested the group beat a white youth, stating *"There goes a white boy; go get him."* The group chased the white boy down and beat him so severely he spent four days in a coma.

After a jury trial, Mitchell was found guilty beyond a reasonable doubt. The same jury concluded that Mitchell had been motivated by racial bias. As a result, Mitchell was sentenced to seven years in prison rather than the maximum two-year sentence for the underlying crime. He appealed, arguing that the hate crime statute that led to his lengthy sentence violated the First Amendment. The Wisconsin Supreme Court agreed, and ruled that the law effectively punished offensive thoughts.

On appeal to the U.S. Supreme Court, the state argued that the statute only punished offensive conduct, not thought (i.e., the offensive conduct of selecting a victim on the basis of race rather than the offensive thought of wanting to select a victim because of his race). The Court concluded that the use of speech as evidence of intent in a criminal prosecution does not violate the Constitution.

However, if the state statute doesn't require that the prosecution prove beyond a reasonable doubt as part of its case in chief that bias was the motivating factor for the crime, the enhanced sentence may not be Constitutional. That's the issue that faced the Supreme Court in *Apprendi v. New Jersey*, 530 U.S. 466 (2000). In 1994, a few days before Christmas, Apprendi, a white resident of the suburb of Vineland, New Jersey, shot several .22-caliber bullets into the home of an African American family who had recently moved into the previously all-white neighborhood. Apprendi was promptly arrested and told police he had fired into the home because he didn't want African Americans in the neighborhood. He was charged under New Jersey law with various offenses, none of which laid out a bias motivation. Apprendi plead guilty to one weapon charge, and the plea was accepted on condition that at sentencing the state could argue for an enhanced sentence due to the alleged racial motivation for the shooting. Apprendi agreed on condition he could raise the constitutionality of the enhanced sentence on appeal.

At the sentencing hearing, the prosecution presented evidence of bias, and the judge found by a preponderance of the evidence that racial bias was the motive for the shooting. The judge then enhanced the sentence as New Jersey's hate crime legislation allowed. He appealed, arguing that the due process clause of the Constitution required that a jury, not a judge, decide whether bias was the motive for the crime, and that the appropriate standard of proof was beyond a reasonable doubt. When the case reached the Supreme Court, a majority of the justices agreed. The Court held that *"The Constitution requires that any fact that increases the penalty for a crime beyond the prescribed statutory maximum, other than the fact of a prior conviction, must be submitted to a jury and proved beyond a reasonable doubt."*[22]

The Court ruled in 2003 that states can make it a crime to burn a cross. Virginia's legislature had passed a law that created a presumption that burning a cross was racially motivated and made it a crime to do so. The Supreme Court struck the presumption, but ruled that the state can charge and convict citizens who burn crosses with the intent to intimidate. Criminalizing cross burning does not violate the First Amendment.[23]

ABDUCTION AND KIDNAPPING

Perhaps no crime sends more chills down a parent's back than the thought of a child being abducted. Yet children disappear at an alarming rate every year. For example, the FBI reported that approximately 725,000 children disappeared in 2001. Not all these cases were stranger abductions, of course. Some were parental or other relative kidnapping, while other cases represent children and teens who have been reported as runaways or children who simply got lost or were the victims of accidents. However, of the total cases, stranger abduction cases (defined as missing in circumstances indicating that the disappearance was not voluntary) stood at 28,765. The figure includes children, teens, and adults.[24]

Because figures include all involuntary abductions, getting a clear picture of how many children really are taken by strangers and placed in grave danger or killed has been difficult. As a result, there has been a public perception that large numbers of young children are abducted and murdered every year. The U.S. Department of Justice has recently announced that it will begin tracking child abductions in a way more likely to paint an accurate picture of the pervasiveness of the problem. As of 2000, accurate data on a national level were being reported from 17 states, and that data indicated that abductions of children rarely result in death (only 1 out of 1,214 child kidnapping cases reported in 1997 from participating states).[25] The study revealed that of the cases looked at, the cases fell into three categories: parental kidnapping, acquaintance kidnapping, and stranger kidnapping. Parental kidnapping was least likely to result in physical harm to the victim, whereas acquaintance kidnapping carried the greatest risk of injury. The most likely victims of stranger kidnapping were young children, who were also most often taken from public places.[26]

Also in 2000, the Department of Justice began a large-scale study to finally get accurate figures for all categories of missing children, including those kidnapped and those who disappear for other reasons. The study is required by the Missing Children's Assistance Act and is ongoing.[27]

All 50 states as well as the federal government have laws in place criminalizing abduction, whether the victim is a child or an adult. In addition, removing a child from a custodial parent or guardian's care outside the parameters of a visitation order is a crime. Transporting a child across state lines in conjunction with a parental or other abduction violates federal law, as is transporting an abducted adult. But for a long time, there was very little coordination of efforts to recover missing children or adults since so many jurisdictions were involved. That all changed after several well-publicized cases involving the abduction and murder of children, including the abduction and murder of Adam Walsh and Polly Klass. Adam was snatched from a store in Florida in 1981, and Polly was abducted from a slumber party in her California home in 1993 and later found murdered.

STATE STATUTES

Kidnapping is generally defined as the crime of taking and detaining a person against his will by force, intimidation, or fraud. **Abduction** is generally defined as the illegal carrying away, by force or deception, of a person. Kidnapping can occur when the person is held even momentarily, whereas abduction requires that the victim be moved from one place to another. Both crimes may involve the demand for a ransom, and may be punished more severely when ransom is demanded.

Many states combine kidnapping and abduction into one offense and then create other offenses to cover situations outside the definition. A typical state kidnapping and abduction statute is Pennsylvania's. It provided that:

A person is guilty of kidnapping if he unlawfully removes another a substantial distance under the circumstances from the place where he is found, or if he unlawfully confines another for a substantial period of time in a place of isolation, with any of the following intentions:

- To hold for ransom or reward, or as a shield or hostage;
- To facilitate the commission of a felony or flight thereafter;
- To inflict bodily injury on or to terrorize the victim or another;
- To interfere with the performance by public officials of any governmental or public function.

The Pennsylvania statute goes on to define confinement or removal as unlawful if ". . . *it is accomplished by force, threat or deception, or, in the case of a person who is under the age of 14 years or an incapacitated person, if it is accomplished without the consent of a parent, guardian or other person responsible for general supervision of his welfare.* "[28]

Pennsylvania also prohibits unlawful restraint,[29] false imprisonment,[30] interfering with custody of children,[31] interfering with custody of committed persons,[32] concealment of whereabouts of child,[33] and luring a child into a motor vehicle.[34] Each crime has its own elements and its own penalty. For example, the crime of luring a child into a motor vehicle does not require proof of the intent to harm that child, only proof that the child was persuaded or threatened and that there was no permission given by a guardian.[35]

HISTORICAL HIGHLIGHT
The Lindbergh Baby Abduction

The first federal kidnapping law was known as the Lindbergh Law, and required that the victim be transported over a state line for federal jurisdiction to attach. Charles Lindbergh was the first man to fly a plane solo across the Atlantic, piloting the *Spirit of St. Louis* across the ocean on May 21, 1927. He would again attract national attention when his son was kidnapped and murdered.

The Lindbergh kidnapping began on March 1, 1932, when Charles Lindbergh's 20-month-old son disappeared from his crib at the family's Princeton, New Jersey, home.[36] A note left by the kidnappers demanded a ransom of $50,000. A baby believed to be the abducted child was found dead after the ransom was paid, and his suspected kidnapper was tried and executed. The FBI, which had no jurisdiction over kidnapping at the time, became involved because the ransom was paid in gold certificates, over which it did have jurisdiction. Its investigation eventually led to the suspect, Bruno Hauptmann, a carpenter who quit his job on the day the ransom was paid and began playing the stock market.

At the time, the trial was referred to as the Trial of the Century.[37] When the Lindbergh baby was kidnapped, it was not yet a federal offense to take and hold a person for ransom, but almost immediately such a law was proposed.[38] The current federal kidnapping statute was originally named the Lindbergh Act. It greatly expanded the influence of the Federal Bureau of Investigations, which used the law to crack down on a nationwide rash of abductions for ransom.[39]

ESSENTIAL ELEMENTS OF KIDNAPPING AND ABDUCTION

To prove kidnapping, the government must show that the victim was taken or detained against his or her will. If the victim is competent to testify and survives and can testify, her testimony can establish that the defendant took or detained her against her will. Of course, witnesses to the event can also testify as to what they observed. In the case of a young victim who cannot be qualified to testify due to his tender years, a witness or circumstantial evidence can be used. For example, it would be enough to show that the child taken was recovered in the defendant's presence or custody when the legal custodian also testifies that the defendant didn't have permission to take the child. Circumstantial evidence can also be used when the victim doesn't survive.

Kidnapping doesn't require that the perpetrator demand a ransom. Since state laws differ, always check the specific statute in your jurisdiction for the essential elements the prosecutor must prove.

FEDERAL STATUTES

Federal law defines a kidnapper as someone who "unlawfully seizes, confines, inveigles, decoys, kidnaps, abducts, or carries away and holds for ransom or reward or otherwise any person . . ." and transports that person ". . . in interstate or foreign commerce, regardless of whether the person was alive when transported across a State boundary if the person was alive when the transportation began."[40] Kidnapping those under the age of 18 carries the potential for a longer sentence than if the victim is an adult. Likewise, if the young victim is subjected to life-threatening treatment or sexual or physical abuse, the penalty may be increased when the defendant's sentence is calculated under the federal Sentencing Guidelines.[41]

CHILD ABUSE AND NEGLECT

When children are concerned, government plays an important role. Since Elizabethan days, government (whether king or state or federal jurisdiction) has served in the role of **parens patriae.** That role has required government to protect the interests of those who cannot protect themselves. As early as 1890, the U.S. Supreme Court held that the *parens patriae* theory was inherent in the power of the state to regulate the treatment of children.[42] In addition, states have rights under their general police powers to regulate the treatment of children within their jurisdictions.

On the other end of the spectrum is the power of parents to regulate family life in accordance with their personal, religious, and ethical belief systems. This constitutionally derived power at times conflicts with the government's view under its *parens patriae* and police powers. There are times that the state may seek to interfere with religious belief when that belief may harm children. Parents cannot in most cases deny life-saving treatment to their children on the basis of religious belief in the power of prayer to heal, for example. Should they choose to do so, they may well face criminal charges for child endangerment. Likewise, harsh punishments meted out on the religious theory that sparing the rod spoils the child may result in criminal charges of assault. Should death result, the parent may be charged with manslaughter or murder.

HISTORICAL HIGHLIGHT
AMBER Alert System May Help Recover Abducted Children

The first few hours following a child abduction are crucial for the safe return of the child. The more time that passes, the less likely it is the child will return home safe. According to the Department of Justice, 74 percent of children who are kidnapped and later found murdered are killed within three hours of being abducted.[43] The AMBER (America's Missing Broadcast Emergency Response) Alert system was created to shorten response time in child abductions and anecdotal evidence seems to point to early success.

The AMBER Alert system began in 1996 in Texas and is named for Amber Hagerman, a young child who was abducted while riding her bike and brutally murdered. The idea behind the program is to quickly use the media to publicize a child's missing status. It has evolved into a program that includes news flashes and broadcasting information along electronic signs on the nation's highways. In mid-2004 the system went national, with many states coordinating their systems. In addition, AMBER Alerts are now available online and via pagers, cell phones, and other wireless devices. Information is available for all states in the program through the Department of Justice AMBER Alert web page at *http://www.ojp.usdoj.gov/amberalert/*.

CORPORAL PUNISHMENT AND CHILD ABUSE

One of the first areas of conflict between the criminal law and parental authority is in the area of corporal punishment. Were an adult to slap another adult across the face, there would be no doubt that the act could be prosecuted as an assault. But if the same adult slaps his child, that may be seen as appropriate punishment by some in law enforcement, but as child abuse in another. Most state criminal assault statutes provide a defense for acts of reasonable corporal punishment. For example, Pennsylvania provides that the use of force on another person is justifiable if:

> The actor is the parent or guardian or other person similarly responsible for the general care and supervision of a minor or a person acting at the request of such parent, guardian, or other responsible person and:
>
> 1. the force is used for the purpose of safeguarding or promoting the welfare of the minor, including the prevention or punishment of his misconduct; and
>
> 2. the force used is not designed to cause or known to create a substantial risk of causing death, serious bodily injury, disfigurement, extreme pain or mental distress or gross degradation.[44]

Slapping a child on the rear as you stop him from running into the street is probably allowable under this statute, while slapping the child until he bruises probably is not. But the reality is that with corporal punishment as a defense, few children on whom the rod is not spared will find their parents prosecuted. The defense allows for a considerable amount of leeway for parents.

HISTORICAL HIGHLIGHT
Child's Abduction and Murder Gives Birth to America's Most Wanted Television Program

On July 27, 1981, 6-year-old Adam Walsh was abducted and murdered. His head was found floating in a river, but his body was never found. His father, John Walsh, discovered that there had been little coordination between police departments when a child is reported missing, and no centralized agency to turn to. As the result of his lobbying, Congress passed the Missing Children Act of 1982 and the Missing Children's Assistance Act of 1984. Those laws led to the creation of the *National Center for Missing and Exploited Children*. The center maintains a toll-free line to report missing children or the sighting of one. John Walsh also went on to host the television show *America's Most Wanted*, which introduces the nation to unsolved crimes and serves as a clearinghouse for tips. Leads garnered through the program have resulted in the capture of over 803 suspects as of July 2004.

HISTORICAL HIGHLIGHT
Child Wins Lawsuit Against Spanking Guardian

In countries bound by the rules of the European Union, parents who want to spank their children may find the wrath of the high court come down on them instead. The nations of the European Union, which includes Austria, Croatia, Cyprus, Denmark, Finland, Latvia, Italy, Norway, Sweden, and the United Kingdom, have all banned corporal punishment of children. The last holdout was the United Kingdom, which had an exception similar to the one common in the United States that allowed parents or guardians to use reasonable corporal punishment.

The United Kingdom was forced to conform its laws to those of the rest of the members of the European Union when the European Court of Human Rights awarded £10,000 in damages and £20,000 in legal fees to a 14-year-old boy who claimed that a beating from his stepfather contravened the European convention on human rights. The court ruled in 1998 that ". . . no one shall be subjected to torture or to inhuman or degrading treatment or punishment," and found that the corporal punishment meted out by the stepfather violated that rule. The United Kingdom's highest court had already ruled that the punishment given the boy did not violate English law.[45] England recently enacted a ban on spanking to comply with the European Union rules.

Generally, if the parent or guardian's conduct goes beyond the defense, he or she can be charged with assault. Of course, a stranger committing the same act as a parent or guardian may be privileged to commit cannot use the defense. Many states apply ordinary criminal prohibitions to physical harm done to children and provide for a greater sentence when the victim is a child.

OTHER DEFENSES

Because child abuse and neglect laws need to balance the interest of the state to protect children and the rights of parents to raise their offspring as they see fit, child abuse laws are often written in a way that makes them susceptible to a wide range of interpretation of what is abuse and what is not. They are intentionally vague. As a result, those charged under the statutes can sometimes successfully claim that the law is so vague as to be unconstitutional. The Supreme Court has ruled on a number of occasions that a criminal law must "define the criminal offense with sufficient definiteness that ordinary people can understand what it prohibits and in a manner that does not encourage arbitrary and discriminatory enforcement."[46] The challenge can be that the statute overall is so vague or overbroad that it has no validity in any case. Defense counsel can also allege that as applied to the conduct a particular defendant is charged with, the statute is arbitrary and vague.

CHILD SEXUAL ABUSE

The medical definition of **child sexual abuse** is very broad. According to the American Academy of Pediatrics, child sexual abuse is *"the engaging of a child in sexual activities that the child cannot comprehend, for which the child is developmentally unprepared and cannot give informed consent, and/or that violate the social and legal taboos of society. The sexual activity may include all forms of oral genital, genital, or anal contact by or to the child, or non-touching abuses, such as exhibitionism, voyeurism, or using the child in the production of pornography. . . ."*[47]

The medical definition encompasses a long list of potential criminal charges, including rape, indecent assault, statutory rape, incest, and sexual assault. Although medically it is all sexual abuse, criminally, each act is a separate and distinct offense. For example, in Wisconsin a defendant commits a first-degree sexual assault when the defendant has had "sexual contact or sexual intercourse with a person who had not attained the age of 13 years," while she commits a second-degree sexual assault if the contact is with a person who is younger than 16 years.[48] In Pennsylvania, *"a person commits a felony of the second degree when that person engages in sexual intercourse with a complainant under the age of 16 years and that person is four or more years older than the complainant and the complainant and the person are not married to each other."*[49]

Depending on the jurisdiction, the fact that the defendant believed a consenting sex partner was over the age of consent in the jurisdiction may or may not be a defense. For example, in Pennsylvania, it is a criminal offense to have indecent contact with a person younger than 13 years old[50] and with a person less than 16 years of age if the defendant is at least four years older and not the victim's spouse.[51] Pennsylvania law proclaims it is not a defense that the defendant thought the victim was older than 14 when the child was 13. However, it is a defense that the defendant thought the child was older than 14 if in fact he or she was between the age of 14 and 16.[52] The defendant would have to prove to the court by a preponderance of the evidence that he reasonably thought the victim was older than 14.

Although most child sexual abuse cases are prosecuted on the state level, there are several federal statutes that may impact a particular case and lead to a federal rather than state prosecution. For example, it is a federal offense to cross state lines with the intent to engage in a sexual act with a child under 12 or to transport a child across state lines in order to engage in criminal sexual activity with that child.[53]

PRACTICE POINTERS

Those representing the interests of domestic violence or sexual assault victims can find information on federal programs, grants, and laws at the Department of Justice's Violence Against Women Office, 810 7th Street, NW, Washington, DC 20531, (202) 307–6026. The website address is *http://www.ojp.usdoj.gov/vawo*. The agency offers a range of publications for those involved in the domestic violence field, including the *Toolkit to End Violence Against Women*, available at *http://toolkit.ncjrs.org/*. Other helpful agencies and publications are:

- National Domestic Violence Hotline: 1–800–799–SAFE (7233) and *http://www.ndvh.org/*
- Publications from the Office of Victims of Crime, Department of Justice, including *Understanding DNA Evidence: A Guide for Victim Service Providers*, available at *http://www.ojp.usdoj.gov/ovc/publications/bulletins/dna_4_2001/welcome.html*
- National Institute of Justice's study, *Extent, Nature, and Consequences of Intimate Partner Violence: Findings From the National Violence Against Women Survey*, 2000 at *http://www.ojp.usdoj.gov/nij/pubs-sum/181867.htm*
- National Institute of Justice's study, *The Sexual Victimization of College Women*, 2000 at *http://www.ojp.usdoj.gov/nij/pubs-sum/182369.htm*
- National AMBER Alert System information can be accessed at *http://www.ojp.usdoj.gov/amberalert/*
- The National Sexual Assault Resource Center at *http://www.nsvrc.org* provides information on sexual assault.
- Other specialized resources include the Battered Women's Justice Project at 800–903–0111, the Health Resource Center on Domestic Violence at 888–792–2873, and the Sacred Circle Center on Violence Against Native Women at 605–341–2050.

Those working with victims of domestic abuse should guard against unrealistic expectations. Inevitably, advocates for the victim will be frustrated when a prosecution falls apart as the couple reconciles or the victim refuses to actively cooperate. Short of forcing victims to testify through subpoena and asking the victim to be held in contempt when he or she doesn't cooperate, there is little that can be done when the victim wants to drop the case.

For those working in law enforcement investigating and prosecuting hate crimes, the Anti-Defamation League collects data on hate crime legislation, available at its website, *http://www.adl.org/*.

HISTORICAL HIGHLIGHT
Forgive Me, Father. The Catholic Church's Child Sexual Abuse Crisis

John Goeghan was found guilty of molesting a child in a swimming pool in January 2002. However, John Goeghan was not the average child molester—he was a well-respected priest in Boston. Over 130 people have accused him of child sexual abuse during his career at six different parishes over a 30-year span. He was eventually convicted and imprisoned, where he was brutally murdered by a fellow inmate. But how could one man have abused so many children over such a long period of time without getting caught?

Paul Shanley, also a priest in the Boston area, was arrested for similar allegations in May 2002. A month after his arrest, the Boston Archdiocese released internal documents that revealed that they had known about allegations of child sexual abuse against Shanley since 1967. Shanley's work records reflected that he had been moved by the Catholic Church from parish to parish as more allegations arose against him.

This practice of moving accused priests to new assignments seems to not have been an isolated incident. In March 2002, Bishop Anthony J. O'Connell resigned from the Diocese of Palm Beach, Florida, after admitting to sexually abusing a seminary student. Archbishop Rembert Weakland of Milwaukee, Wisconsin, resigned under similar allegations in May 2002. In June 2002, J. Kendrick Williams, also accused of child sexual assault, resigned from his post as bishop of the Diocese of Lexington, Kentucky. All three of these priests seem to have been shuffled from one assignment to another as victims came forward.

As these cases are being tried in both criminal and civil courts, many are beginning to speculate about the legal questions arising from them. Statutes of limitations may exist in many jurisdictions that would prevent criminal charges from being filed after a certain period of time has elapsed since the incidents occurred. Already, the U.S. Supreme Court has struck down an attempt by the California legislature to enact a new statute of limitations for childhood sexual abuse as a violation of the *ex post facto* rule.[54] California has had to release or drop charges against about 800 accused child molesters, including several Catholic priests, since the decision.[55] Has the Catholic Church used this method of moving accused priests from one place to the next as a strategy for exhausting these statutes of limitations so that criminal prosecutions can be avoided by the time the occurrences of child sexual abuse are revealed?

Resources for those seeking information on missing or exploited children include:

● The National Center for Missing and Exploited Children, a nonprofit organization working in cooperation with the U.S. Department of Justice, serves as a national resource center and clearinghouse on missing child cases. The Center is linked with clearinghouses in all 50 states, and can be reached at 1–800–843–5678 and online at *www.missingkids.org.*

- The Polly Klass Foundation, dedicated to finding missing children and lobbying for laws protecting children from exploitation, can be reached at 1–800–587–4357 or online at *www.pollyklass.org.*
- Families of missing children may find the booklet "When Your Child is Missing: A Family Survival Guide" helpful. It is available from the Office of Juvenile Justice and Delinquency Prevention, the Department of Justice online at *www.ojjdp.ncjrs.org/pubs/childismissing/* or in pamphlet form from the Department of Justice. It was written by parents of missing and murdered children.

CHAPTER SUMMARY

After reading this chapter, you should have a good understanding of the wide variety of crimes that exist outlawing injury to the person. The criminal law punished a vast range of behavior considered morally repugnant by the majority as expressed through the laws enacted by their legal representatives. Many of the violent criminal offenses described in this chapter are in practice directed against women and children.

Traditionally defined as forced sexual intercourse with a woman, not one's wife, modern rape definitions don't distinguish between male or female victims and have expanded the types of sexual conduct that constitute rape. Most states also allow at least a limited right to bring rape charges against a spouse and no longer require the use of direct force or physical harm. The key elements of rape are that the statute's prohibited sexual activity took place and that there was no consent by the victim.

Consent is a defense to most charges of rape unless the victim is underage, drugged, or otherwise unable to give effective consent. Rape shield laws limit the type of evidence that can be introduced about the victim in a sexual assault case. Only evidence that is directly relevant to the case will be admitted and testimony about the victim's prior sexual history is not admitted unless it directly relates to evidence in the case or to his or her consent to the sexual acts at the heart of the case.

Assault is an act of force or threat of force intended to inflict harm upon a person or to put the person in fear that such harm is imminent. Every state has its own set of rules about which acts constitute assault. To prove that an assault took place, the state must show that there was either an act that resulted in physical harm or a threat that resulted in the fear of imminent physical harm. Most states classify assault in accordance with the type of harm threatened or done and the type of weapon used to threaten or act. Thus, it is a more serious offense to threaten a victim with a gun (because it can cause serious bodily harm or death) than with a fist (which may cause less serious bodily harm unless the assailant is a boxer).

Domestic violence is assault, battery, aggravated assault, harassment, stalking, and other crimes involving physical or mental injury to a victim when perpetrated by the victim's partner. Domestic violence is a serious problem in the United States, but has historically been ignored by many in law enforcement. Today, that is changing as shelters and educational opportunities open up for women (who are the overwhelming majority of domestic violence victims), and more charges are being filed. In addition, the federal government is funding research and programs to help victims of domestic violence start new lives through the authority given them in the Violence Against Women Act.

Hate crimes are offenses motivated by hatred against a victim based on his or her race, religion, sexual orientation, handicap, ethnicity, or national origin. Many states have enacted hate crime laws that enhance the sentence received for the commission of a crime if the motive for the criminal act was animus towards a protected class or member of a protected class. The Supreme Court has ruled that hate crime legislation is legal as long as proving that the motive for a crime's commission is an essential element of the crime, and not a factor to be considered by the sentencing judge.

Kidnapping and abduction are crimes in which the perpetrator takes, holds, and sometimes carries away the victim through force or coercion. Neither kidnapping nor abduction requires that the perpetrator demand a ransom. Today, well over 28,000 children and adults disappear under circumstances that make it likely their disappearance wasn't voluntary. State laws regulate most cases of abduction unless there is evidence that the victim was taken across state lines.

Child abuse is the label given to crimes that are either committed against minors or crimes created to protect children who cannot act in their own best interest. The doctrine of *parens patriae* gives authority to government to protect the vulnerable, while police powers give states the limited right to regulate the civil lives of its citizens. These two doctrines are the basis for special laws regarding children. Examples include statutory rape, incest, and child medical neglect. Some acts that would be crimes if committed against another adult are not crimes if the victim is a child and the perpetrator is a parent or guardian. For example, it would be a crime to spank a neighbor but not to spank one's misbehaving child.

KEY TERMS

Abduction: The illegal carrying away of a person by force or coercion, generally with the intent to do harm to the victim. Today, kidnapping and abduction are generally covered by the same criminal statute.

Assault: An act of force or threat of force intended to inflict harm upon a person or to put the person in fear that such harm is imminent.

Child abuse: Child abuse is the label given to crimes that are either committed against minors or crimes created to protect children who cannot act in their own best interest. Examples include statutory rape, incest, and child medical neglect.

Domestic violence: Assault, battery, aggravated assault, harassment, stalking, and other crimes involving physical or mental injury to a victim when perpetrated by the victim's partner.

Hate crimes: Offenses motivated by hatred against a victim based on his or her race, religion, sexual orientation, handicap, ethnicity, or national origin.

Kidnapping: The crime of taking and detaining a person against his will by force, intimidation, or fraud. Holding the victim for ransom is not required.

Parens patriae: Common Law rule that requires that the crown protect those most vulnerable in society when they cannot protect themselves.

Rape: Traditionally defined as forced sexual intercourse with a woman, not one's wife. Modern rape definitions don't distinguish between male or female victims and have expanded the types of sexual contact that are included in the definition. Most states also allow at least a limited right to bring rape charges against a spouse and no longer require the use of direct force or physical harm.

Rape shield law: Codified rule of evidence that provides for the exclusion of a rape victim's sexual history unless it is directly relevant to his or her consent or other evidence in the case.

VAWA: The Violence Against Women Act, a federal law criminalizing interstate acts of domestic violence and funding research and education programs.

DISCUSSION QUESTIONS

1. Research your state's assault statutes and discuss how assault offenses in your state differ from those illustrated in this chapter. Select one assault offense in your jurisdiction and outline the elements of the offense. Then describe the evidence you would need to present in order to secure a conviction.

2. Research your state's rape and sexual assault laws. Outline the elements of your state's statutory rape and marital rape laws. Then describe the evidence you would need in order to secure a conviction. Then outline the elements of your state's rape law and describe what evidence you would have to present to defend against a charge of rape.

3. Locate your state's rape shield law. What evidence of the victim's past sexual history does it allow into evidence and under what circumstances?

4. What is domestic violence and what is your community doing to prevent it? Research the incident of domestic violence in your jurisdiction.

5. Should corporal punishment by parents and guardians be outlawed as it has been in the European Community?

6. Research the missing child emergency response system set up in your jurisdiction. Does it provide for immediate action or does it require that parents wait before the police become involved in recovery efforts? If it requires a wait, how would you try to persuade local authorities to change their policy?

FURTHER READING

1. Walsh, J. (1998). *Tears of Rage: From Grieving Father to Crusader for Justice.* Pocket Books. This book tells the story of Adam Walsh's kidnapping and murder through his father's perspective and chronicles John Walsh's efforts to make recovering lost and abducted children easier.

2. Those interested in historical materials from the FBI archives, which have been released to the public through the Freedom of Information Act, can visit the agency's Freedom of Information Act Electronic Reading Room. The archives include documents on the Lindbergh kidnapping and other high-profile cases. The website is *http://foia.fbi.gov/*. The Department of Justice maintains a similar virtual reading room at *http://www.usdoj.gov/04foia/index.html*.

3. Temple-Raston, D. (2002). *A Death in Texas: A Story of Race, Murder, and a Small Town's Struggle for Redemption.* Henry Holt. Recounts the hate crime murder of James Byrd, Jr., in Jasper, Texas. The 49-year-old African American man was tied to a pickup truck by three white men and dragged behind until he died.

4. Brownmiller, S. (1975). *Against Our Will: Men, Women, and Rape.* Simon & Schuster. Classic study of rape, its origins, and its effect on women.

QUOTATIONS FOR CHAPTER NINE

1. *It is but reasonable that, among crimes of different natures, those should be most severely punished which are the most destructive of the public safety and happiness.*
   Blackstone, *Commentaries on the Laws of England* (Ed. Cooley) (1899).

2. *The King's Chancelor is the general guardian of all infants, idiots, and lunatics.*
   Blackstone, *Commentaries on the Laws of England* (Ed. Cooley) (1899).

ENDNOTES

1. U.S. Department of Justice, *Report to the Nation on Crime and Justice 29* (2nd ed., 1988).

2. Surgeon General Antonia Novello, "From the Surgeon General," U.S. Public Health Services, 267 *JAMA* 3132 (1992).

3. "Va. House Backs Bill to Outlaw Wife Rape," *Washington Post* (February 8, 2002) and Virginia Code Ann. § 18.2–61 (B).

4. Pennsylvania State Police, Bureau of Drug Law Enforcement, *Date Rape Drugs; Information You Need To Know*.

5. Division of Criminal Justice, New Jersey, Press Release, *Brothers to Be Sentenced for Operating Internet Date Rape Business* (March 22, 2001).

6. Virginia Code § 18.2–67.7.

7. "Deal Proposed for Defendant in Net Sex Case," *New York Times* (November 22, 2000).

8. *Focus on New York's Rape Shield Law: Court Overturns Cybersex Torture Conviction*, Court TV Online (December 22, 1999).

9. "All Charges Dismissed by Judge in Columbia Sex Torture Case," *New York Times* (November 2, 2001).

10. 18 P.S. § 2709(b).

11. 18 P.S. § 2714(a) and (b).

12. 18 P.S. § 2701(a).

13. 18 P.S. § 2301.

14. See, for example, Pennsylvania's aggravated assault statute at 18 P.S. § 2702, which affords protection to a long list of public officials including school board members, public defenders, district attorneys, and probation officers.

15. Bureau of Justice Statistics, U.S. Department of Justice, *Violence Against Women* (1994).

16. Federal Bureau of Investigation, *Uniform Crime Reports of the U.S.* (1996).

17. Bureau of Justice Statistics, U.S. Department of Justice, *Violence by Intimates: Analysis of Data on Crimes by Current or Former Spouses, Boyfriends and Girlfriends* (1998).

18. 42 U.S.C. § 13981(b).

19. *United States v. Morrison*, 529 U.S. 598 (2000).

20. Bureau of Justice Statistics, U.S. Department of Justice, Press Release, *Justice Department Releases 1997 to 1999 Hate Crime Statistics* (September 23, 2001).

21. Bureau of Justice Statistics, U.S. Department of Justice, *Hate Crimes Reported in NIBRS, 1997–99* (2001).

22. *Apprendi v. New Jersey*, 530 U.S. 466 (2000).

23. *Virginia v. Black*, 123 S. Ct. 1536 (2003).

24. The National Center for Missing and Exploited Children, Press Release, *National Center for Missing and Exploited Children Releases 2001 Missing Child Reports* (January 25 2002).

25. U.S. Department of Justice, Juvenile Justice Bulletin, *Kidnapping of Juveniles: Patterns from NIBRS* (June 2000).

26. Ibid.

27. U.S. Department of Justice, Juvenile Justice Bulletin, *Second Comprehensive Study of Missing Children* (April 2000).

28. 18 P.S. § 2901.

29. 18 P.S. § 2902.

30. 18 P.S. § 2903.

31. 18 P.S. § 2904.

32. 18 P.S. § 2905.

33. 18 P.S. § 2909.

34. 18 P.S. § 2910.

35. *Commonwealth v. Nanorta*, 742 A. 2d 176 (1999).

36. "Lindbergh Baby Kidnapped from Home of Parents on Farm near Princeton: Taken from His Crib; Wide Search On," *New York Times* (March 2, 1932).

37. "Haupthmann Guilty; Sentenced to Death for the Murder of Lindbergh Baby," *New York Times* (February 14, 1935).

38. "Federal Aid in Hunt Ordered by Hoover," *New York Times* (March 3, 1932).

39. Federal Bureau of Investigations, *History of the FBI*, online at *www.fbi.gov/fbinbrief/historic/history/historymain.htm*.

40. 18 U.S.C. § 1201 (a).

41. 18 U.S.C. § 1201 (g).

42. *Mormon Church v. United States*, 136 U.S. 1 (1890).

43. Assistant Attorney General Deborah Daniels, National AMBER Alert coordinator.

44. 18 P.S. § 509.

45. "European Court Ruling Bans Corporal Punishment of UK Children," *The Guardian* (London) (September 23, 1998).

46. *Kolender v. Lawson*, 461 U.S. 352 (1983).

47. American Academy of Pediatrics, *Guidelines for the Evaluation of Sexual Abuse of Children*, 87 *Pediatrics* 254, 1991.

48. Wis. Stat. § 948.02 and 948.025.

49. 18 P.S. § 3122.1.

50. 18 P.S. § 3126(a)(7).

51. 18 P.S. § 3126 (a) (8).

52. 18 P.S. § 3102. The defense reads *"Whenever in this chapter the criminality of conduct depends on a child being below the age of 14 years, it is no defense that the defendant did not*

know the age of the child or reasonably believed the child to be the age of 14 years or older. When criminality depends on the child's being below a critical age older than 14 years, it is a defense for the defendant to prove by a preponderance of the evidence that he or she reasonably believed the child to be above the critical age."

53. 18 U.S.C. § 2241(c) and 2423.

54. *Stogner v. California*, 539 U.S. 607 (2003).

55. *High Court: California Can't Prosecute Long-ago Sex Crimes*, CNN online (June 27, 2003).

CHAPTER 10
Crimes Against Property

CHAPTER OBJECTIVES

After studying this chapter, you should be able to:

- Understand what property is and the bundles of rights that accompany each type of property.
- Explain the terms *fee simple, joint tenants with right of survivorship, tenancy by the entireties,* and *tenant in common.*
- Define *theft* and name the different classifications of theft.
- List the essential elements required to prove theft.
- Differentiate embezzlement from other forms of theft.
- Define *robbery.*
- Define *burglary* and describe its common law origins.
- Define *arson* and explain why so few cases are cleared.
- Explain the most common methods of check fraud and forgery.

CHAPTER CONTENTS

> *. . . nor shall any State deprive any person of life, liberty, or property without due process of law.*
>
> *U.S. Constitution*, Amendment 14, Section 1

INTRODUCTION

In order to have a true appreciation for crimes involving property, you must first understand what **property** is and is not. Implicit in any discussion of property is the premise that it can actually be held by individuals at all. Some societies simply don't accept that premise. The Common Law tradition on which American law is largely based recognizes private property rights as an important part of the rules that govern society. In England and the United States, one of the most important rights accorded citizens is the protection of his or her right to property, both real and personal.

In the American Common Law tradition, property consists of a bundle of rights, including the right to possess, use and enjoy, and dispose of something. It is not a material object itself, but a person's right to do what he or she wishes with that object, subject to limitations provided in the law.[1] Thus, the "owner" of a book has the right to possess it (perhaps put it on her bookshelf or nightstand), the right to use it (perhaps to read it and make notes in the margins), and the right to dispose of it (perhaps by selling it or even to burn it).

Understanding the basics of property law is essential to understanding crimes that involve interfering with those rights such as theft, burglary, forgery, and criminal trespass. Each of these crimes involves interference with another's property rights, and requires that the prosecution prove ownership as well as interference with that ownership.

Property comes in two varieties. **Real property** is land and everything permanently attached to it. It includes land, subsurface rights (i.e., the right to mine the land), air rights, timbering and harvesting rights (i.e., the right to farm, harvest, or log the land), and any buildings and structures permanently attached to the land (i.e., house, barn, silo, garage, and the like). Real property can be either private or public. Private property is that which is owned by a private individual, while public property is held by a state government or the federal government on behalf of us all. Examples of public real property are the national seashore and other national parks.

Personal property is everything else the law grants ownership rights to. It is also known as **chattel**.[2] Personal property can be tangible, with a physical presence. For example, a car or a book is personal property. Personal property can also be intangible, without a physical presence. Examples include patents and copyrights. Personal property also includes domestic animals and livestock as well as wild animals that have either been domesticated or placed under control.

Property rights are not without limit. Real property, for example, is subject to seizure by governmental entities as part of the state's power of **eminent domain.** Eminent domain is the state's power to take private property for a public use or public purpose without the owner's consent.[3] Under the Constitution, any such taking must be after due process of law. Private property can't just be seized; some kind of a hearing is required. For example, when a criminal's ill-gotten gains from a criminal enterprise are seized in a drug raid, the state must still afford the defendant a hearing on that seizure before it becomes permanent. Typically, the state must show the court that there was some minimum nexus between the criminal activity and the acquisition of the property by the defendant.

Property can be owned outright. If it is, the owner is said to hold the property in **fee simple.** Fee simple is a legal term for ownership of the entire bundle of rights that go with a piece of property.[4] For example, you may own your house in fee simple. If you do, you have the right to use, possess, or dispose of the property during your lifetime and to pass it on to your heirs. You can dispose of some of your bundle of rights and keep the rest if you desire. For example, if you own a beach house in fee simple, you may periodically transfer your right to possess and enjoy the property to someone else by renting out the house to vacationers. While they rent the house, it is they who have the right to enjoy and possess it.

Ownership is not restricted to one person; many persons can own the same property together. For example, husbands and wives often own property as **tenants by the entireties.** Tenancy by the entirety is a legal joint ownership in which both spouses own an undivided interest in the whole property and in which neither spouse can sell his or her interest without the consent of the other.[5] Other forms of joint ownership are **tenancy in common** and **joint tenancy with right of survivorship.**[6] Tenants in common each own an undivided interest in the whole property. Neither tenant in common can exclude the other from the property, but any of the tenants can sell or will the property to another without the consent of the other joint tenants. If the owners hold property as joint tenants with right of survivorship, the survivor gets the property. However, if one joint tenant sells or gives away his interest before he dies, the property would no longer pass to the other joint tenant. Instead, the new owner would become a tenant in common.

Title to property can be acquired in several ways. Property rights can be bought for a price, inherited, acquired as a gift, or acquired by mere possession. The most common methods of transfer of property rights is through purchase or inheritance. Purchase of property is done by contract and involves the exchange of something of value. For example, if you purchase a CD for $15, you have bought title to that CD. Acquiring property by gift or inheritance requires three things. First, the owner must intend to give the property away. Second, the gift must be delivered to the recipient. Finally, the recipient must accept the gift. Property can also be acquired by possession. For example, a hunter who shoots a deer passing over his land becomes the owner of the deer when he takes possession of it. Before it was shot, the deer belonged to no one. After, it belongs to the hunter. Abandoned property can also be acquired by possession. For example, if a jogger spots a treasure sitting on the curb for garbage collection, she can take possession of it and becomes its owner.

In criminal law, ownership is important for several reasons. For example, a thief can only steal that which does not belong to him; he cannot steal his own property. Nor can he trespass against his own property. Thus, an estranged husband who breaks into the house he still owns jointly with his wife cannot be charged with criminal trespass, nor can he be charged with burglary if he removes personal articles that belong to the couple. Theft also requires that the prosecution prove beyond a reasonable doubt that the defendant intended to permanently deprive the owner of the property taken.

HISTORICAL HIGHLIGHT
Animal Rights Activists' "Emancipation" of Animals Highlights Meaning of Property

When Thomas Jefferson wrote that man had "inalienable rights" such as "life, liberty, and the pursuit of happiness," he was referring quite literally to men, specifically white, land-owning men. Women and people of color were not included. In fact, African American slaves were considered property in the southern colonies. When the Constitution was drafted, their condition was upgraded only slightly; slaves were counted as three-fifths of a person for census purposes.

Clearly, the perception of who is entitled to rights has changed over the last 200+ years. Today, some argue that children should have the right to "divorce" their parents. Rutgers University Law School takes the concept further. They teach an Animal Rights Law course, which attempts to "eradicate the status of non-humans as property, and to recognize that animals should be thought of as *persons* under the law."

Professor Gary Francione, the guiding force behind the Rutgers Animal Rights Law program, is attempting to bring about "animal emancipation." He urges people not to eat meat or dairy products. Additionally, he states on the website Animal Emancipation, Inc., online at *http://www.aeubc-online.org*, that "there is no moral justification for institutionalized animal exploitation," and that animal rights "cannot be sacrificed merely because humans believe . . . [the benefits] for humans . . . outweigh the detriment for animals."

Francione makes no claim to be part of mainstream thought. In fact, he refers to the mainstream as "polluted." He sees animals as the next beneficiaries of a civil rights movement.

HISTORICAL HIGHLIGHT
Who Owns the Rights to Sunken Treasure?

On September 11, 1857, the steamship *Central America* was making the last leg of its journey from Panama to New York when it encountered a hurricane off the coast of South Carolina. The ship developed a leak that became worse as the storm went on. Eventually water flooded the steam boilers, extinguishing the fire and leaving the ship at the mercy of the storm. A few passengers were set afloat in life boats and were safely picked up by another ship. The other 336 people on-board perished when the ship went down.

The *Central America* was a wooden-hulled luxury liner. Most of its passengers had found gold in California, and were carrying it home to families on the East Coast. They had sailed from San Francisco to Panama, crossed the isthmus by train, and boarded the steamer on the Atlantic side. The ship was carrying gold for various companies as cargo, and many of the passengers had large personal amounts of gold. The newspaper reports of the day estimated the ship to be carrying $2 million of gold in 1857 dollars. Estimates of its modern-day equivalent ran as high as $1 billion.

As news of the sinking reached the United States, insurers paid the various claims for the lost gold. Because the ship sank in over two thousand feet of water, the insurers held no hope they would ever salvage the cargo.

In the late 1970s, ocean research scientist Thomas Thompson began studying newspaper accounts of the *Central America* sinking. He became convinced that modern ocean mapping and deep-sea exploration technology could make recovering the *Central America*'s treasure possible. Thompson began putting an investor syndicate together to fund the massive undertaking.

By 1987, Thompson had put together his syndicate, now called the Columbus-America Discovery Group, and began salvage operations. Insurance companies challenged the syndicate's right to the treasure, claiming they had paid for the gold after the shipwreck in 1857. This claim would have been valid if the property were lost property.

However, Thompson and his group argued that it was abandoned property. In court, they showed that even after papers telling of the *Central America*'s location were published, insurers mounted no effort to salvage the gold. Further, no documentation existed from the 1857 claims.

Thompson and his group won in federal district court where the judge ruled that conventional property laws applied, and the property was abandoned and could be given to the first group to recover it. The Appeals Court saw things somewhat differently. Since the shipwreck was in international waters, maritime law applied. It sent the case back to the district court with instructions to apply maritime law.

Maritime laws date from the ancient city of Rhodes. The inhabitants of Rhodes instituted the first maritime code sometime around 900 B.C. When the Romans conquered Rhodes, they preserved the maritime code, and it came down through Anglo-American legal tradition. Maritime law has always held that salvors (those who salvage ships) are entitled to very liberal awards.

In this case, the district judge applied the maritime law and awarded the salvagers 90 percent of the market value from the salvage. Those few insurers whose claims survived would get the remainder. Unfortunately, the gold retrieved from the site is not as much as some predicted. The *Central America* yielded about $21 million in gold. Thompson's group spent over $30 million to retrieve it.

THEFT OR LARCENY

The terms *theft* and *larceny* are interchangeable. Some jurisdictions call the crime theft, while others refer to it as larceny. We will use the term **theft** to refer to the crime. At Common Law, theft was defined as the taking and carrying away of another's personal property with the intent to deprive him or her of it permanently. There are many distinct acts that fit the definition of theft, and every state has its own list. Below are some common theft classifications.

Shoplifting or retail theft: This form of theft includes concealing goods in stores to avoid paying for them or altering the price on an item in order to pay a lower price. Many states have escalating penalties for retail theft. The penalty varies according to the value of the merchandise stolen or the number of prior convictions the defendant has on record.

Purse snatching: This form of theft involves a quick and usually observed taking of a purse, briefcase, or the like in a public place and then fleeing the scene.

Pickpocketing: This form of theft usually involves a secretive snatching of personal property such as a wallet or cash from another person's possession.

Looting: Looting is taking property from or near a building damaged or destroyed by a fire, riot, or natural disasters. Consider two recent examples of looting. When the World Trade Organization held its meeting in Seattle, Washington, in November 1999, there was widespread rioting, and over 500 people were arrested. Protesters smashed store windows, and some (perhaps protesters or just people seeing an opportunity) looted corporate icons like Starbucks coffee house, and department stores Bon Marche and Nordstroms.[7] Similarly, it appears that at least one jewelry store beneath the World Trade Center was looted in the aftermath of the September 11 terror attacks, presumably by rescuers who saw an opportunity to stock up on expensive watches and jewelry.[8]

Library theft: This type of theft is generally defined as theft of a circulating library item such as a book or record that is kept beyond its return date, and after notification that the item must be returned. Library theft can also cover the concealing and taking of rare manuscripts from a library. A recent example of library theft involved a University of Wisconsin student who allegedly stole as many as 50 original documents from a Yale University library where he worked over the summer of 2001. The student was caught when attempting to sell signatures to an autograph dealer, and may have mutilated some documents by cutting away the signatures of famous persons like George Washington.[9]

Theft by deception: When a person commits theft by deception, he or she steals through surreptitious means such as fraud. For example, a marina operator was charged with theft by deception when he knew his lease on the marina would not be renewed, but he continued to collect fees from boat owners for storage.[10]

Theft of services: This form of theft is committed when someone obtains services such as cable television or other utilities by tapping into the source of those utilities with the intention not to pay for those services. Theft of services can also occur when someone uses false information to receive utility services.

Theft by bailee or trustee: This form of theft occurs when someone other than the true owner of property has custody of that property. For example, a jeweler who is going to repair a ring has temporary custody of the property. The owner of the ring has temporarily turned over the property for repair and safekeeping. If the jeweler keeps or sells the ring, she has committed theft. In some jurisdictions, this crime may be known as theft by failure to make required disposition of funds received. For example, a Pennsylvania real estate title insurance agent collected funds from real estate buyers and placed them in an escrow account. He was supposed to distribute those funds in accordance with the real estate settlement. Instead, he took over $195,000 of the funds for his own use. He pled guilty to theft by failure to make required disposition of funds received.[11]

Auto theft: One of the most costly property crimes in the United States is auto theft. The crime is costly because nearly every auto owner is insured for theft, so that most car thefts result in payment of the value of the car by an insurer. In 2000, there were 9 auto thefts per 1,000 households.

The types of theft previously outlined are examples. Many jurisdictions have created other crimes of theft, and will continue to do so as the need arises. For example, 50 years ago there was no need to define theft to include offenses like stealing someone's credit profile and identity in order to apply for fraudulent credit cards. But all these crimes have the basic elements of theft in common. It is to these elements that we now turn.

TAKING AND CARRYING AWAY

The first element of the crime of theft is "taking and carrying away." The prosecution must prove that the defendant took possession of the object of the theft and carried it away. As you have seen in the discussion of specific types of theft, the taking can include keeping possession of something placed in the defendant's custody. But the essence of any theft is that the defendant takes personal property belonging to another and places it under his own control. For example, a customer who tries on a dress in a department store, and then walks out with the dress on, has taken and carried it away (and committed the crime of retail theft). The degree of carrying away can be slight. She would be guilty of retail theft even if she were caught before she got out of the store because she had taken possession of the dress and had begun to take it out of the store.

PERSONAL PROPERTY

Under the Common Law, the only type of property that could be stolen was tangible personal property. Real estate could not be stolen, nor could other intangible things like copyrights, stocks, or bonds. Now all jurisdictions have revised their theft statutes to include intangible personal property under their definitions of theft. That personal property can include such things as electric and cable service, and intangible computer files. In addition, someone who forges a deed to real estate can also be charged with theft (by deception).

OF ANOTHER

The property stolen must belong to someone other than the defendant. The prosecution must therefore prove ownership of the property. Prosecutors need the cooperation of property owners in order to secure theft convictions. In order to constitute theft, the defendant must take the property without the consent of the owner. It would not be theft, for example, to take your friend's ring if she gave it to you. But the prosecutor would have to put your friend on the stand to testify that she both owned the ring and did not give it to you in order for you to be convicted of theft.

Another very real problem is proving that the property the police found the defendant in possession of is actually the victim's property. For example, if the victim claims the defendant stole her diamond ring, she will have to identify the diamond as hers. If the ring is engraved, the victim can identify it. But what if the diamond has been removed from its setting (a common tactic used by gem thieves)? How will she identify the diamond as hers? Unless she has had the diamond marked, mapped, and registered (a service available for rare and high-end gems), she will be unable to tell her diamond from another and the thief will walk away with the gem.

Because stolen property must be positively identified as belonging to the owner, it is crucial that owners keep careful track of serial numbers and other identifying characteristics of their property in case of theft. Without positive proof, the thief may very well walk away with his ill-gotten lot.

WITH THE INTENT TO PERMANENTLY DEPRIVE THE OWNER OF THE PROPERTY

The final element of the crime of theft involves intent. It is not enough that the defendant took possession of property belonging to another. He must also intend to permanently deprive the owner of the property. Intent may be proven with indirect or circumstantial evidence. Thus, a thief's actions may speak of his intent. For example, an art thief who steals a gallery's Monet painting and then displays it in his private study will likely find that a jury can be convinced that his actions indicate he intended to permanently deprive the gallery of the use and enjoyment of the painting. But what about a neighbor who takes a gas grill from down the block and is caught red-handed rolling the grill towards his house? Did he intend to permanently deprive the owner of the grill or did he just borrow it?[12] Other cases where intent is less than clear are cases where absent-minded shoppers claim to have inadvertently placed merchandise in their pockets or bags, and never intended to leave the store without paying. In such cases, credibility plays a major factor.

Embezzlement occurs when someone who has legal possession of property of another uses, converts, or retains that property for his own use or the use of someone other than the owner. It differs from other forms of theft because it does not require proof that the perpetrator took and carried away property of another. That's because the embezzler already lawfully possesses the property, albeit on behalf of the other. Many cases of embezzlement involve a trusted insider stealing from an employer.

Embezzlement tends to be a crime of opportunity, and can often be avoided with proper oversight and financial controls. Take the case of a former Prothonotary and Clerk of Court for Mifflin County, Pennsylvania. Sue Ellen Saxton controlled thousands of dollars submitted to the court in fines, penalties, and other funds. Over the years she managed to divert over $800,000 of funds in her possession and control to her personal use. The funds were allegedly used to fund gambling expeditions to Las Vegas and Atlantic City. The embezzlement was accomplished by marking funds actually diverted to her personal account as having been returned to criminal defendants. She pled guilty to one count of conspiracy under federal law.[13]

Avoiding embezzlement requires putting in place an appropriate check to assure that no one can divert funds without notice. Since discovering it was missing over $800,000, Mifflin County has purchased accounting software to track money coming in and going out of accounts.[14] All businesses should assure that they have in place appropriate safeguards to prevent embezzlement.

HISTORICAL HIGHLIGHT
Episcopal Church Secretary Cooks the Books and Has Them Thrown at Her

No one suspected Ellen Cooke was anything other than what she appeared—wife, mother, and church activist. She had worked for her own church in an affluent New Jersey suburb as well as for the National Episcopal Church. She seemed to be a pillar of the community.

But all wasn't as it appeared to be. Ellen Cooke lived well. She purchased a home in Montclair, New Jersey, and carried out extensive renovations. As time went on, she purchased a farm in Virginia. Her children went to private school. In short, Ellen was living the good life.

As national treasurer for the Episcopal Church from 1986 to 1994, Ellen was responsible for millions of dollars of church funds. Over that time, she diverted over $2 million into her own account. When she was caught, her world came crashing down around her.[15]

The properties purchased with the stolen money were sold and the proceeds given back to the church. She was charged with tax evasion and transporting stolen money across state lines. She pled guilty to the charges, but her lawyer claimed she suffered from bipolar disorder and should receive a lenient sentence.

The judge in the case disagreed. She noted that while Ellen was living the good life, she was destroying the trust parishioners had placed in the Episcopal Church. Following the disclosures of her theft, contributions had fallen for the Episcopal and other churches. Services for the needy were curtailed, and church workers were laid off. The judge sentenced her to five years, 14 months longer than the maximum recommended by federal sentencing guidelines. Ellen will not be eligible for parole during that time and must serve three years of supervised release afterwards.

ROBBERY

Robbery is the taking of personal property from the person of another against his will, by either force or threat of force.[16] It is forcible stealing. To convict a defendant of robbery, the prosecution must prove that there was:

- A taking and carrying away of the property of another
- The intent to steal that property

- Property taken from the person or in the presence of the person
- The use of force or threat of the use of imminent force

Common acts of robbery include stopping someone and demanding his wallet when the demand is accompanied by the threat, either actual or implied, that the robber will harm the victim if he doesn't acquiesce, and demanding a teller in a bank to hand over cash. What distinguishes robbery from other forms of theft is the element of threat to the person. Generally, states have two categories of robbery—simple robbery and armed robbery. Simple robbery is accomplished without weapons, while armed robbery is accomplished with the use of some sort of weapon such as a knife, gun, or other dangerous instrument. Armed robbery is punished more severely than simple robbery. In fact, many states mandate long prison terms for those who commit armed robbery.

CAUTION: FEDERAL LAW DIFFERS FROM COMMON LAW

There are also federal criminal laws prohibiting robbery. In some cases, federal laws do not parallel the common law of robbery. For example, if a banking institution is federally chartered, federal law defines a bank robber as:

> Whoever by force and violence, or by intimidation, takes, or attempts to take, from the person or presence of another, or obtains or attempts to obtain by extortion any property or money or any other thing of value belonging to, or in the care, custody, control, management, or possession of, any bank, credit union, or any savings and loan association.[17]
>
> The Supreme Court has ruled that prosecutors seeking bank robbery convictions under this statute do not have to prove that the robber took or carried away the valuables he attempted to take.[18]

We now turn to the elements of the crime of robbery that differ from those of theft. Remember with most state statutes, the elements of the crime of theft must also be satisfied.

FROM THE PERSON OR IN THE PRESENCE OF THE PERSON

Robbery does not occur if force is neither threatened or used. For example, if you have a party at your house, and a guest picks up a ring you left by the sink, pockets it, and leaves, she has not committed robbery even if you saw her take the ring. However, if she pockets the ring while grabbing a steak knife and bandishes it threateningly towards you while she makes her exit, then she had committed robbery. The difference is in the fear she has inflicted on you. In the first example, she has committed theft, whereas in the second example she has committed robbery.

BY THE USE OF FORCE OR THREAT OF THE USE OF IMMINENT FORCE

Robbery must be committed with the aid of the use of force or the threat of the imminent use of force. A robbery can be committed when a defendant makes a threatening move towards the victim, if it seems to the victim that the defendant is capable of inflicting harm. A demand for "Your money or your life" from an octogenarian weighing 100 pounds would probably not be robbery, but the same demand from a burly 25-year-old weight lifter probably would be.

Generally, if a weapon is displayed in the presence of a victim when a theft is attempted or takes place, the crime committed is armed robbery. A typical statute defines armed robbery as: "*the crime of robbery while armed with a pistol, dirk, slingshot, metal knuckles, razor, or other deadly weapon. . . .*"[19]

There is an interesting line of cases in which toy weapons were used. In most cases, the fact that a toy gun appears real is enough to sustain a charge of armed robbery. However, when the victim realizes the weapon used is fake, the crime committed is simple robbery.

For example, a defendant who entered a bank with two red sticks tied together, asked the teller for money, and lit what appeared to be a fuse was convicted of robbery under federal law and was sentenced to additional jail time for using a dangerous weapon during a robbery. In fact, the bomb was a harmless homemade bundle of sticks and string.[20]

However, in a robbery of a McDonald's restaurant two defendants used a toy water gun and a play M16. The restaurant employees testified that they did not believe that the guns were real. An appeals court sent the case back for reconsideration after the trial court convicted one defendant of armed robbery.[21]

What if the defendant keeps a toy gun hidden during a robbery but it is discovered on him after the arrest? At least under federal law, that would not be armed robbery.[22]

What if the gun used in a bank robbery isn't loaded? Is that still the use of a dangerous weapon during the robbery of a federally chartered bank, qualifying the defendant for a longer sentence than if no weapon was used? According to the Supreme Court, the answer is "yes." The case involved two men who, both wearing stocking masks and gloves, entered a bank in Baltimore. One displayed a dark handgun and ordered everyone in the bank to put their hands up and not to move. While he remained in the lobby area holding the gun, his partner jumped over the counter and put $3,400 in a brown paper bag. The two were apprehended by a police officer as they left the bank. The officers discovered that the gun was unloaded. One defendant was convicted of using a dangerous weapon during a robbery. In a unanimous opinion, the Supreme Court reasoned that " . . . *the display of a gun instills fear in the average citizen; as a consequence, it creates an immediate danger that a violent response will ensue. Finally, a gun can cause harm when used as a bludgeon.*"[23]

BURGLARY

At Common Law, **burglary** was the breaking and entering of the dwelling house of another at night with the intent to commit a felony inside. It was generally punishable by death. The crime required that the perpetrator secure entry by some use of force. That is, it was not burglary to enter an unlocked dwelling. Force must have been used, whether that meant pushing in a door or breaking a window. In addition, the entry had to be to a dwelling house. It was not burglary to break into a warehouse or other storage place.

The crime of burglary is complete when the entry with intent to commit a felony has taken place. It doesn't matter that the burglar doesn't actually commit a crime once inside. In fact, any crime committed once inside will be charged separately whether that crime is an assault, murder, or theft.

HISTORICAL HIGHLIGHT
Armed Robbery of LSAT Test Proves Costly

Law school may be a dream for many, but if you want to go, you have to have good grades and a good score on the Law School Admissions Test. Taking the standardized test is a ritual for all law school hopefuls. Some students are apparently so intent on getting a good score that they will resort to armed robbery.

During the February 8, 1997, exam, a student using fake identification to take the test at the University of California at Los Angeles walked out about 15 minutes into the test. When the proctor followed him onto the street and demanded the test back, the student pulled a switchblade knife, got in a car, and left. Shortly after, Danny Khatchaturian and Dikran Iskendarian, two students taking the test in Hawaii, began receiving the answers on their pagers. The time difference between Hawaii and California meant there was a 2-hour delay in the test.[24] In January, 2001, the two were sentenced to 1-year home detention and 5-years probation as well as to pay $97,000 in restitution to the LSAT.[25] No word is available on their law school applications.

Blackstone, the great English legal commentator, insisted that burglary could only occur at those times of the day when it was too dark to see a man's face without the aid of artificial light or moonlight. He wrote:

> The time must be by night, and not by day: for in the day time there is no burglary. . . . As to what is reckoned night, and what day, for this purpose: anciently the day was accounted to begin only at sun-rising, and to end immediately upon sun-set; but the better opinion seems to be, that if there be daylight or crepusculum enough, begun or left, to discern a man's face withal, it is no burglary. But this does not extend to moonlight; for then many midnight burglaries would go unpunished: and besides, the malignity of the offence does not so properly arise from its being done in the dark, as at the dead of night; when all the creation, except beasts of prey, are at rest; when sleep has disarmed the owner, and rendered his castle defenceless.[26]

Today, states have expanded the definition of burglary to cover just about any unauthorized entry into a structure, at any time of day or night. Some states simply retain the nighttime provision in their statutes and have added other sections to their crimes codes that also punish daytime break-ins. They distinguish between nighttime and daytime break-ins by punishing night activity more severely than the same crime committed in broad daytime. The most common definition today is that burglary is the unlawful entry of a structure to commit a felony or theft. For example, the criminal law of Pennsylvania provides that:

> A person is guilty of burglary if he enters a building or occupied structure, or separately secured or occupied portion thereof, with intent to commit a crime therein, unless the premises are at the time open to the public or the actor is licensed or privileged to enter.[27]

Pennsylvania grades the offense on the basis of how the building or occupied structure is used. If the building isn't set up for overnight accommodations (i.e., it isn't a residence or a hotel or inn) and no one is present during the burglary, the offense carries a lesser penalty than if the building is a home. A burglar who enters a jewelry store to steal the merchandise is subject to a lesser penalty than if the same burglar broke into a private home. However, if the same burglar broke into the jewelry store, and the night watchman was there, he would face the higher penalty.

UNLAWFUL ENTRY INTO PREMISES

What does it mean to unlawfully enter premises? Does the burglar have to physically enter the premises with his whole body or is it enough that he breaks a window and reaches in to help himself to another's belongings? Most states hold that reaching in is enough to constitute burglary. Most states still require that there must be at least some form of unauthorized entry into the premises. That's because the crime of burglary is based in part on the concept of the tort of trespass. Trespass is the unlawful and unprivileged entry or intrusion onto the property of another. If the building entered is normally open to the public, and the defendant is legally present in the building, it is not burglary just as his presence would not constitute the tort of trespass.

DWELLING HOUSE OF ANOTHER

The Common Law definition required that to constitute burglary, the unlawful entry must have been to a dwelling house of another. At Common Law, a dwelling house was a structure in which people lived and slept. States no longer limit burglary to dwelling houses, and include just about any structure, occupied or unoccupied, in their definitions. Some states have expanded the definition to include unoccupied automobiles and even telephone booths. For example, California defines "burglary" so broadly as to include shoplifting and theft of goods from a "locked" but unoccupied automobile.[28]

The requirement that the building entered by a would-be burglar be "of another" is another reflection that the genesis of the crime of burglary is in the tort of trespass. Just as you cannot trespass on your own property, neither can you burglarize your own home. Although this may seem obvious, it is a fairly common problem, and courts must sometimes determine what is meant by "of another." For example, assume a husband and wife have separated, but the husband still is an owner of the marital home in which the wife continues to live. If the husband breaks the window and enters the house with the intent to steal property belonging to his wife, he cannot be charged with burglary. He has not entered the property of another. He could still be charged with theft, of course, if he successfully made off with his wife's property.

In addition to proving that the defendant entered the dwelling house (or other building, depending on the definition used in your state's burglary statute), the prosecution must show that the defendant didn't have permission to be present in the structure. Clearly, a person present in a public place during normal business hours when the facility is open to the public has implied permission to be there. He was invited and therefore isn't trespassing. The prosecution typically puts the property owner or a manager on the stand during trial to testify that the defendant didn't have permission to enter the building.

With Intent to Commit a Felony

A defendant's entry into another's structure, no matter how violent or destructive that entry was, isn't burglary unless the defendant can be shown to have intended to commit a felony while inside. Many states have made proof even easier, as they have specified that the intent that must be shown is merely the intent to commit a crime once inside. That crime does not have to be theft-related. It would still be burglary to break into a home with the intent to kill or rape someone inside. In many cases, there will be direct evidence of intent—as happens when a defendant is caught leaving the site of the burglary with stolen goods.

Sometimes a question is raised as to when the defendant formed the intent to commit a felony or other crime once inside. For example, a homeless person who seeks shelter in what appears to be an empty house but runs into the owner during his visit and then injures that owner may not be guilty of burglary. He may be guilty of a lesser offense like unlawful entry or criminal trespass. He would also likely be guilty of assault, but not burglary.

Proving intent is generally not difficult in burglary cases even if the defendant isn't "caught in the act." Circumstantial evidence is often relied on by juries and judges. Generally, judges and juries can rely on common sense when weighing circumstantial evidence. The fact that the defendant broke into a building that contains personal property and was caught often leads to an inference that he intended to steal some of that property once inside. Unless the defendant testifies and comes up with a plausible explanation for his presence, judge or jury likely will consider his presence and the circumstances surrounding it to satisfy the intent requirement.

ARSON

At Common Law, **arson** was the malicious burning of the dwelling house of another. The building burned had to be the dwelling of another, so that burning down a stable or other outbuilding was not arson. Nor was it a crime to burn down one's own building. In order to curtail insurance fraud (as might happen if an insured homeowner burned down his property and collected the insurance) and so-called spite arson (as might happen when an angry spouse burned down the home previously shared with a spouse and still jointly owned), most states expanded their definition of arson. Today, most states have changed their laws to define arson as the willful and malicious burning of a structure or building.

By setting the standard of intent as willful and malicious burning, arson statutes cover all the common motives for committing the crime. Possible motivation for committing arson include:

- *Arson for profit:* Arson committed in order to collect on insurance carried on the structure burned or by an owner who cannot sell the property and wants to move on. The latter can be a major problem in decaying urban areas with a large concentration of abandoned and boarded-up warehouses and businesses.
- *Arson for revenge:* Arson committed as payback for a failed love affair or marriage or in retaliation for an adverse employment decision.

- *Evidence destruction:* Arson committed to cover up another crime or destroy evidence, such as evidence that a victim in the structure was killed by fire rather than other means, or as a means of eliminating documents sought in a criminal investigation.
- *Political act:* Arson to make a political statement, such as the fire-bombing of abortion clinics by anti-abortion extremists.
- *Arson for thrill:* Some cases of arson are the work of thrill seekers who are frequently juveniles. These cases represent a high proportion of arson cases in which there is an arrest. Other fires may be set by perpetrators plagued by mental illness. Pyromaniacs may start fires as part of a quest for sexual or other excitement.[29]

Arson is a serious crime in the United States. The FBI reports that in 2000 there were over 78,000 cases of arson reported to police. Of these, over 30,000 involved structures, and over 12,700 of these, were single-family homes. The average amount of damages caused by arson directed at a structure was over $19,000. Unfortunately, the clearance rate for arson was only 16 percent. A crime is defined as "cleared" in the FBI crime reports when a suspect is arrested and charged with the crime. That means a great many incidents of arson go unpunished every year.[30]

When arson is politically motivated, the arsonist is sometimes also charged under federal law. For example, after the September 11, 2001, terrorist attacks, there was a flurry of anti-Muslim sentiment that swept through a segment of the population. In Salt Lake City, Utah, a restaurant owned by a man of Pakistani descent was set on fire. The suspect was James Hetrick, who later pled guilty to the crime of using force to attempt to intimidate or interfere with a federally protected activity. The protected activity was working. Herrick told the court he started the fire in response to the attacks of September 11, 2001, and purposely picked the restaurant because of the ethnicity and national origin of the owner.[31]

ESSENTIAL ELEMENTS OF ARSON

The essential elements that the government must prove beyond a reasonable doubt in an arson case are:

- The fire was willfully and maliciously set by the defendant or someone else on his orders. Carelessness isn't enough.
- The fire set by the defendant caused damage. Merely scorching a building is not enough (although the offense charged might instead be attempted arson or criminal trespass and criminal mischief).

Arson cases are not easy to prove. First, the fire itself, if successful, destroys much of the evidence. Second, there are many fires that are accidental and not the result of intentional wrongdoing. Cigarettes left to smolder, careless cooking, faulty electrical systems, and lightning are frequent causes of fires. In addition, getting the appropriate evidence may sometimes be difficult. Fire officials who arrive on the scene can make a preliminary decision whether the fire was intentionally set or not, and can seize any evidence in plain sight.

The Supreme Court has ruled that once a blaze has been extinguished and the firefighters have left the premises, a warrant is required to reenter the premises. The Fourth Amendment protects the owner of the premises from intrusion without probable cause that the fire was deliberately set. In order to get a warrant, a government official must show more than that a fire occurred. However, the firefighters who initially respond may seize evidence that is in plain view and investigate the cause of the fire as part of their efforts to contain it and make the area safe. That evidence can then be used to support an application for a warrant if it reached the level of probable cause. The case *Michigan v. Tyler*[32] involved a fire at a furniture store. When the fire chief arrived, the fire was still smoldering. Discovered in the embers were several plastic containers of flammable liquid, which aroused suspicion. Over the next few weeks, police and fire officials returned several times to gather evidence, all without a warrant. The testimony of fire experts and evidence obtained from the visits were introduced into evidence and the store owners were convicted of arson. The Supreme Court reversed the convictions and ordered any evidence seized after the immediate exigency was over without a warrant be excluded in any retrial.

HISTORICAL HIGHLIGHT
How the FBI Began Collecting Crime Data

Early in the twentieth century it became apparent to law enforcement officials that tracking the type and frequency of criminal activity was important to its containment. The problem was that individual states didn't always share information about criminal activity within their borders with others in the union. In addition, each state had a unique set of criminal laws, and there were as many definitions of specific crimes as there were states.

In the late 1920s the International Association of Chiefs of Police suggested that there should be a national database of crime and criminal activity. Voluntary data collection began in 1930, with information coming from state, county, and city law enforcement agencies. The information is now gathered at the Federal Bureau of Investigation. Law enforcement agencies use uniform definitions when deciding which crimes to report to help overcome differences in state laws. There are eight classifications of crimes reported to the FBI. These are:

1. Murder and nonnegligent manslaughter
2. Forcible rape
3. Robbery
4. Aggravated assault
5. Burglary
6. Larceny-theft
7. Motor vehicle theft
8. Arson

The FBI publishes an annual report of crime in America, which is available at the FBI website *www.fbi.gov*.

FORGERY AND CHECK FRAUD

The number of checks written in the United States every year is staggering. And many of these checks are stolen and altered or counterfeited, resulting in a loss of between $10 billion and $14 billion per year, according to the U.S. Department of the Treasury. **Forgery** is the fraudulent making or altering of any writing in a way that alters the legal rights and liabilities of another. Although many types of documents can be forged, checks are the most common documents. Check fraud includes forgery and other forms of theft accomplished through the misuse of checks or the check processing system.

Check fraud and forgery can be committed in a number of creative ways. The most common forms of check fraud are:

- *Forged signatures:* Forged signature checks are legitimate checks with a forged signature. A thief may steal a checkbook from the owner or intercept an order of checks arriving in the mail and fill out the checks, supplying his signature for that of the account holder.
- *Forged endorsement:* In this form of check fraud, a thief steals an already-made-out check and forges the endorsement signature on the back and cashes or deposits the funds.
- *Altered checks:* In this form of check fraud, a thief alters a check to make it appear the check is made out to someone other than the intended payee or the amount to be drawn against the drawer's account is altered.
- *Check kiting:* In this form of check fraud, criminals deposit a check into one account, which is drawn on another bank's account, and then draws on the deposit knowing that the deposited check is no good.
- *Counterfeit checks:* This form of check fraud involves the creation of fake checks. Today, with the rapid development of computer technology and software, forging checks is easy. All a thief needs is a computer, a checking account number and bank routing number (found on every check), check writing software, and a printer. Software intended to be used by consumers to print their own legitimate checks can churn out checks that look and seem indistinguishable from the real thing.

All states have criminal laws punishing check fraud and forgery, although the language varies from state to state. For example, in Minnesota, a person

> . . . is guilty of check forgery . . . if the person, with intent to defraud, does any of the following:
>
> 1. falsely makes or alters a check so that it purports to have been made by another or by the maker under an assumed or fictitious name, or at another time, or with different provisions, or by the authority of one who did not give authority; or
> 2. falsely endorses or alters a check so that it purports to have been endorsed by another.[33]

In addition, the United States Code has many provisions dealing with forged and counterfeited securities and other commercial documents.[34] Note also that the Uniform Commercial Code, which all states have adopted with some variation, has extensive provisions that govern liability of financial institutions and account holders when a check is forged or altered.

Most states also have laws that criminalize writing checks when there are insufficient funds in the account to cover the checks. Generally, these statutes provide that the maker of the check must be notified that the check has been dishonored and be given an opportunity to make the check good if the account was open. If he or she doesn't, criminal charges can be filed. For example, Pennsylvania provides that the drawer be notified that the check was dishonored within 30 days of presentment, and that the drawer must make the check good within 10 days of notification. If he or she does not, the Commonwealth can rely on the presumption that the maker's intent was fraudulent.[35]

PRACTICE POINTERS

As with most criminal laws covered in this textbook, they are just guidelines and a starting point for research. Always check the exact wording of the criminal code of your state or the U.S. Code if the case you are working on comes under federal jurisdiction. This is especially true of cases involving theft. State statutes vary greatly.

If the client has already been charged, read the statute carefully. This is especially true when the charge is robbery and the statute increases the sentence if the defendant used a dangerous weapon. The nature of the weapon used, especially if it was a fake or a toy, may give rise to an argument that the crime committed was at most simple robbery, and be the basis for a plea bargain to a lesser offense.

If a client faces arson charges, be sure to examine the allegations and the evidence carefully. Evidence seized or observed without a warrant after the immediate exigency of the fire has passed may be inadmissible. If you are working for the prosecution, prepare as if defense counsel will raise the issue and determine what evidence was seized during or immediately after the fire and what was seized later. The earlier evidence may still be enough to allow an expert to conclude that the fire was set.

If you work for the defense, you may want to consider bringing in your own expert to determine if the evidence really indicates that the fire was deliberately set. Also examine the prosecution's indictment carefully. It will typically lay out the alleged motive the defendant had for torching his or another's property. Does the motive put forth by the prosecution make sense? For example, prosecutors will often suggest that insurance is the motivation. That may be logical if the policy was just issued or recently increased, but not if the policy is a long-standing one. Frank discussions should take place about the defendant's financial position. Heavy debt and a failing or underperforming business may be perceived as motivation for arson, but can be countered with evidence that business was on the upswing or that alternative financing was in the works.

Forgery and check fraud cases often depend heavily on expert testimony about the authenticity of a signature. Both the prosecution and the defense are likely to employ experts in document examination. When identifying an expert in arson or document examination, keep these guidelines in place:

- Examine each potential expert's resume and experience carefully. Note membership in relevant professional organizations and publications in juried or peer-reviewed journals. If the expert is affiliated with a major university or other well-respected organization, so much the better.
- Experts who only testify for the prosecution or only testify for the defense are suspect. At best, they appear less credible than those whose testimony has been more evenly spread. At worst, the expert will appear to be a hired gun or in the prosecutor's pocket.

● Check credentials carefully. In recent years there has been a rash of cases involving erroneous or intentionally false testimony by forensic experts. Nothing will sink an expert's testimony faster than evidence that he or she faces professional negligence or even criminal charges arising out of testimony in other cases. This is an area where defense counsel have recently become more proactive, seeking out evidence that a particular laboratory or expert has lied or misled in other cases.

● When preparing the case, note any special rules in your jurisdiction about the exchange of expert testimony or notice of the intended use of an expert's opinion at trial.

CHAPTER SUMMARY

To understand crimes against property, you must first understand what property is. Property consists of a bundle of rights, including the right to possess, use and enjoy, and dispose of something. It is not a material object itself, but a person's right to do what he or she wishes with that object, subject to limitations provided in the law.

Real property is land and everything permanently attached to it. It includes land, subsurface rights, air rights, timbering and harvesting rights, and any buildings and structures permanently attached to the land. Personal property is everything else to which the law grants ownership rights. Property can be owned outright. If it is, the owner is said to hold the property in fee simple. Fee simple is a legal term for ownership of the entire bundle of rights that go with a piece of property.

Property can be held by one or jointly. Tenancy by the entirety is a legal joint ownership in which both spouses own an undivided interest in the whole property and in which neither spouse can sell his or her interest without the consent of the other. It only applies to married couples. Other forms of joint ownership are tenancy in common and joint tenancy with right of survivorship. Tenants in common each own an undivided interest in the whole property. If the owners hold property as joint tenants with right of survivorship, the survivor gets the property in the event of death of a joint tenant.

A basic understanding of the law of property is necessary in order to understand criminal laws that punish interference with property rights. Theft was defined at Common Law as the taking and carrying away of another's personal property with the intent to deprive him or her of it permanently. Laws that make theft a crime require that the person stealing the property intends to permanently deprive the owner of the use, possession, and enjoyment of that property.

Today, states and the federal government have passed many laws that build upon the Common Law definition of theft but apply to special situations. Theft offenses include theft by deception, embezzlement, library theft, shoplifting, auto theft, and many others. Robbery is theft accomplished by the use of force or the threat of force. It differs from theft in that the victim is put in fear before surrendering the property sought by the robber. Robbery carried out with the use or brandishing of a weapon is a more serious offense than robbery without a weapon.

Burglary was defined at Common Law as breaking and entering of the dwelling house of another at night with the intent to commit a felony inside. Today the offense can occur at any time of day and does not require that a dwelling house be the target. A forcible entry into any structure with the intent to commit a felony once inside is all that is required.

Arson was the malicious burning of the dwelling house of another at Common Law. Today the definition has been expanded to cover the intentional and malicious burning of a structure. If the intention of the arsonist is to collect insurance proceeds, it does not matter that the property was his own. Arson is committed for many reasons, including insurance fraud, spite, as a political statement, and for thrill and excitement. Any of these motives are enough to establish that the fire was set intentionally and maliciously.

Forgery is the fraudulent making or altering of any writing in a way that alters the legal rights and liabilities of another. Common forms of forgery involve check fraud. Check fraud includes forging the signature of another on a check, forging an endorsement on the back of a check, altering the amount of a check or to whom it is drawn, check kiting between accounts, and producing counterfeit checks. All are punishable under state laws. In addition, states often make it a crime to write a "bad" check. Once the maker is notified that the check was not honored, he or she generally has a short period of time to make it good before charges are filed.

KEY TERMS

Arson: The intentional and malicious burning of a structure. At Common Law, it was the malicious burning of the dwelling house of another.

Burglary: At Common Law, the breaking and entering of the dwelling house of another at night with the intent to commit a felony inside. Today, burglary is the forcible entry into a structure with the intent to commit a felony once inside.

Eminent domain: The state's power to take private property for a public use or public purpose without the owner's consent. The U.S. Constitution requires that property can only be taken after due process of law.

Fee simple: The legal term for ownership of the entire bundle of rights that go with a piece of property.

Forgery: The fraudulent making or altering of any writing in a way that alters the legal rights and liabilities of another.

Joint tenants with right of survivorship: Form of ownership in which the joint tenant receives the property should the other die. Either may sell their share before death and the new owners then become tenants in common.

Personal property: All property other than real property.

Property: A bundle of rights, including the right to possess, use and enjoy, and dispose of something. It is not a material object itself, but a person's right to do what he or she wishes with that object, subject to limitations provided in the law.

Real property: Consists of land and everything permanently attached to it. It includes land, subsurface rights, air rights, timbering and harvesting rights, and any buildings and structures permanently attached to the land.

Robbery: The taking of personal property from the person of another against his will, by either force or threat of force.

Tenancy by the entirety: The legal joint ownership in which both spouses own an undivided interest in the whole property and in which neither spouse can sell his or her interest without the consent of the other.

Tenants in common: Form of joint ownership in which each owns an undivided interest in the whole property.

Theft: The taking and carrying away of another's personal property with the intent to deprive him or her of it permanently.

DISCUSSION QUESTIONS

1. A community has enacted a law that requires residents to separate their garbage into recyclables and nonrecyclables. The recyclable items are placed in plastic containers marked "Property of the City of Ecology." The city collects the contents of the containers and sells it to a recycling facility, boosting the city budget by several hundred thousand dollars per year. Joe, a homeless man, makes the rounds on garbage day and selects metal cans from the recycling bins, which he crushes and sells to a recycling facility. He is arrested and charged with theft of city property. You have been asked to analyze the case on behalf of the public defender representing Joe. What is Joe's best defense to the theft charges?

2. What form of check fraud has occurred in each of the following factual scenarios?

   A. Carla receives a birthday check from her grandmother and adds a "1" in front of the $10 and writes "One Hundred" in front of the Ten Dollars and no cents on the check.

   B. Sarah buys a copy of "Easy Check" software for her computer and uses the account number and bank routing number from her roommate's checks to print checks, which she then uses to pay her tuition bill.

   C. Jack finds a purse at a bus stop, and takes a check from the checkbook he finds inside. He makes the check out to "cash" and signs the check with the account holder's name.

   D. Smitty maintains two checking accounts at two banks. He will be paid on Friday and has no funds in either account on Wednesday. Wednesday he writes a check for $100 to himself on account number one and deposits it in account number two. He then withdraws $100 from account number two. On Friday he deposits his paycheck in account number one to cover the check.

3. Jessy decides to rob a bank. Jessy dresses up as a clown and carries a child's toy rifle, which has an orange tip, when he approaches a teller and demands cash after brandishing the gun. He is caught a block from the bank as he trips on his clown shoes. Police charge him with armed robbery. How do you approach his defense?

4. Jerry is separated from his wife and still owns a house jointly with her. She has changed the keys to the house, and Jerry breaks a window to enter the house and retrieve personal belongings. He is charged with burglary. How do you defend him? Is your answer different if he takes his wife's possessions rather than his own?

5. Mary has been thinking about remodeling her kitchen. She has contacted several contractors, and has received several estimates. She has also applied for a home equity loan to finance the project, but has been turned down because she does not have enough equity in the home to qualify. Saturday night she fries some chicken and leaves the deep fryer full of oil on in the kitchen. She leaves for a walk. When she returns, she finds the firefighters dowsing a fire in her kitchen. Although the rest of the structure is saved, the kitchen is a total loss. Insurance covers the rebuilding. If you are the local prosecutor, how would you go about putting together a case against Mary? What evidence would you seek, and how would you obtain it?

FURTHER READING

1. Morris, J. (1995). *DSM IV Made Easy.* The Guilford Press. This handbook helps demystify psychiatric diagnosis and is especially helpful for legal professionals working with psychiatric experts.
2. Faith, N. (2000). *Blaze: The Forensics of Fire.* St. Martin's Press. This book describes historic fires and the techniques used to determine their cause.
3. Redsicker, D., and O'Connor, J. (1996). *Practical Fire and Arson Investigation.* CRC Press. A guidebook for fire and arson investigators.
4. Shover, N. (1996). *Great Pretenders, Pursuits and Careers of Persistent Thieves.* Westview Press. This book looks at the career criminal who resumes a life of crime despite efforts to "go straight."
5. Cromwell, P. (editor). (1998). *In Their Own Words: Criminals on Crime.* Roxbury. An anthology in which criminals explain their life of crime.

QUOTATIONS FOR CHAPTER TEN

1. *Private property is held sacred in all good governments, and particularly in our own.*
   Andrew Jackson, addressing officers at New Orleans while defending against the British Army (1815)
2. *The personal right to acquire property, which is a natural right, gives to property, when acquired, a right to protection, as a social right.*
   James Madison, addressing Virginia Convention (1829)
3. *In no other country in the world is the love of property keener or more alert than in the United States, and nowhere else does the majority display less inclination toward doctrines which in any way threaten the way property is owned.*
   Alexis de Tocqueville, *Democracy in America* (1840)

ENDNOTES

1. Ballentine's Law Dictionary.
2. Ibid.
3. Ibid.
4. Ibid.
5. Ibid.
6. Ibid.
7. "Merchants Find Meeting Held Trouble in Store," *Seattle Times* (December 1, 1999).
8. "Two Arrested for Looting WTC Tourneau Store," *Professional Jeweler* (September 24, 2001).
9. "Man Charged in $2m Theft of Rare Books from Yale," *Boston Globe* (December 8, 2001).
10. "Man Charged With Theft By Deception. He Sold Storage Space He Couldn't Provide," *Concord* (New Hampshire) *Monitor* (September 27, 2001).
11. Caster, B. Montgomery County District Attorney's Office Press Release (February 9, 2001).

12. The author's first jury trial involved just such a case. The defendant, who represented himself, told the jury he was merely "borrowing" the grill and intended to return it after a backyard barbecue. He was acquitted.

13. Barasch, D. United States Attorney for the Middle District of Pennsylvania Press Release (February 20, 2001).

14. "Prothonotary's Debts Paid by Commissioners," *The* (Lewistown, PA) *Sentinel* (June 4, 2001). The author began her legal career as an Assistant District Attorney in Mifflin County and never for a moment suspected that there was anything amiss at the courthouse. Embezzlement is notoriously hard to recognize if the embezzler appears to lead a "normal" lifestyle.

15. "Ex-Treasurer of Episcopal Church Sentenced to 5 Years; Crime: Ellen Cooke Admitted Embezzling $1.5 Million from the Denomination. Judge Cites Ex-Official's Greed and Desire for High-living in Imposing the Stiff Sentence," *LA Times* (July 13, 1996).

16. Ballentine's Law Dictionary.

17. 18 U.S.C. § 2113.

18. *Carter v. United States,* 530 U.S. 255 (2000).

19. S.C. Code Ann § 16–11–330.

20. *United States v. Miller,* 206 F. 3d 1051 (11th Cir. 2000).

21. *State of South Carolina v. Gourdine,* 472 S.E.2d 241 (1996).

22. *United States v. Perry,* 991 F.2d 304 (6th Cir. 1993).

23. *McLaughlin v. United States,* 476 U.S. 16 (1986).

24. "LSAT Robbery Prompts Arrests," *The Daily Trojan* (UCLA) (March 27, 1997).

25. "LSAT Cheaters Are Sentenced to Probation," *Corpus Christi Caller Times* (January 28, 2000).

26. 4 W. Blackstone, Commentaries 224.

27. 18 P.S. § 3502.

28. 18 Cal. Penal Code Ann. § 459

29. According to the American Psychiatric Association's *Diagnostic and Statistical Manual of Psychiatric Disorders,* Fourth Edition, patients with pyromania exhibit the following behavior: A patient must have set more than one fire, been tense or excited before setting the fire, have been fascinated by fire in the past, experienced pleasure, gratification, or relief after the fire or while watching it, and not had any of the other common reasons for setting the fire, such as revenge, political agenda, or profit motive.

30. U.S. Department of Justice, Federal Bureau of Investigation Press Release, *Crime in the United States, 2000* (October 22, 2001).

31. U.S. Department of Justice, Federal Bureau of Investigation Online Publication, *No Tolerance for Hate Crimes,* Page Two: Beyond the Headlines (November 19, 2001).

32. *Michigan v. Tyler,* 436 U.S. 499 (1978).

33. Minn. Stat. §609.631(2).

34. 18 U.S.C. §470 et. seq.

35. 18 P.S. § 4105.

CHAPTER 11
Treason, Terrorism, and Wartime Criminal Justice

CHAPTER OBJECTIVES

After studying this chapter, you should be able to:

- Explain the history of wartime criminal laws
- List and explain the provisions in the U.S. Constitution that govern the powers of Congress and the president in time of war
- Define treason and list and explain the provisions in the U.S. Constitution that apply to treason
- Define the elements of treason and sedition
- List two federal laws that define and punish terrorist acts
- Understand the major provisions of the Patriot Act of 2001 as they apply to acts of terror directed against the United States' interests at home and abroad
- Explain the history of presidential orders for military tribunals in time of war or armed conflict

CHAPTER CONTENTS

> *They that can give up essential liberty to obtain a little temporary safety deserve neither liberty nor safety.*
>
> **Benjamin Franklin**

> *The Congress shall have the power . . . to declare war, grant letters of marque and reprisal, and make rules concerning captures on land and water.*
>
> *U.S. Constitution,* **Article I, Section 8**

> *Treason against the United States, shall consist only in levying war against them, or in adhering to their enemies, giving them aid and comfort. No person shall be convicted of treason unless on the testimony of two witnesses to the same overt act, or on confession in open court.*
>
> *U.S. Constitution,* **Article III, Section 3**

INTRODUCTION AND HISTORICAL BACKGROUND

Our history is full of contradictions when it comes to judging loyalty and putting out the welcome mat. On one hand, we are a country made up of a large population of immigrants. With the exception of those among us who can trace our ancestry to members of Native American tribes, we are all descendants of immigrants or first-generation immigrants. The Statue of Liberty extolls us to "Bring me your tired, your poor, your huddled masses yearning to breathe free."[1] On the other hand, as a nation we have been quick to judge and sometimes misjudge the loyalty of new arrivals, particularly in times of war or domestic turmoil.

Treason and sedition are crimes that punish the disloyalty of a country's citizens and resident aliens. A duty of loyalty is assumed by all who reside in a country. Loyalty to one's nation is such an ingrained value that governments punish disloyalty reflexively. Similarly, espionage, whether for economic or ideological reasons, constitutes a breach of trust on both a personal and national level. Our discussion of treason, terrorism, and wartime criminal justice necessarily begins with a discussion of history. As you will see, what was done in the past is often prologue to the present. For example, when President George W. Bush issued an Executive Order on November 13, 2001, calling for secret military tribunals to try suspected terrorists, his supporters pointed to the trial of suspected WWII saboteurs by a military court as precedent for the order.

One of the earliest examples of restrictions borne of doubts about loyalty were the Alien and Sedition Acts of 1798 signed into law by President John Adams. At the time, there was great fear of an enemy within at a time when it appeared we might go to war against France. The problem was that there were a great many French aliens in the young country. Some estimates were that there were 25,000 French in Philadelphia alone. There were also many newly arrived Irish refugees from the Irish Rebellion of 1798.

The Alien Act increased the time needed to qualify for citizenship from 5 to 14 years and gave the president the power to expel any foreigner he considered dangerous. The Sedition Act made it a crime to either make "[f]alse, scandalous, and malicious" writings against the government or to stir up sedition among otherwise loyal Americans. The law was subsequently used to quiet troublesome newspaper editors.[2] Both laws were to be the law of the land for only a few years.

WARTIME POWER

As you have learned, the Constitution sets forth the framework for the American system of justice. The arrangement relies heavily on all three branches of government having a say in running the country. Each branch has powers that serve as a check on the other branches lest any one branch become all powerful. The framers of the Constitution wanted to avoid any possibility that the people would ever again be subject to tyrannical rule by a monarch or that a head of state could assume dictatorial powers.

The framers foresaw that there would inevitably be times when the country would face enemies, internal and external, as well as times of peace. To assure that our form of government would survive the inevitable challenges ahead, the Constitution provides for the **power to declare war.** Among the checks and balances found in the Constitution are power-sharing provisions for just such times. For example, the Constitution grants to Congress "the power . . . to declare war, grant letters of marque and reprisal, and make rules concerning captures on land and water."[3]

Letters of marque and reprisal are letters from a government formerly used to grant a private person the power to seize the subjects of a foreign state. The same clause of the Constitution also gives Congress the power :

- To raise and support armies
- To provide and maintain a navy
- To make rules for the government and regulation of the land and naval forces
- To call up the militia to execute the laws of the Union and suppress insurrections and repel invasions.

The president also plays a role in wartime. The Constitution provides that:

> The President shall be the Commander in Chief of the Army and Navy of the United States, and of the Militia of the several states when called into the actual Service of the United States.[4]

As you can see, it is Congress that has the power to declare war and the president who is in charge of planning, organizing, and executing that war. The limitation of the president's power in time of war has been tested several times, with the deciding vote coming from the Judicial Branch of government. Since 1973, the power to commit troops over-

HISTORICAL HIGHLIGHT
Laws Restricting Freedom in Times of War or National Emergency

In times of war and national emergency, the federal government has historically enacted special legislation designed to protect the people from real or perceived danger. The most infamous of laws was the Executive Order authorizing the federal government to inter Japanese Americans in camps during World War II. Other examples include:

- The Alien and Sedition Acts of 1798. These laws gave the president the authority to exclude any alien he thought was dangerous and made it illegal to make false accusations against the government or to incite citizens to sedition.
- The Sedition Act of 1918. This law made it illegal to criticize the United States' role in the war effort during World War I.
- The Smith Act of 1940. This law made it a crime to "knowingly or willfully advocate, abet, advise, or teach the duty, necessity, desirability, or propriety of overthrowing any government in the U.S. by force or violence or to print, publish, edit, issue, circulate, sell, distribute, or publicly display any written or printed matter advocating, advising, or teaching the duty, necessity, desirability, or propriety of overthrowing governments."
- The McCarren Act of 1950. Also known as the Internal Security Act, this federal law allowed for the establishment of internment camps for use in national emergencies.
- The McCarren-Walter Act of 1952. This law, also known as the Immigration and Nationality Act, tightened restrictions on aliens and reduced immigration from nonwhite countries. It also legalized stripping naturalized citizens who were judged "subversive" of their citizenship and deporting them. In addition, the law allowed deportation of resident aliens engaged in political activity.

seas had also been governed by the War Powers Resolution, passed by Congress. The legislation provides that the president may commit troops when Congress has declared war, when Congress has specifically authorized troops to be deployed, or when the United States has been attacked.

Both Congressional power and presidential power have been fine-tuned with the assistance of the Supreme Court. In times of turmoil, presidents sometimes issue orders citing as authority the inherent power of the president as commander in chief. That was the case during the Korean Conflict. Starting in 1950, North Korea, with the support of the People's Republic of China and the Soviet Union, waged war against South Korea. It was a conflict widely viewed as an attempt by Communist forces to expand their influence. President Harry

Truman bypassed Congress, and did not ask for a declaration of war. Instead, he called the conflict a "police action" and worked with the United Nations in defending South Korea.

By 1952, the conflict in Korea was in full force, and at home steel workers were talking about going on strike. President Truman saw the steel industry as essential to a successful police action in Korea, and to avoid a shutdown, took decisive action. He issued an Executive Order that authorized the secretary of commerce to "take possession of all such plants, facilities, and other property . . . as he may deem necessary in the interests of national defense."[5]

Within hours, the owners of the steel plants seized sought help from federal courts. The case came to the Supreme Court within weeks. The president argued that he had the power as commander in chief to take immediate action in an emergency. The Supreme Court disagreed. Justice Black concluded that "the founders of this Nation entrusted the lawmaking power to the Congress alone in both good and bad times" so that if the president wanted to nationalize an industry he had better get Congress to pass legislation doing so.[6]

At times when Congress has declared war, the Supreme Court has been less reluctant to second-guess presidential Executive Orders. For example, after the Japanese bombed Pearl Harbor in a sneak attack and Congress declared war on Japan, people on the West Coast became concerned about the prospect of either a direct invasion by the Japanese or acts of internal sabotage by Japanese aliens and immigrants and even their American born children. One of the first to call for the internment of Japanese Americans was the Republican congressman from Santa Monica, Leland M. Ford. Congressman Ford insisted that "all Japanese, whether citizens or not, be placed in inland concentration camps." His voice was joined by others, and soon the delegations from California, Oregon, and Washington were calling for internment.

Earl Warren was the California attorney general at the time. He ordered his staff to prepare maps detailing the location of all Japanese and Japanese American landowners in California. These maps revealed that people of Japanese ancestry owned land located near or around what could be considered strategic targets for sabotage, such as beaches, air and oil fields, and water reservoirs.

On February 19, 1942, President Roosevelt signed Executive Order 9066. The order authorized the military to clear sensitive areas of any and all persons and to restrict movement into and out of such areas. Excluded from many areas, the presence of Japanese Americans in communities could, according to Warren, ". . . bring about race riots and prejudice and hysteria and excesses of all kinds." The solution was, allegedly for their own safety, that the displaced should be confined. By March 2, the military designated the western half of California, Oregon, and Washington as a military area and ordered those of Japanese heritage removed.[7]

All in all, over 110,000 people were confined to internment camps until the end of the war. The Supreme Court went on to uphold the evacuation and internment in *Korematsu v. United States*.[8] Many of the internees, most of whom were U.S. citizens, lost their homes and businesses. Although the internment of Japanese Americans is probably best known, the United States also interned Italian and German Americans and resident aliens from Italy, Germany, and Japan. Congress apologized decades later, and President Ronald Reagan signed the Civil Liberties Act of 1988. The Act was passed by Congress to provide a presidential apology and symbolic payment of $20,000 to the internees, evacuees, and persons of Japanese ancestry who lost liberty or property due to the forced internments. Earl Warren, who played such a pivotal role as California attorney general, went on to become chief justice of the Supreme Court. His decisions were to be known as some of the most liberal ever, and included *Brown v. Board of Education* and *Miranda v. Arizona*.

HABEAS CORPUS IN WARTIME AND THE QUESTION OF MILITARY TRIBUNALS

You may recall that **habeas corpus** is a legal term that literally means "have the body." When a court exercises the writ of *habeas corpus,* or the "Great Writ," it literally orders another authority to bring a person held to the court. It was originally used to prevent kings from simply making enemies disappear. Today, *habeas corpus* petitions are commonly filed by prisoners in state systems who want a federal court to review whether the justice they are receiving at the hand of the state meets minimum constitutional standards. Thus, a state prisoner who believes the conditions in his prison cell amount to cruel and unusual punishment can have access to a federal court to hear that complaint by filing a *habeas corpus* petition.

The right of *habeas corpus* is an important one in both English and American jurisprudence. It is seen as a pivotal right. For example, the great English legal scholar Blackstone thought the right of *habeas corpus* as "the bulwark of the British Constitution." He wrote that the right to *habeas corpus* was even more important than the right to be free from the loss of property without due process of law because "confinement of the person, by secretly hurrying him to jail, where his sufferings are unknown or forgotten is a less public, a less striking, and therefore a more dangerous engine of arbitrary government."[9]

The Constitution provides that "The privilege of the Writ of Habeas Corpus shall not be suspended, unless when in cases of rebellion or invasion the public safety may require it."[10] The standard, then, is a tough one. The presumption is that every person held under the control of an agent or unit of government is entitled to some means of judicial review of his confinement, conviction, or sentence. Even during World War II when the federal government tried suspected German saboteurs in a military tribunal, the prisoners had the right to have their case reviewed by courts.

The federal government has employed the use of **military tribunals** during time of war. For example, President Lincoln used a military court to try Lambdin P. Milligan during the Civil War. He was sentenced to hanging by a military tribunal for planning to form a secret military faction to free captured Confederate soldiers, rearm them, and invade Indiana. The case came before the Court on a petition for *habeas corpus* even though President Lincoln had suspended *habeas corpus.* The Supreme Court wrote that only Congress had the authority to set up military tribunals, and then only in time of war. As long as the country's courts are open, concluded the Court, they were the proper venue for trial and reversed the conviction.[11]

MILITARY TRIBUNALS TODAY

In the aftermath of the terrorist attacks on September 11, 2001, President George W. Bush signed an Executive Order authorizing the detention and trial of noncitizens by military tribunals. This order cites as authority by Congress for Authorization for Use of Military Force. That authorization declared:

> That the President is authorized to use all necessary and appropriate force against those nations, organizations, or persons he determines planned, authorized, committed, or aided the terrorist attacks that occurred on September 11, 2001, or harbored such organizations or persons, in order to prevent any future acts of international terrorism against the United States by such nations, organizations or persons.

HISTORICAL HIGHLIGHT
Habeas Corpus *Lends Helping Hand to Imprisoned Student after September 11th Attacks*

Imagine that you are a 21-year-old student from Jordan who is being questioned after the attacks on America on September 11th. You are being asked hundreds of questions while strapped to a lie-detector machine. Imagine further that, although you did not commit any crime and are not being charged with any crime, you might know a few things about what happened, making you a material witness. Would you be nervous or scared?

Osama Awadallah, a student at Grossmont College in El Cajon, California, was in just this situation. After being questioned by the FBI and being identified as a possible material witness for a grand jury, Awadallah was in maximum security prisons for the next three weeks, transported from Southern California, to Oklahoma, and then to Manhattan. During this time, he was shackled, strip-searched, and sometimes kept in solitary confinement. But Osama Awadallah had not been arrested for any crime, he was being held to testify before a grand jury.

Thanks to *habeas corpus,* Shira A. Scheindlin, a judge for the U.S. District Court for the Southern District of New York, was able to find that Awadallah was unlawfully detained and that "since 1789, no Congress has granted the government the authority to imprison an innocent person in order to guarantee that he will testify before a grand jury conducting a criminal investigation." Osama Awadallah was released and his testimony to the grand jury was suppressed.[12]

President Bush's order calls for some suspected terrorists to be tried by military tribunals, and announced that the rules of evidence ordinarily applied to criminal cases tried in federal court would not be followed. The order covers noncitizens designated personally by the president for military tribunal trial after he concludes any of the following:

- If they are or were Al Qaida members.
- If they engaged in, aided or abetted, or conspired to commit acts of international terrorism.
- If they have harbored such individuals.

The order also says the president can designate noncitizens for military trials if "it is in the best interest of the United States that such individual be subject to this order."

Those designated by the president for military trial will be tried either in the United States or abroad under the following conditions:

- The military commission sits as trier of fact and law; roles usually split between the jury and judge.
- The presiding officer can admit any evidence that has "probative value to a reasonable person."

HISTORICAL HIGHLIGHT
FBI Rushes World War II Would-Be Saboteurs to Electric Chair

In 1942 after the United States declared war on Germany, eight would-be Nazi saboteurs left German-occupied France for America. Submarines dropped the two groups off along the Long Island, New York, beach and Ponte Vedra Beach in Florida. Seven were German citizens, but the eighth was a U.S. citizen. One declared to his partner that he intended to turn himself in rather than commit acts of sabotage. He did so, and was questioned for eight days by the FBI. He told the FBI that the Germans were intent on landing others and engaging in a war of terror by leaving bombs in public places and blowing up vital industrial plants.[13]

The FBI arrested all eight men and turned them over to a military commission. They were tried under the Articles of War (military laws authorized by Congress earlier), convicted, and sentenced to death. While the trial was still underway, they filed a request for *habeas corpus* with the Supreme Court, relying on *Ex parte Milligan* to claim that the military tribunal had no jurisdiction and that state or federal courts should handle the case.

The Court agreed to hear the case. The Articles of Law previously enacted by Congress allowed a military commission to try those not ordinarily tried by court martial. Therefore, this time the Court upheld the military tribunal's convictions of spying, conspiracy, and violating the laws of war. It held that those who are unlawful combatants such as these men who entered the country secretly and did not wear uniforms or carry identification weren't prisoners of war, and could be tried by a military commission when Congress has provided for such commissions in legislation. Within a month, all eight men were sentenced and six of them were executed by electrocution in a D.C. jail.[14]

- The secretary of defense designates the prosecutor, and the defendant may have an attorney.
- Conviction need not be unanimous, but can be by vote of two-thirds of the commission, and sentencing agreed upon by two-thirds of the commission.
- Any appeal goes to the president or the secretary of defense, and their decision is final. The order specifies that those tried by military tribunal can't appeal to any court in the United States, foreign country, or any international tribunal.

One problem with the president's order is that it may well interfere with efforts to extradite to the United States or otherwise put suspected terrorists in the hands of U.S. military tribunals. For example, the idea of secret hearings, few rights for the accused, and military officers serving as both judge and jury may violate treaties in force such as the 1950 European Convention on Human Rights. In addition, the European Union countries have all banned capital punishment, and may refuse to extradite suspects without promises that they would not be executed if convicted. Even if an EU country did agree to extradite a suspect, he or she would have the right to appeal to the European Court of Human Rights, whose decision is binding on all EU member countries.

At the time of the writing of this textbook, no suspected terrorist was known to have been tried by military commission although the military has stated that they plan to begin trials soon. It has released some of the prisoners. Some members of Congress as well as civil rights organizations were questioning whether President Bush had the authority to call for tribunals without the express consent of Congress and whether any president or Congress had the authority to suspend the right of *habeas corpus* under the circumstances and in the manner the order purports to.

Now that several years have passed since the events of 9/11, the legal community has begun looking more closely at the need for special tribunals and especially at the idea that "enemy combatants" can be detained indefinitely without charges being filed or their cases being adjudicated. In fact, the U.S. Supreme Court decided two so-called enemy combatant cases during 2004. Both involve American citizens being held by the military as suspected terrorists.

The first case involves Yasir Esam Hamdi, a Saudi national who was born in Louisiana while his parents worked for an oil company. Because he was, he is an American citizen. Hamdi was captured on a battlefield in Afghanistan and eventually moved to the detention center in Guantanamo, Cuba. When the U.S. military discovered he was a citizen, it transferred him to a naval brig in Virginia.

His parents filed a lawsuit, alleging that as a citizen he could not be held indefinitely. The Fourth Circuit Court of Appeals concluded that because he was caught on the battleground as an enemy, he could be held without charges.[15] His parents appealed, and the Supreme Court agreed to decide whether Hamdi was being legally held as an enemy combatant. The Department of Defense argued that Hamdi had been caught on the battlefield, that he was armed and ready to fight other American citizens, and that he had been interrogated by our military. That interrogation gave him the opportunity to challenge his detention, the government argued.

On the last day of the 2003–2004 term, the Court issued its opinion. It told the Bush administration that any American citizen held as an enemy combatant without charges must be given a meaningful opportunity to challenge that designation before an independent and neutral decision-maker. The Court wrote, "An interrogation by one's captor, however, effective as an intelligence-gathering tool, hardly constitutes a constitutionally adequate fact-finding before a neutral decision-maker." The Court did not specify the mechanics of that review, but instead sent the case back to the federal trial court.[16] The Court left open the possibility that a military tribunal like that authorized by the president shortly after 9/11 might be adequate, but reiterated that any decision could be challenged in federal courts.

The government released Hamdi on October 11, 2004 and sent him home to Saudi Arabia. He agreed to renounce his U.S. citizenship, as the government was apparently not prepared to try him.

The second case involves Jose Padilla, a United States citizen from Chicago who was arrested in 2001 after returning on a flight from the Middle East. He was alleged to have been involved with Al Qaida plans to detonate a "dirty bomb" (a bomb capable of dispersing radiological material over a large area, but without a nuclear explosion) in the United States. Rather than charging him with any specific crime, President Bush designated him an "enemy combatant" and had him moved to the naval brig in Charleston, South Carolina. He has been held there since.

An attorney eventually contacted to represent Padilla filed a petition to have him released or charged. On December 18, 2003, the second Circuit Court of Appeals ordered that he be charged or released within 30 days. Solicitor General Theodore Olson (who lost his wife on 9/11—she was a passenger on the plane that hit the Pentagon) filed an appeal to the Supreme Court in order to halt Padilla's release. The Supreme Court accepted this case, also. It decided Padilla's case the same day it issued the *Hamdi* decision. But rather than decide the merits of the case, the Court sent it back to the trial court on the premise that Padilla had filed his case in the wrong federal circuit.[17] His case continues.

The Supreme Court also took up the case of several noncitizens who challenged their internment at Guantanamo Bay, Cuba. They challenged the Bush administration's indefinite detention. The government argued that the facility they are held in is in Cuba and therefore outside federal court jurisdiction. The Court disagreed and ordered their cases to be heard by a federal district judge without expressing an opinion on whether they are entitled to a trial or can be held indefinitely.[18] Like the *Padilla* case, their cases are bound to surface again. When, where, and under what circumstances they can challenge their detention remains unresolved as of this writing, although the government is going ahead with plans to begin military tribunals soon.[19]

DEFINING TREASON AND SEDITION

Treason is the only crime that is specifically defined in the Constitution. The Constitution provides that "Treason against the United States, shall consist only in levying war against them, or in adhering to their enemies, giving them aid and comfort."[20]

The Constitution also specifically singles out treason as a crime that requires the government to produce more evidence against the accused than any other crime. It provides that "No person shall be convicted of treason unless on the testimony of two witnesses to the same overt act, or on confession in open court."[21] Thus, treason requires very solid evidence or a confession in the courtroom before a conviction can be obtained. Why did the framers of the Constitution see fit to accord extraordinary protection to those charged with treason? Perhaps because they saw charges of treason as so serious that a wrongful conviction must be guarded against. Perhaps they feared that unless a confession was repeated in open court, it was susceptible to being obtained fraudulently or through the use of torture. Perhaps the framers simply wanted to avoid the possibility that government officials might prosecute political disagreements as treason without concrete evidence of disloyalty. Whatever the reason, treason was singled out for special attention.

The crime of treason is defined in the U.S. Code as a person "owing allegiance to the United States, levies war against them or adheres to their enemies, giving them aid and comfort within the United States or elsewhere."[22] Traditionally, treason has been viewed as the most serious crime.[23]

Treason is a breach of allegiance to the United States; therefore, only those who the law defines as owing allegiance to the United States can be prosecuted for treason.[24] Allegiance can be either temporary or permanent. U.S. citizens, whether natural-born or naturalized, are viewed as having permanent allegiance to the United States, but aliens residing in the United States are perceived to have only temporary allegiance.[25]

Elements

There are two elements to the crime of treason:

- Adherence to the enemy
- Rendering the enemy aid and comfort

Adherence to the Enemy

Enemies of the United States are defined as any "party who was [a] subject of foreign power in state of open hostility with [the] United States." Adherence to the enemy can take the form of:

- Selling goods to an agent of an enemy of the United States[26]
- Statements praising the enemy[27]
- Residing in an enemy country[28]
- Delivery of prisoners to the enemy, unless under a death threat that was likely to be carried out[29]

Rendering the Enemy Aid and Comfort

Examples of rendering aid and comfort to the enemy are:

- A person who acted as an interpreter at a Japanese mine during World War II where American soldiers were beaten in order to increase production[30]
- Any act that strengthens the enemy or weakens the United States[31]
- Concealing a spy's identity, or supplying him with funds and assistance[32]

In order to commit treason, a person must have not only the intent to commit the overt act in question, but also to betray the country by that act.[33] A person who commits no overt act, but still sides with the enemy, is not guilty of treason. A person who commits an overt act, but without treasonous intent, is also not guilty of treason.[34]

Defenses

Various defenses are available to a person charged with treason. Some of them are:

- Duress
- First Amendment privilege
- Immunity from prosecution

Duress

In order for this defense to succeed, the defendant must demonstrate that he or she was in immediate danger of loss of life or severe bodily harm.[35] Of course, any assertion of duress must be substantiated by facts.[36]

First Amendment Privilege

The First Amendment's guarantee of free speech does not apply to treasonous speech. The First Amendment defense was tried by a man who made short-wave radio broadcasts for the enemy during World War II. The Court ruled that this type of speech fell outside the protection of the First Amendment.[37] A similar fate awaited a man who made anti-American broadcasts on German radio during World War II.[38]

Immunity from Prosecution

If the defendant can demonstrate that he or she is part of a class of people who have been granted immunity, he or she can avoid prosecution. The most notable case of this happening was the blanket amnesty given confederate soldiers after the Civil War.[39]

Very few treason trials have actually taken place in the United States. One of the most significant treason trials in our history is that of Aaron Burr. Aaron Burr served as vice president under Thomas Jefferson. During Jefferson's second term (and after Burr was no longer vice president) President Jefferson charged Burr with treason.[40] Burr faced the prospect of being put to the gallows or a firing squad for activities allegedly involving seeking foreign support for a new country in the western part of the American continent. Burr was caught with a flotilla of armed men, and was accused of treason by Jefferson. During the trial, Jefferson was ordered to turn over private papers concerning his communications with the general who investigated the charges. It was the first time in our history that a president had been ordered to produce documents or appear in court. Justice Marshall, who heard the case, told the jurors that "levying war" meant more than making plans to go to war, it meant "the actual assembling of men for the treasonable purpose." In the end, the jury did not convict Burr, since there was no confession in court, nor evidence presented by two witnesses to the same act.[41]

Recently, the Department of Justice debated whether it should charge John Walker Lindh, the alleged "American Taliban" picked up in Afghanistan with other Taliban fighters, with treason. In the end, it elected not to charge him, most likely because Lindh probably would never confess in open court to acts of treason. In addition, it seems unlikely that two witnesses can be found willing to testify that he committed an act of treason. Instead, the "American Taliban" has been charged with violating federal antiterrorism laws and pled guilty in a plea agreement.

Sedition is a conspiracy "to overthrow, put down, or to destroy by force the Government of the United States, or levy war against them, or to oppose the authority thereof, or by force to prevent, hinder, or delay the execution of any law of the United States, or by force to seize, take, or possess any property of the United States contrary to the authority thereof."[42]

Elements

The elements of sedition are:

- Conspiracy
- Overthrow of the United States
- Oppose by force the authority of the United States
- Prevent, hinder, or delay execution of law
- Use of force

Conspiracy

A **conspiracy** is an agreement between two or more persons to engage in a criminal act.[43] For purposes of sedition, the conspirators must agree among themselves to commit an act of sedition.[44]

Overthrow of the United States

Any group who states that their goal is the overthrow of the government of the United States by unconstitutional means would possess this element. The Communist Party met this requirement in a 1922 case.[45]

Oppose by Force the Authority of the United States

This element is satisfied if a person or persons attempts by force to prevent actual exercise of federal authority. Merely disobeying a law is not sufficient to satisfy this element.[46]

Prevent, Hinder, or Delay Execution of Law

To satisfy this element the person or persons involved must forcibly resist the government's execution of the law. As an example, when Chinese immigrants became the target of violence in the American West in the 1880s, the U.S. government entered into two treaties with China that obligated the U.S. government to protect Chinese citizens residing in the United States. Those who opposed the U.S. government's efforts to protect Chinese immigrants were charged with sedition. However, their actions were taken against the Chinese, but not in actual defiance of the civil authority; therefore, their actions did not constitute sedition.[47]

During World War I, draft resistors were prosecuted under the sedition statute.[48]

Use of Force

Any seditious conspiracy must contemplate the use of force.[49] However, no overt act must necessarily take place for a sedition prosecution, merely the planning of one.

DEFINING TERRORISM

Because treason is a crime singled out for special protection, and can be hard to prove given the Constitution's restrictions, Congress has enacted other laws designed to punish activities that serve the same purpose as treasonous behavior, but fall short of fitting the definition of treason. Espionage, terrorism, and other subversive activities may amount to treason, but are separate crimes. Here are some samples of acts that are federal crimes:

- **Espionage** includes: *[w]hoever knowingly and willfully communicates, furnishes, transmits, or otherwise makes available to an unauthorized person, or publishes, or uses in any manner prejudicial to the safety or interest of the United States or for the benefit of any foreign government to the detriment of the United States any classified information.*[50]
- **Rebellion or insurrection** includes: *Whoever incites, sets on foot, assists, or engages in any rebellion or insurrection against the authority of the United States or the laws thereof, or gives aid or comfort thereto.. . . .* [51]

HISTORICAL HIGHLIGHT
Hanssen Betrays His Country

On July 6, 2001, former FBI agent Robert Hanssen pled guilty in federal court to 15 counts of espionage and conspiracy. He did so pursuant to a plea agreement with prosecutors that saved him from a potential death sentence. Hanssen, who worked for the FBI for 15 years, admitted to spying for the former Soviet Union and later for Russia between 1979 and 1999. Prosecutors alleged that the father of six and long-time FBI agent was paid about $1.4 million in cash and diamonds in exchange for intelligence information. The information included identities of American spies, classified information about eavesdropping technology, and nuclear secrets. Hanssen was accused of compromising dozens of Soviet spies who were working for the United States, some of whom were executed.

Hanssen was caught after leaving a package under a wooden footbridge in a Virginia park when the United States had been given the tip-off by an informant in Russian intelligence that the FBI had a double agent.

The plea agreement provided that in exchange for a guilty plea, Hanssen would receive a life sentence with no possibility of parole and would be required to cooperate with both the FBI and the CIA. He is currently serving his sentence in the Allenwood federal prison in Pennsylvania. His wife will receive part of the pension he would have earned had he retired.

- **Advocating overthrow of government** includes: *Whoever knowingly or willfully advocates, abets, advises, or teaches the duty, necessity, desirability, or propriety of overthrowing or destroying the government of the United States or the government of any State, Territory, District or Possession thereof, or the government of any political subdivision therein, by force or violence, or by the assassination of any officer of any such government....* [52]

There are also federal laws against acts of **terrorism,** generally defined as the unlawful use or threat of violence especially against the state or the public as a politically motivated means of attack or coercion, which we examine next. We will examine both international and domestic terrorism, as those terms are defined in federal criminal laws.

Terrorism is not a new problem for the United States. In fact, terrorist acts have been the focus of law enforcement with some frequency in the last century and appears likely to continue to be well into the first decade of the new century.

For example, during the years 1919 and 1920, the nation found itself facing an internal security threat: anarchists who sought to destroy the American government and a modern capitalist world. The most outward sign of this revolutionary fervor was a series of attempted bomb attacks on American institutions and government officials. Beginning in the spring of 1919, government officials like Supreme Court Justice Oliver Wendell Holmes and Attorney General A. Mitchell Palmer received bombs (which did not injure either man). A post office clerk discovered over 30 bombs awaiting delivery in the system in New York.

Later the next year, a bomb did go off in the New York City financial district. It had been left in a horse-drawn wagon between a U.S. Treasury office and J.P. Morgan & Company office.

Attorney General Palmer's response was to crack down on those perceived to be radicals. Recent immigrants from southern and eastern Europe were deported, and over 6,000 people were arrested in a roundup Attorney General Palmer alleged would prevent a large-scale terror attack. When no new terror attacks emerged, the crisis ended.[53]

Until recently, the deadliest terror attack on the United States happened in Oklahoma City, Oklahoma. Timothy McVeigh, a disaffected former soldier who claimed to engage in terror as retaliation for alleged FBI wrongdoing, blew up the Alfred P. Murrah Federal Courthouse with a homemade fertilizer bomb. The explosion killed 168 people, including 19 children, and injured hundreds. McVeigh was tried under federal law and executed by lethal injection on June 11, 2001. He became the first federal prisoner executed since 1963.

On September 11, 2001, the United States faced the worst attack on its civilian population in its history. Quickly it became obvious that the hijacking of four airliners and their use as missiles to bring down the Twin Towers of the World Trade Center, destroy a portion of the Pentagon, and crash into a field in rural Pennsylvania, was the work of international terrorists. As the identities of the hijackers became known, it became clear the terror acts were probably the work of Osama bin Laden and his Al Qaida terrorist network. Congress quickly authorized the president to take military action against the terrorists and the nation that provided them shelter, Taliban-ruled Afghanistan.

At the same time, Congress also passed tough new amendments to the Antiterrorism and Effective Death Penalty Act of 1996. The amendments are commonly referred to as the Patriot Act of 2001. The Act provides that:

- Wiretaps can be obtained to follow the persons whose conversations are sought, rather than being linked to a specific phone. This provision allows investigators to track the conversations of a suspect whether he is using his own phone, a cell phone, or another phone.
- Law enforcement, armed with a subpoena, are allowed to seize voice mail and other electronic communication and to obtain information about the means of payment and account numbers.
- Aliens are allowed to be detained for seven days without charges being filed.
- The federal criminal code is amended to: (1) revise the definition of **international terrorism** to include activities that appear to be intended to affect the conduct of government by mass destruction; and (2) define **domestic terrorism** as activities that occur primarily within U.S. jurisdiction, that involve criminal acts dangerous to human life, and that appear to be intended to intimidate or coerce a civilian population, to influence government policy by intimidation or coercion, or to affect government conduct by mass destruction, assassination, or kidnapping.
- Harboring any person knowing or having reasonable grounds to believe that such person has committed or is about to commit a terrorism offense is prohibited.
- There is no statute of limitations for terrorist offenses.

The federal penal code provisions dealing with terrorism are extensive and reach out beyond our borders. In most cases, criminal acts that involve the use of bombs, chemical, biological, or nuclear weapons against Americans abroad or in the United States and that kill those targets are punishable by death. The specific provisions and definitions are found in Title 18, Part I, Chapter 113B of the U.S. Code.

HISTORICAL HIGHLIGHT
Eric Rudolph Caught After Years on the Run

The strange tale of Eric Rudolph underscored that all terrorism isn't international, but very frequently is of the home-grown variety. Rudolph was a suspect in a string of abortion clinic and nightclub bombings and may have been involved in the bomb that went off in Atlanta during the 1996 Summer Olympic Games as well. The Olympic bombing killed one woman and injured many others. In one of the clinic bombings an off-duty police officer was killed and a receptionist badly injured. Not much is known about his political leanings.

Rudolph was on the run and believed to be hiding in the Nantahala National Forest in North Carolina. He was on the FBI's ten most wanted list, with a $1 million prize on his head. The last known sighting was in 1998, when Rudolph likely stole a pickup truck with 75 pounds of food and supplies in it, until he was caught May 31, 2003, by an off-duty police officer. Rudolph was caught while rooting through a dumpster.

He now faces charges for the bombings in Alabama and in Georgia.[54]

HISTORICAL HIGHLIGHT
Attorney General Listens in on Attorney-Client Conversations

On October 30, 2001, U.S. Attorney General John Ashcroft approved a Justice Department rule that allows federal agents to listen in on some conversations between inmates in the federal prison system and their attorneys. The rule provides that in cases where the attorney general has certified that reasonable suspicion exists to believe that an inmate may use communications with attorneys or investigators to further or facilitate acts of violence or terrorism, those conversations may be monitored. The rule applies to anyone held in federal custody, including convicts, detainees, those awaiting trial, and anyone held as a material witness.

Critics point out that the rule is sure to stifle legitimate conversations between attorneys, support staff, and clients and that the rule may go too far insofar as it allows the Executive Branch with no judicial oversight to make the determination of who is monitored.[55]

PRACTICE POINTERS

Legal assistants and investigators who work for criminal defense attorneys, prosecutors, or public defenders probably won't see many terrorism cases in any given year. But if a client does face possible charges, those preparing the defense or prosecution should keep these statistics, prepared by the Transactional Records Access Clearinghouse of Syracuse University,[56] in mind:

- In the five-year period ending September 30, 2001, there were a total of 1,338 cases federal prosecutors classified as involving domestic or international terrorism.
- Prosecutors elected not to bring charges in 68 percent of the terrorism cases referred to them for prosecution.
- Convictions were won against just 178 persons. Twenty-four of those were classified as international cases, and 154 as domestic terror.
- The median prison term in international cases was 10 months, and in domestic cases was 37 months.

The bottom line? Few cases are prosecuted, and convictions don't usually result in long sentences. Of course, that may change as new laws are enacted following the terror attacks of September 11, 2001. A harder line approach to terrorism is likely.

Since few legal offices have much experience with cases involving either domestic or international terrorism, those who find themselves working on such cases will have to get up to speed quickly. That's equally true no matter which side of the fence they work for.

Legal professionals involved in interviewing or questioning defendants represented by their firms should be aware that conversations conducted in federal detention facilities may be monitored. Ordinarily, any conversations dealing with legal matters between an attorney and a client is considered confidential. The attorney-client privilege generally extends to conversations the client has with support staff also. Consult your supervising attorney about what to tell the client about confidentiality of conversations.

ASSISTANCE WITH CASES INVOLVING IMPORTANT PUBLIC POLICY QUESTIONS

Those who work at defending suspects accused of planning or committing terror acts or of aiding and abetting such acts may want to seek information or assistance from several groups interested in the larger issues raised by new enforcement realities like the Patriot Act and the prospect of military tribunals. In addition to many state and local bar associations, help may be available from:

- Center for Constitutional Rights, a New York group initially organized to defend civil rights protesters in the 1960s, at *www.humanrightsnow.org*
- The Cato Institute, a group known for championing "conservative" causes, at *www.cato.org*
- People for the American Way, a Washington area group known for championing "liberal" causes, at *www.pfaw.org*
- The American Civil Liberties Union at *www.aclu.org*
- National Association of Criminal Defense Lawyers at *www.nacdl.org*

CHAPTER SUMMARY

The U.S. Constitution provides the framework for much of the law that applies in times of war or domestic turmoil. First, the Constitution sets forth the power of both Congress and the president in time of war. It gives to Congress the power to make declarations of war and to the president the role of commander in chief. Once Congress has declared war, the president exercises his power as commander in chief to set, execute, and achieve war goals.

The power to conduct war has led presidents to order groups suspected of disloyalty into internment camps and suspected saboteurs tried by military commissions. In each of these two examples, the Supreme Court upheld the presidents' actions by finding that the procedures were authorized by Congressional legislation.

The Constitution also defines treason and sets strict standards required to find someone guilty of treason. Treason is levying war against the United States, or in adhering to their enemies, giving them aid and comfort. Treason must be proven by the testimony of two witnesses to the same overt act, or the defendant's confession in open court.

Congress has passed other laws designed to punish activities that fall short of treason, but that harm the security of the country or its citizens. Examples include criminal laws punishing the disclosure of classified information to unauthorized persons or foreign countries.

Congress has also passed federal criminal laws outlawing activities that may be crimes under state law but the commission of which has as an intention undermining governmental authority or intimidating the population. Thus, the bombing of abortion clinics by domestic terrorists, the leveling of a federal building in Oklahoma City, or the destruction of U.S. embassies overseas have been labeled as terrorist acts and prosecuted accordingly.

KEY TERMS

Domestic terrorism: Activities that occur primarily within U.S. jurisdiction, that involve criminal acts dangerous to human life, and that appear to be intended to intimidate or coerce a civilian population, to influence government policy by intimidation or coercion, or to affect government conduct by mass destruction, assassination, or kidnapping.

Espionage: Knowingly and willfully communicating, furnishing, transmitting, or otherwise making available to an unauthorized person, or publishing, or using in any manner prejudicial to the safety or interest of the United States, or for the benefit of any foreign government to the detriment of the United States, any classified information.

Letters of marque and reprisal: A letter from a government formerly used to grant a private person the power to seize the subjects of a foreign state.

Habeas corpus: The "Great Writ," which orders another authority to bring a person held to the court. It was originally used to prevent kings from simply making enemies disappear.

International terrorism: Activities that occur primarily outside U.S. jurisdiction, and involve criminal acts dangerous to human life, including acts of mass destruction, intended to influence the policy of a government by intimidation or coercion or to affect the conduct of a government by assassination or kidnapping.

Military tribunal: A military court convened in times of emergency to try those accused of war-related crimes, such as terrorism, espionage, or treason.

Power to declare war: The power reserved by Congress in the Constitution. Congress can declare war on a belligerent, and then the Executive Branch conducts the war.

Terrorism: The unlawful use or threat of violence, especially against the state or the public as a politically motivated means of attack or coercion.

Treason: Levying war against the United States, or in adhering to their enemies, giving them aid and comfort. Treason must be proven by the testimony of two witnesses to the same overt act, or the defendant's confession in open court.

DISCUSSION QUESTIONS

1. Is it appropriate to subject noncitizens to military trials for acts allegedly carried out against American interests at home or abroad?
2. Under what circumstances, if any, should subjects be tried and convicted with an evidentiary standard short of reasonable doubt?
3. Should civil liberties be restricted in time of war?
4. Why do you think the founding fathers set such high standards for conviction of treason?
5. Should a person be prosecuted for espionage if he or she is spying for one of our allies? (Examples: Julius and Ethel Rosenberg, and Jonathan Pollard)

FOR FURTHER READING AND VIEWING

BOOKS

1. Junger, S. (2001). *Fire.* W. W. Norton. Covers first-hand account of an American traveling with the Afghan resistance forces who sought to rid the country of the Taliban and Osama bin Laden.
2. Chapin, B. (1971). *American Law of Treason: Revolutionary and Early National Origins.* University of Washington Press.
3. Hurst, J. W. (1971). *The Law of Treason in the United States: Collected Essays (Contributions in American History, No. 12).* Greenwood Publishing.
4. Vise, D. (2001). "The Bureau and the Mole: The Unmasking of Robert Philip Hanssen, the Most Dangerous Double Agent in FBI History." *Atlantic Monthly.*
5. Vidal, G. (2000). *Burr.* Vintage Books. Fictional account of the Burr affair.
6. Goldenberg, E. (1993). *The Spy Who Knew Too Much: The Government Plot to Silence Jonathan Pollard.* SPI Book. Another true spy-catching story.
7. Scottoline, L. (2004). *Killer Smile.* Harper Collins. Legal thriller set in 2004, but exploring what happened to an Italian immigrant interned during WWII. Ms. Scottoline's parents were required to register as alien enemies during WWII even though they had made their home in Philadelphia for decades.
8. Dobbs, M. (2004). *Saboteurs: The Nazi Raid on America.* Alfred A. Knopf. This recent account of the Nazis tried by military tribunals during WWII includes recently unearthed material from the National Archives.

FILMS

1. *The Wind and the Lion,* a 1975 film telling the story of an American woman and her children who were kidnapped by a Berber tribe in 1904 and rescued by the application of Teddy Roosevelt's Big Stick policy, stars Candice Bergen, Brian Keith, and Sean Connery.

2. *The Spy Who Came in From the Cold*, a 1965 classic Cold War thriller based on John LeCarre's book of the same name, stars Richard Burton.

3. *Black Sunday*, a 1976 thriller in which Palestinian terrorists try to wipe out the crowd at the Super Bowl, stars Robert Shaw and Bruce Dern.

4. *The Day of the Jackal,* a 1973 thriller, deals with an attempted assassination of Charles de Gaulle and is a chilling look at the cool composure of someone capable of terrorist acts.

5. *The Eye of the Needle* stars Donald Sunderland as a Nazi spy in England who must deliver information about Britain's military capacity directly to Hitler. This 1981 thriller has a surprise ending.

6. *The Year of Living Dangerously* is a 1983 Mel Gibson, Linda Hunt, and Sigourney Weaver film set in 1965 Jakarta during the political upheavals that were threatening to collapse the unstable government of President Sukarno.

7. *The Ugly American*, featuring Marlon Brando, is the film adaptation of Eugene Burdick's Cold War thriller based loosely on Vietnam.

8. *The Little Drummer Girl* stars Diane Keaton as a left-wing pro-Palestinian actress recruited to spy for Israel.

QUOTATIONS FOR CHAPTER ELEVEN

1. *We'd be in a bad way if we won the war and lost our civil liberties.*
   Earl Warren, then California attorney general on the dismissal of all Japanese Americans from civil service positions after the Japanese bombing of Pearl Harbor

2. *Hardships are part of war, and war is an aggregation of hardship.*
   Justice Black in *Korematsu v. United States*

3. *As nightfall does not come at once, neither does oppression. In both instances, there is a twilight when everything remains seemingly unchanged. And it is in such twilight that we all must be most aware of change in the air—however slight—lest we become unwitting victims of the darkness.*
   Justice William O. Douglas

4. *. . . the rule of law is essential to our American freedoms.*
   Patrick Leahy in letter to Attorney General John Ashcroft

ENDNOTES

1. The inscription was written by Emma Lazarus (1849–1887).
2. D. McCullough, *John Adams* (Simon & Schuster, 2001).
3. *U.S. Constitution,* Article I, Section 8.
4. *U.S. Constitution,* Article II, Section 2.
5. Executive Order No. 10340 (April 8, 1952).
6. *Youngstown Sheet & Tube Co. v. Sawyer*, 343 U.S. 579 (1952).
7. E. Cray, *Chief Justice. A Biography of Earl Warren* (Simon & Schuster, 1997).
8. *Korematsu v. United States*, 323 U.S. 214 (1944).
9. Blackstone, *Commentaries on the Laws of England* (1765).

10. *U.S. Constitution*, Article I, Section 9.

11. *Ex parte Milligan*, 71 U.S. (4 Wall) 2 (1866).

12. *United States v. Awadallah*, 202 F. Supp. 2d 55 (2002).

13. J. Curt, *Edgar Hoover: The Man and the Secrets* (W. W. Norton & Company, 1991).

14. *Ex parte Quirin et al.,* 317 U.S.1 (1942).

15. *Hamdi v. Rumsfeld*, 337 F. 3d 335 (4th Cir. 2003).

16. *Hamdi v. Rumsfeld*, 124 S. Ct. 2633 (2004).

17. *Rumsfeld v. Padilla*, 124 S. Ct. 2711 (2004).

18. *Rasul v. Bush*, 124 S. Ct. 2711 (2004).

19. "U.S. to tell detainees of rights; Pentagon outlines new procedures," *Washington Post* (July 10, 2004).

20. *U.S. Constitution*, Article III, Section 3.

21. Ibid.

22. 18 U.S.C. § 2381.

23. *Stephan v. United States*, 133 F.2d 87 (6th Cir. 1943), cert den 318 U.S. 781, reh den 319 U.S. 783 (1943).

24. *Young v. United States*, 97 U.S. 39 (1878).

25. *Carlisle v. United States*, 8 Ct. Cl 153 (1872).

26. *Hanauer v. Doane*, 79 U.S. 342 (1871); *Carlisle v. United States,* 83 U.S. 147 (1873).

27. *Kawakita v. United States*, 343 U.S. 717 (1952).

28. *United States v. Chandler*, 72 F. Supp. 230 (DC Mass 1947).

29. *United States v. Hodges*, F. Cas No 15374 (CC Md 1815).

30. *Kawakita v. United States*, 343 U.S. 717 (1952).

31. *United States v. Haupt*, 47 F. Supp. 836 (DC Ill 1942).

32. *United States v. Fricke*, 259 F. 673 (DC NY 1919).

33. *Cramer v. United States*, 325 U.S. 1 (1945).

34. *Kawakita v. United States*, 343 U.S. 717 (1952).

35. *D'Aquino v. United States,* 1922 F.2d 338 (9th Cir 1951), cert den 343 U.S. 935 (1952).

36. *Miller v. The Ship Resolution* (1781, F CC Pa) 2 U.S. 1, later op (F CC Pa) 2 US 19.

37. *United States v. Chandler*, 72 F. Supp. 230 (DC Mass 1947).

38. *United States v. Burgman*, 87 F. Supp. 568 (DC 1949) cert den 342 U.S. 838 (1950).

39. *Young v. United States*, 97 U.S. 39 (1878); *United States v. Morrison,* 30 F. Cas No 18270 (1869).

40. Burr was involved in another scandal as well. He killed Alexander Hamilton in a duel.

41. W. Burger, *It Is So Ordered: A Constitution Unfolds* (William Morrow and Company, 1995).

42. 18 U.S.C. § 2384.

43. Ballentine's Law Dictionary.

44. *Wright v. United States*, 108 F. 805 (5th Cir. 1901), cert den 181 U.S. 620 (1901).

45. *Skeffinton v. Katzeff*, 277 F. 129 (1st Cir. 1922).

46. *Baldwin v. Franks*,120 U.S. 678 (1887).

47. Ibid.

48. *Wells v. United States*, 257 F. 605 (9th Cir. 1919); *Enfield v. United States*, 261 F. 141(8th Cir. 1919); *Orear v. United States*, 261 F. 257 (5th Cir. 1919).

49. *Hays v. American Defense Soc.*, 252 N.Y. 266, 169 N.E. 380 (1929).

50. 18 U.S.C. § 798.

51. 18 U.S.C. § 2383.

52. Ibid.

53. M. Sullivan and D. Rather, eds., *Our Times: America at the Birth of the 20th Century* (New York: Scribner, 1996).

54. "$13.4 million later, no trace of bombing suspect; Eric Robert Rudolph may be dead, or lying low in North Carolina or parts unknown, but searchers call the money well spent," *The Atlanta Journal and Constitution* (May 17, 2001).

55. "A Question of Confidentiality; Eavesdropping in the lockup poses a potential threat to attorney-client privilege. Some lawyers fear the post-Sept. 11 climate may further erode privacy rights," *LA Times* (December 7, 2001).

56. The Transactional Records Access Clearinghouse is a nonprofit, nonpartisan group associated with Syracuse University. The information was gleaned from computer tapes released by the Justice Department after the group won a court order for the information under the Freedom of Information Act.

CHAPTER 12
Crimes Against the State

CHAPTER OBJECTIVES

After studying this chapter, you should be able to:

- Understand the significance of perjury
- Explain the essential elements of obstruction of justice
- Understand the different types of contempt
- Know what constitutes bribery
- Explain the ways that the government seeks to control corrupt organizations
- Know the steps in the impeachment process
- Appreciate the special problems that offenses against the state pose for society and the rule of law

CHAPTER CONTENTS

> *A single witness shall not rise up against a man on account of any iniquity or any sin he has committed; on the evidence of two or three witnesses a matter shall be confirmed.*
>
> **Deuteronomy 19:15**

INTRODUCTION

Every system of government must establish laws that protect its own integrity. The American system drew heavily on its English heritage to enact laws that preserve the public's trust in its institutions. Crimes like perjury, obstruction of justice, and contempt are carried out by those who seek to thwart the proper operation of our judicial system. If no steps were taken to counter these crimes, the system could not function.

The natural law tradition that governments exist by the consent of the governed demands that political officials have a duty to the people. Bribery, the selling of an office, constitutes a betrayal of that duty. In addition, much of the proper functioning of government relies on the integrity of the people and institutions who work within it. When corrupt officials lack that integrity and refuse to leave office voluntarily, government must use its impeachment power to remove them and restore integrity to the system.

Corrupt organizations also pose a threat to government, often by seeking to usurp government's role. Organized crime operations may, for example, offer "protection" for businesses in exchange for a "contribution." Legitimate government's battle with organized crime has been a long and arduous one. We will examine some of the laws crafted to disrupt the operations of corrupt organizations and punish the operators.

Unfortunately, the very guarantees that undergird a free society sometimes create a refuge for criminals. When writing laws governing crimes against the state, the battle has always been to structure laws that prevent corruption and preserve liberty. As you will see, that means that those engaged in sophisticated criminal activities are sometimes difficult to catch and punish.

PERJURY

Perjury is defined as "giving false testimony in a judicial proceeding or an administrative proceeding, lying under oath as to a material fact, swearing to the truth of anything one knows or believes to be false."[1] Obviously telling the truth is vital to the integrity of the judicial system. Judges and juries often base decisions on the testimony of witnesses, and false testimony may mean unjust conviction. False convictions impair the integrity of the justice system, and is an injury to us all. Therefore, perjury is a very serious crime against the state.

Under federal law there are three types of perjury. The first type, often referred to as section 1621 perjury (for the section of the U.S. code describing it—18 U.S.C. § 1621), is a general giving of false testimony. This is the broadest of the three types of perjury. It applies to all material statements or information provided under oath "to a competent tribunal, officer, or person, in any case in which a law of the United States authorizes an oath to be administered." It is not limited to testimony in court, but includes any sworn statement to a government official or representative. Students seeking federal financial aid, for example, may commit perjury if they provide false or misleading information on the FAFSA, the Free Application for Federal Student Aid.

The second type of perjury is section 1623 perjury (18 U.S.C. § 1623). Section 1623 perjury is false testimony given in court or before a grand jury. Unlike the general giving of false testimony, this type is limited to court and grand jury testimony.

The third type is subornation of perjury (18 U.S.C. § 1622). **Subornation of perjury** is defined as convincing or seeking to convince another person to commit perjury. In order to be convicted of subornation of perjury, a person must convince another to commit perjury, and that person must then actually perjure himself or herself.

Every state has its own set of criminal laws punishing perjury and other forms of dishonest testimony or representation. For example, Pennsylvania has a criminal offense called "Unsworn Falsification to Authorities," which provides that a

> . . . person commits a misdemeanor of the second degree if, with intent to mislead a public servant in performing his official function, he . . . makes any written false statement which he does not believe to be true.[2]

DIFFERENCES BETWEEN SECTION 1621 AND 1623 PERJURY

The Two-Witness Rule

Section 1621 perjury has its origins in Common Law concepts of perjury. Under Common Law, a person could not be convicted of perjury unless two people testified that the alleged perjurer's statements were not true. This is called the **two-witness rule.** The 1621 section carries on this Common Law tradition, but with some modifications. For example, physical evidence that corroborates testimony satisfies the two-witness rule. That is, if the prosecution presents one witness who testifies that the defendant lied and an additional piece of physical evidence that corroborated the testimony, the rule is satisfied.

Section 1623 requires that *proof beyond a reasonable doubt . . . is sufficient for conviction.*[3] In other words, the proof may take any form—physical evidence, testimony, or any other type of proof. The standard of proof is thus lower than for section 1621 perjury. Stated another way, proving section 1621 perjury requires a stricter standard than is required for most other crimes. The two-witness rule specifically does not apply to section 1623 cases. You may recall from the last chapter that there is another crime that requires this higher level of proof for conviction—treason.

Another key difference between section 1621 and section 1623 is what occurs when a witness recants his or her testimony. **Recantation** is the retraction of testimony. Under section 1621, even if a witness recants his or her testimony, he or she can still be prosecuted for perjury.[4] However, under section 1623, a witness can recant testimony during the same proceeding as long as that testimony has not "substantially affected the proceeding."[5]

Another important difference comes into play when a witness contradicts himself or herself on the stand. Under section 1621, the government must prove which of the contradictory statements is false. However, section 1623 places no such burden on the prosecution. Contradictory statements are sufficient for conviction in and of themselves.[6]

Elements of Perjury

The elements of perjury are:

- An oath
- Intent
- Falsity
- Materiality

An Oath

Perjury can only occur if a false statement is made under oath to speak truthfully. There is no standard wording for the oath, but it must be administered by a legally authorized person. The authority for administering the oath can be derived from law, rules, or regulation. Rules and regulations often govern administrative proceedings, but the oath is just as valid in these cases as it would be in a courtroom. Consequently, sworn false statements in administrative hearings can be prosecuted under perjury statutes.

Intent

Under both sections 1621 and 1623, the person giving the false testimony must be aware that what he or she is saying is false and must intend to mislead by giving the false testimony.

Falsity

In any perjury or subornation of perjury case, the falsity of the statement in question must be proved beyond a reasonable doubt in order to secure a conviction.

Materiality

In order to qualify as perjury a statement must be material to a case. Lying about something of no consequence is not a crime. A statement is material if it is likely that the case or matter in which the falsehood was presented was influenced by it. In other words, if the statement had the possibility of influencing the outcome of a proceeding, it is material. A witness who tells the court that he had scrambled eggs for breakfast when he had pancakes is not guilty of perjury unless what he had for breakfast is relevant to the case.

Defenses to Perjury

The defenses to perjury are:

- Recantation
- Assistance of counsel
- Double jeopardy
- The "perjury trap"
- Fifth Amendment

Recantation

Recantation, as noted earlier, is the retraction of earlier testimony. Recantation traditionally has not done well as a defense, but is most effective when the defendant uses recantation to demonstrate that there was no criminal intent in testifying falsely. In other words, recantation is used to clarify statements later discovered to have been misleading or in error. A defendant, in effect, explains away his or her earlier statements by "clarifying" them.

Assistance of Counsel

Sometimes witnesses called to testify don't consult with an attorney before testifying, and thus may never know that being less than truthful can be a crime. There is no requirement, however, that a witness be told he or she can consult with an attorney. However, a witness can assert that he or she testified on the advice of counsel. In this case, the defendant eliminates the element of intent if he or she can prove the testimony was given in good faith on bad advice.

Double Jeopardy

The double jeopardy defense can be raised when the defendant's acquittal in a criminal trial was based on the jury believing his or her untrue testimony.[7] Prosecutions for perjury after an acquittal sometimes give the appearance of being a vindictive prosecution. There is no blanket prohibition against prosecuting someone for perjury in a case where he or she was the defendant. As a practical matter, it seldom happens.

HISTORICAL HIGHLIGHT
Bill Clinton Loses Law License

Former president Bill Clinton admitted on his last day in office that he testified falsely in testimony in a 1998 lawsuit. As a consequence of his admission, he had his license to practice law suspended for five years and was struck from the United States Supreme Court's list of attorneys qualified to argue cases before it. The actions stem from testimony Bill Clinton provided in a deposition in the Paula Jones sexual harassment lawsuit. Ms. Jones had sued Clinton for alleged acts of sexual harassment he committed against her while he was the governor of Arkansas. In the deposition, he was asked whether he had been sexually involved with White House intern Monica Lewinsky. His answers, he later conceded, were evasive. In a news release, he stated that "I tried to walk a fine line between acting lawfully and testifying falsely, but I now recognize that I did not fully accomplish this goal and am certain my responses to questions about Ms. Lewinsky were false."[8]

The suspension of Clinton's license to practice law was part of an agreement between the former president and Independent Counsel Robert Ray. In exchange, Clinton will not face criminal charges, including possible obstruction of justice or perjury charges. U.S. District Judge Susan Webber Wright had earlier found Clinton in civil contempt of court for willful failure to testify truthfully in the Jones case.

The Perjury Trap

Grand juries often serve an investigative function. They can call witnesses and seek out evidence in a case in order to decide whether there are grounds to charge someone with a crime. The power of a grand jury can sometimes be used by a zealous prosecutor to attempt to force a witness to provide testimony that contradicts what he or she told investigators or others in law enforcement. He or she is then caught in the **perjury trap.** If he tells the truth this time, he is trapped into confessing that he lied earlier. If he lies again, he runs the risk of additional charges. If he can prove that the main purpose for which he has been called to testify is to force him into the perjury trap, he may be able to defend against any subsequent perjury prosecution.

Fifth Amendment

As you learned earlier, the Fifth Amendment to the Constitution protects an accused person from self-incrimination. If testifying means a witness will perjure himself or prove he committed perjury earlier, he can raise the Fifth Amendment and refuse to testify.

OBSTRUCTION OF JUSTICE

Closely related to perjury is **obstruction of justice.** Obstruction of justice is defined as "the crime of impeding or hindering the administration of justice in any way." Obstruction of justice is a broad term that may apply to many different types of activities. Witness tampering or intimidation, jury tampering, or even suborning perjury can be forms of obstruction of justice. At the heart of the crime is interfering with the full and fair administration of justice. For example, prosecutors or police officers who hide, tamper with, or destroy evidence can be charged with obstruction of justice, as can defendants who threaten or bribe witnesses.

Elements

In order to prove the crime of obstruction of justice, the following elements must be satisfied:

- There is a pending judicial proceeding.
- The defendant knew of the proceeding.
- The defendant acted corruptly with the specific intent to obstruct or interfere with the proceeding or due administration of justice.[9]

Pending Proceedings

A proceeding must be pending in order to charge obstruction of justice. A person believing that an investigation may begin can be convicted of obstruction of justice if he or she takes action that may destroy evidence. Consider this example. A police department is running out of space to keep evidence collected over the years, including evidence used in prior cases that have concluded and the final appeal completed. If the department decided to dispose of old evidence, they may do so. However, if the department has reason to believe the evidence in a particular case is tainted, has been tampered with, or will be needed in a pending appeal, it would be obstruction of justice to destroy it.

In recent years, there has been a dramatic improvement in the use of scientific evaluation of evidence. There have been cases in which new scientific tests on old evidence have either confirmed to a high degree of probability that the convicted individual was guilty or proven that he was innocent. These new tests have been performed on evidence that in some cases had been in storage for decades. Because of this, some legislatures have proposed extending the time that those holding evidence must store and maintain it.

Knowledge

Very simply, the defendant must have known a judicial proceeding was pending in order to form the intent to obstruct justice; no knowledge, no intent, no crime.

Acting Corruptly with Intent to Obstruct Justice

The defendant must commit an act that has as its intent disruption of a judicial proceeding. The act must occur in a time frame that is consistent with that purpose. In order to act "corruptly," the act must be done with the intent of obstructing justice. The term *corruptly* means acting with an improper purpose, personally or by influencing another, including making a false or misleading statement, or withholding, concealing, altering, or destroying a document or other information.[10]

The defendant need not succeed in obstructing justice, but only in attempting to. He or she must "endeavor" to obstruct justice.[11] Endeavor is loosely defined to mean any effort carried out with the intent of obstructing justice. It is not limited to any one or group of activities, but applies generally to any attempt to obstruct justice.[12]

Types of Obstruction

Obstruction of justice can take many forms, but the actions generally prosecuted under the federal statute fall into three groups. The first group involves hiding, changing, or destroying relevant documents such as court records, and the second is encouraging or giving false testimony. The third group are offenses that involve intimidation, threats, or other harm to witnesses, jurors, judges, or others involved in legal proceedings or investigations in an attempt to prevent or shape their testimony or judgment. Examples of obstruction under federal law include:

> 18 U.S.C. § 1503. Influencing or Injuring Officer or Juror Generally
> 18 U.S.C. § 1504. Influencing Juror by Writing
> 18 U.S.C. § 1505. Obstruction of Proceedings Before Departments, Agencies
> 18 U.S.C. § 1506. Theft or Alteration of Record or Process
> 18 U.S.C. § 1509. Obstruction of Court Orders
> 18 U.S.C. § 1510. Obstruction of Criminal Investigations
> 18 U.S.C. § 1511. Obstruction of State or Local Law Enforcement
> 18 U.S.C. § 1512. Tampering with a Witness, Victim, or an Informant
> 18 U.S.C. § 1513. Retaliating Against a Witness, Victim, or an Informant

HISTORICAL HIGHLIGHT
Did Chemists Obstruct Justice?

The legal system depends on the integrity of the participants. This is especially true of those who are called to testify as experts about scientific evidence. In many criminal cases, the outcome of the case depends on the scientific analysis of bits of evidence found at the scene of the crime implicating the defendant. Take DNA evidence. Scientific analysis of hair, body fluids, and other organic matter can exclude or implicate the defendant. What happens if the presumably neutral scientists, who perform the tests and inform the jury of their conclusions, do sloppy and unreliable work or even lie? In several recent cases, that may have been what happened.

Take, for example, the work of serologist Fred Zain. Mr. Zain has twice been tried by the state of West Virginia for defrauding the state and lying under oath in dozens of criminal cases. He headed up the serology unit of the West Virginia State Police crime lab. So far, no jury has convicted him. Both times, the jury was hung six-six on all charges. However, five men have had their convictions overturned because of errors in the tests Zain performed on evidence used to convict them. Many others are asking for new DNA testing of the evidence used to convict them.[13]

Then there is the mess in which Oklahoma had found itself. There, chemist Joyce Gilchrist is alleged to have falsified evidence reports in perhaps hundreds of cases before she was fired in September 2001. Reexamination of her work has freed a convicted rapist, a death row inmate, overturned another death sentence, and may call into question the guilt of one man who was executed. Malcolm Johnson was executed in January 2000 for the rape and murder of an Oklahoma City woman. He claimed that he was innocent, but Gilchrist had testified that semen found at the scene was consistent with Johnson's blood type. Later examination of the slides Gilchrist reviewed showed no semen present.[14] Other cases are also undergoing review.

18 U.S.C. § 1516. Obstruction of Federal Audit
18 U.S.C. § 1517. Obstructing Examination of Financial Institution
18 U.S.C. § 1518. Obstruction of Criminal Investigations of Health Care Offenses

States have similar statutes in place that apply to state investigations and legal proceedings.

CONTEMPT

Contempt is defined as "Conduct that brings the authority and administration of the law into disrespect or that embarrasses or obstructs the court's discharge of its duties."[15] Contempt is descended from English Common Law where disobedience to a writ under the king's seal was considered contempt. The federal rule on contempt states that:

A court of the United States shall have power to punish by fine or imprisonment, at its discretion, such contempt of its authority, and none other, as—

1. Misbehavior of any person in its presence or so near thereto as to obstruct the administration of justice;
2. Misbehavior of any of its officers in their official transactions;
3. Disobedience or resistance to its lawful writ, process, order, rule, decree, or command.[16]

There are two forms of contempt—civil and criminal. Civil contempt findings can be issued on the spot by judges. In most cases, civil contempt cases involve a finding by the presiding judge that an individual is in contempt of court, and an order for the payment of a fine. The proof required is simple: The individual knew there was a court order directing him to do something, and he did not comply. For example, a witness who was served with a subpoena for records and does not bring those records can be held in contempt. Sometimes judges issue civil contempt orders to attorneys involved in a case who do not behave appropriately in the court room in accordance with the standards of decorum the judge has set. In those cases, the punishment is typically a fine.

Civil contempt orders can also order an individual to comply with a court order and impose incarceration until the person held in contempt complies with the order or demand. He or she can be jailed until he or she complies. In essence, civil contempt proceedings are remedial in nature, meant to force compliance with the court's will and the incarcerated individual holds the "keys to the jailhouse."

Persons charged with and convicted of criminal contempt, however, cannot purge themselves of that contempt by later complying. That is, criminal contempt is a separate crime for which the individual is being punished, rather than a mechanism to force someone to comply. Criminal contempt can be either a summary offense or a felony. Criminal contempt requires both a contemptuous act and a wrongful state of mind.[17]

Criminal contempt is reserved for obstinance, and does not cover a good-faith disagreement.[18] Summary criminal contempt can be imposed by a judge with no due process for charges of misconduct, in open court, in the presence of the judge, which disturbs the court's business. Recall that the right to a jury trial in criminal cases does not apply in every case, only in those where the punishment includes a substantial prison term. Felony contempt would require a trial by jury and finding of guilt beyond a reasonable doubt since it could be punished by a substantial jail term.

Defenses

Some of the more popular defenses against contempt are:

- Absence of warning by court
- Attorney-client privilege
- Double jeopardy
- Reporter's privilege

Absence of Warning by Court

While a warning by the court that certain behavior will result in a contempt citing is not absolutely necessary, the absence of a warning has been successfully used as a defense. The defense has worked on at least one occasion when the defendant claimed to have no idea the behavior in question would result in contempt.[19]

HISTORICAL HIGHLIGHT
The Chicago Eight Minus One: The Story of Bobby Seale

It was the last week of August in 1968. America was weary of the Vietnam War. The Democrats gathered in Chicago to nominate their candidate for president. Chicago was at the crossroads of epochs. The era of big-city boss politics was about to end, and the quintessential big-city boss, Richard Daley, was hosting the convention. He fully expected to have his man, Vice-President Hubert Humphrey, nominated.

Outside the convention, a well-organized anti-war protest was taking place in Chicago's Grant Park. When the protesters attempted to leave the park and march to the convention center, the Chicago police reacted with reckless violence. They began beating the protesters with clubs, often attacking innocent bystanders and members of the press.

Despite the fact that a national study labeled the event a "police riot," eight demonstration organizers were charged with violating anti-riot statutes. The eight were long-time liberal activist David Dellinger; two of the founders of the Students for a Democratic Society, Rennie Davis and Tom Hayden; the cofounders of the Youth International Party or Yippies, Abbie Hoffman and Jerry Rubin; student Lee Weiner; Professor John Froines; and Black Panther activist Bobby Seale.

In court, seven of the defendants were represented by activist attorney William Kunstler. Bobby Seale had retained the services of California attorney Charles Garry. But Garry had to have gallbladder surgery, and asked for a six-week continuance. Judge Julius Hoffman denied the motion because local attorneys had put in appearances for Seale with the understanding they were only to help with the pretrial preparation. Judge Hoffman replied that "there was no such thing as a limited appearance in a criminal case."[20]

The strategy of the Chicago eight was called "guerilla theater." This was a confrontational style pioneered by defendant Jerry Rubin. Rubin had used it successfully when he was subpoenaed by the House Un-American Activities Committee during the Red Scare. Rubin showed up to testify dressed in eighteenth-century colonial costume. The hearing adjourned and Rubin's subpoena was forgotten.

The eight viewed the trial as an attempt by the Nixon administration to intimidate them. Their suspicion had some basis in fact. As the investigation of the Chicago riots concluded in the waning days of the Johnson administration, Attorney General Ramsey Clark felt that the eight should not be prosecuted. Clark, however, left the decision to the new administration. Nixon's Attorney General John Mitchell wanted to prosecute.[21] He even went so far as to have the FBI monitor communications between the defendants and their lawyers.

At the trial, Seale repeatedly protested his not being allowed to have the counsel of his choice. Seale attempted to represent himself. The exchanges between Seale and Hoffman grew more heated. Seale, noting that all the white defendants had the counsel of their choice, called Hoffman a racist, fascist pig. Finally, Hoffman ordered Seale to be gagged and chained to his chair.

Eventually, Hoffman severed Seale's case from the others. When he severed the case, he cited Seale for 16 counts of contempt for which he was to serve three months each.

The Court of Appeals saw this as an abuse of power. Under the law at that time, a judge could not impose a contempt sentence for longer than six months without a jury trial. The appeals court saw Hoffman's action as an attempt to circumvent the law. Seale's case was remanded for a jury trial, but by then news of the FBI's monitoring of the attorney-client communications was public. The government elected to drop the charges rather than reveal the contents of the taped conversations.

Attorney-Client Privilege

An attorney cannot be forced to reveal privileged information communicated to him or her by a client. In other words, an attorney can't be charged with contempt for refusing to disclose information she received while discussing a case with a client. However, for this defense to work, an attorney must provide independent evidence that the communications in question are attorney-client communications. The attorney's mere assertion that they are is not enough.[22]

Double Jeopardy

Double jeopardy defenses for contempt seldom prevail. The defense has been raised when the same conduct resulted in both civil and criminal contempt charges, but was unsuccessful.[23] Courts are free to charge each incident of contemptuous behavior as a separate count of contempt.[24] Even acts that are punishable by other crimes can also be cited as contempt. For example, a defendant who assaulted the prosecutor in court was successfully charged with both assault on a federal officer and contempt.[25]

Reporter's Privilege

Over the years, journalists seeking to protect sources have sometimes asserted that they cannot be forced to testify about those sources. Sometimes courts have held them in contempt for refusing to provide the information. For example, a Los Angeles Herald-Examiner reporter who refused to disclose his source of material related to the Charles Manson trial was jailed for 46 days in 1972.

In a federal criminal case or grand jury proceeding, the United States attorney general is required to review each subpoena for a journalist's testimony before it is sought. The regulations require that the Department of Justice, when reviewing the request, "strike the proper balance between the public's interest in the free dissemination of ideas and information and the public's interest in effective law enforcement and the fair administration of justice."[26]

HISTORICAL HIGHLIGHT
Freelance Writer Breaks Record for Time in Jail for Contempt

A freelance writer and adjunct lecturer at the University of Houston holds the record for the longest time spent in jail for refusing to reveal or turn over notes gathered in the course of researching a book. Vanessa Leggett has refused to turn over her notes in a murder case being investigated by a federal grand jury.

The case involves the 1997 murder of Doris Angleton, the wife of Texas millionaire Robert Angleton. Mr. Angleton was acquitted in state court of hiring his brother to kill Mrs. Angleton. The brother, Roger, committed suicide in his Harris County, Texas, jail cell before Mr. Angleton went on trial. He left behind a note claiming sole responsibility for the killing. Vanessa Leggett had interviewed Roger in prison before he killed himself, and it is the notes of those meetings that the Department of Justice seeks.

She was served with a subpoena to appear before the federal grand jury, but refused to turn over the notes. A federal court ordered her to, and then held her in contempt when she continued to refuse. She was jailed on July 20, 2001. An appeal to the Fifth Circuit Court of Appeals did not succeed. She faced the possibility of remaining in jail for up to 18 months, or until she complies, whichever came first. She was finally released on January 4, 2002, when the grand jury expired.[27]

BRIBERY

Bribery is defined as "the crime of giving something of value with the intention of influencing the action of a public official."[28]

Elements

The elements of bribery are:

- The recipient or target of the bribe must be a governmental official.
- A bribe in the form of money, goods, favors, or something of value was offered or given.
- The bribe was meant to induce an action or inaction.

A Recipient of the Bribe

A bribe recipient can be any government official ranging from a congressman to a clerk issuing permits or licenses. For example, after the September 11 terror attacks, investigators discovered that a number of men of Middle Eastern heritage had received special permits allowing them to transport hazardous material via truck across the nation's highways. The licensees had not taken the special test required of applicants. Eventually, a clerk working in the Pennsylvania Department of Transportation was charged with accepting bribes in exchange for issuing the licenses without examinations. Though a low-level clerk, he held a government position, and was in a position to take official action. In this case, he could issue or deny a license to applicants.

A Bribe

The bribe itself is money or something of value that is given to the recipient in return for certain action or, in some cases, inaction. The crime of bribery is complete when the offeror expresses ability and desire to pay, assuming he intends the proffered payment will lead to a favorable decision by the offeree.[29] Therefore, the bribe doesn't have to be given directly to the government official. It can be given to someone else, if that's what the recipient wants. The bribe itself can be anything of value such as cash, paid vacations, jewelry, or anything else other than a fee charged to all. In fact, some states even regulate the type and value of gifts that can be given to government officials such as holiday and appreciation gifts. The U.S. Postal Service prohibits gifts to carriers and others that are worth more than $20.

Action Meant to Result from the Bribe

The action meant to result from the bribe need not be illegal in and of itself. The government must merely show that the receipt of the bribe influenced the decision. For example, it would still be bribery to offer a passport clerk a $500 "bonus" if he or she issues you a passport today instead of tomorrow.

Bribery can also be prosecuted despite the fact that the recipient lacks the authority to accomplish the action desired by the offeror. It also doesn't matter if the recipient of the bribe never delivers what he or she promises to do for the bribe.

State of Mind

The person offering the bribe must intend that his offer will result in favorable action on the part of the recipient. So long as the bribe was intended as *quid pro quo* for a favor, the intent requirement has been met.

Defenses

A frequently raised defense to bribery charges is:

- Entrapment or extortion by public official

Entrapment

Entrapment can be claimed as a defense where it can be proven that the government agent initiated the bribery scheme, and forced the defendant into a course of action he or she normally would not have taken. An entrapment defense has two elements: government inducement and the defendant's lack of predisposition to commit the crime.[30] Keep in mind that proving entrapment in any case is difficult; the defendant must prove that he or she wasn't predisposed to paying a bribe or was unaware that the requested payment was a bribe rather than the customary fee for a government service. Even in cases where a government official demands payment before carrying out official duties, the person from whom the bribe is being extorted has other avenues for recourse. He or she can, for example, file a mandamus action, which is a lawsuit seeking to compel government to do something they are required to do. The target can also report the attempted extortion to police or other law enforcement.

What happens if a defendant pays money as a bribe, and then raises entrapment as a defense? Does he get his money back? In at least one case, the answer was no even though there was no bribery conviction.[31]

CORRUPT ORGANIZATIONS

For many years government has sought to control and eliminate corrupt organizations. One of the most comprehensive pieces of legislation in this battle is the Organized Crime Control Act. Part of this act is the Racketeering Influenced and Corrupt Organizations Act or **RICO,** which was passed in 1970.[32] RICO was originally intended to prosecute organized crime, but was drafted very broadly. The original intention was to provide a way to prosecute organized crime activities run through both illegitimate business enterprises and through legitimate-appearing businesses. Sometimes legitimate businesses serve as a shield for illegitimate activities or a way to funnel earnings from crime to make the profits appear legitimate. However, in recent years RICO has been applied to business activities far removed from organized crime syndicates.

Under RICO, it is a federal crime to acquire or maintain an interest in, use income from, or conduct or participate in the affairs of an "enterprise" through a pattern of "racketeering activity."
An enterprise can be:

- A corporation
- A partnership
- A sole proprietorship
- Any business or organization
- The government

Racketeering activity includes many crimes and activities such as:

- Bribery
- Embezzlement
- Gambling
- Arson
- Counterfeiting money, recordings, copyrighted materials, and computer programs
- Trafficking in contraband cigarettes
- Harboring illegal aliens

At least two acts must be committed by the organization being charged with racketeering within a 10-year period. In addition to fines and imprisonment, persons or organizations convicted under RICO are subject to seizure of property obtained with illegally acquired funds. For example, a partnership that used a pizza shop as a front for dealing in cigarettes on which the partnership hasn't paid cigarette taxes may find that the pizza shop will be seized and sold, with the proceeds going to the government.

IMPEACHMENT

Impeachment is an indictment of a federal official charging him or her with "treason, bribery, and high crimes and misdemeanors."[33] Once an official is impeached, he or she is tried and, if found guilty, removed from office.

The form of impeachment outlined in the U.S. Constitution owes much to its English predecessor. Although impeachment is no longer used in the United Kingdom (all officials now serve at the pleasure of Parliament), in the days of a strong executive, in the form of a king, it was necessary to have a mechanism to remove corrupt royal appointees.

Impeachment articles are voted upon by the House of Representatives (House of Commons in England), and then a trial is held in the Senate (House of Lords in England). In order to be removed from office the Senate must vote to convict by a two-thirds supermajority.

Impeachment was intended to be a seldom-used remedy. The standard of "high crimes and misdemeanors," while vague, does imply that the framers intended it to be a remedy for very serious infractions by public officials. The widened context of "treason, bribery, high crimes and misdemeanors" leads to the conclusion that the founding fathers were concerned about officials selling their office or betraying the citizens to whom they must ultimately answer.

One reason there have been few impeachment cases in our history is that in many cases public officials have simply been voted out when their term expired. We have not had to resort to impeachment. There is one group of officials for whom impeachment is the only avenue for removal, absent death or voluntary retirement. Recall that federal judges are appointed for life. Thus, a federal judge can only be forced out of office by impeachment.

The most high-profile impeachment cases are those of presidents. Two U.S. presidents, Andrew Johnson and Bill Clinton, have been impeached, but neither have been removed from office. A third president, Richard Nixon, lost an impeachment vote in the U.S. House of Representatives Judiciary Committee, where the process begins, but resigned before the matter came before the full House.

PROCEDURES

The procedures in an impeachment are not spelled out in the Constitution or Code. Congress can decide on procedures on an ad hoc basis. In modern times, Congress has initiated two presidential impeachment proceedings, against Presidents Nixon and Clinton.

When proceedings began against President Nixon, Congress found that the Constitution offered little guidance. The House Judiciary Committee developed rules of evidence and procedures for the impeachment proceedings. However, those rules only bound Congress for the duration of the Nixon impeachment process.

HISTORICAL HIGHLIGHT

Impeachment After Acquittal: The Story of Alcee Hastings

Alcee Hastings was a pioneer for African Americans. He was the first black to be named United States District Judge for the Southern District of Florida. Unfortunately, he also became the first black federal official ever to be impeached. He was also the first federal official of any race to be impeached and removed from office after being acquitted in federal court on the same charges.

How this strange turn of events came to be owes much to Hastings's magnetic personality. He is a bright, articulate, persuasive speaker. At his trial he spoke convincingly in his own behalf and the jury did not convict. The Senate trial was different.

A judicial inquiry had produced voluminous evidence that Hastings had solicited a $150,000 bribe from two racketeers. He had allegedly solicited it through an intermediary to maintain deniability, but an undercover agent impersonated one of the racketeers.

Balancing this damning information was the acquittal in court. The U.S. House of Representatives was faced with a dilemma. African American Congressman John Conyers of Michigan was chosen to head the House's investigation. He gravely weighed the evidence and came to the conclusion that Hastings was guilty. Conyers addressed Congress and said: "We did not wage (the) civil rights struggle merely to replace one form of judicial corruption for another. . . . The principle of equality requires that a black public official be held to the same standard that other public officials are held to." The House voted 413 to 3 for impeachment.

Hastings' supporters were optimistic about the Senate vote. The Senate is required to vote for impeachment by a two-thirds majority before an official can be removed from office. The consensus was that Hastings could charm, cajole, and convince the requisite number of Senators to assure an acquittal.

The Senate, however, had to view the facts. The undercover agent testified that he asked the contact to demonstrate that he could get Hastings to do what he wanted; the contact arranged for Hastings to have dinner at a Miami hotel, and appear in the lobby at a specific time. Hastings did just as the agent requested. When the money was paid, Hastings made his law clerk stay late to finish the paperwork releasing seized property belonging to the man the agent was impersonating.

In the end, despite the acquittal in court, the Senate voted to convict on October 20, 1989.[34] A visibly shaken Hastings left the chamber in tears. However, within a few years, he was elected to the House of Representatives from his south Florida district. Hastings now belongs to the body that voted for his impeachment.

When Congress began impeachment proceedings against President Clinton, it did not immediately establish its procedures. It did so only after receiving the report of Special Prosecutor Kenneth Starr. Congressional critics charged that Congress appeared to be shaping the procedures to the evidence, instead of designing them to impartially evaluate the evidence.

Impeachment in Congress is no guarantee that the elected official will not have to face charges in state or federal court. During President Nixon's impeachment ordeal, he faced a parallel prosecution in federal court. In fact, it was his loss before the U.S. Supreme Court that forced him to reveal the most damaging evidence against him, the Oval Office tapes. Had Mr. Nixon not resigned, those tapes would have been used against him in his Senate trial.

In the same vein, President Clinton was forced to relinquish his law license as part of the settlement of the perjury charges against him. President Clinton was accused of lying under oath concerning his affair with Monica Lewinsky during testimony in a civil suit brought against him for sexual harassment by Paula Jones. (See historical highlight earlier in this chapter.)

AMBIGUITIES

Unlike criminal proceedings where the burden of proof is "guilt beyond a reasonable doubt," or civil actions where the "preponderance of evidence" standard applies, the burden of proof is not codified in impeachment proceedings. Congress has never specified what standard is to be used, but has left it up to the individual senator when voting to convict.

Additionally, the definition of "high crimes and misdemeanors" is nebulous. President Clinton's supporters argued that perjury in a civil case did not rise to the level of "high crimes and misdemeanors" as intended in the Constitution. They apparently convinced enough of the Senate to prevent conviction.

President Clinton's impeachment also raised another question. Can a president or federal judge be impeached for activities not related to the duties of his or her office? President Clinton's questionable conduct was carried out as a private citizen. None of the impeachment articles alleged that he abused the privileges of his office. Almost all previous impeachments were prosecuted against office holders who acted illegally in the execution of their office.

CONCLUSION

Impeachment was designed to be a seldom-used tool. Despite having the form of a legal proceeding, it is in reality a political exercise. The Founding Fathers recognized this and put the safeguard of requiring a two-thirds majority to convict. Even though this section has focused on federal impeachment proceedings, the states each have impeachment proceedings.

Some states also use a process known as a recall vote. A recall vote is where the citizens choose to remove or recall an official through a referendum. Usually it is necessary to get a certain number of signatures on a petition to get the issue on the ballot. If a majority of the citizens vote to recall the individual, he or she must leave office.

Impeachment is a process fraught with ambiguity. It can be open to political manipulation. Some historians have noted that when impeachment is abused, the public loses its appetite for it for years afterward.[35] House Minority Leader Richard Gephart referred to the Clinton impeachment as part of "the politics of personal destruction." Despite its possible misuse, impeachment is a process deeply ingrained in American jurisprudence.

PRACTICE POINTERS

Legal professionals in paralegal or investigative positions who work for attorneys representing business owners, partnerships, and corporations will find themselves working on cases involving possible criminal charges typically considered "white collar crimes." These clients pose special challenges since they are generally educated and understand how the legal system works. Many seek representation while the case is still under investigation or even before. Representation often involves cooperation with investigations and plea bargaining negotiation. These are processes in which members of the professional support staff often play a significant role.

Clients often want to know how likely it is that they could face charges. The U.S. Department of Justice has issued guidelines for their attorneys to use in determining when to start investigations, bring charges, or negotiate a plea agreement when a corporation and its owner or principal is the target.[36] These guidelines include:

- The nature and seriousness of the misconduct
- The pervasiveness of the wrongdoing
- The company's history of wrongdoing
- Cooperation by principals
- Voluntary disclosure of wrongdoing
- Willingness to make restitution
- Whether civil sanctions are enough

In the event federal charges are filed against a client, the odds of conviction after trial are high, often over 90 percent. If the case goes to trial, significant time and resources will be spent preparing documents and testimony to support efforts to reduce the sentence to be served. You may be actively involved, for example, in seeking out mitigating factors that support an argument for deviation from the federal sentencing guidelines. This preparation may mean the difference between a prison sentence or supervised release and house detention.

The possible charges available to U.S. attorneys are far more extensive than those covered in this chapter. In addition to RICO charges, business owners may face mail and security fraud charges, accusations of environmental violations, antitrust and tax charges, and many more. Those investigating possible charges should remember that often there are also state crime code violations possible.

CHAPTER SUMMARY

The basis of civilization is the nation-state, or polis. The ancient Athenians had an almost poetic affection for the polis. At Pericles' funeral oration for Athens' honored war dead, he spoke of Athens as "a pattern to others" because Athenians were subservient to the rule of law.[37] Every democratic society since Athens has held that "no man is above the law." Unlike monarchies and oligarchies, the legitimacy of democratic government is based on the principle that a state's political leaders were ultimately answerable to the people.

Some 2,500 years after Pericles, another leader paid homage to a field of honored dead when he said that "the government of the people, by the people, and for the people shall not perish from the earth."[38] To both Pericles and Lincoln, allegiance to the state was the highest duty of a citizen in a free society. The betrayal of that allegiance, whether that took the form of treason or simply bribery, profaned the graves of the men who had given their lives in its service.

Most of the criminal offenses described in this chapter are offenses against the rule of law in the sense that they go to the heart of the integrity of the system. Perjury, bribery, and obstruction of justice do more than harm an individual. Gone undetected and unpunished, they ultimately destroy the rule of law.

KEY TERMS

Bribery: The crime of giving something of value with the intention of influencing the action of a public official.

Conspiracy: An agreement between two or more persons to engage in a criminal act.

Contempt: Conduct that brings the authority and administration of the law into disrespect or that embarrasses or obstructs the court's discharge of its duties.

Impeachment: An indictment of a public official that leads to a trial to determine whether he or she should be removed from office.

Obstruction of justice: The crime of impeding or hindering the administration of justice in any way.

Perjury: Giving false testimony in a judicial or administrative proceeding; lying under oath as to a material fact; swearing to the truth of anything one knows or believes to be false.

Perjury trap: A situation where a grand jury subpoenas a witness for the sole purpose of obtaining perjured testimony.

Recantation: The retraction of testimony.

RICO: Racketeering Influenced and Corrupt Organizations Act is legislation that enables the government to prosecute individuals and organizations for a pattern of criminal activity. Originally meant to target organized crime.

Subornation of perjury: Convincing or seeking to convince another person to commit perjury.

Two-witness rule: The Common Law rule that requires two witnesses to testify to another's perjury in order for a conviction to take place.

DISCUSSION QUESTIONS

1. Should the government run "sting operations" where they offer bribes to politicians? Is this entrapment? Is this creating crime where none existed?
2. Do elected officials (or for that matter, attorneys) have a "higher duty" to the law than the average citizen? How would this apply to President Clinton's statements in Paula Jones's civil suit?
3. Should the RICO statutes be applied to areas other than just organized crime? Is that law written too broadly?

4. Does the Constitution's definition of "bribery, treason, high crimes, and misdemeanors" as the basis for impeachment refer to actions taken before an official took office? What level of offense meets this standard?

FOR FURTHER READING

1. Mass, P. (1997). *Underboss: Sammy the Bull Gravano's Story of Life in the Mafia.* HarperCollins.
2. Jackson, D. D. (1973). *Judges: An Inside View of the Agonies and Excesses of an American Elite.* Antheneum.
3. Black, C. L. (1998). *Impeachment: A Handbook.* Yale University Press.
4. Caplan, G. M. (1983). *ABSCAM Ethics: Moral Issues and Deception in Law Enforcement.* HarperInformation.
5. Noonan, J. T. (1984). *Bribes.* Macmillan.

QUOTATIONS FOR CHAPTER TWELVE

1. *But who is to guard the guard themselves?*
   Juvenal in *Satires* (circa 115)

2. *The whole art of government consists in the art of being honest.*
   Thomas Jefferson

3. *Moral principle is a looser bond than pecuniary interest.*
   Abraham Lincoln

4. *A government of laws, not men.*
   John Adams

5. *The greater the power, the more dangerous the abuse.*
   Edmund Burke

6. *The United States Attorney is the representative not of an ordinary party to a controversy, bit of a sovereignty whose obligation to govern impartially is as compelling as its obligation to govern all; and whose interest, therefore, in a criminal prosecution is not that it shall win a case, but that justice shall be done. As such, he is in a peculiar and very definite sense the servant of the law, the twofold aim of which is that guilt shall not escape or innocence suffer. He may prosecute with earnestness and vigor—indeed, he should do so. But, while he may strike hard blows, he is not at liberty to strike foul ones. It is as much his duty to refrain from improper methods calculated to produce a wrongful conviction as it is to use every legitimate means to bring about a just one.*
   Justice Sutherland in *Berger v. United States*, 295 U.S. 78 (1935)

ENDNOTES

1. Ballentine's Law Dictionary.
2. 18 P.S. § 4904.
3. 18 U.S.C. § 1623(e).
4. *United States v. Norris*, 300 U.S. 564 (1937).

5. 18 U.S.C. § 1623(d).

6. 18 U.S.C. § 1623(c).

7. *United States v. Gugliaro*, 501 F. 2d 68 (2nd Cir. 1974).

8. Clinton statement issued by the White House, January 18, 2001.

9. *United States v. Wood*, 6 F. 3d 692 (10th Cir. 1993).

10. 18 U.S.C. § 1515.

11. *United States v. Wood*, 6 F. 3d 692 (10th Cir. 1993).

12. *United States v. Cammisano*, 917 F. 2d 1057 (8th Cir. 1990).

13. "How much has Fred Zain cost the state?" *Sunday Gazette-Mail* (September 23, 2001).

14. "Police chemist's missteps cause Oklahoma scandal," *Washington Post* (November 11, 2001).

15. Ballentine's Law Dictionary.

16. 18 U.S.C. § 401.

17. *In re Farquhar*, 160 U.S. App DC 295, 492 F. 2d 561 (1973).

18. *Floersheim v. Engman*, 161 U.S. App DC 30, 494 F. 2d 949 (1973).

19. *United States v. Seale*, 461 F. 2d 345 (7th Cir. 1972).

20. Ibid.

21. "Lessons of the 60's: 'We'd do it again,' say the Chicago Seven's lawyers," *ABA Journal* (May 18, 1987).

22. *In re Bonanno*, 344 F. 2d 830 (2nd Cir. 1965).

23. *Yates v. United States*, 355 U.S. 66 (1957).

24. *Bullock v. United States*, 265 F. 2d 683 (6th Cir. 1959), cert den 360 U.S. 909 (1959).

25. *United States v. Rollerson*, 145 U.S. App DC 338, 449 F. 2d 1000 (1971).

26. 28 C.F.R. 50.10(a).

27. "Who counts as a journalist for First Amendment purposes?" Cable News Network Online (January 10, 2002).

28. Ballentine's Law Dictionary.

29. *United States v. Hernandez*, 731 F. 2d 1147 (5th Cir. 1984).

30. *United States v. Daniel*, 3 F. 3d 775 (4th Cir. 1993).

31. *United States v. Kim*, 870 F. 2d 81 (2d Cir.1989).

32. 18 U.S.C. & 1961 et seq.

33. United States Constitution, Article II Section 4.

34. "Senate convicts, removes Hastings from judgeship," *Wall Street Journal* (October 23, 1989).

35. M. J. Gerhardt, *Review: The Perils of Presidential Impeachment*. 67 U. Chi. L. Rev. 293.

36. J. M. Nolan, *White Collar Crime: Department of Justice Issues Guidance to U.S. Attorneys Regarding Criteria for Criminally Charging Corporations*. Findlaw Library, *http://www.findlaw.com*, 2000.

37. M. Cohen and N. Fermon, *Princeton Readings on Political Thought*. Princeton University Press, 1996.

38. A. Lincoln, *The Gettysburg Address*.

CHAPTER 13
Social Crimes

CHAPTER OBJECTIVES

After studying this chapter, you should be able to:

- Understand the history of social crimes
- Define prostitution and explain the elements required to be proven in a prosecution
- Understand the history of laws criminalizing out-of-wedlock sexual relationships and their impact today
- Understand the Supreme Court's position on sodomy and its impact
- Describe some of the laws that regulate gambling
- Understand the problem of drug abuse and law enforcement efforts to curtail the use and trafficking in illegal drugs

CHAPTER CONTENTS

QUOTATIONS FOR CHAPTER 13
ENDNOTES

> *Of all tyrannies a tyranny sincerely exercised for the good of its victims may be the most oppressive. It may be better to live under robber barons than under omnipotent moral busybodies. The robber baron's cruelty may sometimes sleep, his cupidity may at some point be satiated; but those who torment us for our own good will torment us without end for they do so with the approval of their own conscience.*
>
> **James Madison, *The Federalist No. 51***

INTRODUCTION

Every society has generally accepted rules of conduct for its members. Those rules vary from place to place and time to time. In some societies, the rules are strict and plentiful, while in others they are few and far between. Conduct rules often have their roots in religious doctrines, but sometimes have more practical origins. For example, the prohibition against prostitution has its origin in religion, but some counties in the United States allow prostitutes to operate in licensed brothels where presumably regular health checks help prevent the spread of disease that might flourish in an unsupervised setting.

Most rules of conduct in modern societies don't carry criminal penalties, but instead rely on self-censorship or public ostracism for enforcement. Some violations of the rules do carry criminal sanctions, and it is those we now turn our attention to. The list of social offenses that have at one time or another been considered crimes include:

- Adultery and fornication
- Bestiality and buggery
- Miscegenation (mixed-race marriage)
- Seduction and alienation of affections

PROSTITUTION

Prostitution is generally defined as engaging in sexual intercourse or other sexual activity for pay. It can be engaged in by either sex, although most prostitutes are women. It was widespread across the ancient world in Greece, Egypt, and Rome, and is sometimes referred to as the world's oldest profession. For some practitioners, selling sex acts supports a drug habit. Others who may have few job or social skills turn to prostitution for economic reasons. Still others are runaway teens who find themselves on the streets with no money or shelter and few support systems available. Prostitutes are also frequent targets for criminal acts, including murder. In fact, some of the most notorious serial killers in our history specifically targeted prostitutes.

Most states outlaw sex for money and make it a crime for both parties involved. It has long been a federal crime to transport someone over state lines for immoral purposes,[1] as the original language of the Mann Act is read. The law now defines "immoral purposes" with precision, and provides that:

HISTORICAL HIGHLIGHT
Sex Workers Try to Dispel Stereotypes About Prostitution

Not everyone involved in prostitution and related activities do so out of desperation or the need to feed an addiction. Some claim their choice of profession was made freely and have formed organizations aimed at improving working conditions and gaining respect and legal protection for members. Many of these participants in prostitution and related acts such as acting in pornographic films, working in massage parlors, and dancing in strip clubs prefer to be called **sex workers.**

The North American Task Force on Prostitution is a network of sex workers and sex workers' rights organizations, and individuals and organizations that support the rights of sex workers to ply their trades without interference from law enforcement, and with the ability to organize into what amounts to trade unions or guilds. There are member organizations in many large cities offering education, health screening, and even legal assistance to sex workers.

Other groups operate on a model designed less to make prostitution a legitimate business, and more to assure that sex workers are safe and healthy and able to receive medical treatment or drug counseling if desired. For example, in the nation's capital, HIPS (Helping Individual Prostitutes Survive) runs an outreach van nightly to assist sex workers. HIPS also operates a toll-free national hotline.

> Whoever knowingly transports any individual in interstate or foreign commerce, or in any Territory or Possession of the United States, with intent that such individual engage in prostitution, or in any sexual activity for which any person can be charged with a criminal offense, or attempts to do so, shall be fined under this title or imprisoned not more than 10 years, or both.

At one point, the U.S. Supreme Court went as far as to say that a man who "transported a woman in interstate commerce so that she should become his mistress or concubine" was transporting her with an "immoral purpose" within the meaning of the Mann Act.[2] Over the years, the act was also used to convict a Mormon practitioner of polygamy from bringing his brides home over state lines.[3] Eventually, the language was changed to its present wording to assure that only those transported over state lines to engage in the sale of sex for money would run afoul of the law.

State criminal laws outlawing prostitution generally outlaw two distinct behaviors: soliciting someone to engage in sex for money in a public place, and working in a brothel or other private setting selling sex for money. For example, in Pennsylvania a person is guilty of prostitution if he or she:

> is an inmate of a house of prostitution or otherwise engages in sexual activity as a business; or loiters in or within view of any public place for the purpose of being hired to engage in sexual activity.[4]

Many states have graduated penalties for engaging in prostitution, with each additional conviction resulting in a longer prison term and fine. Many states, in recognition that prostitution can be a factor in the spread of sexually transmitted diseases, make selling sexual favors by those who know they are infected with the human immunodeficiency virus (HIV) a felony offense.

Those who hire prostitutes also commit a criminal offense in most states. In addition, anyone who works to procure clients for a prostitute (the definition of a "**pimp**") can also be prosecuted. Although it was not always so, most states now punish pimps, prostitutes, and their clients equally. In addition, those who patronize prostitutes are sometimes subject to publicity. For example, in Pennsylvania, the second conviction for soliciting a prostitute carries with it a requirement that the conviction shall be published in a local newspaper (at the defendant's expense).[5]

There is only one state in the United States in which prostitution is legal. Since 1971, counties in Nevada have been able to elect to allow brothels within their borders.[6] The state requires that counties with brothels license their prostitutes, and also requires that all clients wear condoms. It is still illegal to sell sex outside of brothels and in Las Vegas itself.

FORNICATION, ADULTERY, AND POLYGAMY/POLYANDRY

Both **fornication** and **adultery** were originally crimes in all states. Fornication is defined as voluntary sexual intercourse between two unmarried persons.[7] Adultery is sexual intercourse by a married person with someone not his or her spouse.[8]

Today, statutes criminalizing adultery and fornication are generally limited to situations where the acts take place between people who otherwise cannot marry and in cases where there is independent verification of the offense. For example, in Mississippi it is a crime punishable by up to 10 years in prison to commit even one act of adultery or fornication with someone you could not marry because he or she was too close of a blood relative.[9] North Carolina outlaws fornication and adultery but does not allow the testimony of either of the participants against the other. Those in the military can still face a court martial for committing adultery.

Polygamy, or having several wives, and polyandry, or having several husbands, is a practice that today exists in some parts of the world, but a practice that has been outlawed in all states. The term **bigamy** is used to describe the criminal act of marrying when one already has a spouse, and applies to both polygamists and polyandrists. In the United States, it was officially practiced by Mormons until the Church of Jesus Christ of Latter-Day Saints prohibited it in 1890.[10] Outlawing polygamy was made a condition of joining the United States when western territories that had accepted the practice sought entry, as was the case for Utah's admission to the Union in 1896.

Some states even criminalize the teaching of bigamy. For example, in Mississippi, you may be fined up to $500 and imprisoned up to 6 months if you:

> teach another the doctrines, principles, or tenets, or any of them, of polygamy; or shall endeavor so to do; or shall induce or persuade another by words or acts, or otherwise, to embrace or adopt polygamy, or to emigrate to any other state, territory, district, or country for the purpose of embracing, adopting, or practicing polygamy. . . .[11]

HISTORIC HIGHLIGHT
"Religious Duty" to Have Multiple Wives Lands Man in Jail

Tom Green believes he has the religious duty to practice multiple marriage. To that end, he has been living in a polygamous household with five wives and several dozen children. The family lives in the Utah desert in a compound of trailers. But Mr. Green isn't shy about his unusual living arrangements. In fact, he touted what he calls his "original Mormonism" in daytime talk shows and challenged state prosecutors to charge him. They did.

When Green's case was tried, a jury took three hours to find him guilty of four counts of bigamy and one count of criminal failure to pay child support. On August 24, 2001, the 53-year-old was sentenced to five years in prison and ordered to repay $78,000 in welfare payments his wives and children had collected over the years. He has appealed the conviction but remains in jail pending the outcome. He also awaits trial in a related rape case. Prosecutors say he impregnated one of his wives while she was 13, and below the age of consent.

Anyone charged under this act could likely defend by arguing that this statute is contrary to the First Amendment prohibition against curtailing free speech and religious freedom of thought, even though practicing bigamy may be punished. The Supreme Court early on upheld the right of a state to outlaw polygamy and bigamy even if it was practiced as part of a sincerely held religious belief.[12]

ABORTION

Perhaps no issue divides America as does the legalization of **abortion.** Abortion is the termination of pregnancy by something other than birth. During most of the late nineteenth and early to mid-twentieth century, states held that those who performed abortions were guilty of murder. These rigid rules have not historically been in place, however. Greek and Roman women practiced abortion without fear of retribution or punishment. However, the Hippocratic Oath, which has long been the source of medical ethics rules, does warn physicians not to induce abortions.

Nonetheless, abortion was not considered a violation of the Common Law in England. At Common Law, an abortion performed before "quickening" was not an indictable offense.[13] It wasn't until the mid-1800s that abortion became a crime, and then only after "quickening." Quickening was generally believed to occur around the fifteenth to eighteenth week of pregnancy, and was the time a woman first felt her child move. But by the 1950s virtually every state had enacted abortion laws outlawing all abortions that weren't performed to save the life of the mother. It is against this backdrop that the controversial Supreme Court abortion decisions were made.

Until the 1973 Supreme Court decision in *Roe v. Wade*,[14] every state but four had on its books laws that criminalized abortion. In *Roe*, the plaintiff was a pregnant woman who sought an abortion, but could not get one in her home state of Texas because it was a criminal offense to procure an abortion if the mother's life was not in danger. She sued, arguing that the state law that would let her face possible criminal sanctions were she to procure an abortion in Texas violated her constitutional right to privacy.

The Supreme Court concluded that a woman's right to privacy and personal liberty encompassed allowing her to make the determination of whether she desires children. That right, however, was balanced against the state's right to protect her life and that of the fetus she carries by regulating the conditions under which she can seek an abortion. The Court came up with a three-prong decision, summarized as follows:

1. During the first trimester of pregnancy, the decision to have an abortion rests with the woman and her physician.
2. During the second trimester, the state can regulate the procedure in ways consistent with protecting maternal health.
3. During the final trimester, the state may prohibit abortions except to save the life of the mother.

The Court's decision in *Roe* has been one of the most controversial. In the nearly three decades since the initial decision, the Court has heard related cases many times and settled some questions left open. The Court has on several occasions refused to overrule itself. Since then, the Court has decided that a state cannot require notification to a husband as a condition for an abortion, but allowed to stand laws that require a short waiting period, parental notification with an alternative judicial petition in some cases, pre-abortion counseling and informed consent, and strict recordkeeping requirements.[15] It also removed the strict trimester approach, and instead stated that abortion laws can't "unduly burden" a woman's right to choose. The Supreme Court also stuck down a Nebraska law criminalizing so-called "partial-birth" abortions.[16]

The federal government has also entered the abortion rights battle. For example, Congress attempted to pass a partial-birth abortion ban in 2000, only to find the legislation vetoed by then-President William Clinton. New bills have been introduced since, and are under consideration. Congress also is considering a bill that criminalizes transporting a minor across state lines to procure an abortion if she could not obtain one in her home state if transportation is not provided by a parent.

SODOMY

Sodomy is generally defined as sexual relations between members of the same sex, sexual conduct *per anus* or *per os* between unmarried persons of the opposite sex, and sexual intercourse with animals.[17] Historically, sodomy laws played a large role in controlling homosexual behaviors. The proscription of sodomy goes back at least as far as Roman times, where it was a capital offense.[18] In England, sodomy was an offense handled by the Catholic Church until the time of the Reformation when Henry VIII transferred all ecclesiastic offenses over to the King's Court.[19] All thirteen states made sodomy a crime at the time the Bill of Rights became the law of the land.[20] Many state laws criminalizing sodomy have been challenged on the basis that they interfere with the constitutional right to privacy.

The Supreme Court heard one such challenge in *Bowers v. Hardwick*.[21] In that case, Hardwick, the defendant, was charged with engaging in sodomy with another male in the privacy of his bedroom. Sodomy was against the law in Georgia. After his preliminary hearing on the charges, at which the district attorney announced he would not prosecute the case unless more evidence surfaced, Hardwick sued. He asserted that he was a practicing homosexual, and that the Georgia sodomy statute placed him in imminent danger of arrest. He argued that the Constitution granted him a right to privacy in his bedroom, and that the state had no business charging him with committing a sex act with another consulting adult. The Court, in a 5–4 vote, concluded that homosexuals did not have a constitutional right to violate state sodomy laws, and that states were free to criminalize such behavior if they saw fit to.

Many states then repealed their sodomy laws, making any kind of sexual contact (other than prostitution) between consenting adults of any sex legal. The following states have either abolished their sodomy laws or had them declared unconstitutional by their state's highest court: Alaska, California, Colorado, Connecticut, Delaware, District of Columbia, Hawaii, Illinois, Indiana, Iowa, Maine, Montana, Nebraska, Nevada, New Hampshire, New Jersey, New Mexico, New York, North Dakota, Ohio, Oregon, Pennsylvania, South Dakota, Tennessee, Texas, Vermont, Washington, West Virginia, Wisconsin, and Wyoming.

In 2003, the Supreme Court made an abrupt about face on the question of criminalized sodomy. In a 6–3 decision, the Court overturned its decision in *Hardwick* and concluded that community standards have changed. They cited the states that had since decriminalized sodomy and found that remaining laws were unconstitutional as a denial of due process and violation of privacy. The case is *Lawrence v. Texas,* 539 U.S. 558 (2003). The decision is viewed by many as a milestone recognition by the Court of an inherent right to privacy.

PUBLIC INDECENCY OR LEWDNESS

All states have laws that criminalize behavior that constitutes **public indecency** or lewdness. Public indecency is generally defined as lewd or lascivious conduct that is open to public view.[22] Typical actions punished under these types of statutes include nude dancing, performing sex acts in a public place (where there is no reasonable expectation of privacy), and exposing one's genitals in a public place.

Public indecency charges typically don't result in long sentences or large fines, and tend to be viewed as catchall provisions of penal codes unless the defendant has been arrested on several occasions for the same conduct, or appears to be threatening or dangerous. For example, a male suspect who makes it a habit to expose his genitalia to young children may have a greater likelihood of prosecution and punishment than a first-time offender caught masturbating in a dirty movie theater or engaging in sexual behavior in a parked car.

Perhaps the public lewdness case that has garnered the most publicity in recent history is that of children's program creator Pee Wee Herman, or Paul Reubens. In 1991, he was caught in an adult theater while allegedly exposing his genitals and masturbating. He later pleaded no contest to a charge of indecent exposure and was sentenced to perform 75 hours of community service and to pay a fine.[23] The episode lost him his television show and made him a social outcast for nearly a decade.

GAMBLING _____

Gambling and games of chance have been with us for most of history. Gambling is generally defined as the act of taking a monetary risk on the chance of receiving a monetary gain. Gambling therefore involves chance, rather than skill.[24] It is the taking of a chance as opposed to the use of skill that distinguishes gambling from a game of skill or a contest. For example, suppose you wanted to sell your house in a hurry. If you held a raffle, and charged every entrant $200, could you award the house to the lucky holder of the winning ticket? Probably not, because a game of chance such as your raffle would be gambling under most state laws (and as you will see later, might be a federal crime if you used the Internet to sell your raffle tickets).

But what if you held a contest with a $200 entry fee and awarded the house to the person who wrote the best essay? Would that qualify as a skill contest rather than a game of chance? The answer is unclear. At best the contest would have to comply with state sweepstake and contest laws. But the owners would still risk having their raffle declared an illegal lottery or numbers game.

Today, most states[25] run their own gambling operations in the form of lotteries or otherwise permit limited legal gambling while churches run bingo games and Monte Carlo nights regularly to raise funds. Some states have funded entire new social programs with lottery proceeds. For example, Pennsylvania's lottery provided nearly $700 million in funding to programs that benefit older citizens in 2000, after taking in almost $1.7 billion in ticket sales. The programs funded include prescription drug discounts, transportation, and property tax breaks for senior citizens that might otherwise be funded with tax dollars. Gamblers buying tickets won back $868 million in prizes.[26]

Gambling also takes place at racetracks, on Indian reservations that have established casinos, and in states that have legalized casinos and riverboat gambling. But legal gambling isn't the only form of gambling taking place. Many billions of dollars are spent every year on illegal games of chance, including Internet gambling. Internet gambling alone is expected to exceed $2 billion in 2001.[27]

What is the impact of gambling? In 1996, Congress wanted answers to that question and authorized the creation of the national Gambling Impact Study Commission. The commission released its study in June 1999, and made a number of findings and recommendations. These included:

- A recommendation that there be a moratorium on the expansion of gambling until a more complete assessment of the social harm that may result from expansion can be studied.
- A recommendation that federal law be considered to regulate the new area of Internet gambling, but that states, local authorities, and tribal leaders can best determine what restrictions should be placed on gambling within their jurisdictions.

States that have legalized some forms of gambling nonetheless regulate it carefully. Bingo and other small games of chance are generally allowed. Tempting as it might be to assume that legal, state-run, or state-supervised gambling would end criminal involvement in gambling, that does not appear to be the case. A significant amount of illegal gambling takes place as sports gambling, or gambling on the outcome of sporting events. Illegal gambling also takes the form of "numbers" games.[28] These illegal operations work much like the legal state-sponsored ones, except that the winnings aren't taxed, nor are the profits taxed or returned to the community in the form of social program funding or additions to the general funds.

In areas where legal casinos and legal lotteries exist, there is also a thriving illegal business in loan sharking, as gamblers seek ready access to cash.

Illegal gambling operations can be prosecuted under federal law if they meet the following criteria:

- The gambling operation violates state law where it is operated.
- It involves five or more persons who conduct, finance, manage, supervise, direct, or own all or part of the business.
- It has been or remains in substantially continuous operation for a period in excess of 30 days or has a gross revenue of $2,000 in any single day.[29]

The types of gambling operations covered by the law include lotteries, slot machines, pool selling, bookmaking, roulette wheels, and dice tables. The law also explicitly excludes bingo games and other similar gambling devices operated by organizations recognized as a tax-exempt organization by the Internal Revenue Service.

HISTORICAL HIGHLIGHT
Internet Gambling Operation Not Outside Reach of Federal Law

What happens when a bright young man working in the technology field decides he wants a piece of the Internet gold rush? If he sets up an overseas Internet sports bookmaking operation, he lands in jail. Consider the case of Jay Cohen. As a young man in San Francisco, he enjoyed a rewarding career as a derivatives trader. But in 1996 he saw that the Internet was about to take off, and went in search of the fast lane. He dreamed of creating an e-company and settled on the idea of an offshore betting business model. He left his trading job and set up shop on the Caribbean island of Antigua.

There he started World Sports Exchange, a business organized solely to bookmake on American sporting events. The business operated like this: Customers opened an account with WSE in Antigua and deposited at least $300 in the account. To bet, customers would call or contact WSE on the Internet. WSE would confirm the bet and manage the details for a 10 percent commission or fee. Millions flowed into the operation. The operation was entirely legal on Antigua.

FBI agents then opened accounts, placed bets, and arrested Cohen. A jury convicted him of violating 18 U.S.C. § 1084, and the second Circuit Court of Appeals upheld the conviction.[30] The federal law, known as the Wire Communications Act, was enacted years before the birth of the Internet and was designed to prevent bookies from taking bets over the phone. Cohen was sentenced to 21 months in prison. Several other principals in the operation are still at large.

Another section of the U.S. Code has recently been used to prosecute those involved in Internet gambling. 18 U.S.C. § 1084 provides that:

> Whoever being engaged in the business of betting or wagering knowingly uses a wire communication facility for the transmission in interstate or foreign commerce of bets or wagers or information assisting in the placing of bets or wagers on any sporting event or contest, or for the transmission of a wire communication which entitles the recipient to receive money or credit as a result of bets or wagers, or for information assisting in the placing of bets or wagers, shall be fined under this title or imprisoned not more than two years, or both.

Other federal laws that attempt to control illegal interstate gambling include 18 U.S.C. § 1952, which prohibits interstate or foreign travel to further gambling or other illegitimate business dealings, and 18 U.S.C. § 1953, which outlaws the interstate transportation of gambling paraphernalia. More legislation involving Internet gambling is likely to surface as Congress and state legislatures cope with this new means of operating gambling businesses.

DRUG PRODUCTION AND USE

Drug use in the United States is a considerable problem. According to the federal agency responsible for developing a national drug policy, the Office of National Drug Control Policy, in 1999, there were 14.8 million Americans aged 12 or older who had used illegal drugs in the last month. That number represents 6.7 percent of the population over the age of 12. Other statistics include:

- 3.6 million Americans met the medical diagnostic criteria for drug dependency.
- 800,000 teens between the ages of 12 and 17 were drug dependent.
- Children who smoke "pot" at an early age are less likely to finish school and more likely to commit crimes than those who don't.
- More than 1.5 million Americans were arrested for drug-law violations in 1999.[31]

Clearly, illicit drug use and abuse is a serious problem for law enforcement. Today, the "war on drugs" has taken on a new urgency as it has become clear that terrorist organizations abroad have a hand in the production and distribution of illicit drugs in the United States. The profits from these operations in turn may be providing valuable cash for terrorist organizations across the globe.

Those who use illicit drugs violate a variety of state and federal criminal laws, and those who produce, import, and sell those drugs face the harshest penalties. We will focus on federal drug laws, but every state has similar laws on its books. A few states have experimented with decriminalizing the usage, possession, and sale of some controlled substances, primarily marijuana.

A **controlled substance** is defined as a drug considered dangerous under the law because of its effects, including intoxication, stupor, or addictive potential.[32] That is, the drug is listed on either a state or federal directory of controlled substances, and may in some cases be available by prescription to treat medical conditions. Examples include many commonly prescribed pharmaceuticals like Dilantin and Ritalin. Some controlled substances are so dangerous that they are not legally available at all. Examples include heroin and, in most states, marijuana.

HISTORICAL HIGHLIGHT
DEA Reports on Drug Trafficking

Much of the job of ending drug trafficking into the United States falls on the Drug Enforcement Agency, or DEA. Recently the agency released a report detailing how and from where illegal drugs not produced or grown domestically enter the country.[33] The report calls the illegal drug market in the United States one of the most profitable in the world and claims it attracts the most ruthless, sophisticated, and aggressive drug traffickers.

Who is supplying the drug market in the United States? One source is South America, from where drug traffickers smuggle cocaine and heroin over land through Mexico and by sea through the Caribbean as well as via the air. Mexican criminal groups smuggle cocaine, heroin, methamphetamine, amphetamine, and marijuana through our southern border.

The source of Ecstacy (3, 4-methylenedioxymethamphetamine), a popular party drug, is thought to be Israeli and Russian drug syndicates. The drug is manufactured in clandestine laboratories in Western Europe and smuggled in on commercial air flights and via courier service. Heroin is smuggled in from organized criminal groups in Southeast and Southwest Asia through New York City and down the eastern seaboard and into the Midwest.

PENALTIES

Most criminal cases brought against drug abusers are state violations. As a practical matter, federal law enforcement officials handle cases involving trafficking of controlled substances across our borders and across state lines while local law enforcement handles individual drug use and drug distribution and dealing on a local level. However, agents from federal agencies like the Drug Enforcement Agency (DEA) and the FBI work closely with state attorneys general and local police departments to coordinate the war on drugs. For example, in areas designated as High Intensity Drug Trafficking Areas (HIDTAs), the federal government takes a lead role in coordinating federal, state, and local law enforcement efforts. There are 26 such areas in the United States.

Arrests for drug use are quite common. In 1999, there were over 1.5 million arrests by state and local law enforcement agencies.[34] More than four-fifths of drug law violation arrests are for possession violations, and drug abuse violations in 1999 accounted for 11 percent of all arrests. The most frequent drug possessed by the defendants was marijuana, followed by heroin and cocaine. Marijuana and heroin are Schedule I drugs (see the following list) while cocaine is a Schedule II drug. Approximately 87 percent of drug defendants handled by the court system during 1999 were convicted.[35]

There are five schedules of controlled substances catalogued by the federal drug laws and additions are made when new drugs surface or a previously unscheduled drug is determined to belong on the list. Almost every state has adopted the same schedules. The penalty for possession of a substance on the list depends on which schedule the substance is on, and how much of the substance with which the defendant was caught. The schedules can be found at 21 U.S.C. § 811 and at the DEA website, *www.dea.gov.* The major categories are:

Schedule I.
(A) The drug or other substance has a high potential for abuse.
(B) The drug or other substance has no currently accepted medical use in treatment in the United States.
(C) There is a lack of accepted safety for use of the drug or other substance under medical supervision.

Schedule II.
(A) The drug or other substance has a high potential for abuse.
(B) The drug or other substance has a currently accepted medical use in treatment in the United States or a currently accepted medical use with severe restrictions.
(C) Abuse of the drug or other substances may lead to severe psychological or physical dependence.

Schedule III.
(A) The drug or other substance has a potential for abuse less than the drugs or other substances in Schedules I and II.
(B) The drug or other substance has a currently accepted medical use in treatment in the United States.
(C) Abuse of the drug or other substance may lead to moderate or low physical dependence or high psychological dependence.

Schedule IV.
(A) The drug or other substance has a low potential for abuse relative to the drugs or other substances in Schedule III.
(B) The drug or other substance has a currently accepted medical use in treatment in the United States.
(C) Abuse of the drug or other substance may lead to limited physical dependence or psychological dependence relative to the drugs or other substances in Schedule III.

Schedule V.
(A) The drug or other substance has a low potential for abuse relative to the drugs or other substances in Schedule IV.
(B) The drug or other substance has a currently accepted medical use in treatment in the United States.
(C) Abuse of the drug or other substance may lead to limited physical dependence or psychological dependence relative to the drugs or other substances in Schedule IV.

The statute then delineates the chemical name for each substance classified on the list. The penalties are found in 21 U.S.C. § 841 through 863. For example, the penalty for simple possession of some controlled substance ranges from up to a year in prison for the first offense to a minimum of five years in prison for the possession of more than five grams of cocaine. For those engaged in trafficking in drugs, the penalties include life in prison. If the quantities are very high, or if the defendant attempted to kill another to evade detection or arrest, the law authorizes the imposition of the penalty of death.[36] The average sentence in 1999 for drug trafficking was 4.5 years in prison.

PRACTICE POINTERS

Some of the offenses described in this chapter will seldom be encountered by most legal professionals working in a private law firm. Those who work in state or local agencies, district attorneys' offices, or public defenders' offices may encounter cases involving defendants charged with sodomy, indecent exposure, and prostitution on a fairly regular basis. They should keep in mind that social offenses such as these aren't a priority for most law enforcement agencies, but are nuisances that must be dealt with.

Legal professionals working with firms, organizations, or agencies that provide abortion or abortion information need to familiarize themselves with the law in their state regarding abortion. For example, representing health clinics that provide abortions or assistance obtaining abortions must make sure they stay within the requirements of their state's abortion laws. If they do not, they risk criminal prosecution. In the area of abortion regulation, it is imperative that legal professionals keep up with legislative and judicial developments, since it is unlikely either those in favor of abortion rights or against such rights will let up their efforts to shape the debate in the legislature or the courts.

Legal professionals who work for firms or government agencies concerned with the gaming industry must be well versed in both federal, state, and local laws on gambling. This is no small task. Every state has laws in place either outlawing all gambling, or authorizing limited gambling by the state or a state-supervised business, and outlawing all other forms of gambling. Prosecutors also appear willing to apply old laws to contests and variations on games of chance in an attempt to clarify what the rules are, especially on the Internet. They don't intend to wait until new legislation is passed. That means legal professionals researching the law of gambling need to think like a creative prosecutor. Try to imagine new uses for existing legislation, and you will serve the client well. New legislation is also likely as states grapple with the reality of gambling.

Legal professionals who work in the area of drug addiction and interdiction must keep abreast of changing laws and conditions in the war on drugs. Drugs, like fashion, go in and out of style, and the approach to charging or defending those involved in the trade changes accordingly. Expertise in pharmacology may be necessary in some cases involving clandestine laboratories and drug production. Cases involving trafficking in large amounts of dangerous drugs are the most difficult, because penalties can include life in prison or even death. Those working with clients and attorneys to assess the likely outcome of drug cases will want to check with the Bureau of Justice Statistics. The agency's website provides access to a wealth of data, including information on the likelihood of prosecution, release on bond, conviction, and type and length of sentence. The website is at *http://www.ojp.usdoj.gov/bjs/*.

CHAPTER SUMMARY

In this chapter we have explored social crimes. Many of these are what some refer to as "victimless" crimes. While that may be a fair characterization for crimes like sodomy committed by consenting adults in the privacy of their bedroom, the reality is that many of the other offenses discussed in this chapter are associated with large-scale social problems like drug addiction, gambling addiction, and the commission of petty crimes.

Prostitution is generally defined as engaging in sexual intercourse or other sexual activity for pay. It can be engaged in by either sex, although most prostitutes are women. Most states punish both prostitutes and those who patronize their services as well as anyone who works to procure clients for a prostitute. Prostitution is only legal in selected counties in Nevada.

Fornication and adultery are now seldom criminalized. Bigamy, or having more than one wife, is illegal in all states. It was once practiced by Mormons in the West, but was outlawed as a condition of admission of those states to the Union. Today, there are still occasional prosecutions for bigamy.

Sodomy, defined as sexual relations between members of the same sex, sexual conduct *per anus* or *per os* between unmarried persons of the opposite sex, and sexual intercourse with animals, can and is still outlawed by some states. But in light of the Supreme Court decision in *Lawrence v. Texas*, many of those restrictions are bound to fall. States also have the right to punish public exposure or lewdness.

The Supreme Court has ruled that a woman may terminate a pregnancy, but that states can set reasonable limits about the time, place, and conditions for abortion. States cannot unreasonably interfere with a woman's right to choose, but can require her to receive counseling, notify parents or petition a court before the procedure is performed if she is a minor, and otherwise place administrative requirements on the process. States can also limit the right to an abortion if the pregnancy has progressed far into its term unless the mother's life is in danger. This is an area of the law that stirs emotions and is constantly undergoing challenge. For example, at the time of this writing, Congress had approved a ban on so-called partial-birth abortions and the president had signed it, but several federal courts have ruled the measure unconstitutional. More litigation is sure to follow.

Gambling, which is defined as engaging in a game of chance by wagering money for the chance of a financial payoff, is now a source of revenue for most states. Gambling that isn't approved, controlled, or run by state governments is still illegal and can be a state or federal offense. Internet gambling has successfully been prosecuted under statutes forbidding the wagering of bets over telephone lines in states where wagering is illegal.

Illegal drug trafficking and use is a substantial problem in the United States today. State, local, and federal law enforcement agencies are working together to interdict drugs as they enter the United States and to prosecute those who traffic in controlled substances. The penalties for possession range from fines and short prison terms while trafficking can net a defendant life in prison or even the death penalty.

KEY TERMS

Abortion: The termination of pregnancy by something other than birth.

Adultery: Sexual intercourse by a married person with someone not his or her spouse.

Bigamy: The criminal act of marrying when one already has a spouse.

Controlled substance: A drug considered dangerous under the law because of its effects, including intoxication, stupor, or addictive potential.

Fornication: Voluntary sexual intercourse between two unmarried persons.

Gambling: The act of taking a monetary risk on the chance of receiving a monetary gain.

Pimp: One who works to procure clients for a prostitute.

Prostitution: Engaging in sexual intercourse or other sexual activity for pay.

Public indecency: Lewd or lascivious conduct that is open to public view.

Sex workers: A term preferred by some working in the sex industry such as prostitutes, porn actresses or actors, exotic dancers, and the like.

Sodomy: Sexual relations between members of the same sex, sexual conduct *per anus* or *per os* between unmarried persons of the opposite sex, and sexual intercourse with animals.

DISCUSSION QUESTIONS

1. Is prostitution a victimless crime? Why, or why not?
2. Do you believe the Supreme Court went too far in its abortion decisions? Or did it not go far enough?
3. Should states have the right to dictate what types of sexual activities go on between consenting adults in private? Would your answer change if the activity in question were dangerous or even deadly?
4. Should states be in the business of gambling?
5. Do states and the federal government do enough to curb the availability of illegal drugs?
6. Should casual drug users be imprisoned or should they be required to undergo addiction treatment instead?
7. Should drug use be decriminalized?

FOR FURTHER READING AND VIEWING

1. Albert, A. (2001). *Brothel: Mustang Ranch and Its Women*. Random House. This book is an inside look at what went on at the Mustang Ranch in Nevada until it closed.
2. Solinger, R. (2001). *Abortion Wars: A Half Century of Struggle, 1950–2000*. University of California Press. A collection of essays on abortion by writers who are pro-choice. Includes extensive discussion of *Roe v. Wade* and *Planned Parenthood v. Casey.*
3. Hull, N. E., and Hoffer, P. C. (2001). *Roe v. Wade: The Abortion Rights Controversy in American History*. University Press of Kansas. An overview of the abortion rights controversy.
4. Gordon, S. B. (2001). *The Mormon Question: Polygamy and Constitutional Conflict in Nineteenth-Century America*. University of North Carolina Press. A look at the history of polygamy in the West.
5. Goldstein, A. (2001). *Addiction: From Biology to Drug Policy*. Oxford University Press. Explores the nature of addiction to categories of drugs and the laws and policies needed to fight addiction.
6. Schlosser, E. (2003). *Reefer Madness: Sex, Drugs and Cheap Labor in the American Black Market*. Houghton Mifflin. An inside look at the illegal drug and adult entertainment industries and how demand has spurred a black market economy in sin.

7. Krakauer, J. (2003). *Under the Banner of Heaven: A Story of Violent Faith*. Doubleday. Expose of religious fanaticism in the United States, especially in Utah.

QUOTATIONS FOR CHAPTER THIRTEEN

1. *A crime not fit to be named.*
   William Blackstone on the subject of sodomy

2. *Laws are made for the government of actions, and while they cannot interfere with mere religious belief and opinions, they may with practices.*
   Chief Justice Waite in *Reynolds v. United States*, 98 U.S. 145 (1878)

3. *I will neither give a deadly drug to anybody if asked for it, nor will I make a suggestion to this effect. Similarly, I will not give to a woman an abortive remedy.*
   Hippocratic Oath

4. *We know that terrorist organizations routinely launder the proceeds from drug trafficking and use the funds to support and expand their operations internationally.*
   Senator Orrin Hatch (R–UT)

5. *It's so important for Americans to know that the traffic in drugs finances the work of terror, sustaining terrorists, that terrorists use drug profits to fund their cells to commit acts of murder. If you quit drugs, you join the fight against terror in America.*
   George W. Bush, President of the United States (December 14, 2001)

ENDNOTES

1. The Mann Act, 18 U.S.C. § 2421.
2. *Caminetti v. United States*, 242 U.S. 470 (1917).
3. *Cleveland v. United States*, 329 U.S. 14 (1946).
4. 18 P.S. § 5902.
5. 18 P.S. § 5902(e.2).
6. 15 N.R.S. § 201.354.
7. Ballentine's Law Dictionary.
8. Ballentine's Law Dictionary.
9. 97 Miss. Code § 97-29.5.
10. *Toncray v. Budge*, 95 P. 26.
11. 97 Miss. Code § 97-29-43.
12. *Reynolds v. United States*, 98 U.S. 145 (1878).
13. Blackstone, *Commentaries*.
14. 410 U.S. 113 (1973).
15. *Planned Parenthood of Southeastern Pa. v. Casey*, 505 U.S. 833 (1992).
16. *Stenberg v. Carhart*, 530 U.S. 914 (2000).
17. Ballentine's Law Dictionary.
18. Code Theod. 9.7.6; Code Just. 9.9.31.

19. 25 Hen.VIII, ch. 6.

20. *Survey on the Constitutional Right to Privacy in the Context of Homosexual Activity,* 40 U. Miami L. Rev. 521 (1986).

21. *Bowers v. Hardwick,* 478 U.S. 186 (1984).

22. Ballentine's Law Dictionary.

23. B. Hardy, "Return from Planet Pee-wee," *Vanity Fair* (September 1999).

24. Ballentine's Law Dictionary.

25. Utah, Tennessee, and Hawaii are the holdouts.

26. Pa. Lottery Annual Report June 30, 2001.

27. *National Gambling Impact Study Commission Final Report,* June 1999.

28. R. Dunstan, *Gambling in California,* California Research Bureau, 1997.

29. 18 U.S.C. § 1955.

30. *USA v. Cohen,* F. 3d (2nd Cir. 2001).

31. Office of National Drug Control Policy, *The National Drug Control Strategy: 2001 Annual Report.*

32. Ballentine's Law Dictionary.

33. Drug Enforcement Agency, *Drug Trafficking in the United States* (September 2001).

34. Federal Bureau of Investigations, *Uniform Crime Reports, Crime in the United States,* 1999.

35. Department of Justice, Bureau of Justice Statistics, *Drug Crime and Facts,* 2001.

36. 18 U.S.C. § 3591.

CHAPTER 14
Common Law Defenses

CHAPTER OBJECTIVES

After studying this chapter, you should be able to:

- Know the Common Law defenses, and their essential elements
- Understand the concept of self-defense and be able to explain when non-deadly and deadly force can be used
- Explain under what circumstances consent is a defense
- Explain when mistake of law and mistake of fact are defenses
- Explain entrapment
- Differentiate between the consequences of voluntary and involuntary intoxication
- Explain the different standards for the insanity defense and how each operates

CHAPTER CONTENTS

For Further Reading

Quotations for Chapter Fourteen

Endnotes

> *(The intoxicated) shall have no privilege by this voluntarily contracted madness, but shall have the same judgment as if he were in his right senses.*
>
> M. Hale

INTRODUCTION

In every criminal trial the prosecution has the burden of proof and must prove the case against the defendant beyond a reasonable doubt. The defendant isn't required to answer the charges except to plead not guilty or guilty.

As we have seen, every crime can be broken down into its essential elements, and the government is required to prove each element beyond a reasonable doubt. We have already examined the elements of many crimes. A prosecutor who proves these elements will generally get a conviction unless the defendant raises a defense to the crime. The law provides legitimate defenses that, if proven, dictate an acquittal.

Depending on the crime, a number of defenses may be available to defendants. Defenses take their legitimacy from Common Law, constitutional law, and statutory law. For instance, the insanity defense, known as the M'Naghten Rule, takes its name from the defendant in a seventeenth-century English case that established the precedent. The defense became codified into law in the United States, and has been altered by statute in some states. The *ex post facto* defense is written plainly in the Constitution. Anglo-American law has a rich tradition of limiting the power of the state, protecting the rights of the accused, and recognizing a defendant's right to use specific defenses to crimes.

JUSTIFICATION DEFENSES

Justification defenses can be used where the commission of the proscribed act is justified and, therefore, not appropriate for criminal sanctions. In other words, the person accused of the crime had a legitimate reason for committing the act and was therefore justified in committing an act that would otherwise be a crime. The justification defense most people are familiar with is **self-defense** in what would otherwise be a murder case. It is far from the only justification defense available.

Individuals have the right to defend themselves, innocent people, and their property from harm from others. Citizens trying to prevent a crime from occurring may also have a defense if their actions otherwise violate the law. The circumstances of each case dictate whether the actions taken are protected by a justification defense. There are no hard and fast rules; the case depends on the facts faced by the person seeking to justify his or her actions.

A person may always use **non-deadly force** to prevent an attacker from committing a crime against them. The person may use a reasonable amount of force to restrain or render harmless the attacker, but may not use deadly force unless the following requirements are met. Persons using non-deadly force are not required to retreat at any time during the use of force. Consider this example. A woman walking down a busy street feels someone brush by her. She then feels her handbag's shoulder strap tighten and realizes the youth who brushed by her is trying to steal her purse. She can hit him over the head with her purse to subdue him, tie him to the nearest lamp post with her belt, and wait for the police to arrive. She has used non-deadly force to subdue and hold him and will be able to defend her actions if criminal assault and kidnapping charges are filed against her.

However, the use of **deadly force** is much more tightly controlled. A person may only use deadly force in self-defense when it reasonably appears necessary to prevent immediate death or serious injury or prevent the commission of a serious felony involving risk to human life. Deadly force may only be used against an attacker who has initiated the aggression using unlawful force. Consider the following example. You are on a flight over the Atlantic when you notice that the man in the next seat is attempting to light his shoes. On closer observation, you notice that the shoe lace resembles a fuse. You call attention to his behavior by summoning the cabin crew. Together, you and other passengers attempt to subdue the passenger, but he struggles to light the shoe. You hit him over the head with a wine bottle and kill him. It turns out his shoes were loaded with plastic explosives. Your actions involved the use of deadly force, but you were justified because it appears he was attempting to blow up the plane. You used deadly force to prevent death and destruction. However, if the first blow knocked the passenger out, and the rest of the crew tied him to a chair and removed his shoes, you cannot continue to hit him over the head until he is dead.

Often in deadly force situations, there is a question of whether a person could have or should have retreated from the situation when the opportunity arose. A **retreat rule** has grown out of Common Law decisions through the years. The rule has two parts:

- A person must retreat rather than use deadly force unless the person is at his or her home or business.
- Most states have adopted the rule that there is no duty to retreat unless the retreat can be made in complete safety.

Consider the shoe bomb case again. You were under no duty to retreat since to do so would be impossible. You can't get off the plane.

Oddly enough, aggressors can avail themselves of the self-defense argument under certain circumstances. Aggressors can regain the right to self-defense if they remove themselves from the fight. This is referred to as **withdrawal**.

Consider the following scenario. An armed gunman enters a store with the intent of robbing it. He pulls his gun and demands cash. The owner of the store instead pulls his gun. Shots are exchanged, but no one is hit. The gunman flees and throws his gun in a nearby dumpster. The store owner pursues the gunman and begins firing at him. At this point, the gunman has regained his right to self-defense. The store owner is now the aggressor.

Similarly, initial aggressors are protected under the doctrine of **sudden escalation**. If a fight that was not life-threatening suddenly becomes life-threatening, the initial aggressor can take whatever action is necessary to protect himself. As an example, one teenager approaches another and picks a fight. The second teenager at first defends himself in like fashion. However, at some point, the attacked teenager becomes enraged, picks up a sharp object lying nearby, and attacks the aggressor. The aggressor now has the right to take whatever steps necessary to defend himself. If the attacked teenager is now using deadly force, the initial aggressor may use deadly force to stop the attack.

Another Common Law defense is the **defense of others**. A defendant can use the defense of others defense when he acts in the belief the intended victim had a legal right to act in his or her own defense. There need not be any special relationship between the defendant and the intended victim. In this case, the defendant need not retreat unless he is sure the victim is safe.

This could be played out as follows. A man is walking down the street and sees a perpetrator attacking a woman. The man can use appropriate force to stop the attack. If the attacker is using deadly force, the man can use deadly force to stop him. However, if his initial interference is enough to drive off the attacker, and the intended victim is now safe, the man may not pursue the attacker with the intent of doing him bodily harm.

The law delineates between what force may be used to defend people and what may be used to defend property. For instance, it is not permissible to kill an unarmed purse snatcher. It is legal to try to catch him and hold him for police. Deadly force may only be used in property crimes where the aggressor is placing people in imminent danger.

Deadly force is permissible in the act of crime prevention if the crime is a serious felony that may endanger human life. For other less dangerous crimes, non-deadly force is appropriate. You cannot, for example, rig a deadly trap to prevent break-ins to your home or hunting camp. For example, in *Katko v. Briney*, 183 N.W.2d 657 (1971), the Iowa Supreme Court let stand a jury verdict for actual and punitive damages against the owner of an abandoned farmhouse who had rigged a rifle to go off if an intruder entered. An intruder did, and sued successfully when he was injured.

Sometimes breaking the law is necessary to protect human life or property. For instance, a person may trespass on a property to save a person from imminent danger. In order for the **necessity defense** to work, the defendant must reasonably believe his or her action was necessary to avoid harm to society, which is greater than any harm caused to the property. The necessity defense may never be used to justify a death to protect property. In any use of the necessity defense, the defendant must be without fault. For example, a co-conspirator to burn down a house cannot break into a neighbor's house to phone the fire department.

Bear in mind that Common Law defenses may have been modified in your jurisdiction. Always check local laws before using or advising the use of deadly force to protect either people or property.

DURESS DEFENSES

Defendants sometimes commit acts under duress and can then use the **duress defense**. Duress is a defense if the defendant committed the crime out of a well-grounded fear of death or serious bodily harm. For instance, it would be illegal for a bank teller to hand a bag of cash to her best friend, but not to a robber with a gun in his hand. The difference is that the teller hands the money to the robber under duress. In these cases, the defendant is arguing that she is the victim of the crime, not the perpetrator. Hostages who are made to commit crimes such as bank robberies while under the control of their captors can also use the defense.

The following conditions must be met for the duress defense to apply:

- The actor was wrongfully threatened by another to perform an act that he or she otherwise would not have performed.
- The threat was of serious bodily harm or death to the person or an immediate family member.

- The threat was immediate and there was no way for the threatened person to escape or avoid the threatened action.
- The harm threatened was greater than the harm from the crime committed.
- The threatened person wasn't intentionally involved in the situation.

Cases like these are seldom prosecuted if the police and prosecutors are convinced that the hostage acted out of fear and the threat was real. The person in question must be under threat of death to herself or a family member. The threat must be immediate and real. The duress defense is generally not a defense to murder. That's because the crime committed under duress (murder) isn't greater than the harm threatened (death if the threatened person doesn't kill as ordered). In other words, you can't kill to avoid being killed, but you can rob to avoid being killed. Duress may be a defense to felony murder, if the person was under duress to commit the underlying felony. (See Chapter 8 for a discussion of the felony-murder rule.)

OTHER COMMON LAW DEFENSES

The **mistake of fact** defense can be used when a defendant honestly believes something to be true that isn't. For instance, a person retrieving a piece of luggage at an airport that looks exactly like his or hers may be guilty of not checking the claim check, but not of stealing someone's luggage. The mistake of fact defense applies to different crimes differently. For instance, for general intent crimes the mistake must be a reasonable mistake. But for specific intent crimes, any mistake of fact may be used as a defense. You could not form the specific intent to commit a crime if you are mistaken about the facts. For example, in a hypothetical jurisdiction it is a specific intent crime to have sexual contact with a brother or sister. You and your twin brother were separated at birth and placed in different foster homes. Thirty years later, you meet but do not know you are related. You fall in love and have sexual relations. The fact that you don't realize you are related is a defense to criminal charges of incest. Once you find out you are sister and brother, however, the defense is no longer available. The mistake of fact defense may not be used for strict liability crimes.

The **mistake of law** defense can generally be used when a person in good faith relied on an interpretation of law from a person charged with administering the law. For instance, an IRS official tells you that the cost of your "Home of the Whopper" boxer shorts are a legitimate entertainment deduction. You take the deduction, but it is later disallowed. You could use the mistake of law defense to avoid any criminal penalty. Most likely though you will have to pay the tax due.

The mistake of law defense can also be used if an interpretation of the law changed. For instance, in the above scenario the IRS agent was accurate at the time he gave you the interpretation, but the interpretation changes the following year to only allow deductions for Elvis "Hunka Hunka Burning Love" boxers. If this were the case, you could avoid criminal liability for deducting the "Whopper" boxers. The mistaken interpretation of law may not come from an attorney. They deal in briefs, not boxers.

Entrapment is a defense used when law enforcement officials lure a person into committing a crime. Most frequently, this occurs in bribery cases. To work, the entrapment defense must pass a two-prong test. First, the criminal design must have originated with law enforcement. Second, the defendant must not be predisposed to commit the crime.

Depending on the case law in your jurisdiction, one of two tests for predisposition are used. Most jurisdictions use the **subjective standard**, also known as the **majority rule**. The subjective standard revolves around the answer to one question, "Was the defendant predisposed to commit the crime?" Other jurisdictions use the **objective standard** or the **minority rule**. The objective standard focuses on the government's inducement and asks the question, "Would an innocent person be induced to commit the crime by the officer's acts?"

The Supreme Court answered that question in a case involving the receipt of child pornography. It ruled that the entrapment defense prohibited prosecution of a defendant who ordered child pornography after a 26-month mail campaign by the government to induce him to order a catalog. The campaign included personal letters from a postal inspector posing as another male interested in seeing nude teenage boys, solicitations to join associations dedicated to freedom of the press, and requests that he purchase magazines depicting boys. When his order from the sting operation arrived, he was arrested. A search of his house turned up nothing but the materials the government had sent him. The Supreme Court ruled that the government's campaign to get him to order was entrapment.[1]

A defendant may use the victim's **consent** as a defense in some circumstances. For instance, a defendant accused of rape is not guilty if the sex was consensual. The consent defense is unavailable for statutory rape. A victim's consent is not valid if:

- The victim is a minor
- The victim has a mental disease or defect
- The victim is intoxicated to the point he or she is unable to make a reasonable judgment
- Consent is obtained by force or duress
- Consent is obtained by fraudulent or deceptive means
- The victim has been judged to be legally incompetent
- The consent defense is precluded by the law in question

Generally consent is not a defense to crimes involving grievous bodily harm or death. For example, it isn't a defense to murder that the victim wanted to die, or a defense to assault that the victim wanted to be beaten or disfigured. These acts would be crimes whether the victim wanted the acts to take place or not, unlike rape, which wouldn't be a crime if the other party consented.

CAPACITY DEFENSES

Capacity defenses may be used when the defendant lacks the capacity or ability to control his or her actions or understand that the act was criminal in nature. Age, mental disabilities, intoxication, and insanity can affect the ability to understand the law and control one's actions. Capacity defenses shield from liability those who can't understand right from wrong or control their actions.

INFANCY DEFENSE

For instance, debate rages about how to try minors who commit violent crimes. Under the Common Law, children of tender age could not be held liable for criminal acts under the presumption that they lacked the capacity to tell right from wrong. Although some states have sought to modify the standard by statute, the Common Law standard for the **infancy defense** is as follows:

- Children under 7 years of age are conclusively presumed to be incapable of knowing the wrongfulness of their crimes.
- Children 7 to 14 years of age have a rebuttable presumption of incapacity. The burden of proof is on the prosecutor to prove beyond a reasonable doubt that the defendant appreciated the quality and nature of his or her actions.
- Children over 14 were treated as adults and presumed to fully appreciate the difference between right and wrong.

Keep in mind that capacity is only part of the story. Children who have the capacity to commit crimes can be tried in the state's juvenile court system or in the adult system. Before a child is tried in adult court, a hearing is held. That hearing may include a discussion of the child's capacity as well as an examination of the charges and any prior record. Some states have recently enacted legislation that allows more children to be charged as adults in response to demands by the public that "doing adult crime ought to mean doing adult time." A full discussion of the treatment of juveniles as adults is beyond the scope of this text.

INTOXICATION DEFENSE

The intoxication defense is most successfully used in cases of **involuntary intoxication**. This happens when a person unknowingly ingests an intoxicating substance. Date-rape drugs are an example of this. This defense may be made to both specific and general intent crimes. Persons who are involuntarily intoxicated are treated the same as insane defendants. They must meet whatever test the jurisdiction uses for insanity. (See the next section in this chapter.)

Voluntary intoxication is quite another matter. It may never be used as a defense to a general intent crime. It also cannot be used as an excuse or justification of a crime of homicide. It cannot be used as a defense to crimes involving negligence, recklessness, or strict liability. Voluntary intoxication has been used as a defense to specific intent crimes where the intoxication prevents the defendant from formulating the requisite intent. If successful, this can reduce a charge of first-degree murder to second-degree murder.

INSANITY

Courts have long wrestled with the concept of trying the mentally ill or handicapped. Just as young children do not understand the nature of their actions, mentally ill or handicapped people may not either. Over the years, courts have recognized several defenses based on the defendant's inability to distinguish right from wrong when committing a crime.

The most common of these defenses is the **insanity defense**. In essence, a defendant using the insanity defense is claiming he or she lacked the mental state to understand the nature and consequences of the crime. The insanity defense is often used when the evidence against the defendant is overwhelming. Under these circumstances, the defendant cannot deny committing the crime, but can argue insanity. If the defendant is successful, he or she would be committed to a mental hospital rather than prison. The defendant would remain there until the state determined the person to be sane.

HISTORICAL HIGHLIGHT
The Move Away from Capital Punishment for the Mentally Retarded

In 2002, Virginia became the eighteenth state to outlaw execution of the mentally retarded. Under Virginia law, convicts with an IQ below 70 may not be executed. Twelve other states have no capital punishment. Virginia's decision may have tipped the scales for the Supreme Court. Later the same year, the Court ruled that applying the death penalty to mentally retarded persons was cruel and unusual punishment in violation of the Eighth Amendment. The case was *Atkins v. Virginia*, 536 U.S. 304 (2002). States who still have the death penalty will now have to come up with standards to determine who is mentally retarded and who is not.

Several high-profile executions of prisoners with very low IQs brought the capacity question to the fore of the debate over capital punishment. Since people with very low IQs never develop the equivalent of "adult minds," the question of whether they can form intent or understand the consequences of their actions cannot be answered clearly. Some even argue that trying and convicting these people amounts to trying a child in an adult court.

Additionally, the "deterrent" aspects of capital punishment may very well be lost on a person who neither understands what he is doing or its consequences. Nor is there a general deterrent effect that would likely dissuade other mentally retarded persons to refrain from criminal acts, given diminished capacity to understand the connection between the criminal act and the consequences. Persons with low IQs may also lack the ability to aid their own defense at trial, resulting in false convictions. Given the permanent nature of the death penalty, life imprisonment would seem a better alternative.[2] The Supreme Court seems to agree.

HISTORICAL HIGHLIGHT
Guns and Alcohol: The James Allen Egelhoff Story

James Allen Egelhoff was camping and picking mushrooms in northwestern Montana when he met Roberta Pavlova and John Christenson. They sold their mushrooms and went to a bar for some drinks. After drinking at the bar, they proceeded to a private party where more drinking occurred. Sometime during the evening Egelhoff gave his gun to Pavlova to store in the car's glove compartment.

That night around midnight Montana state troopers were called to the scene of a car that had gone off the road into a ditch. In the front seat were Pavlova and Christenson. Each had been shot in the head once and killed. In the back seat was Egelhoff, yelling obscenities and behaving wildly. His gun lay on the floor at his feet with two discharged rounds.

The policemen arrested Egelhoff. His hands tested positive for gunshot residue, and his blood alcohol level an hour after his arrest was .36, over four times the intoxication level.

Egelhoff was charged with two counts of deliberate homicide. However, he had no memory of committing the crimes. Under Montana law, a person is guilty of deliberate homicide if he purposely or knowingly causes the death of another human being.

At trial, Egelhoff maintained that he was so drunk, he could not have committed the crimes. He argued that some fourth person must have pulled the trigger, and he was too intoxicated to remember the incident. In the charge to the jury, the judge informed them that they could not take Egelhoff's intoxication into account when "determining the existence of a mental state which is an element of the offense." The jury convicted him of both homicides and sentenced him to 84 years in prison.

Egelhoff appealed to the Montana Supreme Court. He argued that his intoxication was relevant to his ability to form intent. If he could not form intent, he was not guilty of deliberate homicide, but some lesser offense such as manslaughter. The Montana Supreme Court agreed and reversed the conviction. The case was appealed to the U.S. Supreme Court.

This case proved to be a very divisive one for the justices. At issue was whether excluding the intoxication evidence from consideration as it affected his ability to form intent was a denial of due process. By a 5–4 margin, the Court ruled that the trial judge had not erred in instructing the jury to determine Egelhoff's intent without taking his intoxication into account. In other words, his voluntary intoxication could never be an excuse for committing homicide.[3]

The insanity defense was first used successfully in 1843. The defendant in that case was named Daniel M'Naghten. Hence, future insanity cases would be governed by the **M'Naghten rule**. If a defendant at the time of the crime was "laboring under such a defect of reason, from diseases of the mind, as not to know the nature and quality of the act he was doing, or, if he did know it, that he did not know that what he was doing was wrong," no conviction is warranted. The burden of proof for the insanity defense is as follows:

> Every man is presumed to be sane and to possess a sufficient degree of reason to be responsible for his crimes, until the contrary be proved to (the jury's) satisfaction; and that to establish a defense on the ground of insanity, it must be clearly proved.[4]

BEYOND M'NAGHTEN

Some American states have modified the M'Naghten rule. In 1886, Alabama adopted the more liberal "irresistible impulse" test. In effect, this created a "temporary insanity" for people who committed "crimes of passion."[5]

HISTORICAL HIGHLIGHT
The M'Naghten Case

Sir Robert Peel was the British Home Secretary in the mid-1840s. Mr. Peel was a crusader in the fight against crime. In fact, he is generally considered to be the father of the British police. Hence, the nickname "Bobbies."

Of course, not everyone appreciated Sir Robert's passion. One individual in particular did not take kindly to the war on crime. His name was Daniel M'Naghten, and he believed that Sir Robert Peel was the head of a conspiracy to kill him. In his paranoid rage he shot and killed Edward Drummond, Peel's private secretary. M'Naghten mistook Drummond for Peel.

At trial, his attorney argued that M'Naghten was insane at the time he shot Drummond, and should be hospitalized, not imprisoned. The jury agreed, and M'Naghten was found "not guilty by reason of insanity."

M'Naghten was expanded even further in the 1954 *Durham v. United States* case. In this case, the District of Columbia Appeals Court ruled that "an accused is not criminally responsible if his unlawful act was the product of mental disease or defect."[6] Where M'Naghten required a complete lack of capacity, the **Durham test** only required a "substantial lack of capacity." The "substantial lack of capacity" test is part of the Model Penal Code, but has not been adopted by all states.

GUILTY, BUT MENTALLY ILL

The insanity defense debate has paralleled the capital punishment debate in the United States for most of its history. Very shortly after the Supreme Court outlawed the death penalty as it was practiced in 1972, states began working on new death penalty laws, and tighter restrictions on the insanity defense.

Illinois enacted a "**guilty, but mentally ill**" statute in the wake of the acquittal of a defendant by reason of insanity and subsequent repeat murders. But the national spotlight shone on the subject after the 1980 assassination of John Lennon by a deranged fan, and the 1981 attempt on President Reagan's life by the delusional John Hinckley. The thought of releasing either Hinckley or Lennon's assassin, Mark David Chapman, was more than many could bear. In response, several states enacted "guilty, but mentally ill" statutes.

Under "guilty, but mentally ill" laws, defendants who do not meet the M'Naghten standard of a complete lack of capacity, but fall under the substantial lack of capacity standard, are convicted and sent to a mental hospital. If they recover, they are sent to prison for the rest of their term.

COMPETENCY TO STAND TRIAL

A variation on the insanity defense is to claim that the defendant is **incompetent to stand trial**. Common Law has long held that a person must be able to understand the proceedings against him and be able to interact with his attorneys in order have a fair trial. However, a defendant who is incompetent today may be competent tomorrow. Can the state hold someone indefinitely until they can stand trial?

This question came before the Supreme Court in 1972. In that case, *Jackson v. Indiana*, the High Court ruled that defendants can only be held for a reasonable amount of time. Subsequent decisions have generally held that defendants cannot be held more than the lesser of 18 months or the maximum sentence for the crime they are charged with. At that point, the state must:

- try the defendant, if he or she is competent to stand trial,
- dismiss the charges, or
- commence civil proceedings to have the defendant committed to a mental institution.[7]

The standard for competency in many jurisdictions comes from Justice Thurgood Marshall's dissent in *White v. Estelle*, where he stated: "This Court has approved a test of incompetence which seeks to determine whether the defendant 'has sufficient present ability to consult with his lawyer with a reasonable degree of rational understanding—and whether he has a rational as well as factual understanding of the proceedings against him' " [*Dusky v. United States*, 362 U.S. 402 (1960)].[8]

In recent years, older defendants have avoided trial temporarily or permanently due to their health condition. Often this is a combination of senility, or overall health condition. This concept is recognized in international law as well. In 2000, former Chilean dictator Augusto Pinochet was arrested in England for crimes committed during his reign. The indictment had been issued by a Spanish court. An English judge ruled that the man was in too ill health to stand trial, and released him.

In the United States, the cases of Thomas E. Blanton Jr. and Bobby Frank Cherry, accused of bombing the 16th St. Baptist Church in Birmingham, Alabama, in 1963, were delayed because of the defendant's age. Blanton was not convicted until 2001, and Cherry's trial was delayed when he was at first ruled incompetent to stand trial, and later ruled competent.

HISTORICAL HIGHLIGHT
Bombingham: The Death Throes of Segregation

It was April 1963. Dr. Martin Luther King Jr. set his sights on Birmingham, Alabama, the last bastion of southern segregation. Almost nine years after the famous *Brown v. Board of Education* decision, Birmingham's schools were still segregated. Neither the city nor downtown merchants employed African Americans. In addition to segregated drinking fountains, restrooms, and dressing rooms, local ordinances required separate taxi cabs, ambulances, hospitals, cemeteries, elevators, eating places, hotels, and theaters. Marriage between the races was a felony.

Dr. King's arrival was designed to help the city's already growing civil rights movement headed by local minister, the Rev. Fred Shuttlesworth. At the time, the African American community was being terrorized by local officials and members of the Ku Klux Klan. Black homes were frequently bombed leading to the city's nickname "Bombingham." King's plan was to train large groups of protesters to protest nonviolently, and be arrested in large numbers. The mass arrests would overwhelm local law enforcement, and focus national attention on segregation.

Shuttlesworth's church, the 16th Street Baptist Church, was the epicenter of the movement. After Dr. King was arrested for illegally demonstrating, teenagers left the church in waves of 50 only to be arrested. As each group was arrested, another took their place. Eventually, the city had to turn fire hoses and dogs on the protesters because they had no place to incarcerate them. When it happened, the TV cameras were rolling.

City merchants, fearing the city's reputation would be forever sullied, relented. They met with Dr. King and ended the protests, as well as the accompanying black boycott of the stores. But the segregationists were not finished. That September, Klansmen set off a bomb in the basement of the 16th Street Baptist Church, killing four young girls.

Law enforcement officials suspected four men, Robert "Dynamite Bob" Chambliss, Herman Cash, Thomas Blanton, Jr., and Bobby Frank Cherry. Chambliss was the first to go to trial, and was convicted in 1977. Herman Cash was never charged and died in 1994. The case seemed dead until the FBI received new evidence in 1997. Charges were eventually brought against Blanton and Cherry. Blanton was convicted in 2001 and sentenced to life in prison. Cherry was charged based partly on evidence provided by his son, who claimed Cherry was not home the night before the bombing as he had told police.[9]

Cherry, however, was now old and in poor health. Initially, Cherry was found incompetent to stand trial. After receiving medical treatment, his condition improved. Cherry's case went to trial in 2002. He was found guilty and sentenced to life in prison. The story of Cherry's relationship with his son is told in the television movie "Sins of the Father."

INCAPACITY AND PUNISHMENT

In cases where the death penalty has already been imposed, convicts can postpone execution by claiming **insanity just prior to execution.** The Common Law basis for this defense also goes back to England. The legal scholar Blackstone opined that this safeguard was necessary because the condemned prisoner may be able to produce some valid reason that execution should be stayed. In the United States, this standard was upheld by the Supreme Court in 1958.[10]

Prisons tend to have a damaging effect on a person's sanity. Consequently, prisoners may become insane during their prison term. Should **insanity during incarceration** occur, prisoners are moved to a psychiatric hospital for the remainder of their term. Should they still be insane at the end of their term, they may be committed to a mental hospital until they recover.

PRACTICE POINTERS

Every criminal charge should be examined closely for the possibility of raising a defense to the charges. This is true whether you are working for the prosecution or the defense. In many cases, the evidence will be strong enough to assure a conviction, but for the assertion of a defense. The examination process should proceed as follows:

- Examine the charges and outline the essential elements of each charge. Evaluate the evidence and determine whether it appears the prosecution can prove every element of the offense beyond a reasonable doubt. It may help to use a checklist and check off each element.
- List possible defenses based on your knowledge of the defendant and the allegations made by the police. Is there a question of self-defense? Is there evidence of entrapment? Does the defendant suffer from a mental impairment?
- Once you have identified possible defenses, list the elements required to prove the defense and outline the facts you believe will prove the defense.
- If you believe a defense is available, but you don't yet have the evidence needed to support the defense, come up with an investigative plan to gather the evidence.
- Be sure to check the law in your jurisdiction. Some states require prior notification to the prosecution if certain defenses like the insanity defense will be used.

CHAPTER SUMMARY

Common Law has carved out several defenses for defendants who would otherwise be found guilty. Justification defenses can be used where the person accused of the crime had a legitimate reason for committing the act. The most common justification defense in murder cases is the self-defense justification. Individuals have the right to defend themselves, innocent people, and their property. Individuals also have some protection when they are attempting to prevent a criminal act from occurring. A person may use nondeadly force to prevent an attacker from committing a crime against him or her.

A person may only use deadly force in self-defense when it reasonably appears necessary to prevent immediate death or serious injury or prevent the commission of a serious felony involving risk to human life. The retreat rule defines criminal behavior when the option of using deadly force or retreating exists. The rule has two parts:

1. A person must retreat rather than use deadly force unless the person is at his or her home or business.
2. Most states have adopted the rule that there is no duty to retreat unless the retreat can be made in complete safety.

Aggressors who withdraw from a fight may defend themselves from subsequent charges by showing they backed down. Aggressors may also protect themselves from the sudden escalation of a fight. The defense-of-others defense allows defendants to protect innocent citizens from criminal attack.

Deadly force may only be used in property crimes where the aggressor is placing people in imminent danger. Deadly force is permissible in the act of crime prevention if the crime is a serious felony that may endanger human life. A person may use the necessity defense when the crime was committed in the process of saving human life or property.

Defendants may use the duress defense if someone is threatening to kill the person or a family member if the crime is not committed.

The mistake-of-fact defense can be used when a defendant honestly believes something to be true that isn't. The mistake-of-fact defense may not be used for strict liability crimes. Similarly, the mistake-of-law defense can generally be used when a person in good faith relied on an interpretation of law from a person charged with administering the law. The mistaken interpretation of law may not come from an attorney.

Entrapment is a defense used when law enforcement officials lure a person into committing a crime. The entrapment defense must pass a two-prong test. First, the criminal design must have originated with law enforcement. Second, the defendant was not predisposed to commit the crime.

A defendant may use the victim's consent as a defense in some circumstances. For instance, a defendant accused of rape is not guilty if the sex was consensual. The consent defense is unavailable for statutory rape and crimes involving death or serious bodily injury.

Capacity defenses may be used when the defendant lacks the capacity or ability to control his or her actions or understand that the act was criminal in nature. The Common Law standard for the infancy defense says that children under 7 years of age may not be tried, and children 7 to 14 years of age have a rebuttable presumption of incapacity. The prosecutor must prove beyond a reasonable doubt the defendant appreciated the quality and nature of his or her actions. Children over 14 are treated as adults for purposes of capacity. Juvenile courts may authorize trying the defendant as an adult.

Involuntary intoxication occurs when a person unknowingly ingests an intoxicating substance. This defense may be made to both specific and general intent crimes. Persons who are involuntarily intoxicated are treated the same as insane defendants. They must meet whatever test the jurisdiction uses for insanity.

Voluntary intoxication may never be used as a defense to a general intent crime. It cannot be used as an excuse or justification of a specific intent crime such as murder. It cannot be used as a defense to crimes involving negligence, recklessness, or strict liability.

Under the insanity defense, a defendant claims he or she lacked the mental state to understand the nature and consequences of the crime. The Common Law insanity defense derives from the M'Naghten case. The M'Naghten rule states that a defendant "is presumed to be sane and to possess a sufficient degree of reason to be responsible for his crimes, until the contrary be proved to (the jury's) satisfaction" beyond a reasonable doubt.

Some American states have modified the M'Naghten rule employing "irresistible impulse" or "temporary insanity" defense for people who committed "crimes of passion." More liberal interpretations include the Durham test, which is the "substantial lack of capacity" test.

Some states have a "guilty, but mentally ill" statute where defendants who do not meet the M'Naghten standard of a complete lack of capacity, but fall under the substantial lack of capacity standard, are convicted and sent to a mental hospital. If they recover, they are sent to prison for the rest of their term.

Some defendants are judged to be incompetent to stand trial. Generally, defendants cannot be held more than the lesser of 18 months or the maximum sentence for the crime they are charged with. At that point, the state must try the defendant, if he or she is competent to stand trial, dismiss the charges, or commence civil proceedings to have the defendant committed to a mental institution.

The standard for competency in many jurisdictions is whether the defendant "has sufficient present ability to consult with his lawyer with a reasonable degree of rational understanding—and whether he has a rational as well as factual understanding of the proceedings against him."

Older defendants may not be competent for trial due to their overall health condition. They have the same rights as other defendants judged to be incompetent to stand trial.

In cases where the death penalty has already been imposed, convicts can postpone execution by claiming "insanity just prior to execution." Prisoners who become insane during their prison term are moved to a psychiatric hospital for the remainder of their term. Should they still be insane at the end of their term, they may be committed to a mental hospital until they recover.

KEY TERMS

Consent defense: Usually used in rape cases, argues the defendant had the "victim's" consent to perform the acts.

Deadly force: Force intended to cause death or likely to result in death.

Defense of others: The defense used when otherwise criminal activities are done to save other people from harm.

Duress defense: The defense that a person acted under threat of bodily harm to themselves or a family member. It may not be used to justify killing. The crime committed must be less serious than the harm threatened.

Durham test: Test of insanity that only requires a "substantial lack of capacity" on the part of the defendant.

Entrapment: A defense used when law enforcement officials lure a person into committing a crime.

Guilty, but mentally ill: Defendants who do not meet the complete lack of capacity standard, but fall under the substantial lack of capacity standard are convicted and sent to a mental hospital. If they recover, they are sent to prison for the rest of their term.

Incompetent to stand trial: A person unable to understand the proceedings against him and be able to interact with his attorneys.

Infancy defense: The defense that a child is too young to either be prosecuted, or stand trial as an adult.

Insanity defense: States that the defendant lacked the mental state to understand the nature and consequences of the crime.

Insanity during incarceration: Prisoners who become insane are generally removed to mental hospitals. If they are still insane at the conclusion of their prison term, they are generally committed.

Insanity just prior to execution: Most jurisdictions will not execute an insane person. Persons whose sanity returns are rewarded with death.

Involuntary intoxication: The condition of a person who unknowingly ingests an intoxicating substance. Generally treated like insanity.

Justification defenses: A legal excuse for committing an act that otherwise would be a tort or a crime.

Mistake of fact: A defense used when a defendant honestly believes something to be true that isn't.

Mistake of law: A defense used when a person in good faith relied on an interpretation of law from a person charged with administering the law.

M'Naghten rule: Holds that a defendant "is presumed to be sane and to possess a sufficient degree of reason to be responsible for his crimes, until the contrary be proved to (the jury's) satisfaction" beyond a reasonable doubt.

Non-deadly force: Force used to subdue a criminal or prevent a crime without risking death.

Objective standard (minority rule) for entrapment: Asks the question, "Would an innocent person be induced to commit the crime by the officer's acts?"

Retreat rule: The rule governing when a person must retreat rather than use deadly force.

Self-defense: The use of force to protect oneself from death or imminent bodily harm at the hands of an aggressor.

Subjective standard (majority rule) for entrapment: Asks the question, "Was the defendant predisposed to commit the crime?"

Sudden escalation: The concept that a conflict that was not life-threatening escalates to the point that it is.

Voluntary intoxication: The condition where a person knowingly ingests an intoxicating substance. Not a defense to murder or most crimes.

Withdrawal: The act of removing oneself from a conflict.

DISCUSSION QUESTIONS

1. Explain the differences between the M'Naghten rule, the Durham test, and guilty but mentally ill. If you were advising a client who wants to raise the insanity defense, which defense would be most advantageous for her?
2. Research the insanity defense in your jurisdiction. Which defense or defenses does your jurisdiction use?
3. When is the defense of entrapment available in your jurisdiction?
4. Explain when you can use nonlethal force and when you can use lethal force to protect yourself from criminal activity.
5. Should the insanity defense be eliminated?

FOR FURTHER READING

1. Smith, R. (1981). *Trial by Medicine: The Insanity Defense in Victorian England*. Edinburgh University Press. Discusses the advances in the jurisprudence of insanity in Victorian England.
2. Moran, R. (1981). *Knowing Right from Wrong: The Insanity Defense of Daniel M'Naghten*. Free Press. Recounts the story of the insanity defense.
3. Bonnie, R. (1986). *Trial of John W. Hinckley, Jr.: A Case Study in the Insanity Defense*. Foundation Press.

QUOTATIONS FOR CHAPTER FOURTEEN

1. *No man has a wholly undiseased mind; in one way or another all men are mad.*
   Mark Twain, *The Memorable Assassination*

2. *Where does the violet tint end and the orange tint begin? Distinctly we see the difference of the colors, but where exactly does the one first blending enter into the other. So with sanity and insanity.*
   Herman Melville

3. *Government agents may not originate a criminal design, implant in an innocent person's mind the disposition to commit a criminal act, and then induce commission of the crime so that the Government may prosecute.*
   Justice White in *Jacobson v. United States*, 503 U.S. 540 (1992)

ENDNOTES

1. *Jacobson v. United States*, 503 U.S. 540 (1992).
2. "*Va. moves to limit executions: Senate approves shielding retarded,*" *Washington Post* (February 9, 2002).
3. *Montana v. Egelhoff*, 518 U.S. 116 (1996).
4. *Rex v. M'Naghten*, House of Lords. 10 Cl. & F. 200, 8 Eng, Rep. 718.
5. *Parsons v. State*, 81 Ala. 577. 2 So. 854 (1887).
6. *Durham v. United States*, 94 U.S. App. D. C. 228. 214 F. 2d 862 (1954).
7. *Indiana v. Jackson*, 406 U.S. 715 (1972).
8. *White v. Estelle*, 459 U.S. 1118 (1983).
9. Editorial. "*1963 Birmingham bombing: Another man's time to answer,*" *The Durham Herald* (Durham, NC) (January 7, 2002).
10. *Caritativo v. California*, 359 U.S. 549 (1958).

APPENDIX A
The Constitution of the United States of America

WE THE PEOPLE of the United States, in Order to form a more perfect Union, establish Justice, insure domestic Tranquility, provide for the common defence, promote the general Welfare, and secure the Blessings of Liberty to ourselves and our Posterity, do ordain and establish this Constitution for the United States of America.

ARTICLE ONE

Section 1.

All legislative powers herein granted shall be vested in a Congress of the United States, which shall consist of a Senate and House of Representatives.

Section 2.

The House of Representatives shall be composed of members chosen every second year by the people of the several States, and the electors in each State shall have the qualifications requisite for electors of the most numerous branch of the State legislature.

No Person shall be a Representative who shall not have attained to the age of twenty five years, and been seven years a citizen of the United States, and who shall not, when elected, be an inhabitant of that State in which he shall be chosen.

Representatives and direct taxes shall be apportioned among the several States which may be included within this Union, according to their respective numbers, which shall be determined by adding to the whole number of free persons, including those bound to service for a term of years, and excluding Indians not taxed, three fifths of all other persons. The actual enumeration shall be made within three years after the first meeting of the Congress of the United States, and within every subsequent term of ten years, in such manner as they shall by law direct. The number of Representatives shall not exceed one for every thirty thousand, but each State shall have at least one Representative; and until such enumeration shall be made, the State of New Hampshire shall be entitled to choose three, Massachusetts eight, Rhode Island and Providence Plantations one, Connecticut five, New York six, New Jersey four, Pennsylvania eight, Delaware one, Maryland six, Virginia ten, North Carolina five, South Carolina five and Georgia three. When vacancies happen in the Representation from any State, the executive authority thereof shall issue writs of election to fill such vacancies.

The House of Representatives shall choose their Speaker and other officers; and shall have the sole power of Impeachment.

Section 3.

The Senate of the United States shall be composed of two Senators from each State, chosen by the legislature thereof, for six years; and each Senator shall have one Vote.

Immediately after they shall be assembled in consequence of the first election, they shall be divided as equally as may be into three classes. The seats of the Senators of the first class shall be vacated at the expiration of the second year, of the second class at the expiration of the fourth year, and of the third class at the expiration of the sixth year, so that one third may be chosen every second year; and if vacancies happen by resignation, or otherwise, during the recess of the legislature of any State, the executive thereof may make temporary appointments until the next meeting of the legislature, which shall then fill such vacancies.

No person shall be a Senator who shall not have attained to the age of thirty years, and been nine years a citizen of the United States, and who shall not, when elected, be an inhabitant of that State for which he shall be chosen.

The Vice-President of the United States shall be President of the Senate, but shall have no vote, unless they be equally divided.

The Senate shall choose their other officers, and also a President pro tempore, in the absence of the Vice-President, or when he shall exercise the office of President of the United States.

The Senate shall have the sole power to try all impeachments. When sitting for that purpose, they shall be on oath or affirmation. When the President of the United States is tried, the Chief Justice shall preside: And no Person shall be convicted without the concurrence of two thirds of the members present.

Judgment in cases of impeachment shall not extend further than to removal from office, and disqualification to hold and enjoy any office of honor, trust or profit under the United States: but the party convicted shall nevertheless be liable and subject to indictment, trial, judgment and punishment, according to law.

Section 4.

The times, places and manner of holding elections for Senators and Representatives, shall be prescribed in each State by the legislature thereof; but the Congress may at any time by law make or alter such regulations, except as to the places of choosing Senators.

The Congress shall assemble at least once in every year, and such meeting shall be on the first Monday in December, unless they shall by law appoint a different day.

Section 5.

Each house shall be the judge of the elections, returns and qualifications of its own members, and a majority of each shall constitute a quorum to do business; but a smaller number may adjourn from day to day, and may be authorized to compel the attendance of absent members, in such manner, and under such penalties as each house may provide.

Each house may determine the rules of its proceedings, punish its members for disorderly behavior, and, with the concurrence of two-thirds, expel a member.

Each house shall keep a journal of its proceedings, and from time to time publish the same, excepting such parts as may in their judgment require secrecy; and the yeas and nays of the members of either house on any question shall, at the desire of one fifth of those present, be entered on the journal.

Neither house, during the session of Congress, shall, without the consent of the other, adjourn for more than three days, nor to any other place than that in which the two Houses shall be sitting.

Section 6.

The Senators and Representatives shall receive a compensation for their services, to be ascertained by law, and paid out of the Treasury of the United States. They shall in all cases, except treason, felony and breach of the peace, be privileged from arrest during their attendance at the session of their respective houses, and in going to and returning from the same; and for any speech or debate in either house, they shall not be questioned in any other place.

No Senator or Representative shall, during the time for which he was elected, be appointed to any civil office under the authority of the United States which shall have been created, or the emoluments whereof shall have been increased during such time; and no person holding any office under the United States, shall be a member of either house during his continuance in office.

Section 7.

All bills for raising revenue shall originate in the House of Representatives; but the Senate may propose or concur with amendments as on other bills.

Every bill which shall have passed the House of Representatives and the Senate, shall, before it become a law, be presented to the President of the United States; If he approve he shall sign it, but if not he shall return it, with his objections to that house in which it shall have originated, who shall enter the objections at large on their journal, and proceed to reconsider it. If after such reconsideration two thirds of that house shall agree to pass the bill, it shall be sent, together with the objections, to the other house, by which it shall likewise be reconsidered, and if approved by two thirds of that house, it shall become a law. But in all such cases the votes of both houses shall be determined by yeas and nays, and the names of the persons voting for and against the bill shall be entered on the journal of each house respectively. If any bill shall not be returned by the President within ten days (Sundays excepted) after it shall have been presented to him, the same shall be a law, in like manner as if he had signed it, unless the Congress by their adjournment prevent its return, in which case it shall not be a law.

Every order, resolution, or vote to which the concurrence of the Senate and House of Representatives may be necessary (except on a question of adjournment) shall be presented to the President of the United States; and before the same shall take effect, shall be approved by him, or being disapproved by him, shall be repassed by two thirds of the Senate and House of Representatives, according to the rules and limitations prescribed in the case of a bill.

Section 8.

The Congress shall have power to lay and collect taxes, duties, imposts and excises, to pay the debts and provide for the common defence and general welfare of the United States; but all duties, imposts and excises shall be uniform throughout the United States; To borrow money on the credit of the United States; To regulate commerce with foreign nations, and among the several States, and with the Indian tribes; To establish an uniform rule of naturalization, and uniform Laws on the subject of bankruptcies throughout the United States; To coin money, regulate the value thereof, and of foreign coin, and fix the standard of weights and measures; To provide for the punishment of counterfeiting the securities and current Coin of the United States; To establish post-offices and post-roads; To promote the progress of science and useful arts, by securing for limited times to authors and inventors the exclusive right to their respective writings and discoveries; To constitute tribunals inferior to the Supreme Court; To define and punish piracies and felonies committed on the high seas, and offenses against the law of nations; To declare war, grant letters of marque and reprisal, and make rules concerning captures on land and water; To raise and support armies, but no appropriation of money to that use shall be for a longer term than two years; To provide and maintain a navy; To make rules for the government and regulation of the land and naval forces; To provide for calling forth the militia to execute the laws of the union, suppress insurrections and repel invasions; To provide for organizing, arming, and disciplining, the militia, and for governing such part of them as may be employed in the service of the United States, reserving to the States respectively, the appointment of the officers, and the authority of training the militia according to the discipline prescribed by Congress; To exercise exclusive legislation in all cases whatsoever, over such district (not exceeding ten miles square) as may, by cession of particular States, and the acceptance of Congress, become the seat of the Government of the United States, and to exercise like authority over all places purchased by the consent of the legislature of the State in which the same shall be, for the erection of forts, magazines, arsenals, dockyards, and other needful Buildings; and To make all laws which shall be necessary and proper for carrying into execution the foregoing powers, and all other powers vested by this Constitution in the Government of the United States, or in any department or officer thereof.

Section 9.

The migration or importation of such persons as any of the States now existing shall think proper to admit, shall not be prohibited by the Congress prior to the Year one thousand eight hundred and eight, but a tax or duty may be imposed on such importation, not exceeding ten dollars for each person.

The privilege of the writ of habeas corpus shall not be suspended, unless when in cases of rebellion or invasion the public safety may require it.

No bill of attainder or ex post facto law shall be passed.

No capitation, or other direct tax shall be laid, unless in proportion to the census or enumeration herein before directed to be taken.

No tax or duty shall be laid on articles exported from any State.

No preference shall be given by any regulation of commerce or revenue to the ports of one State over those of another: nor shall vessels bound to, or from, one State, be obliged to enter, clear, or pay duties in another.

No money shall be drawn from the Treasury, but in consequence of appropriations made by law; and a regular statement and account of the receipts and expenditures of all public money shall be published from time to time.

No title of nobility shall be granted by the United States; and no person holding any office of profit or trust under them, shall, without the consent of the Congress, accept of any present, emolument, office, or title, of any kind whatever, from any king, prince or foreign State.

Section 10.

No State shall enter into any treaty, alliance, or confederation; grant letters of marque and reprisal; coin money; emit bills of credit; make anything but gold and silver coin a tender in payment of debts; pass any bill of attainder, ex post facto law, or law impairing the obligation of contracts, or grant any title of nobility.

No State shall, without the consent of the Congress, lay any imposts or duties on imports or exports, except what may be absolutely necessary for executing its inspection laws: and the net produce of all duties and imposts, laid by any State on imports or exports, shall be for the use of the Treasury of the United States; and all such laws shall be subject to the revision and control of the Congress.

No State shall, without the consent of Congress, lay any duty of tonnage, keep troops, or ships of war in time of peace, enter into any agreement or compact with another State, or with a foreign power, or engage in war, unless actually invaded, or in such imminent danger as will not admit of delay.

ARTICLE TWO

Section 1.

The executive power shall be vested in a President of the United States of America. He shall hold his office during the term of four years, and, together with the Vice-President chosen for the same term, be elected, as follows:

Each State shall appoint, in such manner as the legislature thereof may direct, a number of electors, equal to the whole number of Senators and Representatives to which the State may be entitled in the Congress: but no Senator or Representative, or person holding an office of trust or profit under the United States, shall be appointed an elector.

The electors shall meet in their respective States, and vote by ballot for two persons, of whom one at least shall not lie an inhabitant of the same State with themselves. And they shall make a list of all the persons voted for, and of the number of votes for each; which list they shall sign and certify, and transmit sealed to the seat of the government of the United States, directed to the President of the Senate. The President of the Senate shall, in the presence of the Senate and House of Representatives, open all the certificates, and the votes shall then be counted. The person having the greatest number of votes shall be the President, if such number be a majority of the whole number of electors appointed; and if there be more than one who have such majority, and have an equal number of votes, then the House of Representatives shall immediately choose by ballot one of them for President; and if no person have a majority, then from the five highest on the list the said House shall in like manner choose the President.

But in choosing the President, the votes shall be taken by States, the representation from each State having one vote; a quorum for this purpose shall consist of a member or members from two thirds of the States, and a majority of all the States shall be necessary to a choice. In every case, after the choice of the President, the person having the greatest number of votes of the electors shall be the Vice-President. But if there should remain two or more who have equal votes, the Senate shall choose from them by ballot the Vice-President.

The Congress may determine the time of choosing the electors, and the day on which they shall give their votes; which day shall be the same throughout the United States.

No person except a natural born citizen, or a citizen of the United States, at the time of the adoption of this Constitution, shall be eligible to the office of President; neither shall any person be eligible to that office who shall not have attained to the age of thirty five years, and been fourteen years a resident within the United States.

In case of the removal of the President from office, or of his death, resignation, or inability to discharge the powers and duties of the said office, the same shall devolve on the Vice-President, and the Congress may by law provide for the case of removal, death, resignation or inability, both of the President and Vice President, declaring what officer shall then act as President, and such officer shall act accordingly, until the disability be removed, or a President shall be elected.

The President shall, at stated times, receive for his services, a compensation, which shall neither be increased nor diminished during the period for which he shall have been elected, and he shall not receive within that period any other emolument from the United States, or any of them.

Before he enter on the execution of his office, he shall take the following oath or affirmation:

"I do solemnly swear (or affirm) that I will faithfully execute the office of President of the United States, and will to the best of my ability, preserve, protect and defend the Constitution of the United States."

Section 2.

The President shall be Commander-in-Chief of the Army and Navy of the United States, and of the militia of the several States, when called into the actual service of the United States; he may require the opinion, in writing, of the principal officer in each of the executive departments, upon any subject relating to the duties of their respective offices, and he shall have power to grant reprieves and pardons for offenses against the United States, except in cases of impeachment.

He shall have power, by and with the advice and consent of the Senate, to make treaties, provided two thirds of the Senators present concur; and he shall nominate, and by and with the advice and consent of the Senate, shall appoint ambassadors, other public ministers and consuls, judges of the Supreme Court, and all other officers of the United States, whose appointments are not herein otherwise provided for, and which shall be established by law: but the Congress may by law vest the appointment of such inferior officers, as they think proper, in the President alone, in the courts of law, or in the heads of departments.

The President shall have power to fill up all vacancies that may happen during the recess of the Senate, by granting commissions which shall expire at the end of their next session.

Section 3.

He shall from time to time give to the Congress information of the State of the Union, and recommend to their consideration such measures as he shall judge necessary and expedient; he may, on extraordinary occasions, convene both houses, or either of them, and in case of disagreement between them, with respect to the time of adjournment, he may adjourn them to such time as he shall think proper; he shall receive ambassadors and other public ministers; he shall take care that the laws be faithfully executed, and shall commission all the officers of the United States.

Section 4.

The President, Vice-President and all civil officers of the United States, shall be removed from office on impeachment for, and conviction of, treason, bribery, or other high crimes and misdemeanors.

ARTICLE THREE

Section 1.

The judicial power of the United States, shall be vested in one Supreme Court, and in such inferior courts as the Congress may from time to time ordain and establish. The judges, both of the supreme and inferior courts, shall hold their offices during good behavior, and shall, at stated times, receive for their services, a compensation, which shall not be diminished during their continuance in office.

Section 2.

The judicial power shall extend to all cases, in law and equity, arising under this Constitution, the laws of the United States, and treaties made, or which shall be made, under their authority; to all cases affecting ambassadors, other public ministers and consuls; to all cases of admiralty and maritime jurisdiction; to controversies to which the United States shall be a party; to controversies between two or more States; between a State and citizens of another State; between citizens of different States; between citizens of the same State claiming lands under grants of different States, and between a State, or the citizens thereof, and foreign States, citizens or subjects.

In all cases affecting ambassadors, other public ministers and consuls, and those in which a State shall be party, the Supreme Court shall have original jurisdiction. In all the other cases before mentioned, the Supreme Court shall have appellate jurisdiction, both as to law and fact, with such exceptions, and under such regulations as the Congress shall make.

Trial of all crimes, except in cases of impeachment, shall be by jury; and such trial shall be held in the State where the said crimes shall have been committed; but when not committed within any State, the trial shall be at such place or places as the Congress may by law have directed.

Section 3.

Treason against the United States, shall consist only in levying war against them, or in adhering to their enemies, giving them aid and comfort. No person shall be convicted of treason unless on the testimony of two witnesses to the same overt act, or on confession in open court.

The Congress shall have power to declare the punishment of treason, but no attainder of treason shall work corruption of blood, or forfeiture except during the life of the person attainted.

ARTICLE FOUR

Section 1.

Full faith and credit shall be given in each State to the public acts, records, and judicial proceedings of every other State. And the Congress may by general laws prescribe the manner in which such acts, records and proceedings shall be proved, and the effect thereof.

Section 2.

The citizens of each State shall be entitled to all privileges and immunities of citizens in the several States.

A person charged in any State with treason, felony, or other crime, who shall flee from justice, and be found in another State, shall on demand of the executive authority of the

State from which he fled, be delivered up, to be removed to the State having jurisdiction of the crime. No person held to service or labor in one State, under the laws thereof, escaping into another, shall, in consequence of any law or regulation therein, be discharged from such service or labor, But shall be delivered up on claim of the party to whom such service or labor may be due.

Section 3.

New States may be admitted by the Congress into this Union; but no new States shall be formed or erected within the jurisdiction of any other State; nor any State be formed by the junction of two or more States, or parts of States, without the consent of the legislatures of the States concerned as well as of the Congress.

The Congress shall have power to dispose of and make all needful rules and regulations respecting the territory or other property belonging to the United States; and nothing in this Constitution shall be so construed as to prejudice any claims of the United States, or of any particular State.

Section 4.

The United States shall guarantee to every State in this Union a republican form of government, and shall protect each of them against invasion; and on application of the legislature, or of the executive (when the legislature cannot be convened) against domestic violence.

ARTICLE FIVE

The Congress, whenever two thirds of both houses shall deem it necessary, shall propose amendments to this Constitution, or, on the application of the Legislatures of two thirds of the several States, shall call a convention for proposing amendments, which, in either case, shall be valid to all intents and purposes, as part of this Constitution, when ratified by the Legislatures of three fourths of the several States, or by conventions in three fourths thereof, as the one or the other mode of ratification may be proposed by the Congress; provided that no amendment which may be made prior to the Year One thousand eight hundred and eight shall in any manner affect the first and fourth Clauses in the Ninth Section of the first Article; and that no State, without its consent, shall be deprived of its equal suffrage in the Senate.

ARTICLE SIX

All debts contracted and engagements entered into, before the adoption of this Constitution, shall be as valid against the United States under this Constitution, as under the Confederation.

This Constitution, and the laws of the United States which shall be made in pursuance thereof; and all treaties made, or which shall be made, under the authority of the United States, shall be the supreme law of the land; and the judges in every State shall be bound thereby, anything in the Constitution or laws of any State to the contrary notwithstanding.

The Senators and Representatives before mentioned, and the members of the several State Legislatures, and all executive and judicial officers, both of the United States and of the several States, shall be bound by oath or affirmation, to support this Constitution; but no religious test shall ever be required as a qualification to any office or public trust under the United States.

ARTICLE SEVEN

The ratification of the Conventions of nine States, shall be sufficient for the establishment of this Constitution between the States so ratifying the same.

BILL OF RIGHTS

AMENDMENT I (1791)

Congress shall make no law respecting an establishment of religion, or prohibiting the free exercise thereof; or abridging the freedom of speech, or of the press; or the right of the people peaceably to assemble, and to petition the government for a redress of grievances.

AMENDMENT II (1791)

A well regulated militia, being necessary to the security of a free State, the right of the people to keep and bear arms, shall not be infringed.

AMENDMENT III (1791)

No soldier shall, in time of peace be quartered in any house, without the consent of the owner, nor in time of war, but in a manner to be prescribed by law.

AMENDMENT IV (1791)

The right of the people to be secure in their persons, houses, papers, and effects, against unreasonable searches and seizures, shall not be violated, and no warrants shall issue, but upon probable cause, supported by Oath or affirmation, and particularly describing the place to be searched, and the persons or things to be seized.

AMENDMENT V (1791)

No person shall be held to answer for a capital, or otherwise infamous crime, unless on a presentment or indictment of a Grand Jury, except in cases arising in the land or naval forces, or in the militia, when in actual service in time of war or public danger; nor shall any person be subject for the same offence to be twice put in jeopardy of life or limb; nor shall be compelled in any criminal case to be a witness against himself, nor be deprived of life, liberty, or property, without due process of law; nor shall private property be taken for public use, without just compensation.

AMENDMENT VI (1791)

In all criminal prosecutions, the accused shall enjoy the right to a speedy and public trial, by an impartial jury of the State and district wherein the crime shall have been committed, which district shall have been previously ascertained by law, and to be informed of the nature and cause of the accusation; to be confronted with the witnesses against him; to have compulsory process for obtaining witnesses in his favor, and to have the assistance of counsel for his defence.

AMENDMENT VII (1791)

In suits at common law, where the value in controversy shall exceed twenty dollars, the right of trial by jury shall be preserved, and no fact tried by a jury, shall be otherwise re-examined in any court of the United States, than according to the rules of the common law.

AMENDMENT VIII (1791)

Excessive bail shall not lie required, nor excessive fines imposed, nor cruel and unusual punishments inflicted.

AMENDMENT IX (1791)

The enumeration in the Constitution, of certain rights, shall not be construed to deny or disparage others retained by the people.

AMENDMENT X (1791)

The powers not delegated to the United States by the Constitution, nor prohibited by it to the States, are reserved to the States respectively, or to the people.

AMENDMENT XI (1798)

The judicial power of the United States shall not be construed to extend to any suit in law or equity, commenced or prosecuted against one of the United States by Citizens of another State, or by citizens or subjects of any foreign State.

AMENDMENT XII (1804)

The electors shall meet in their respective States, and vote by ballot for President and Vice-President, one of whom, at least, shall not be an inhabitant of the same State with themselves; they shall name in their ballots the person voted for as President, and in distinct ballots the person voted for as Vice-President, and they shall make distinct lists of all persons voted for as President, and of all persons voted for as Vice-President and of the number of votes for each, which lists they shall sign and certify, and transmit sealed to the seat of the Government of the United States, directed to the President of the Senate; The President of the Senate shall, in the presence of the Senate and House of Representatives, open all the certificates and the votes shall then be counted; the person having the greatest number of votes for President, shall be the President, if such number be a majority of the whole number of Electors appointed; and if no person have such majority, then from the persons having the highest numbers not exceeding three on the list of those voted for as President, the House of Representatives shall choose immediately, by ballot, the President. But in choosing the President, the votes shall be taken by States, the representation from each State having one vote; a quorum for this purpose shall consist of a member or members from two-thirds of the States, and a majority of all the States shall be necessary to a choice. And if the House of Representatives shall not choose a President whenever the right of choice shall devolve upon them, before the fourth day of March next following, then the Vice-President shall act as President, as in the case of the death or other constitutional disability of the President.

The person having the greatest number of votes as Vice-President, shall be the Vice-President, if such number be a majority of the whole number of Electors appointed, and if no person have a majority, then from the two highest numbers on the list, the Senate shall choose the Vice-President; a quorum for the purpose shall consist of two-thirds of the whole number of Senators, and a majority of the whole number shall be necessary to a choice. But no person constitutionally ineligible to the office of President shall be eligible to that of Vice-President of the United States.

AMENDMENT XIII (1865)

Section 1.

Neither slavery nor involuntary servitude, except as a punishment for crime whereof the party shall have been duly convicted, shall exist within the United States, or any place subject to their jurisdiction.

Section 2.

Congress shall have power to enforce this article by appropriate legislation.

AMENDMENT XIV (1868)

Section 1.

All persons born or naturalized in the United States, and subject to the jurisdiction thereof, are citizens of the United States and of the State wherein they reside. No State shall make or enforce any law which shall abridge the privileges or immunities of citizens of the United States; nor shall any State deprive any person of life, liberty, or property, without due process of law; nor deny to any person within its jurisdiction the equal protection of the laws.

Section 2.

Representatives shall be apportioned among the several States according to their respective numbers, counting the whole number of persons in each State, excluding Indians not taxed. But when the right to vote at any election for the choice of Electors for President and Vice-President of the United States, Representatives in Congress, the executive and judicial officers of a State, or the members of the Legislature thereof, is denied to any of the male inhabitants of such State, being twenty-one years of age, and citizens of the United States, or in any way abridged, except for participation in rebellion, or other crime, the basis of representation therein shall be reduced in the proportion which the number of such male citizens shall bear to the whole number of male citizens twenty-one years of age in such State.

Section 3.

No person shall be a Senator or Representative in Congress, or elector of President and Vice-President, or hold any office, civil or military, under the United States, or under any State, who, having previously taken an oath, as a member of Congress, or as an officer of the United States, or as a member of any State legislature, or as an executive or judicial officer of any State, to support the Constitution of the United States, shall have engaged in insurrection or rebellion against the same, or given aid or comfort to the enemies thereof. But Congress may by a vote of two-thirds of each House, remove such disability.

Section 4.

The validity of the public debt of the United States, authorized by law, including debts incurred for payment of pensions and bounties for services in suppressing insurrection or rebellion, shall not be questioned. But neither the United States nor any State shall assume or pay any debt or obligation incurred in aid of insurrection or rebellion against the United States, or any claim for the loss or emancipation of any slave; but all such debts, obligations and claims shall be held illegal and void.

Section 5.

The Congress shall have power to enforce, by appropriate legislation, the provisions of this article.

AMENDMENT XV (1870)

Section 1.

The right of citizens of the United States to vote shall not be denied or abridged by the United States or by any State on account of race, color, or previous condition of servitude.

Section 2.

The Congress shall have power to enforce this article by appropriate legislation.

AMENDMENT XVI (1913)

The Congress shall have power to lay and collect taxes on incomes, from whatever source derived, without apportionment among the several States and without regard to any census or enumeration.

AMENDMENT XVII (1913)

The Senate of the United States shall be composed of two senators from each State, elected by the people thereof, for six years; and each Senator shall have one vote. The electors in each State shall have the qualifications requisite for electors of the most numerous branch of the State legislature. When vacancies happen in the representation of any State in the Senate, the executive authority of such State shall issue writs of election to fill such vacancies: Provided, That the legislature of any State may empower the executive thereof to make temporary appointments until the people fill the vacancies by election as the legislature may direct.

This amendment shall not be so construed as to affect the election or term of any senator chosen before it becomes valid as part of the Constitution.

AMENDMENT XVIII (1919)

Section 1.

After one year from the ratification of this article, the manufacture, sale, or transportation of intoxicating liquors within, the importation thereof into, or the exportation thereof from the United States and all territory subject to the jurisdiction thereof for beverage purposes is hereby prohibited.

Section 2.

The Congress and the several States shall have concurrent power to enforce this article by appropriate legislation.

Section 3.

This article shall be inoperative unless it shall have been ratified as an amendment to the Constitution by the legislatures of the several States, as provided in the Constitution, within seven years from the date of the submission hereof to the States by Congress.

AMENDMENT XIX (1920)

The right of citizens of the United States to vote shall not be denied or abridged by the United States or by any States on account of sex. The Congress shall have power by appropriate legislation to enforce the provisions of this article.

AMENDMENT XX (1933)

Section 1.

The terms of the President and Vice-President shall end at noon on the twentieth day of January, and the terms of Senators and Representatives at noon on the third day of January, of the years in which such terms would have ended if this article had not been ratified; and the terms of their successors shall then begin.

Section 2.

The Congress shall assemble at least once in every year, and such meeting shall begin at noon on the third day of January, unless they shall by law appoint a different day.

Section 3.

If, at the time fixed for the beginning of the term of the President, the President-elect shall have died, the Vice-President-elect shall become President. If a President shall not have been chosen before the time fixed for the beginning of his term, or if the President-elect shall have failed to qualify, then the Vice-President-elect shall act as President until a President shall have qualified; and the Congress may by law provide for the case wherein neither a President-elect nor a Vice-President-elect shall have qualified, declaring who shall then act as President, or the manner in which one who is to act shall be selected, and such person shall act accordingly until a President or Vice-President shall have qualified.

Section 4.

The Congress may by law provide for the case of the death of any of the persons from whom the House of Representatives may choose a President whenever the right of choice shall have devolved upon them, and for the case of the death of any of the persons from whom the Senate may choose a Vice-President whenever the right of choice shall have devolved upon them.

Section 5.

Sections 1 and 2 shall take effect on the 15th day of October following the ratification of this article.

Section 6.

This article shall be inoperative unless it shall have been ratified as an amendment to the Constitution by the legislatures of three-fourths of the several States within seven years from the date of its submission.

AMENDMENT XXI (1933)

Section 1.

The eighteenth article of amendment to the Constitution of the United States is hereby repealed.

Section 2.

The transportation or importation into any State, Territory, or possession of the United States for delivery or use therein of intoxicating liquors, in violation of the laws thereof, is hereby prohibited.

Section 3.

The article shall be inoperative unless it shall have been ratified as an amendment to the Constitution by conventions in the several States, as provided in the Constitution, within seven years from the date of the submission hereof to the States by the Congress.

AMENDMENT XXII (1951)

Section 1.

No person shall be elected to the office of the President more than twice, and no person who has held the office of President, or acted as President for more than two years of a term to which some other person was elected President shall be elected to the office of the President more than once. But this Article shall not apply to any person holding the office of President when this Article was proposed by the Congress, and shall not prevent any person who May be holding the office of President, or acting as President, during the term within which this Article becomes operative from holding the office of President or acting as President during the remainder of such term.

Section 2.

This article shall be inoperative unless it shall have been ratified as an amendment to the Constitution by the legislatures of three-fourths of the several States within seven years from the date of its submission to the States by the Congress.

AMENDMENT XXIII (1961)

Section 1.

The District constituting the seat of government of the United States shall appoint in such manner as the Congress may direct:

A number of electors of President and Vice-President equal to the whole number of Senators and Representatives in Congress to which the District would be entitled if it were a State, but in no event more than the least populous State; they shall be in addition to those appointed by the States, but they shall be considered, for the purposes of the election of President and Vice-President, to be electors appointed by a State; and they shall meet in the district and perform such duties as provided by the twelfth article of amendment.

Section 2.

The Congress shall have power to enforce this article by appropriate legislation.

AMENDMENT XXIV (1964)

Section 1.

The right of citizens of the United States to vote in any primary or other election for President or Vice-President, for electors for President or Vice-President, or for Senator or Representative in Congress, shall not be denied or abridged by the United States or any State by reason of failure to pay any poll tax or other tax.

Section 2.

The Congress shall have power to enforce this article by appropriate legislation.

AMENDMENT XXV (1967)

Section 1.

In case of the removal of the President from office or of his death or resignation, the Vice-President shall become President.

Section 2.

Whenever there is a vacancy in the office of the Vice-President, the President shall nominate a Vice-President who shall take office upon confirmation by a majority vote of both Houses of Congress.

Section 3.

Whenever the President transmits to the President pro tempore of the Senate and the Speaker of the House of Representatives his written declaration that he is unable to discharge the powers and duties of his office, and until he transmits to them a written declaration to the contrary, such powers and duties shall be discharged by the Vice-President as Acting President.

Section 4.

Whenever the Vice-President and a majority of either the principal officers of the executive departments or of such other body as Congress may by law provide, transmit to the President pro tempore of the Senate and the Speaker of the House of Representatives their written declaration that the President is unable to discharge the powers and duties of his office, the Vice-President shall immediately assume the powers and duties of the office as Acting President.

Thereafter, when the President transmits to the President pro tempore of the Senate and the Speaker of the House of Representatives his written declaration that no inability exists, he shall resume the powers and duties of his office unless the Vice-President and a majority of either the principal officers of the executive department or of such other body as Congress may by law provide, transmit within four days to the President pro tempore of the Senate and the Speaker of the House of Representatives their written declaration that the President is unable to discharge the powers and duties of his office. Thereupon Congress shall decide the issue, assembling within forty-eight hours for that purpose if not in session. If the Congress, within twenty-one days after receipt of the latter written declaration, or, if Congress is not in session, within twenty-one days after Congress is required to assemble, determines by two-thirds vote of both Houses that the President is unable to discharge the powers and duties of his office, the Vice-President shall continue to discharge the same as Acting President; otherwise, the President shall resume the powers and duties of his office.

AMENDMENT XXVI (1971)

Section 1.

The right of citizens of the United States, who are eighteen years of age or older, to vote shall not be denied or abridged by the United States or by any State on account of age.

Section 2.

The Congress shall have power to enforce this article by appropriate legislation.

Index